Southern Living

2019 Annual Recipes

VANILLA LAYER CAKE
WITH A FLOWER CUFF
(PAGE 64)

Southern Living
BOOKS

CARROT-AND-FENNEL
SALAD (PAGE 31)

ROASTED BEEF
TENDERLOIN
(PAGE 28)

CAULIFLOWER WITH
CHEESE SAUCE
(PAGE 31)

LEMON-LIME MERINGUE
PIE (PAGE 31)

CLOCKWISE FROM TOP LEFT:

• ROASTED TOMATO-CHEDDAR SOUP (PAGE 33)

• SMOKY SPLIT PEA-AND-SAUSAGE SOUP (PAGE 35)

• BUTTERY CHIVE-AND-MUSTARD DROP BISCUITS (PAGE 37)

• LENTIL SOUP WITH SWEET POTATOES AND BACON (PAGE 36)

SKILLET VEGETABLE
PIE WITH GOAT CHEESE
(PAGE 40)

CLOCKWISE FROM TOP LEFT:

• RASPBERRY-ALMOND
CRUMBLE BARS (PAGE 48)

• BROWN BUTTER-CARAMEL
BLONDIES (PAGE 48)

• SPICED PECAN PIE BARS
(PAGE 45)

• CAPPUCCINO SWIRL BARS
(PAGE 46)

CLOCKWISE FROM TOP LEFT:

• LEMON-GARLIC BUTTER
SHRIMP AND BROCCOLI
(PAGE 53)

• OVEN-FRIED PORK CHOPS
WITH SWEET POTATOES AND
GREEN BEANS (PAGE 52)

• CHEESY SHEET PAN PASTA
(PAGE 54)

• CRISPY CATFISH TACOS
WITH SLAW (PAGE 51)

"NAKED" LEMON CAKE
WITH A FLOWER CROWN
(PAGE 61)

CHOCOLATE BUNDT CAKE
(PAGE 64)

MINI CONFETTI CAKES
(PAGE 61)

CLOCKWISE FROM TOP LEFT:

- TOASTED ISRAELI COUSCOUS
  AND SHRIMP (PAGE 65)

- ROSEMARY CHICKEN THIGHS
  AND VEGETABLES (PAGE 66)

- LEEK-AND-MUSHROOM
  GRITS FRITTATA (PAGE 69)

- CHEESY BEEF-AND-SPINACH
  RAVIOLI (PAGE 69)

SHAVED CARROT,
ASPARAGUS, AND
APPLE SALAD
(PAGE 83)

STRAWBERRY GELATO
WITH ALMOND
SHORTBREAD AND
ELDERFLOWER CRÈME
(PAGE 79)

HAZELNUT FINANCIERS
WITH STRAWBERRY
JAM AND LEMON PUREE
(PAGE 79)

CHOCOLATE-COCONUT
PAVLOVA CAKE (PAGE 91)

Our Year at
Southern Living®

Dear Friends,

The 2019 edition of *Southern Living Annual Recipes* brings you every amazing recipe that has graced the pages of our magazine. Throughout the year, our editors research the latest culinary trends, identify great restaurants, and highlight up-and-coming regional chefs to bring you the best of the South every month. As we've done for over 50 years, our Test Kitchen pros methodically fine-tune every recipe, so you can always cook with confidence. If you find it in the pages of *Southern Living*, you know it's worth making and sharing.

We believe in inspiring and guiding our readers to cook together, eat together, and create memories around the table. Our "Quick Fix" recipes show you easy shortcuts that never skimp on flavor, so you can enjoy hearty dinners night after night. Our ever-popular "What Can I Bring?" features portable, crowd-pleasing dishes that will win rave reviews at your next get-together. And of course, "Save Room" features the showstopping desserts for which *Southern Living* is famous. This year's edition includes the "Favorite Holiday Recipes" bonus section that will help you plan your menus effortlessly.

We are excited to share our year with you, and we know you'll love having this collection of *Southern Living* recipes at your fingertips.

Sid Evans
Editor in Chief
Southern Living magazine

Contents

17 Our Year at *Southern Living*
20 Top-Rated Recipes

23 January
24 Award-Winning Gumbo
26 A Matter of Taste
32 Tastes Like Comfort
38 Go for the Greens
39 Bananas for Sticky Buns
40 Winter Layers
41 Just Add Sunshine
42 *SL* Cooking School

43 February
44 Raising the Bar
50 Weeknight Cheat Sheets
55 Soup's On
56 Chicken in a Snap
57 Make Your Famous Dip!
58 *SL* Cooking School

59 March
60 Garden Party
65 Skillet Sensations
70 A Quick Shrimp Supper
71 Hot Potato
72 Party Perfect
74 *SL* Cooking School

75 April
76 Virginia's Sweet Spot
81 Back to Your Roots
84 Easter Brunch for a Bunch
89 Pretty Tasty Pot Pie
90 Speedy Sheet Pan Salmon
91 Fabulous and Flourless
92 *SL* Cooking School

93 May
94 The House That Mama Built
98 Eat Your Peas
102 Hooked on Shrimp
107 A New Spin on Chicken Spaghetti
108 Pork Perfection
109 It's Shortcake Season
110 *SL* Cooking School

111 June
112 Veggie Delights
116 Fresh in a Flash
120 Steak Salad with a Kick
121 Sunrise Sliders
122 *SL* Cooking School

123 July
124 The Bradford Melon
130 Gather Round the Grill
136 Time for Tomato Pie!
138 Heavenly Corn
140 Tortellini with a Twist
141 Berry Delicious
142 *SL* Cooking School

143 August
144 Just Add Fizz
150 5-Ingredient Suppers
155 Berry Good Breakfast
156 Fresh from the Garden
157 Break Out the Broccoli
158 Peaches and Cream
159 *SL* Cooking School

193 September

194 For the Love of Apple Pie
196 Finding Her Groove
202 Game Day Snack Trays
205 Kickin' Chicken
206 Fix & Freeze
210 Easy, Cheesy Meatballs
211 Going Dutch
212 *SL* Cooking School

213 October

214 Boiled-Peanut Perfection
216 The Oyster Feast
221 Pumpkin Picking Time!
224 Bring Out the Beef
227 Falling for Persimmons
228 Sweet on Shortbread
229 The Instant Pot Roast
230 Mushrooms Make It Better
231 Not Your Ordinary Oatmeal
232 *SL* Cooking School

233 November

234 A Texas-Size Thank-You
236 Picture-Perfect Pies
242 Tastes Like Home
254 Roll Call
255 The Giving Tree
260 Thanksgiving Classics
268 *SL* Cooking School

269 December

270 Spectacular Party Starters
276 Bring a Side
280 The Art of the Roast
283 Spirited Desserts
286 The Gift of Cookies
294 Christmas in Bloom
299 Pralines' Rich History
300 Renaissance Woman
302 Bake Another Batch
303 Good to the Last Crumb
304 *SL* Cooking School

321 Bonus: Our Favorite Holiday Recipes

350 Altitude Adjustments and Metric Equivalents

352 Indexes

352 Recipe Title Index
356 Month-by-Month Index
360 General Recipe Index

Top-Rated Recipes

We cook, we taste, we refine, we rate, and at the end of each year, our Test Kitchen shares the highest-rated recipes from each issue exclusively with *Southern Living Annual Recipes* readers.

January

- Lemon-Lime Meringue Pie (page 31) Tangy lime zest adds zip to this all-time favorite. It'll be the hit of any family dinner or casual get-together.
- Creamy Chicken-and-Rice Soup with Collard Greens (page 32) Satisfy your soul with this tasty spin on a comfort-food classic. It's ready to serve in under 40 minutes—start to finish.
- Buttery Chive-and-Mustard Drop Biscuits (page 37) You'll want to make a double batch of these amazing biscuits! They are a perfect sidekick to any brunch, lunch, or dinner. They also make a great snack or lunchbox treat.
- Mini Bananas Foster Sticky Buns (page 39) We are bananas for these tiny treats. The recipe calls for refrigerated crescent roll dough, making them super easy to whip up for any occasion.

February

- Peanut Butter-Fudge Bars (page 45) Our Test Kitchen struck gold when the cooks created these dreamy chocolate bars. They are ooey-gooey delicious! Whip up a batch to enjoy and one to share. Your friends will love you for it.
- Sheet Pan Chicken with Dressing (page 50) Sheet pan dinners are all the rage, and this recipe tops our list when we're asked for a recommendation. We use chicken thighs, but you can sub any bone-in chicken and get the same foolproof results.
- Lemon-Garlic Butter Shrimp and Broccoli (page 53) Everyone will ask for seconds when you serve this simple shrimp dish. The red pepper adds a nice kick, and the lemon brings out the flavor of the shrimp.
- Slow-Cooker Winter Vegetable Soup with Bacon (page 55) Step up your weeknight dinner with the help of your slow cooker. This veggie-packed soup only cooks for 5 hours, so if you start at lunchtime, dinner will be ready by 5.
- Creamy Southwest Black-Eyed Pea Dip (page 57) Look no further for your perfect potluck go-to. This cheesy appetizer will be the talk of the Super Bowl party. Make sure to keep it in mind when tailgating season rolls around.

March

- Chocolate Bundt Cake (page 64) We use boxed mixes for this Bundt, making it easy to pull off. It's so elegant and impressive—nobody will ever know it all started with a mix.
- Salmon with Lemony Greens and Grains (page 66) This salmon dinner comes together in under 30 minutes and only uses one pan. Easy prep, easy cleanup. And it tastes like you've been cooking for hours.
- Cheesy Beef-and-Spinach Ravioli (page 69) If you have picky eaters in your family, you can leave out the spinach and you'll still get a hearty, healthy, great-tasting meal. You can replace the beef with ground turkey or chicken. This versatile dish is delicious any way you decide to make it.
- Spring Shrimp-and-Orzo Salad with Lemon Dressing (page 70) We love using lemon with shrimp—it really maximizes the flavor of this seaside favorite. The salad is great as a meal or in smaller portions as a side dish, and you can serve it warm or chilled.

April

- Hazelnut Financiers with Strawberry Jam and Lemon Puree (page 79) These fancy little cakes are as amazing as their name implies. Their nutty flavor and chewy texture combine to make them truly irresistible. Top them with sliced strawberries and powdered sugar for an extra-special presentation. They look almost as great as they taste.
- Strawberry-Rhubarb Crisps with Sweet-and-Savory Granola (page 80) The crunchy topping takes a bit of time to make, but it's worth it. Serve them in individual ramekins for a partyworthy treat.
- Huevos Rancheros Bake (page 84) We created this dish with an Easter brunch in mind, but it's perfect for any time of the year when you're looking for a satisfying start to your day.
- Company Quiche (page 86) We use a mix of eggs and egg whites in this Southern staple to make it a bit lighter. Asparagus and onions give it a nice pop of color, and it'll look impressive on your buffet table. Be sure to prebake the crust for best results.
- Skillet Pot Pie with Chicken and Spring Vegetables (page 89) This is not your ordinary chicken pot pie. It's wholesome, satisfying, and packed with fresh seasonal veggies to satisfy any craving. We cooked it in a skillet for a modern flair.

May

- Smoky Field Pea-and-Greens Dip (page 101) Be sure to use fresh field peas for this recipe if you can find them at your local farmers' market—otherwise frozen will work very nicely. Serve this bubbly-hot masterpiece with crusty baguette slices or your favorite crackers.
- Jambalaya Skewers (page 105) Celebrate the arrival of warm weather with a backyard barbecue and make these skewers the star of the show! They cook quickly, so there's no need to even soak the wooden skewers beforehand.
- Creamy Chicken Spaghetti (page 107) We lightened up this comforting classic so you can enjoy all the amazing flavor without any of the guilt. It's the perfect Sunday supper. No side dishes needed!
- Favorite Strawberry Shortcakes (page 109) We love using pure vanilla for the whipped cream. But if you're pressed for time, simply add a few drops of vanilla extract.

June

- Chocolate-Zucchini Cake (page 114) Chocolate and zucchini blend beautifully together in this moist and impressive cake. Our secret to getting the perfect texture is using a box grater to shred the zucchini.
- Pico de Gallo Pork Chops (page 117) All the fresh flavors of the seasons combine in one beautiful and hearty dish that's ready in under 30 minutes. Be sure to make some extra salsa. Pop it in the fridge to enjoy throughout the week.
- Grilled Chicken with Quick-Pickled Squash Salad (page 118) If you're looking for a fast, fresh, healthy dish to enjoy on a warm summer evening, look no further! We like to use a mix of yellow and green squash for the salad, but feel free to use any kind that's in season.
- Pasta with Summer Beans and Bacon (page 119) Add grilled chicken, shrimp, or sliced steak

to this summer salad to take it from side dish to main dish. It's sure to become your new go-to when asked to bring something to a backyard barbecue or casual potluck.
- Sausage, Egg, and Cheddar Biscuit Sandwiches (page 121) The classic egg casserole has been reinvented for a breakfast on the go! Prepare the casserole the night before and reheat in the microwave for a protein-packed, satisfying start to the day.

July

- Watermelon-Ginger Mojitos (page 127) Watermelon and ginger complement each other beautifully in these refreshing summer cocktails. Garnish with a slice of fresh watermelon and mint. Cheers!
- Watermelon Chiffon Pie (page 128) We just love watermelon and can't get enough of it during the hot summer months. This pie is one of our all-time favorites and looks just as impressive as it tastes. Don't let summer slip away without giving it a try.
- Smashed Bacon Cheeseburgers (page 134) By pressing the burger patties down on a hot griddle, you'll get thin burgers with nice crispy edges. Use one, two, or three patties per bun depending on your appetite. Then pile on the bacon and fresh tomato slice!
- Heirloom Tomato Pie with Parmesan-Buttermilk Crust (page 136) Our secret to perfection in this tasty tomato pie is to roast the tomatoes ahead of time. It'll keep the filling from becoming too wet and will also caramelize the tomatoes, intensifying their flavor.
- Black-and-Blue Buttermilk Tart (page 141) This beautiful berry tart is surprisingly simple to make. Your hands-on time is only 25 minutes, and it looks like you've spent all day in the kitchen. If you don't have a tart pan, use a standard pie plate.

August

- Dr Pepper Texas Sheet Cake (page 147) We combined two of our loves into one showstopping dessert. The cake has the fragrant flavors of the beloved beverage topped with a chocolate frosting that will melt in your mouth.
- Grilled Salmon Panzanella Salad (page 151) Day-old bread never tasted this good. Choose your favorite seasonal fresh tomatoes, add a few other ingredients, and you're all set. Ready in a flash and so delicious.
- Chicken Salad-Stuffed Tomatoes (page 154) This is one of our favorite ways to dress up a rotisserie chicken. Meaty beefsteak tomatoes work best, but you can also use smaller tomatoes to create bite-size appetizers.
- "Any-Berry" Muffins with Cornmeal Streusel (page 155) Any combination of berries that you have on hand will do. If you use larger berries, it's best to chop them into smaller pieces so the fruit is evenly distributed.
- Crispy Chicken-and-Broccoli Salad (page 157) We have tested and tasted a lot of broccoli salad over the years, but this is truly one the best. We use chicken tenders in our recipe, but you can leave them out if you're looking for a vegetarian dish.

September

- Smoky Kimchi Pimiento Cheese (page 202) Most Southern cooks have their favorite version of pimiento cheese. We chose this as one of our favorites because of the special kick we get from the kimchi. If you've never tried it, we urge you to give it a taste. We think you'll love it!
- Baked Chicken Wings with Pepper Jelly Glaze (page 204) Nobody will ever guess these oven-baked wings weren't fried. The pepper jelly glaze gives them a surprising new flavor. Dip them into blue cheese dressing and serve alongside celery and carrots at your next tailgate.

- Curried Chicken Pot Pie (page 208) This is sure to become a new family favorite. The best part is that you can make it ahead of time and freeze it. Thaw it out and you'll have dinner in under 30 minutes.
- Smoked-Pork-Stuffed Shells (page 209) You'll love our Southern spin on this traditional Italian dish. It calls for jarred marinara and barbecue sauce, making it a tasty, quick, and easy weeknight meal.
- Bacon-Cheddar Dutch Baby (page 211) A Dutch Baby is a fancy name for skillet pancake. The pastry shell puffs up as it bakes, and it looks super impressive on your brunch table. Cook and serve in a cast-iron skillet.

October

- Classic Boiled Peanuts (page 215) If you're not from the South, boiling peanuts may seem like a strange concept. But it is an artform that we have perfected with this recipe. It's an investment timewise, but we think it's well worth the wait.
- Beefy Butternut Squash Pasta (page 225) This one-pan dinner makes enough for two meals, so you can cook once and eat twice! And the best part is that it's on your table in less than 30 minutes.
- Diner-Style Patty Melts (page 226) Sourdough bread works best because it's hearty enough to stand up to the juicy meat and gooey cheese. One pan does the trick– use a cast-iron skillet to cook the patties and toast the bread.
- Persimmon Pudding (page 227) We haven't heard much about the persimmon since the days of the community cookbook, but it's back. And we've made it better than ever. We found that pudding is the best way to enjoy the fruit. It's a rich, cakelike dessert that's spicy, fruity, and tastes like fall.
- Baked Apple-Cranberry-Pecan Oatmeal (page 231) The overnight chilling will be worth the wait. This not-your-ordinary oatmeal makes a large batch, so you can feed a crowd or enjoy breakfast for the week.

November

- Spiced Coconut-Pumpkin Pie (page 237) We've given the pumpkin pie a tasty twist! The coconut milk adds a rich flavor and just a hint of tropical sweetness that complements the spicy filling very well.
- Creamy Baked Macaroni and Cheese with Bacon (page 244) A Southern Thanksgiving calls for the best, and this recipe fits the bill. We take the standard stove-top version up a notch to be worthy of a special-occasion side dish.
- Simple Mashed Rutabagas and Potatoes (page 245) We believe this lesser-known vegetable deserves a place at your Thanksgiving table. Our recipe brings out the natural sweetness of the rutabaga. It pairs nicely with Yukon Gold potatoes for a creamy, smooth texture.
- Fluffy Corn Pudding (page 249) Make this ahead of time and keep it in the fridge until you're carving the turkey. It cooks for about 40 minutes, making the timing perfect for serving with your meal.
- Buttermilk Spoon Bread (page 252) Spoon bread has been around since the late 18th century, with many versions making their way to the sideboard over the years. Ours calls for a different method of adding the eggs, which adds height and a little glamour to the dish.
- Baked Brie with Honeyed Five Spice Pecans (page 257) Baked Brie is the star of any appetizer platter, and this version takes it a step further. The pecans are sweet and spicy at the same time, making them a perfect partner for the cheese. Serve with crackers and apple slices.

December

- Chipotle Cheese Straws (page 270) Cheese straws are a must-have for the holiday entertaining season. Our version can be ready in under an hour, and it's definitely worth the effort. Almost as easy and picking up a bag of store-bought straws!
- Sweet-and-Spicy Meatballs (page 272) No holiday buffet is complete without meatballs. This recipe calls for chile-garlic sauce, soy, and ginger giving the sauce that perfect combination of sweet and salty. Reserve a bit of sauce for dipping before you add it to the slow cooker.
- Smoked Sausage Pretzel Bites (page 273) These tasty treats will soon become a holiday open house staple. We include a recipe for a mustard dipping sauce, but if you're pressed for time, simply serve with your favorite Dijon.
- Melting Sweet Potatoes with Walnuts (page 278) Give this new spin on a classic recipe a try this holiday season. It's ready for the oven in only 10 minutes!
- Prime Rib with Herbes de Provence Crust and Red Wine Sauce (page 281) Serve this elegant dish for Christmas dinner this year. The presentation is just as impressive as a holiday turkey or ham. Leftovers taste great on a sandwich the next day.
- Candy Cane Cake Bars (page 288) It's difficult to pick a "favorite" cookie. We have so many worthy of calling out, but these tasty treats fit the bill. Take them to your cookie swap, share with friends and family, or just enjoy them yourself. They are a must-try this season.
- Pralines (page 299) We use molasses and heavy cream in our recipe, making the pralines thick, chewy, and extra decadent. Make a batch to share and one to keep!

January

24 **Award-Winning Gumbo** Simmering stock, stirring roux, gathering crowds

26 **A Matter of Taste** For the past five decades, Nathalie Dupree has been one of our region's biggest culinary stars

32 **Tastes Like Comfort** Warm up weeknights with delicious spins on five soul-satisfying classics

38 **Go for the Greens** Toss up a salad with fresh seasonal ingredients

39 **Bananas for Sticky Buns** Turn New Orleans' famous dessert into a sweet brunch treat

40 **Winter Layers** Crisp, buttery phyllo makes a beautiful crust for this veggie-filled skillet pie–no dough-making required

41 **Just Add Sunshine** A rainbow of grapefruit gives a bright note to this rich, creamy cheesecake

42 **SL Cooking School** Our Test Kitchen professionals share flavorful ways to update four favorites

Award-Winning Gumbo

Simmering stock, stirring roux, gathering crowds

Smoked Turkey-and-Andouille Gumbo

Beau Beaullieu and Andy Soileau's New Iberia Kiwanis Club team has taken first place 11 times at the World Championship Gumbo Cookoff. This recipe for their mélange gumbo won in 2015, 2017, and 2018. Beaullieu likes to serve it alongside potato salad and garlic bread. Leftovers taste better the second day, Beaullieu says, and this gumbo freezes well.

ACTIVE 2 HOURS · TOTAL 13 HOURS
SERVES 12

- 1   (10-lb.) smoked turkey
- 10   celery stalks, divided
- 1   medium-size yellow onion
- 2   small yellow onions
- 3   green bell peppers, divided
- 1¾   cups all-purpose flour
- 1¾   cups canola oil
- 2   lb. andouille sausage, cut into bite-size pieces
- 3   garlic cloves, minced (about 1½ Tbsp.)
- 1½   tsp. garlic powder
- 1½   tsp. kosher salt
- 1   tsp. ground bay leaf (or 4 bay leaves)
- ¾   tsp. cayenne pepper
- ¾   tsp. white pepper
- ¾   tsp. black pepper
- 1   Tbsp. hot sauce (such as Tabasco)
- ¼   cup very finely chopped scallions
- ¼   cup very finely chopped fresh flat-leaf parsley
- Cooked white rice, for serving

1. Debone smoked turkey, trying not to shred meat. Cut turkey meat into manageable bite-size pieces, about 1 inch in size. Refrigerate turkey meat for later use in recipe. Place turkey carcass in a large (14-quart) stockpot.

2. Remove and reserve ends from celery. Remove and reserve ends and skins from all onions. Quarter medium-size onion. Quarter all bell peppers, and remove and reserve membranes; discard seeds. Add celery ends, pepper membranes, and onion ends and skins to pot, along with quartered onion, 4 whole celery stalks, and quarters from 1 pepper. Store remaining vegetables, covered, in refrigerator for later use.

3. Cover with water, and bring to a roaring boil over high; reduce heat to medium, and bring mixture to a simmer. Cook, at a steady simmer, until reduced to 8 quarts of stock, which will take up to 8 hours. Remove turkey carcass and vegetable pieces, and discard. Pour stock through a wire-mesh strainer over a large bowl to remove remaining solids; return strained stock to stockpot.

4. Stir together flour and oil in a medium-size cast-iron pan with a slotted, flat spatula. Stir until mixture is thoroughly combined and lumps or bits of flour are no longer visible. Cook mixture over medium, stirring constantly, until it is dark brown in color (think of an aged penny), between 35 minutes and 1 hour and 15 minutes. (This process depends on the heat, which varies from stove-top to stove-top, and the aggressiveness of the cook. Patience is very important.) If the roux burns, throw it away and start over. A burned roux cannot be used. The spatula should constantly rub or scrape the bottom of the pot to prevent mixture from sticking and burning. If the roux begins to clump, whisk out the clump with an aluminum whisk. Once roux has reached desired color, remove pan from heat; continue stirring until slightly cooled, about 10 minutes. (The roux will continue to cook as it cools.)

5. Bring stock to a light boil, and carefully stir in cooled roux. Stir until roux has completely dissolved into stock, giving stock a dark brown color. (At this stage, mixture will be very bitter and taste flat.)

6. Lightly boil mixture, stirring constantly, 45 minutes. Continue to cook, stirring occasionally, 25 minutes longer.

7. Add andouille sausage, in batches, to stock mixture. (Adding in batches prevents mixture from cooling down too much.) Cook, stirring occasionally, 45 minutes.

8. Meanwhile, dice remaining refrigerated celery (6 stalks, about 1½ cups), peppers (2 peppers, about 1 cup), and onions (2 small onions, about 2 cups). Keep diced vegetables separated.

9. Stir the minced garlic into the stock; stir in the "trinity" (diced celery, peppers, and onions), 1 vegetable at a time, adding onions last. Be careful not to cool down the gumbo. It is wise to add 1 vegetable and then wait 5 minutes, allowing the gumbo to heat back up before adding the next vegetable. Note the change in terminology: It's now a gumbo that is still in its infancy. Cook, stirring occasionally, 30 minutes.

10. Add turkey pieces slowly so the gumbo does not cool down. Lightly boil, stirring occasionally, 30 minutes. Stir gently to avoid breaking up the turkey pieces.

11. Add seasonings and hot sauce. If your taste buds are sensitive to seasonings, add only half of each seasoning (except the garlic powder) and hot sauce.

12. With a small aluminum ladle, begin to remove grease from top of gumbo. If additional grease rises to the surface, remove before serving. (Removing the grease is a key step.) Taste the gumbo. If it still seems flat, cook it longer for a greater depth of flavor. The amount of heat under the gumbo and the number of times it is stirred either shortens or lengthens the process.

13. Once you have settled on the taste and the gumbo is ready for serving, add scallions and parsley. Serve over rice, making sure you do not see the rice in your bowl and removing bay leaves (if using). It's not meant to be like a stew or rice and gravy. It should be served like a soup with rice at the bottom of the bowl.

A Matter of Taste

For the past five decades, Nathalie Dupree has been one of our region's biggest culinary stars, spreading the gospel of Southern food far and wide and inspiring generations of cooks, including author Virginia Willis

"Oh, hello, you're here for the meringue lesson."

The year was 1992, and just a few days earlier, I had presented Nathalie Dupree—cookbook author, queen of Southern cuisine, and my professional idol—with a plate of soggy meringue kisses while working behind the scenes on her PBS show, *Nathalie Dupree Cooks for Family and Friends*. In her typical way, Nathalie was gracious about my flop, saying only, "You know, Virginia, it's nearly impossible to make a meringue when it's raining," and then invited me over to her house for a one-on-one tutorial.

So there I was, in her Atlanta home stuffed with cookbooks, dishes, and folk art, learning to scour a large copper mixing bowl with a combination of kosher salt and lemon halves; to add the sugar in a slow, steady stream so it dissolves properly; and to whip the egg whites with a giant balloon whisk until they cling to the side of the bowl (which Nathalie demonstrated by holding it upside down over my head).

When the opportunity to work as an unpaid apprentice on Nathalie's cooking show came around, I jumped at it. When taping ended, I became a part-time apprentice in her home kitchen, testing recipes, shopping, and beginning the actual process of learning how to cook. My grandmother was excellent in the kitchen, and my mother is still an incredible cook, but Nathalie exposed me to things I had never seen and certainly never made, like homemade béchamel sauce and puff pastry.

Unlike many Southern women, Nathalie didn't learn to cook at her mother's or grandmother's elbow. Her parents' marriage ended when she was in elementary school, and her mother went to work to help support the family. So she figured out how to feed herself. After growing up in Virginia, she later moved to Texas for college. Nathalie transferred to George Washington University in Washington, D.C. Then she moved to Boston, where (at age 19) while living in international-student housing, she volunteered to step in for the house cook, who was ill. Not realizing that not

all recipes can be scaled up to feed a crowd, on her first night, she produced a tuna casserole that she describes as layers of grease, tuna, and gloppy sauce. But she stuck out her troubled tour in the kitchen and realized she actually enjoyed it. Nathalie told her mother that she had found her calling. Her mother's reply: "Ladies don't cook."

Thankfully, Nathalie didn't listen. Her marriage to David Dupree, whom she lovingly calls "her favorite former husband," set her on the path from home cook to trained professional. In the 1960s, his work took them to London. Nathalie used this opportunity to take a series of "bride's courses" at Le Cordon Bleu, which led her to earning an advanced diploma at age 30. David's work ended soon after, and a detour took them to Majorca, Spain. On her

Best Biscuit-Making Tips

Whisk the flour while it is still in the bag to fluff it up before measuring.

- -

Use a large, wide, and shallow bowl (not a deep one) for mixing the dough ingredients together.

- -

Rub your fingers and thumb together in a quick snapping motion when working fat into the flour.

- -

Make folding and shaping biscuit dough much easier and keep your countertop clean with a flexible plastic cutting sheet.

- -

And never twist a biscuit cutter—it will make crooked biscuits.

- -

third day there, someone approached her while she was swimming in a pool and said a local restaurant needed a chef for the season. The place had no window screens (so she was stung by wasps); she fought with the maître d'; and she served oversalted mussels to the owners. Though she once again had a rocky start, she persisted.

The couple moved to Atlanta, and Nathalie resumed cooking out of their tiny rental kitchen, supplying two carrot cakes a day to the historic Castle restaurant in Midtown. Soon after, she and David moved to rural Social Circle, Georgia, where they bought 15 acres of land with a warehouse that they transformed into a combination restaurant and antiques store called Nathalie's. In addition to cooking and managing the restaurant, Nathalie took on a newspaper route to help satisfy the bank loan.

Working with local farmers, neighbors with garden surpluses, and the nearby grocery store, Nathalie quickly developed a reputation for building a bridge between the Southern cuisine she grew up with and the European food she learned to cook while abroad. "I served the salad after the meal and bought sweetbreads from the local butcher," she says, adding, "I had only one menu a night, so the early guests got to decide what we were having each evening."

Satisfied regulars started requesting cooking classes, and soon after, Rich's downtown department store in Atlanta recruited her to open the Rich's Cooking School, where she taught for 10 years. Thousands of students (including author Pat Conroy and biochemist turned cookbook writer Shirley Corriher) learned her methods for French classics such as brioche and Southern staples like her light-as-air biscuits, which became one of her most beloved recipes. Nathalie was one of the first to talk about the gluten levels in flour and why Southern self-rising flour is ideal for making biscuits—ideas that are now widely known.

It wasn't long before the rest of the country took notice. Nathalie hosted

television segments for Atlanta's *PM Magazine* and PBS (which led to shows on The Learning Channel and Food Network) while writing cookbooks, most famously *New Southern Cooking* and *Mastering the Art of Southern Cooking*, which she coauthored with Cynthia Graubart. While her work has earned her a slew of accolades and four James Beard Awards, her philosophy remains simple: "I've always wanted people to be able to cook easily using accessible ingredients."

Now, at 79 years old, Nathalie shows no signs of slowing down. She spends her days with her husband, author and journalist Jack Bass, in a Single House nestled in downtown Charleston, South Carolina. There, surrounded by an abundance of cookware (including an enviable collection of asparagus tongs), she continues her work, shooting food videos for *The Post* and *Courier*, testing new recipes, and hosting visiting authors as well as dignitaries.

Last spring, I found myself back in the kitchen with Nathalie. I was in Charleston on a book tour, and she was throwing one of her famous parties for me. I stay with her often when I'm in town, but I rarely see her, as she is always on the go. This visit, however, was different. She had a foot injury with doctor's orders to stay off of it. As she sat in her chair in the den, I was in the adjacent kitchen cooking for the 75 guests expected that evening. It felt like old times, when just the two of us were together in the kitchen.

As I prepped the menu, I realized I needed to modify my Peach Upside-Down Cake recipe to feed the crowd. Fortunately, Nathalie helped me troubleshoot. "What do you think about a caramel sauce to serve on top of the cake instead of caramelizing the peaches in a skillet?" I asked. "Oh, yes, that sounds wonderful," she replied, adding, "I don't think you have to peel the peaches." "That's brilliant. What about the pan? Instead of a cake pan, I think I should use the Pyrex and double the recipe," I responded. Nodding, she agreed. Our entire day was filled with culinary banter, and as the dishes were ready, I would take her samples to taste. This time, everything met with her approval.

VIDALIA ONION-AND-VINEGAR SAUCE

A Few of Her Favorites

Roasted Beef Tenderloin

ACTIVE 10 MIN. - TOTAL 40 MIN.
SERVES 8 TO 10

- 1 (3- to 5-lb.) beef tenderloin, trimmed
- 1 Tbsp. olive oil
- 2 tsp. black pepper, plus more to taste
- 1½ tsp. kosher salt, plus more to taste Vidalia Onion-and-Vinegar Sauce (recipe follows)

1. Preheat oven to 500°F. Place tenderloin in a roasting pan; rub with oil, and sprinkle with pepper and salt. Tuck bottom end, or "tail," underneath the tenderloin.
2. Place in oven, and immediately reduce heat to 400°F; roast tenderloin until a thermometer inserted in thickest portion registers 130°F for rare or 140°F for medium-rare, 20 to 25 minutes. Sprinkle with additional salt and pepper to taste. Let rest 10 minutes before slicing.
3. Serve hot or cold with Vidalia Onion-and-Vinegar Sauce. May be made ahead, wrapped in aluminum foil, and then reheated 15 minutes in a 350°F oven. (It is easier to slice when cold.)

CARROT-AND-FENNEL
SALAD (PAGE 31)

ROASTED BEEF
TENDERLOIN

CAULIFLOWER WITH
CHEESE SAUCE (PAGE 31)

Vidalia Onion–and–Vinegar Sauce

ACTIVE 45 MIN. - TOTAL 1 HOUR
MAKES 2½ CUPS

- ¼ cup plus 3 Tbsp. unsalted butter, divided
- ¼ cup all-purpose flour
- 2 cups beef stock or broth
- ¾ tsp. kosher salt, plus more to taste
- ½ tsp. black pepper, plus more to taste
- 2 medium Vidalia onions, sliced (about 9 oz. each)
- ¼ cup dry white wine
- ¼ cup red wine vinegar

1. Melt ¼ cup of the butter in a large saucepan over medium. Whisk in flour; cook, whisking constantly, until mixture is the color of caramel, 5 to 6 minutes.
2. Gradually whisk in stock, salt, and pepper. Cook, stirring often, until heated through and smooth, 3 to 4 minutes. Keep warm over low heat until ready to use, up to 30 minutes. (This base sauce can be refrigerated or frozen for later use.)

3. Melt remaining 3 tablespoons butter in a heavy skillet over medium-low. Add onions. Cook, stirring constantly, until rich brown, 30 to 40 minutes.
4. Stir in wine and vinegar. Bring to a boil; cook until liquid has almost evaporated, about 3 minutes. Add warm base sauce to onion-and-vinegar mixture; bring to a boil. Cook until hot and bubbly, about 5 minutes. Sprinkle with additional salt and pepper to taste.

LEMON-LIME
MERINGUE PIE

Carrot-and-Fennel Salad

ACTIVE 20 MIN. - TOTAL 1 HOUR, 20 MIN.
SERVES 4

- 3 carrots, grated (about 2½ cups)
- 2 fennel bulbs, thinly sliced (about 3 cups)
- 2 medium shallots, finely chopped (about ¼ cup)
- ¼ cup red wine vinegar
- 1 Tbsp. finely chopped fresh herbs (such as thyme or dill)
- 1 Tbsp. Dijon mustard
- 1 tsp. granulated sugar
- ½ tsp. kosher salt
- ¼ tsp. black pepper
- ¼ cup olive oil
- 6 bacon slices, cooked crisp and crumbled
   Chopped fennel fronds, for topping

1. Place carrots and fennel in a large bowl, and set aside.
2. Whisk together shallots, vinegar, herbs, mustard, sugar, salt, and pepper in a small bowl until combined. Whisk in olive oil until emulsified.
3. Pour shallot vinaigrette over carrots and fennel; toss to coat. Let stand at room temperature 1 hour to marinate. Top with crumbled bacon and chopped fennel fronds just before serving.

Cauliflower with Cheese Sauce

ACTIVE 20 MIN. - TOTAL 30 MIN.
SERVES 4 TO 6

- 1 cup water
- 1 head cauliflower (about 2 lb.)
   Cheese Sauce (recipe follows)
- 1 oz. Cheddar cheese, grated (about ¼ cup)
- 2 Tbsp. unsalted butter
- ⅓ cup coarse fresh breadcrumbs
   Chopped fresh parsley, for topping

1. Preheat oven to 350°F. Heat water in a saucepan with a steamer basket over medium. Cut off thick stem of cauliflower, and remove all but the smallest green leaves. Using a sharp knife, make an X in the remaining core. Place cauliflower, core side down, in steamer basket. Cover and steam until tender, about 15 minutes. Drain. Cut into florets. Transfer cauliflower to an ovenproof serving bowl.

2. Top cauliflower with Cheese Sauce, and sprinkle with grated cheese. Bake in preheated oven until cauliflower is heated through, cheese is melted, and sauce is light brown and bubbling, 5 to 10 minutes.
3. Heat butter in a skillet over medium. Add breadcrumbs; cook, stirring occasionally, until brown. Sprinkle breadcrumbs over melted cheese. Top with chopped parsley.

Cheese Sauce

ACTIVE 5 MIN. - TOTAL 5 MIN.
MAKES ABOUT 2 CUPS

Melt 2 Tbsp. **unsalted butter** in a medium saucepan over medium. Whisk in 2 Tbsp. **all-purpose flour** until combined. Whisk in 1½ cups **whole milk**, and cook, whisking constantly, until mixture comes to a boil, about 2 minutes. Remove from heat, and stir in 2 oz. grated **Cheddar cheese** (about ½ cup), 1 tsp. **Dijon mustard**, ¾ tsp. **kosher salt**, and ¼ tsp. **black pepper** until smooth.

Lemon-Lime Meringue Pie

ACTIVE 30 MIN. - TOTAL 3 HOURS, 15 MIN.
SERVES 8

CRUST
- 1½ cups crushed graham crackers (about 11 rectangles)
- 6 Tbsp. unsalted butter, melted
- ¼ cup granulated sugar
- 1 large egg white, beaten until foamy

FILLING
- 1 cup granulated sugar
- 6 Tbsp. cornstarch
- ¼ tsp. salt
- 1 cup water
- 5 large egg yolks
- 1 Tbsp. lemon zest plus ¼ cup fresh juice (from 1 large lemon), divided
- 1 Tbsp. lime zest plus ¼ cup fresh juice (from 2 limes), divided
- 2 Tbsp. unsalted butter

MERINGUE
- 6 large egg whites
- ½ tsp. cream of tartar
- ¾ cup granulated sugar

1. Prepare the Crust: Preheat oven to 350°F. Stir together crushed graham crackers, butter, and sugar in a medium bowl until combined.

2. Transfer Crust mixture to a 9-inch tart pan or pie plate. (If using a tart pan with removable bottom, surround bottom of pan with aluminum foil to prevent Filling from leaking.) Press mixture evenly in bottom and up sides of pan. Freeze until set, 5 to 10 minutes. Brush bottom and sides of Crust with egg white. Bake in preheated oven 10 minutes. Cool on a rack while preparing Filling.
3. Prepare the Filling: Whisk together sugar, cornstarch, and salt in a medium saucepan. In a medium bowl, whisk together water, egg yolks, lemon juice, and lime juice. Gradually whisk yolk mixture into sugar mixture until combined. Cook over medium-high, whisking often, until Filling thickens and just begins to bubble, 6 to 8 minutes. Cook, whisking constantly, 1 minute more.
4. Remove from heat. Whisk in butter, lemon zest, and lime zest. Allow to cool 30 minutes before pouring into Crust.
5. Prepare the Meringue: Beat together egg whites and cream of tartar with an electric mixer on medium speed until soft peaks form. Gradually add sugar, 1 tablespoon at a time, beating until stiff peaks form.
6. Spread Meringue over Filling, being sure to spread to outside of Crust to seal in Filling and prevent shrinkage. Bake at 350°F until Meringue is golden brown, 14 to 15 minutes. Cool before serving.

> "She taught me to never apologize for any food I serve. Be proud of what you cook, no matter what it is!"
>
> Rebecca Lang, *Southern Living* Contributing Editor and author of *The Southern Vegetable Book*

Tastes Like Comfort

Warm up weeknights with delicious spins on five soul-satisfying classics

TIME-SAVER
Cut down on cleanup by making this chicken soup with leftover cooked white rice or with one package of microwavable white rice, such as Uncle Ben's.

Creamy Chicken-and-Rice Soup with Collard Greens

ACTIVE 35 MIN. - TOTAL 35 MIN.
SERVES 8

- 3 Tbsp. unsalted butter
- 2 large leeks, thinly sliced (white and light green parts only, 4 cups)
- 2 medium carrots, thinly sliced (1 cup)
- 2 celery stalks, finely chopped (½ cup)
- 2 large garlic cloves, minced (1 Tbsp.)
- ¼ cup all-purpose flour
- 8 cups lower-sodium chicken broth
- 3 cups shredded rotisserie chicken (from 1 whole chicken)
- 1 Tbsp. chopped fresh thyme, plus more for garnish
- 4 cups chopped collard greens (from 1 bunch)
- 2 cups cooked white rice
- ½ cup heavy cream
- 1 Tbsp. kosher salt
- ¼ tsp. black pepper

Melt butter in a large Dutch oven over medium. Add leeks, carrots, celery, and garlic. Cook, stirring often, until softened, about 5 minutes. Add flour; cook, stirring constantly, 1 minute. Add broth, chicken, and thyme. Bring to a boil over medium-high. Reduce heat to medium-low, and simmer 10 minutes. Stir in collard greens; cook until just tender, about 5 minutes. Remove from heat; stir in cooked rice, cream, salt, and pepper. Garnish servings with additional thyme.

Roasted Tomato–Cheddar Soup

ACTIVE 10 MIN. - TOTAL 55 MIN.
SERVES 6

- 3 lb. plum tomatoes, halved (about 14 or 15 medium tomatoes)
- 1 medium-size yellow onion, quartered
- 6 large garlic cloves, smashed
- 10 thyme sprigs
- 2 Tbsp. olive oil
- ¼ tsp. black pepper, plus more for serving
- 1 Tbsp. kosher salt, divided
- 3 cups lower-sodium chicken broth
- 1½ Tbsp. balsamic vinegar
- 6 oz. sharp Cheddar cheese, shredded (about 1½ cups), plus more for serving
- Chopped fresh chives

1. Preheat oven to 425°F. Toss together tomatoes, onion, garlic, thyme, oil, pepper, and ½ tablespoon of the salt on a large rimmed baking sheet. Arrange tomatoes evenly, cut sides down, on baking sheet. Bake in preheated oven until tomato skins begin to blister, 25 to 30 minutes.

2. Peel and discard skins from cooked tomatoes; discard thyme from baking sheet. Transfer peeled tomatoes, onion, garlic, and any accumulated juices from baking sheet to a Dutch oven. Add broth, vinegar, and remaining ½ tablespoon salt. Process mixture with an immersion blender until smooth, about 2 minutes. Bring to a simmer over medium; simmer 10 minutes.

3. Remove from heat; stir in cheese until melted and smooth. (If soup is not completely smooth, process once more with immersion blender.) Spoon soup evenly into 6 bowls; sprinkle with additional cheese, pepper, and chives.

COOKING TIP

An immersion blender makes pureeing soup a snap. If you don't have this kitchen tool, simply transfer the hot soup in batches to a blender and process until smooth. Fill the blender no more than halfway so steam can escape.

Instant Pot Beef-and-Barley Soup with Mushrooms

ACTIVE 20 MIN. - TOTAL 1 HOUR
SERVES 6

- 2 medium-size yellow onions, divided
- 4 celery stalks, divided
- 2 lb. boneless beef short ribs, trimmed and cut into 2-inch pieces
- 1 tsp. kosher salt
- ¾ tsp. black pepper, divided
- 3 Tbsp. olive oil
- 8 oz. fresh cremini mushrooms, sliced
- 3 large garlic cloves, minced (1½ Tbsp.)
- 8 cups beef broth
- 1 large carrot, halved crosswise
- 10 thyme sprigs (tied together with kitchen twine)
- 1 cup uncooked quick-cooking barley
  Fresh thyme leaves

1. Chop 1 of the onions into 1-inch pieces, and chop 2 of the celery stalks into ½-inch pieces; set aside. Cut remaining onion and 2 celery stalks in half crosswise; set aside.

2. Preheat Instant Pot (or other programmable pressure cooker) to the "Sauté" setting. Sprinkle beef with salt and ½ teaspoon of the pepper. Add oil to preheated pot. Add beef; cook, turning occasionally, until browned on all sides, about 10 minutes. Remove from pot; set aside. Add mushrooms; cook, stirring often, until tender and browned, about 5 minutes. Remove from pot; set aside. Add the chopped onion and celery pieces; cook, stirring often, until softened, about 5 minutes. Add garlic; cook, stirring constantly, until fragrant, about 1 minute. Return beef and mushrooms to pot. Stir in broth, carrot, tied thyme sprigs, the halved onion and celery, and remaining ¼ teaspoon pepper.

3. Close lid on the Instant Pot, making sure valve is in the sealed position. Select "Manual," and set the pot to 30 minutes on high pressure.

4. Meanwhile, fill a medium saucepan with water; add barley. Bring to a boil over high; cook until tender, about 10 minutes. Drain.

5. When the cook time on the Instant Pot ends, carefully flip the valve to do a quick release. Once the pressure has come down, remove the lid.

6. Remove and discard carrot, onion and celery halves, and tied thyme sprigs. Skim fat from top of soup. Stir in cooked barley. Sprinkle with thyme leaves.

STOVE-TOP METHOD

No Instant Pot? No problem! Prepare recipe as directed in Steps 1 and 2, substituting a Dutch oven over medium-high for an Instant Pot. Omit Step 3. Bring mixture in Dutch oven to a boil over high. Reduce heat to medium-low, and simmer, covered, until beef is fork-tender, about 1 hour and 45 minutes. Proceed with recipe as directed in Steps 4 and 6, omitting Step 5.

Smoky Split Pea-and-Sausage Soup

ACTIVE 15 MIN. - TOTAL 55 MIN.
SERVES 6

- 1 tsp. extra-virgin olive oil, plus more for serving
- 1 lb. smoked sausage (such as Conecuh), sliced into ½-inch rounds
- 1 large yellow onion, chopped (2 cups)
- 2 medium carrots, chopped (⅔ cup)
- 2 celery stalks, chopped (½ cup)
- 2 large garlic cloves, minced (1 Tbsp.)
- 1 lb. dried split peas, rinsed and picked over
- 6 cups lower-sodium chicken broth
- 1 tsp. kosher salt
- ¼ tsp. black pepper, plus more for serving
- 2 bay leaves

1. Heat oil in a large Dutch oven over medium-high. Add sausage; cook, stirring often, until browned, 5 to 6 minutes. Remove sausage, and set aside.

2. Add onion, carrots, celery, and garlic to Dutch oven. Cook, stirring often, until tender, about 5 minutes. Stir in split peas, broth, salt, pepper, and bay leaves. Bring to a boil over medium-high.

3. Stir in cooked sausage. Reduce heat to medium-low. Simmer, stirring occasionally, until peas are tender, about 40 minutes. Remove and discard bay leaves. Spoon soup evenly into 6 bowls.

4. Drizzle with additional oil, and sprinkle with additional pepper.

Lentil Soup with Sweet Potatoes and Bacon

ACTIVE 20 MIN. - TOTAL 1 HOUR
SERVES 6

- 8 thick-cut bacon slices, cut into ½-inch pieces
- 1 medium-size yellow onion, chopped (1½ cups)
- 2 celery stalks, finely chopped (½ cup)
- 3 large garlic cloves, minced (1½ Tbsp.)
- 1 tsp. ground cumin
- 1 large sweet potato, peeled and chopped into ¾-inch cubes (3 cups)
- 1½ cups dried brown lentils
- 8 cups lower-sodium chicken broth
- 1 (14.5-oz.) can fire-roasted diced tomatoes, undrained
- 2 tsp. kosher salt
- ¼ tsp. black pepper
  Chopped fresh flat-leaf parsley

1. Cook bacon pieces in a large Dutch oven over medium-high, stirring often, until crisp, about 10 minutes. Drain on paper towels, and set aside. Remove and discard all but 2 tablespoons drippings from Dutch oven.

2. Add onion, celery, and garlic to Dutch oven. Cook over medium-high, stirring often, until softened, about 5 minutes. Add cumin, and cook, stirring constantly, until toasted, about 1 minute. Stir in sweet potato, lentils, broth, tomatoes, salt, and pepper. Bring to a boil over medium-high. Reduce heat to medium-low; simmer until lentils are tender, 45 to 50 minutes. Spoon soup evenly into 6 bowls. Top with reserved bacon pieces, and sprinkle with parsley.

MAKE AHEAD
This rich, smoky soup can be prepared up to three days in advance and stored in the refrigerator. It tastes even better when the flavors have had extra time to marry.

Buttery Chive-and-Mustard Drop Biscuits

ACTIVE 15 MIN. - TOTAL 35 MIN.
MAKES 24

- 3 cups all-purpose flour
- 2 oz. Parmesan cheese, grated on smallest holes of a box grater (about ½ cup)
- ¼ cup sliced fresh chives, plus more for garnish
- 1 Tbsp. baking powder
- 1 tsp. black pepper
- ¾ tsp. kosher salt
- ¾ tsp. garlic powder
- ¾ tsp. baking soda
- 1¾ cups whole buttermilk
- 3 Tbsp. whole-grain mustard
- ¾ cup unsalted butter, frozen, plus melted butter for serving

1. Preheat oven to 475°F. Stir together flour, cheese, chives, baking powder, pepper, salt, garlic powder, and baking soda in a large bowl. Whisk together buttermilk and mustard in a small bowl. Grate frozen butter into flour mixture using the large holes of a box grater; stir until well coated. Add buttermilk mixture; stir until just combined.
2. Drop batter in 2½- to 3-tablespoonful rounds onto 2 baking sheets lined with parchment paper, leaving 3 inches between rounds.
3. Bake in preheated oven until biscuits are golden brown, 14 to 18 minutes, rotating baking sheets between top and bottom racks halfway through baking time. Brush biscuits with melted butter; garnish with sliced chives. Serve warm.

Go for the Greens

Toss up a salad with fresh seasonal ingredients

Clementine-and-Collard Salad

ACTIVE 20 MIN. - TOTAL 20 MIN.
SERVES 4

Squeeze juice from 1 **clementine** into a small bowl. (You should have about 2 tablespoons juice.) Add 1 tablespoon **apple cider vinegar**, 2 teaspoons **Dijon mustard**, 1 teaspoon **sorghum syrup** (or honey), ¼ teaspoon **black pepper**, and ½ teaspoon **kosher salt**. Slowly add ¼ cup **extra-virgin olive oil**, whisking to combine. Place 1 pound **collard greens**, stemmed and cut into thin strips (8 cups), and 2 small sliced **shallots** (⅓ cup) in a large bowl. Add 2 tablespoons dressing, and gently massage into greens mixture with hands until greens are wilted and tender, 1 minute. Reserve remaining dressing. Peel and slice 2 **clementines** into rings, and set aside. Place the greens mixture on a serving platter; top with 1½ cups shredded **rotisserie chicken** (about 6 ounces), ½ cup chopped toasted **pecans**, 3 ounces crumbled **goat cheese** (about ¾ cup), and sliced clementines. Drizzle reserved dressing over salad, and sprinkle with ¼ teaspoon **kosher salt**.

Nutritional information: Calories: 413; Protein: 24g; Carbs: 16g; Fiber: 6g; Fat: 30g

COOKING TRICK
Massage some of the dressing into the collards to tenderize the greens and make them more flavorful.

Bananas for Sticky Buns

Turn New Orleans' famous dessert into a sweet brunch treat

Mini Bananas Foster Sticky Buns

Refrigerated crescent roll dough makes these sticky buns easy to whip up.

ACTIVE 25 MIN. · TOTAL 1 HOUR
MAKES 2 DOZEN

- 6 Tbsp. butter, divided
- ¾ cup firmly packed light brown sugar, divided
- 2 medium-size ripe bananas, thinly sliced (about 12 oz.)
- 1½ Tbsp. (¾ oz.) light rum, divided
- ½ tsp. ground cinnamon
- 6 Tbsp. granulated sugar, divided
- 2 (8-oz.) cans refrigerated crescent rolls
- ½ cup butter, very softened
- ¼ cup heavy cream
- ¼ tsp. kosher salt
- ½ cup plus 1 to 3 Tbsp. powdered sugar, sifted
- ⅓ cup chopped toasted pecans

1. Melt 2 tablespoons of the butter in a medium skillet over medium; stir in ¼ cup of the brown sugar until combined. Stir in bananas and ½ tablespoon of the rum; cook, stirring often, until bananas soften and begin to break down, 3 to 4 minutes. Set aside; let cool completely, about 20 minutes.

2. Preheat oven to 375°F. Stir together cinnamon, ¼ cup of the brown sugar, and 2 tablespoons of the granulated sugar in a small bowl. Unroll 1 can of crescent roll dough on a lightly floured surface. Separate dough piece along center perforation to form 2 (7½- x 6-inch) rectangles; press perforations to seal. Repeat with remaining can.

3. Spread the 4 dough rectangles evenly with the softened butter, and sprinkle each with about 2 tablespoons of the cinnamon-sugar mixture. Dollop each rectangle with one-fourth of cooled banana mixture, and carefully spread a thin layer of the mixture to within ¼ inch of edges. Roll up each rectangle, jelly-roll fashion, starting at long end.

PICKING POINTERS

Choose bananas that are starting to show signs of ripeness (small brown dots). They will have just the right amount of sweetness and won't turn to mush when cooked.

4. Gently cut each dough log into 6 even slices using a serrated knife. Place rolls in 2 (12-cup) mini muffin pans lined with miniature paper baking cups. Bake in preheated oven until golden brown, 14 to 16 minutes. Let cool on wire racks 15 minutes.

5. Place cream, salt, and remaining ¼ cup each butter, brown sugar, and granulated sugar in a small saucepan over medium. Bring to a boil, whisking constantly; boil 1 minute. Remove from heat, and whisk in remaining 1 tablespoon rum. Gradually whisk in ½ cup of the powdered sugar until smooth. Whisk in remaining 1 to 3 tablespoons powdered sugar, 1 tablespoon at a time, until desired consistency is reached. Drizzle slightly warm buns with glaze, and sprinkle with toasted pecans.

Winter Layers

Crisp, buttery phyllo makes a beautiful crust for this veggie-filled skillet pie—no dough-making required

Skillet Vegetable Pie with Goat Cheese

ACTIVE 30 MIN. - TOTAL 2 HOURS

SERVES 6

-   5 Tbsp. olive oil, divided
-   1 small (8-oz.) yellow onion, chopped (1 cup)
-   2 cups (10 oz.) cubed butternut squash (from 1 medium squash)
-   1 lb. Broccolini, chopped (4½ cups)
-   4 oz. fresh cremini mushrooms, chopped (1¾ cups)
-   2 small garlic cloves, chopped (1 tsp.)
-   1¼ oz. Parmesan cheese, shredded (about ½ cup)
-   1 large egg, beaten
-   1 tsp. kosher salt
-   ½ tsp. black pepper
-   ½ tsp. crushed red pepper
-   6 Tbsp. unsalted butter, melted
-   12 (9- x 14-inch) sheets frozen phyllo dough, thawed
-   2 oz. goat cheese, crumbled (about ½ cup)

1. Preheat oven to 350°F. Heat 2 tablespoons of the oil in a 9-inch cast-iron skillet over medium. Add onion, and cook, stirring often, until softened, about 6 minutes. Add squash; cover and cook, stirring occasionally, until almost tender, about 8 minutes. Transfer mixture to a medium bowl. Add remaining 3 tablespoons oil to skillet over medium-high. Add Broccolini, mushrooms, and garlic. (Skillet will be very full, but vegetables will cook down.) Cook, stirring occasionally, until almost tender, about 8 minutes. Transfer to bowl with squash mixture. Wipe skillet clean. Let vegetable mixture cool 30 minutes. Add Parmesan, egg, salt, black pepper, and crushed red pepper to squash mixture; stir to combine.

2. Brush skillet lightly with butter. Fit 1 phyllo sheet into skillet, allowing the edges to hang over the sides. (Cover remaining sheets with a damp paper towel to prevent them from drying out.) Quickly brush sheet lightly with butter, and turn skillet 45 degrees. Continuing to work quickly, top with a second sheet; brush lightly with butter. Repeat with remaining sheets and butter, reserving 1 tablespoon of the butter.

3. Spoon vegetable mixture evenly over phyllo layers in skillet. Sprinkle goat cheese over top. Fold edges of phyllo sheets up and over filling toward center, overlapping slightly, leaving center exposed. Brush top of phyllo with remaining tablespoon butter. Bake in preheated oven until crust is golden brown, about 40 minutes. Transfer skillet to a wire rack. Cool 15 minutes before serving.

Foolproof Phyllo Crust

Fit 1 phyllo sheet into the buttered skillet so the edges hang over the sides. Brush the entire sheet lightly with melted butter, making sure to coat the edges.

Turn the skillet 45 degrees. Quickly top with a second sheet; brush lightly with butter. Repeat until all sheets are used, reserving 1 tablespoon butter.

Spoon the filling over the phyllo layers. Fold the edges up and over the filling, overlapping slightly and leaving center exposed. Brush top of phyllo with remaining butter.

Just Add Sunshine

A rainbow of grapefruit gives a bright note to this rich, creamy cheesecake

Grapefruit Cheesecake

ACTIVE 20 MIN. - TOTAL 4 HOURS, 20 MIN., PLUS
8 HOURS CHILLING

SERVES 12

CRUST

- 2½ cups finely crushed crisp almond cookies (from 2 [3.5-oz.] pkg.)
- 5 Tbsp. butter, melted
- 2 Tbsp. granulated sugar

CHEESECAKE

- 5 (8-oz.) pkg. cream cheese, softened
- 1¾ cups granulated sugar
- 3 Tbsp. all-purpose flour
- 5 large eggs
- 2 large egg yolks
- 1 Tbsp. grapefruit zest plus ¼ cup fresh juice (from 1 grapefruit)
- 1 tsp. vanilla extract

TOPPING

- ¼ cup grapefruit marmalade (such as Stonewall Kitchen)
- 1 Tbsp. fresh grapefruit juice
- 3 grapefruit, peeled, sliced, and patted dry

1. Prepare the Crust: Preheat oven to 325°F. Wrap outside of a lightly greased 9-inch springform pan with heavy-duty aluminum foil. Stir together cookies, butter, and sugar. Press onto bottom and 1 inch up sides of pan. Bake until set, 7 to 8 minutes. Transfer to a wire rack; cool completely, 30 minutes.

2. Prepare the Cheesecake: Beat cream cheese with a heavy-duty stand mixer on medium speed until creamy, 3 minutes. Gradually add sugar and flour, beating until smooth. Add eggs, 1 at a time, beating after each addition. Add egg yolks, 1 at a time, beating after each addition. Beat in zest, juice, and vanilla on low speed just until combined. Pour into prepared pan (it will be full); place on a rimmed baking sheet.

3. Bake at 325°F until center is almost set but still wobbly, 1 hour and 10 minutes to 1 hour and 20 minutes. Transfer to rack; cool completely, 2 hours. Cover with aluminum foil; chill 8 to 12 hours. Run a knife around outer edge; remove sides of pan.

4. Prepare the Topping: Stir together marmalade and juice in a microwavable bowl. Microwave on HIGH, about 45 seconds; stir to make a glaze. Arrange grapefruit slices on Cheesecake; brush with glaze.

SERVING TIP

To keep the cheesecake from getting soggy, arrange the grapefruit on top just before eating. If you have leftover cheesecake, remove the grapefruit and store separately in the refrigerator.

[3]

[2]

[1]

[4]

Segment Citrus Like a Pro

1

Slice off the top and bottom of the fruit with a paring knife.

2

Cut off the peel and pith in vertical strips, working your way around the entire fruit.

3

Hold the peeled fruit over a bowl, and then slice in between the membranes (toward the center of the fruit). Let the sections fall into the bowl.

The Secret to Better Soup

Our Test Kitchen professionals share flavorful ways to update four favorites

1
CREAM-STYLE CORN

"Canned cream-style or pureed fresh corn will give a velvety texture to chowder—no flour or cornstarch needed."

—Pam Lolley

2
PARMESAN RIND

"I cook minestrone soup with a Parmesan cheese rind. It adds richness and infuses the broth with a subtle nutty flavor."

—Paige Grandjean

3
LONG-GRAIN RICE

"I prefer long-grain rice because it won't break down in chicken soup. Cook it separately, and add to soup before serving."

—Robby Melvin

4
SAN MARZANO TOMATOES

"These canned tomatoes have a well-balanced flavor that I prefer for tomato soup or bisque."

—Karen Rankin

February

44   **Raising the Bar** Seven sweet ideas—from pecan pie bars to chocolate brownies—that are easy to make and fun to share

50   **Weeknight Cheat Sheets** One pan, five delicious suppers, and very little cleanup

55   **Soup's On** Packed with veggies and flavored with a little bacon, this recipe will warm you up on a chilly day

56   **Chicken in a Snap** This tasty 30-minute meal comes together in one pan

57   **Make Your Famous Dip!** This cheesy appetizer will be the talk of the Super Bowl gathering

58   **SL Cooking School** Our Test Kitchen professionals share tips to help you cut perfect bars every time

PEANUT BUTTER-
FUDGE BARS

Raising the Bar

Seven sweet ideas—from pecan pie bars to chocolate brownies—that are easy to make and fun to share

When cookies seem too casual and layer cakes feel too fancy, dessert bars stand in the gap, delivering surprising flavors in portable packaging. For generations of bakers, these handheld treats have been the go-to choice for bridal showers, birthday parties, potlucks, and any other celebratory gatherings. Why do we love them? Let us count the ways: They can be made ahead of time, baked and served out of one pan, and transported with ease. Plus, they're great for feeding a crowd.

In the July 1966 issue of *Southern Living*, we published our first bar recipe, Seven-Layer Cookies, which called for graham cracker crumbs, pecans, flaked coconut, and chocolate and butterscotch chips. Fifty-three years later, our Test Kitchen is still dreaming up tasty new creations, developing time-saving shortcuts, and sharing smart grocery store substitutions that make baking easier and sweeter than ever.

SPICED PECAN PIE BARS

Peanut Butter-Fudge Bars

Allow enough time for the top layer of melted chocolate to firm up before slicing these triple-decker bars. Leftovers can be covered and stored in the refrigerator up to three days.

ACTIVE 15 MIN. - TOTAL 3 HOURS
MAKES 32

    Baking spray with flour
1 (18¾-oz.) pkg. brownie mix (such as Ghirardelli)
1 (10-oz.) pkg. peanut butter chips (about 1¾ cups)
1 (14-oz.) can sweetened condensed milk
½ cup creamy peanut butter
1 tsp. vanilla extract
    Pinch of salt
1½ cups semisweet chocolate chips
¾ cup heavy cream
½ cup roasted salted peanuts, chopped

1. Preheat oven to 350°F. Spray a 13- x 9-inch baking pan with baking spray with flour. Prepare brownie mix according to package directions in prepared pan, baking at 350°F until a wooden pick inserted in the middle comes out clean, about 25 minutes. (Baking times may vary among brownie mixes.) Cool completely, about 1 hour.
2. Place peanut butter chips, sweetened condensed milk, peanut butter, vanilla, and salt in a medium microwavable bowl. Microwave on HIGH 1 minute. Stir until smooth. Spoon over cooled brownies, spreading in an even layer.
3. Place chocolate chips and cream in a small microwavable bowl. Microwave on HIGH until chocolate is melted and mixture is smooth, about 2 minutes, stirring every 30 seconds. Pour over peanut butter mixture on brownies, spreading in an even layer. Refrigerate brownies until top chocolate layer is firm, about 1 hour. Sprinkle with peanuts. Slice into 32 bars.

Spiced Pecan Pie Bars

Two pantry staples—ground cinnamon and ginger—give the traditional pecan pie filling an unexpected and flavorful twist. For an impressive dessert, serve each bar on a plate with a scoop of ice cream and a drizzle of caramel sauce.

ACTIVE 10 MIN. - TOTAL 2 HOURS
MAKES 32

CRUST
    Baking spray with flour
3 cups all-purpose flour
1 cup cold unsalted butter, cubed
¾ cup unsifted powdered sugar
1 tsp. kosher salt
FILLING
4 large eggs
1 cup light corn syrup
⅔ cup packed light brown sugar
½ cup honey
¼ cup all-purpose flour
¼ cup unsalted butter, melted
1 tsp. ground cinnamon
½ tsp. kosher salt
½ tsp. ground ginger
3 cups pecans, coarsely chopped

1. Prepare the Crust: Preheat oven to 350°F. Spray a 13- x 9-inch baking pan with baking spray with flour. Line bottom and sides of pan with parchment paper, leaving a 2- to 3-inch overhang on 2 sides. Place flour, butter, powdered sugar, and salt in a food processor. Pulse until coarse crumbs form, 6 to 7 times. Firmly press mixture into bottom of prepared pan. Bake in preheated oven until light golden brown, about 20 minutes. (Crust will have cracks.)
2. Prepare the Filling: Whisk together eggs, corn syrup, brown sugar, honey, flour, melted butter, cinnamon, salt, and ginger in a bowl until smooth. Stir in pecans. Pour over warm Crust. Bake at 350°F until Filling is set, 25 to 30 minutes. Cool completely in pan, about 1 hour. Slice into 32 bars.

CAPPUCCINO
SWIRL BARS

Cappuccino Swirl Bars

Don't be fooled: These look fancy, but store-bought wafer cookies are the secret to the chocolate crust. Make these coffee-flavored beauties in advance, and refrigerate up to three days.

ACTIVE 15 MIN. - TOTAL 45 MIN., PLUS 4 HOURS CHILLING

MAKES 32

CRUST

Baking spray with flour
3 cups chocolate wafer cookie crumbs (from 2 [9-oz.] pkg. chocolate wafer cookies, such as Nabisco Famous)
½ cup butter, melted
⅓ cup granulated sugar
1 Tbsp. instant espresso granules
1 large egg white, lightly beaten

FILLING

3 (8-oz.) pkg. cream cheese, softened
1⅓ cups granulated sugar
1 cup heavy cream, divided
2 Tbsp. instant espresso granules
1 Tbsp. unsweetened cocoa

GARNISH

Chocolate-covered espresso beans, chopped

1. Prepare the Crust: Preheat oven to 325°F. Coat a 13- x 9-inch baking pan with baking spray with flour. Stir together cookie crumbs, melted butter, sugar, espresso granules, and egg white in a large bowl until combined. Firmly press mixture into bottom of prepared pan. Bake in preheated oven until Crust is set, about 14 minutes. Cool completely, about 30 minutes.

2. Prepare the Filling: Beat cream cheese and sugar in a stand mixer fitted with a paddle attachment on medium-high speed until smooth and creamy, about 3 minutes. Reduce speed to low; beat in ¾ cup of the heavy cream. Increase speed to high; beat until stiff peaks form, about 2 minutes. Transfer 2 cups of the cream cheese mixture to a medium bowl; set aside. Dollop remaining 3 cups cream cheese mixture over cooled Crust.

3. Place remaining ¼ cup heavy cream in a small microwavable bowl; microwave on HIGH until just warm, about 20 seconds. Stir in espresso granules and cocoa until dissolved. Place in freezer; cool 10 minutes. Beat cooled mixture into reserved cream cheese mixture on medium speed until smooth and thickened, about 1 minute. Dollop over cream cheese mixture in Crust. Using a spoon, swirl espresso-cream cheese and plain cream cheese mixtures together to edges of Crust.

4. Cover and refrigerate until very cold, at least 4 hours. Slice into 32 bars. Garnish bars with chopped chocolate-covered espresso beans.

Ultimate Dark Chocolate Brownies

Bourbon and espresso make these rich, fudgy brownies even more decadent. For a kid-friendly—but still delicious—option, you can skip those two ingredients.

ACTIVE 30 MIN. - TOTAL 2 HOURS
MAKES 32

Baking spray with flour
3 (4-oz.) bittersweet chocolate bars (such as Ghirardelli), chopped (about 2 cups)
1 cup unsalted butter
4 large eggs
¾ cup granulated sugar
¾ cup packed light brown sugar
3 Tbsp. (1½ oz.) bourbon
2 Tbsp. instant espresso granules
1½ cups all-purpose flour
½ tsp. kosher salt
3 (4-oz.) semisweet chocolate bars, chopped (about 2 cups), divided
1 tsp. flaky sea salt

1. Preheat oven to 350°F. Coat a 13- x 9-inch baking pan with baking spray with flour. Bring a medium pot with 1 inch of water to a simmer over low. Set a medium-size heatproof glass bowl over pot. Add chopped bittersweet chocolate and butter to bowl; cook, stirring occasionally, until melted, about 2 minutes. Remove from heat; cool slightly, about 10 minutes.

2. Whisk eggs, granulated sugar, brown sugar, bourbon, and espresso granules into cooled chocolate-butter mixture until well combined. Stir in flour and kosher salt until combined. Pour half of the batter into prepared pan. Sprinkle with 1 cup of the chopped semisweet chocolate. Top with remaining batter, smoothing with an offset spatula. Sprinkle with remaining 1 cup chopped semisweet chocolate.

3. Bake in preheated oven until center is set, about 25 minutes. Remove from oven; sprinkle with flaky sea salt. Cool completely in pan, about 1 hour. Slice into 32 bars.

ULTIMATE DARK
CHOCOLATE BROWNIES

Brown Butter-Caramel Blondies

(Photo, page 7)

ACTIVE 40 MIN. - TOTAL 1 HOUR, 50 MIN.
MAKES 32

CARAMEL

1½   cups granulated sugar
¼   cup light corn syrup
¼   cup water
½   cup heavy cream
3   Tbsp. unsalted butter, softened
¼   tsp. salt

BLONDIES

  Baking spray with flour
1½   cups unsalted butter
4   large eggs
2½   cups packed light brown sugar
1   tsp. vanilla extract
3½   cups all-purpose flour
2   tsp. baking powder
1   tsp. salt
¾   cup chopped walnuts, divided
1   (4-oz.) semisweet chocolate bar, chopped, divided

1. Prepare the Caramel: Bring granulated sugar, corn syrup, and water to a boil in a medium saucepan over medium-high. Boil, undisturbed, until mixture turns amber in color, about 10 minutes. Remove from heat; carefully stir in cream, butter, and salt until smooth. Cool until slightly thickened, about 30 minutes.

2. Prepare the Blondies: Preheat oven to 350°F. Coat a 13- x 9-inch baking pan with baking spray with flour. Melt butter in a medium saucepan over medium, swirling occasionally, until butter browns and has a nutty aroma, about 10 minutes. Transfer to a large bowl; cool slightly, about 30 minutes. Whisk eggs, brown sugar, and vanilla into brown butter until shiny, about 30 seconds. Stir together flour, baking powder, and salt in a separate bowl until combined. Gradually add flour mixture, ½ cup of the walnuts, and 2 ounces of the chocolate to brown butter-egg mixture, stirring until combined. Spoon half of the batter into prepared pan. Bake 10 minutes.

3. Remove pan from oven; drizzle with 1 cup cooled Caramel. Spoon remaining batter over top. Sprinkle with remaining ¼ cup walnuts and 2 ounces chocolate. Return to oven; bake at 350°F until mixture is golden and set, about 25 minutes. Cool completely in pan, about 1 hour. Slice into 32 bars. Drizzle with remaining Caramel just before serving.

Lemon-Coconut Chess Bars

Coconut milk adds a hint of tropical flavor to these delightfully tangy bars. For the smoothest filling, whisk together the dry ingredients, and then stir in the wet ingredients until smooth. This will prevent tiny lumps of flour from forming. (Photo, page 6)

ACTIVE 15 MIN. - TOTAL 3 HOURS, 45 MIN.
MAKES 32

CRUST

  Baking spray with flour
2½   cups all-purpose flour
¾   cup unsifted powdered sugar
½   cup sweetened flaked coconut
1½   tsp. kosher salt
1   cup cold unsalted butter, cubed

FILLING

2   cups granulated sugar
2   Tbsp. plain yellow cornmeal
2   Tbsp. all-purpose flour
½   tsp. kosher salt
5   large eggs
1   large egg yolk
1¼   cups well-shaken and stirred coconut milk (from 1 [13½-oz.] can)
½   cup unsalted butter, melted
1   Tbsp. lemon zest plus ½ cup fresh juice (from 3 lemons)
1   tsp. vanilla extract

GARNISH

  Toasted shaved coconut

1. Prepare the Crust: Preheat oven to 350°F. Coat a 13- x 9-inch baking pan with baking spray with flour. Pulse next 4 ingredients in a food processor until combined, 5 or 6 times. Add cold butter; pulse until coarse crumbs form, 6 or 7 times. Firmly press into bottom of prepared pan. Bake until light golden brown, about 25 minutes. Cool slightly, about 10 minutes.

2. Prepare the Filling: Whisk together first 4 ingredients in a bowl. Add next 6 ingredients; stir until smooth. Pour over Crust.

3. Bake at 350°F until set, about 25 minutes. Remove from oven; cool completely in pan, about 1½ hours. Chill 1 hour. Slice into 32 bars. Garnish with shaved coconut.

Raspberry-Almond Crumble Bars

To give these bars an extra-thick layer of fruit, we added berries to the mixture. For the neatest squares, cool completely before cutting—or refrigerate up to two hours.

ACTIVE 25 MIN. - TOTAL 4 HOURS, 10 MIN.
MAKES 32

FILLING

6   cups (26 oz.) fresh or thawed frozen raspberries
¾   cup seedless raspberry jam
½   cup granulated sugar
6   Tbsp. cornstarch
1½   tsp. lemon zest (from 1 lemon)

CRUMBLE

  Cooking spray
2   cups all-purpose flour
1½   cups uncooked old-fashioned regular rolled oats
1½   cups packed light brown sugar
1   cup sliced almonds
½   tsp. ground cinnamon
¼   tsp. baking soda
1   cup butter, melted

1. Prepare the Filling: Stir together first five ingredients in a saucepan. Bring to a boil over medium-high, stirring occasionally. Reduce heat to medium-low; cook, stirring often, until thickened and reduced to 3½ cups, 8 to 10 minutes. Cool completely, about 1 hour.

2. Prepare the Crumble: Preheat oven to 350°F. Spray a 13- x 9-inch baking pan with cooking spray. Line bottom and sides of pan with parchment, leaving a 2-inch overhang on all sides. Stir together flour, oats, brown sugar, almonds, cinnamon, and baking soda in a large bowl. Stir in melted butter until combined. Firmly press 4 cups of the Crumble mixture into bottom of prepared pan. Bake until lightly browned around edges, 10 to 12 minutes. Cool 5 minutes.

3. Spread cooled Filling over warm crust; sprinkle with remaining Crumble. Bake at 350°F until filling is bubbly, 35 to 40 minutes. Cool completely in pan, about 2 hours. Lift bars out of pan using parchment as handles. Slice into 32 bars.

RASPBERRY-ALMOND
CRUMBLE BARS

Weeknight Cheat Sheets

One pan, five delicious suppers, and very little cleanup

PREP TIP
Cut the apple
and vegetables as
directed so they all
cook in the same
amount of time.

Sheet Pan Chicken with Dressing

ACTIVE 20 MIN. - TOTAL 45 MIN.
SERVES 4

- 8 (6-oz.) bone-in, skin-on chicken thighs
- 4 Tbsp. olive oil, divided
- 3 tsp. kosher salt, divided
- 1¾ tsp. chopped fresh thyme (divided), plus 5 whole sprigs
- 1½ tsp. black pepper, divided
- 1 fennel bulb, cut into 1-inch pieces (1½ cups)
- 1 red onion, cut into 8 wedges
- 1 Honeycrisp apple, cut into 1½-inch pieces (¾ cup)
- 2 celery stalks, cut at an angle into ½-inch slices (¾ cup)
- 2 carrots, peeled and cut into ⅓-inch slices (¾ cup)
- 8 oz. cornbread, cut into 1-inch cubes (about 4 cups)

1. Preheat oven to 400°F. Rub chicken thighs with 1 tablespoon of the oil, 1½ teaspoons of the salt, and ¾ teaspoon each of the chopped thyme and pepper. Place chicken on a baking sheet lined with aluminum foil. Bake 15 minutes. (Chicken will not be cooked through.)
2. Meanwhile, combine fennel, onion, apple, celery, carrots, thyme sprigs, 2 tablespoons of the oil, 1 teaspoon of the salt, ½ teaspoon of the pepper, and remaining 1 teaspoon chopped thyme in a large bowl; toss to coat. Arrange vegetable mix evenly around chicken. Bake at 400°F until vegetables are almost tender, about 20 minutes.
3. Toss cornbread with remaining 1 tablespoon oil, ½ teaspoon salt, and ¼ teaspoon pepper. Arrange around chicken; bake at 400°F until a thermometer inserted in thickest portion of chicken registers 165°F, about 5 minutes. Increase oven temperature to broil; cook until chicken and cornbread are golden brown, 4 to 5 minutes.

Crispy Catfish Tacos with Slaw

ACTIVE 20 MIN. - TOTAL 55 MIN.
SERVES 4

- 1 lb. skinless catfish fillets, cut into 16 pieces
- ¾ cup whole buttermilk
- ½ cup fine yellow cornmeal
- ½ cup panko breadcrumbs
- 2 Tbsp. Cajun seasoning (such as Slap Ya Mama)
- ¾ tsp. kosher salt, divided
- ¼ cup mayonnaise
- 2 Tbsp. fresh lime juice (from 1 lime)
- ¼ tsp. black pepper
- 2 cups shredded napa or green cabbage (from 1 small cabbage)
- 8 (6-inch) yellow corn tortillas, warmed
- 2 radishes, cut into matchsticks (¼ cup)
- 1 ripe avocado, thinly sliced
- 2 Tbsp. fresh cilantro leaves
- 2 Tbsp. minced fresh chives
  Lime wedges
  Hot sauce

1. Preheat oven to 450°F with oven rack 6 inches from heat. Combine catfish and buttermilk in a medium bowl; cover and chill 20 minutes or up to 1 hour.

2. Whisk together cornmeal, panko, Cajun seasoning, and ¼ teaspoon of the salt in a shallow dish. Drain catfish; discard buttermilk. Working in batches, dredge fish in cornmeal mixture. Place fish on a wire rack set inside a rimmed baking sheet. Bake in preheated oven until it's golden brown and flakes with a fork, 20 to 25 minutes.

3. Meanwhile, whisk together mayonnaise, lime juice, pepper, and remaining ½ teaspoon salt in a medium bowl. Add cabbage; toss to coat.

4. Place 2 pieces of catfish in each tortilla. Top with cabbage mixture, radishes, avocado, cilantro, and chives. Serve with lime wedges and hot sauce.

SEAFOOD SWAP

If catfish is not available, use any firm white fish such as cod, tilapia, or grouper.

Oven-Fried Pork Chops with Sweet Potatoes and Green Beans

ACTIVE 25 MIN. - TOTAL 55 MIN.
SERVES 4

- 3 Tbsp. country-style Dijon mustard
- 1 Tbsp. chopped fresh thyme
- 1 Tbsp. chopped fresh rosemary
- 1½ tsp. black pepper
- 3 tsp. kosher salt, divided
- 1 cup panko breadcrumbs
- 6½ Tbsp. olive oil, divided
- 4 (12-oz.) 1-inch-thick, bone-in, center-cut pork chops
- 1 lb. sweet potatoes, peeled and cut into ¾-inch pieces (3 cups)
- 4 shallots, halved
- 8 oz. haricots verts (French green beans)
- 1 Tbsp. apple cider vinegar

1. Preheat oven to 425°F with oven rack 6 inches from heat. Stir together mustard, thyme, rosemary, pepper, and 1½ teaspoons of the salt in a small bowl. Reserve 2 teaspoons of the mixture.

2. Stir together panko, 2 tablespoons of the oil, and 1 teaspoon of the salt in a shallow dish. Rub pork chops with mustard mixture, and dredge 1 side of each in panko mixture, pressing to adhere. Place pork on a baking sheet lined with aluminum foil, with dredged sides facing up.

3. Toss together potatoes, shallots, 1½ tablespoons of the oil, and remaining ½ teaspoon salt in a bowl. Arrange potato mixture around pork chops. Bake in preheated oven until a thermometer inserted in thickest portion of pork registers 118°F, 18 to 20 minutes.

4. Increase oven temperature to broil. Toss haricots verts with 1 tablespoon of the oil, and scatter around pork chops. Broil until pork registers 135°F and vegetables are tender, about 5 minutes. Let pork rest 10 minutes (internal temperature will increase to 145°F). Whisk together vinegar, reserved 2 teaspoons mustard mixture, and remaining 2 tablespoons oil; drizzle over vegetables.

PORK POINTER
Dredge only one side of each pork chop in the panko mixture to keep the underside of the meat from becoming soggy.

TIME-SAVER
Make this dish come together even faster by using bagged precut broccoli florets.

Lemon-Garlic Butter Shrimp and Broccoli

ACTIVE 20 MIN. - TOTAL 40 MIN.
SERVES 4

- 6 Tbsp. unsalted butter
- 4 garlic cloves, finely chopped (1 Tbsp.)
- 1 Tbsp. fresh lemon juice (from 1 lemon)
- ½ tsp. black pepper
- ½ tsp. crushed red pepper
- 1½ tsp. kosher salt, divided
- 1 (6-oz.) box long-grain and wild rice mix
- 2¼ cups lower-sodium chicken broth
- 3 cups broccoli florets (from 1 head)
- 3 Tbsp. olive oil
- 1 medium lemon, thinly sliced
- 12 oz. large peeled, deveined raw shrimp

1. Preheat oven to 450°F. Combine butter, garlic, lemon juice, black and red peppers, and 1 teaspoon of the salt in a small microwavable bowl. Microwave on HIGH until melted, about 45 seconds; set aside.

2. Cook rice according to package directions, substituting broth for water. Fluff with a fork; stir in 1 tablespoon of the butter mixture. Cover to keep warm.

3. Meanwhile, toss together broccoli, oil, lemon slices, and remaining ½ teaspoon salt on a rimmed baking sheet; spread in a single layer. Bake in preheated oven until broccoli is crisp-tender, about 13 minutes.

4. Arrange shrimp on baking sheet with broccoli. Drizzle with remaining butter mixture. Bake at 450°F until shrimp are pink, about 5 minutes. Serve with rice.

Cheesy Sheet Pan Pasta

ACTIVE 20 MIN. - TOTAL 1 HOUR, 5 MIN.
SERVES 4

- 6   **thick-cut bacon slices**
- 12 **oz. uncooked fusilli pasta**
- 4   **cups baby spinach, roughly chopped (4 oz.)**
- 1   **(15-oz.) container refrigerated Alfredo sauce**
- 1   **cup cherry tomatoes, halved**
- 1   **tsp. Dijon mustard**
- ½ **tsp. lemon zest (from 1 lemon)**
- 6   **oz. pre-shredded Italian six-cheese blend (about 1½ cups)**
- 2   **Tbsp. chopped fresh flat-leaf parsley**

1. Preheat oven to 350°F. Place bacon on a wire rack set in a 10- x 15-inch rimmed baking sheet lined with aluminum foil. Bake in oven until bacon is crispy, 25 to 30 minutes. Roughly chop; set aside. Reserve bacon drippings in pan; remove wire rack.

2. Increase oven temperature to 425°F. Cook pasta to al dente according to package directions. Drain, reserving ½ cup cooking water. Return hot pasta to pot. Add spinach and reserved cooking water to pasta; stir until wilted, 1 to 2 minutes. Add Alfredo sauce, tomatoes, mustard, lemon zest, and bacon; stir to combine.

3. Spread pasta mixture in an even layer in reserved drippings in rimmed baking sheet. Sprinkle with cheese. Bake at 425°F until cheese is melted and golden brown in spots, about 15 minutes. Garnish with parsley.

Soup's On

Packed with veggies and flavored with a little bacon, this recipe will warm you up on a chilly day

Slow-Cooker Winter Vegetable Soup with Bacon

ACTIVE 15 MIN. - TOTAL 5 HOURS, 50 MIN.
SERVES 8

- 4 thick-cut bacon slices, cut into ½-inch pieces
- 1½ lb. baby Yukon Gold potatoes, halved
- 1½ cups chopped yellow onion (from 1 medium onion)
- 1 cup ¼-inch-thick carrot slices (from 3 medium carrots)
- 1 cup dried navy beans
- ¾ cup ¼-inch-thick parsnip slices (from 2 medium parsnips)
- ¾ cup ¼-inch-thick celery slices (from 2 stalks)
- 6 cups chicken broth
- 1 Tbsp. minced garlic (from 3 garlic cloves)
- ½ tsp. black pepper, plus more for garnish
- ¼ tsp. kosher salt
- 3 cups chopped curly kale (from 1 bunch)
- 1 Tbsp. fresh lemon juice (from 1 lemon)
- Fresh thyme leaves

1. Cook bacon in microwave until crisp according to package directions. Crumble bacon.
2. Place potatoes, onion, carrots, beans, parsnips, celery, broth, garlic, pepper, salt, and bacon in a 5- to 6-quart slow cooker. Cover and cook on LOW until potatoes and beans are tender, 5½ to 6 hours.
3. Uncover and stir in kale. Cook, uncovered, until kale is tender, about 2 minutes. Stir in lemon juice. Ladle soup into serving bowls, and garnish with pepper and thyme leaves.

EASY SWAPS
Substitute collards for the kale, use another type of small dried beans, or add heat with red pepper flakes.

Chicken in a Snap

This tasty 30-minute meal comes together in one pan

Skillet Chicken with Beans and Greens

ACTIVE 30 MIN. - TOTAL 30 MIN.
SERVES 4

- 1 Tbsp. olive oil
- 4 (6-oz.) boneless, skinless chicken breasts
- ¾ tsp. kosher salt
- ½ tsp. black pepper
- 1 medium yellow onion, chopped (1½ cups)
- 6 cups chopped fresh turnip greens (7 oz.)
- 1 (14.5-oz.) can diced fire-roasted tomatoes
- 1 (15-oz.) can cannellini beans, drained and rinsed
- ½ cup unsalted chicken stock
- 1 Tbsp. red wine vinegar
- 2 tsp. granulated sugar
   Hot pepper vinegar

1. Heat oil in a large skillet over medium-high. Sprinkle chicken with salt and pepper. Cook, turning occasionally, until evenly browned, 6 to 8 minutes. Remove from skillet.

2. Add onion to skillet; cook, stirring often, until tender, about 5 minutes. Add greens, tomatoes, beans, and stock. Bring to a boil; stir in red wine vinegar and sugar. Return chicken to pan, cover, and reduce heat to medium. Simmer until thermometer inserted in thickest portion of chicken registers 160°F and greens are just tender, about 10 minutes. Serve with pepper vinegar.

Nutritional information: Calories: 390; Protein: 47g; Carbs: 31g; Fiber: 9g; Fat: 8g

EASY ADDITION

Make this meal even heartier by serving it over steamed rice or cooked orzo.

Make Your Famous Dip!

This cheesy appetizer will be the talk of the Super Bowl gathering

Creamy Southwest Black-Eyed Pea Dip

ACTIVE 15 MIN. - TOTAL 1 HOUR
SERVES 12

- 1 (8-oz.) pkg. cream cheese, softened
- 2 (15-oz.) cans black-eyed peas, rinsed, drained, and divided
- 1½ Tbsp. fresh lime juice, divided
- 1 tsp. hot sauce
- ½ tsp. kosher salt, divided
- 1 cup diced ham
- ¼ cup finely chopped scallions
- ¼ cup finely chopped roasted red bell pepper
- 1 (8-oz.) block Monterey Jack cheese, shredded and divided
- 2 (4-oz.) fresh tomatoes, chopped (about 1 cup)
- 2 Tbsp. finely chopped fresh cilantro
- 1 Tbsp. olive oil
- 1 Tbsp. minced fresh jalapeño
  Tortilla chips

1. Preheat oven to 375°F. Process cream cheese, 1 cup black-eyed peas, ½ tablespoon lime juice, hot sauce, and ¼ teaspoon salt in a food processor until creamy and smooth (about 1 minute). Place mixture in a large bowl.
2. Stir remaining black-eyed peas, diced ham, scallions, bell pepper, and 4 ounces Monterey Jack cheese (1 cup) into cream cheese mixture. Spread mixture into a lightly greased 2-quart baking dish. Sprinkle with remaining 4 ounces cheese.
3. Bake, covered with aluminum foil, in preheated oven 20 minutes. Remove foil, and bake 10 to 15 more minutes or until hot and bubbly. Let stand 10 minutes.
4. Stir together tomatoes, cilantro, olive oil, jalapeño, remaining 1 tablespoon lime juice, and remaining ¼ teaspoon salt in a small bowl. Top black-eyed pea dip with tomato mixture using a slotted spoon. Serve with tortilla chips.

MAKE IT AHEAD
Prepare through Step 2 (omit preheat); chill overnight. Let stand at room temperature 30 minutes before baking; add 10 minutes to covered bake time.

COOKING (SL) SCHOOL

KNOW-HOW

Perfect Squares? Yes, Please

Test Kitchen tips for even cuts every time

LINE THE PAN
Before adding batter, cover pan with aluminum foil. Make sure to leave about a 3-inch overhang on two sides, which you can use as handles to lift the bars once they have baked.

COOL COMPLETELY
It's tempting to cut (and eat) the bars as soon as they come out of the oven, but the longer they cool, the neater your slices will be. Speed up the process by refrigerating them for two hours.

USE A RULER
For the most precise results, measure the bars with a ruler and use a toothpick (or tip of a knife) to make small marks where you'll slice. This is especially helpful if you need an exact number of treats.

SPRAY THE BLADE
A chef's knife is the best tool for slicing bar cookies. Before you cut, coat the blade with cooking spray and wipe it clean with a paper towel. Repeat this process between slices if the bars are extra gooey.

SLICE RIGHT
When it's time to cut, press the blade of the knife down firmly, and then drag it back in a single motion. Moving the blade back and forth (like a saw) creates jagged edges.

> "When baking a layer cake, wrap the cooled layers in plastic wrap, and refrigerate four to six hours before frosting. This will prevent crumbs from getting into the frosting."
>
> **—Pam Lolley**
> Test Kitchen Professional

BAKING TIP

The Secret to Even Cake Layers

When you're dividing cake batter between two or more pans, do it gradually, going back and forth between the pans rather than filling them one by one.

March

60   **Garden Party**   Edible flowers turn simple cakes into showstoppers—no decorating skills required

65   **Skillet Sensations**   Five hearty weeknight suppers that come together in just one pan

70   **A Quick Shrimp Supper**   This simple pasta is tossed with seasonal veggies and a bright, tangy dressing

71   **Hot Potato**   This cheesy soup feeds a crowd and freezes well too

72   **Party Perfect**   A fluted tart pan makes this store-bought crust extra special

74   **SL Cooking School**   Prevent food from getting caked on cast-iron, nonstick, and stainless-steel pans

"NAKED" LEMON CAKE WITH A
FLOWER CROWN

Garden Party

Edible flowers turn simple cakes into showstoppers—no decorating skills required

"Naked" Lemon Cake with a Flower Crown

ACTIVE 40 MIN. - TOTAL 1 HOUR, 50 MIN.
SERVES 16

- 2 (15¼-oz.) pkg. lemon cake mix (such as Betty Crocker Super Moist Delights Lemon Cake Mix)
  Lemon-Vanilla Buttercream (recipe, page 64)
  Edible flowers (such as tuberous begonias, stock, violas, English daisies, and pansies)
  Fresh mint leaves

1. Preheat oven to 350°F. Stir together all wet ingredients needed to prepare cake batters (per package directions) in 1 large bowl. Stir together all dry ingredients from cake mix packages in a separate bowl. Add dry ingredients to wet ingredients; stir together until well blended. Divide combined batter among 3 greased and floured 9-inch round cake pans. Bake until a wooden pick inserted in centers comes out clean, 25 to 30 minutes. Cool cake layers in pans on a wire rack 10 minutes. Invert cake layers onto racks, and cool completely, about 45 minutes.
2. Prepare Lemon-Vanilla Buttercream.
3. Using a serrated knife, trim domed tops of cake layers to make them flat and even. Spread Lemon-Vanilla Buttercream between layers and on top and sides of cake, allowing some of the cake to remain visible on the sides. Smooth with an offset spatula. Arrange a ring of edible flowers and mint leaves around top edge of cake to form a "flower crown."

Mini Confetti Cakes

A round cutter turns a sheet cake into these pretty two-layer minis. (Photo, page 11)

ACTIVE 45 MIN. - TOTAL 2 HOURS, 10 MIN.
SERVES 15

- 1 (15¼-oz.) pkg. vanilla cake mix (such as Betty Crocker Super Moist Favorites Vanilla Cake Mix)
- 3 Tbsp. pink candy sprinkles (pink jimmies)
  Sweetened Whipped Cream (recipe, page 64)
  Edible flowers (such as violas, tuberous begonias, English daisies, and pansies)

1. Preheat oven to 350°F. Prepare cake batter according to package directions, stirring pink candy sprinkles into batter. Pour batter into a greased and floured 13- x 9-inch baking pan. Bake until a wooden pick inserted in center comes out clean, 28 to 33 minutes. Cool cake in pan on a wire rack 10 minutes. Invert cake onto rack; cool completely, about 45 minutes.
2. Prepare the Sweetened Whipped Cream.
3. Cut out 15 mini cakes from cooled cake using a 2½-inch round cutter. Slice each mini cake in half horizontally, making 2 layers per mini cake. Using a small offset spatula, spread Sweetened Whipped Cream on half of layers, and top with remaining layers. Cover tops and sides of cakes with whipped cream. Press edible flowers directly onto cakes.

Edible Flower Facts

Dress desserts with the safest blooms of the bunch

Choose flowers labeled as edible, which you can find in the produce section of specialty food stores. Or order them online at melissas.com.

Use caution whenever eating flowers, and ensure petals are clean and free of pesticides, fertilizers, and bugs.

Be aware that several plants may go by the same name; always make sure you are consuming one that's safe to eat.

Some edible blooms may have a bitter taste and are best used for decoration only.

When in doubt, don't eat them!

SAFE TO EAT

Carnation, English daisy, freesia, lavender, nasturtium, pansy, peony, rose, stock, sweet William, tuberous begonia, violet

ROSE PETAL CUPCAKES
(PAGE 64)

CHOCOLATE BUNDT CAKE
(PAGE 64)

Vanilla Layer Cake with a Flower Cuff

For a smooth finish, dip a knife or offset spatula in hot water; then wipe it dry before frosting the cake. (Photo, page 1)

ACTIVE 30 MIN. - TOTAL 1 HOUR, 50 MIN.
SERVES 10

- 1 (15¼-oz.) pkg. yellow cake mix (such as Duncan Hines Classic Yellow Cake Mix)
  Vanilla Buttercream (recipe follows)
  Small edible flower petals (such as sweet Williams, roses, and tuberous begonias)
- 1 large edible flower (such as a peony or rose)

1. Preheat oven to 350°F. Prepare cake batter according to package directions. Divide batter among 3 greased and floured 6-inch round cake pans. Bake until a wooden pick inserted into centers comes out clean, about 25 minutes. Cool cake layers in pans on a wire rack 10 minutes. Invert cake layers onto rack; cool completely, about 45 minutes.
2. Prepare Vanilla Buttercream.
3. Using a serrated knife, trim domed tops of cake layers to make them even. Spread buttercream between layers and on top and sides of cake. Arrange a ring of edible flower petals around base of cake to form a cuff. Place large edible flower on top of cake.

Rose Petal Cupcakes

Pick petals that coordinate with your party's signature colors. (Photo, page 62)

ACTIVE 35 MIN. - TOTAL 1 HOUR, 15 MIN.
SERVES 24

- 1 (16¼-oz.) pkg. white cake mix (such as Betty Crocker Super Moist Favorites White Cake Mix)
  Rose-Vanilla Buttercream (recipe follows)
  24 edible rose petals

1. Preheat oven to 350°F. Prepare cake batter according to package directions. Divide batter among 24 muffin cups lined with paper baking cups. Bake until a wooden pick inserted in centers comes out clean, 14 to 19 minutes. Cool cupcakes in pans on a wire rack 10 minutes. Remove cupcakes to racks, and cool completely, about 30 minutes.

2. Prepare Rose-Vanilla Buttercream.
3. Spoon Rose-Vanilla Buttercream into a piping bag fitted with a large star tip; pipe onto cooled cupcakes. Gently press an edible rose petal into the side of each cupcake.

Chocolate Bundt Cake

Made with boxed cake and brownie mixes, this Bundt is decadent, yet easy to pull off. (Photo, page 63)

ACTIVE 25 MIN. - TOTAL 2 HOURS, 45 MIN.
SERVES 16

- 1 (15¼-oz.) pkg. chocolate fudge cake mix (such as Betty Crocker Super Moist Favorites Chocolate Fudge Cake Mix)
- 1 (18-oz.) pkg. double-chocolate brownie mix (such as Ghirardelli Double Chocolate Brownie Mix)
- 5 oz. milk chocolate, chopped
- 2½ oz. bittersweet chocolate, chopped
- 1½ cups unsalted butter, softened
- ¼ cup powdered sugar
- ¼ cup Dutch-process cocoa
- 2 Tbsp. sour cream
- 1 tsp. vanilla extract
  Edible pansy flowers

1. Preheat oven to 350°F. Stir together all wet ingredients needed to prepare cake and brownie batters (per package directions) in 1 large bowl. Stir together dry ingredients from cake and brownie mix packages in a separate bowl. Add dry ingredients to wet ingredients, and stir together until well blended. Pour combined batter into a greased and floured 12-cup Bundt pan. Bake until a wooden pick inserted in center comes out clean, 50 to 55 minutes. Cool cake in pan on a wire rack 30 minutes. Invert onto rack, and cool completely, about 1 hour.
2. Place chopped milk chocolate and bittersweet chocolate in a medium-size microwavable bowl. Microwave on HIGH until melted and smooth, about 1 minute, stirring after 30 seconds. Cool 5 minutes.
3. Place butter in bowl of a heavy-duty stand mixer fitted with the paddle attachment. Beat on medium speed until creamy, 1 to 2 minutes. Reduce speed to low; gradually add powdered sugar and cocoa, beating until smooth, about 1 minute, stopping to scrape sides of bowl as needed. Beat in sour cream and vanilla;

gradually beat in cooled melted chocolate. Increase speed to medium; beat until smooth, 2 to 3 minutes.
4. Spoon mixture into a piping bag fitted with a ¼-inch round tip; pipe frosting onto the top of the cooled cake in a decorative pattern. Press edible flowers onto frosting to decorate cake as desired.

Sweetened Whipped Cream

ACTIVE 15 MIN. - TOTAL 15 MIN.
MAKES 6 CUPS

- 2 cups heavy cream
- 1 tsp. vanilla extract
- 6 Tbsp. unsifted powdered sugar

Beat cream and vanilla in a bowl with an electric mixer on medium-high speed until foamy. Gradually add powdered sugar, and beat until stiff peaks form.

Vanilla Buttercream

ACTIVE 15 MIN. - TOTAL 15 MIN.
MAKES ABOUT 6 CUPS

- 1½ cups unsalted butter, softened
- 5 cups unsifted powdered sugar
- 1 tsp. vanilla extract
- ¼ cup heavy cream

Beat butter in bowl of a heavy-duty stand mixer fitted with the paddle attachment on medium speed until creamy, 1 to 2 minutes. Reduce speed to low; gradually add powdered sugar, beating until smooth, about 2 minutes, stopping to scrape sides of bowl as needed. Beat in vanilla. Gradually add cream, beating on medium speed until fluffy and spreadable, about 30 seconds.

Lemon-Vanilla Buttercream

Reduce cream to 2 tablespoons. Beat in 2 tablespoons **lemon juice** (from 1 lemon) with cream.

Rose-Vanilla Buttercream

Stir 1 tablespoon **rose water** into frosting after beating in cream.

Skillet Sensations

Five hearty weeknight suppers that come together in just one pan

Toasted Israeli Couscous and Shrimp

ACTIVE 20 MIN. - TOTAL 30 MIN.
SERVES 4

- 1¼ lb. medium peeled, deveined raw shrimp
- 1 Tbsp. finely chopped garlic (from 3 garlic cloves)
- ¼ tsp. black pepper
- 6 Tbsp. extra-virgin olive oil, divided
- 3 Tbsp. fresh lemon juice (from 2 lemons), plus 1 lemon, cut into wedges, divided
- 1¼ tsp. kosher salt, divided
- 1 medium-size red bell pepper, thinly sliced
- 1 medium-size yellow bell pepper, thinly sliced
- 1 cup uncooked Israeli couscous
- 1½ cups chicken stock
- ¼ cup fresh flat-leaf parsley leaves
- ¼ cup torn fresh basil leaves
- ¼ tsp. crushed red pepper

1. Combine shrimp, garlic, black pepper, 3 tablespoons of the olive oil, 1 tablespoon of the lemon juice, and ½ teaspoon of the salt in a medium bowl; toss to coat. Let stand at room temperature until ready to use.
2. Heat 1 tablespoon of the olive oil in a 10-inch cast-iron skillet over medium-high. Add bell peppers; cook, stirring occasionally, until tender-crisp and charred, about 5 minutes. Sprinkle with ¼ teaspoon of the salt. Transfer to a plate.
3. Add couscous to skillet; cook over medium-high, stirring constantly, until toasted and fragrant, about 2 minutes. Add stock and remaining ½ teaspoon salt; bring to a boil. Cover, and reduce heat to medium-low; simmer until tender and almost all liquid is absorbed, about 10 minutes.
4. Uncover skillet, and top couscous with bell peppers and shrimp. Increase heat to medium; cover, and cook until shrimp are just cooked through, 5 to 7 minutes. Remove from heat, and drizzle with

remaining 2 tablespoons each olive oil and lemon juice. Garnish with parsley, basil, and crushed red pepper. Serve with lemon wedges.

SEAFOOD SECRET

Remove the pan from the stove right after the shrimp turn pink. They'll finish cooking in the hot skillet without turning rubbery.

SALMON WITH LEMONY
GREENS AND GRAINS

Salmon with Lemony Greens and Grains

ACTIVE 25 MIN. - TOTAL 25 MIN.
SERVES 4

- 2   lemons, halved
- 3   Tbsp. unsalted butter, divided
- 4   (6-oz.) skin-on salmon fillets
- ¼   tsp. black pepper
- 1   tsp. kosher salt, divided
- ¼   cup chicken stock
- 4   cups thinly sliced collard greens (about 10 oz.)
- 2   (8.5-oz.) pkg. microwavable farro (such as Simply Balanced)
- 1   (14.5-oz.) can black-eyed peas, drained and rinsed
- 2   Tbsp. chopped fresh chives, divided
- 2   Tbsp. chopped fresh dill, divided

1. Squeeze juice from 3 lemon halves to equal 2½ tablespoons; set juice aside. Cut remaining lemon half into 8 wedges; set aside. Heat 1 tablespoon of the butter in a large nonstick skillet over medium-high. Sprinkle salmon fillets evenly with pepper and ½ teaspoon of the salt. Place salmon in skillet, skin sides down, and cook until skin is crisp, about 4 minutes. Flip salmon, and cook to desired degree of doneness,

2 to 3 minutes for medium. Transfer salmon to a plate; wipe skillet clean.
2. Add stock, collard greens, farro, and remaining 2 tablespoons butter and ½ teaspoon salt to skillet. Cook, stirring often, until collards are wilted, about 3 minutes. Add black-eyed peas to skillet, and cook until heated through. Remove skillet from heat, and stir in reserved lemon juice and 1 tablespoon each of the chopped chives and dill.
3. Spoon collard mixture evenly onto 4 serving plates. Top each serving with a salmon fillet. Garnish with remaining chives and dill. Serve with reserved lemon wedges.

Rosemary Chicken Thighs and Vegetables

ACTIVE 25 MIN. - TOTAL 40 MIN.
SERVES 4

- 4   Tbsp. olive oil, divided
- 4   (6-oz.) bone-in, skin-on chicken thighs
- 2½ tsp. kosher salt, divided
- 1   tsp. black pepper, divided
- 2   medium lemons, halved
- ¼   cup water
- 2   medium sweet potatoes, cut into 3-inch wedges (4 cups)
- 12 oz. Brussels sprouts, trimmed and halved (3 cups)
- 2   large shallots, halved
- 1   large garlic clove, grated (about 1 tsp.)
- 1   Tbsp. whole-grain mustard
- 1   tsp. honey
- 1   tsp. Worcestershire sauce
- 1   tsp. chopped fresh rosemary Rosemary sprigs

1. Preheat oven to 400°F with oven rack in bottom third of oven. Heat 1 tablespoon of the oil in a large cast-iron skillet on stovetop over medium-high. Pat chicken dry with a paper towel; sprinkle evenly with 1½ teaspoons of the salt and ½ teaspoon of the pepper.
2. Place chicken, skin sides down, in hot oil. Add lemon halves, cut sides down, to skillet. Cook until chicken skin is golden and crisp and lemons are charred, about 10 minutes. Transfer lemons to a rimmed baking sheet. Flip chicken, and continue cooking until golden on both sides, 4 to 5 minutes. Transfer chicken to baking sheet with lemons. Pour drippings from skillet into a small bowl, and reserve. Add water to skillet, and stir to loosen browned bits on bottom with a wooden spoon. Discard liquid; wipe skillet clean.
3. Heat remaining 3 tablespoons of the oil in skillet over medium-high. Add sweet potatoes, and cook 2 minutes. Add Brussels sprouts and shallots to skillet. Sprinkle vegetables with remaining 1 teaspoon salt. Cook until charred, about 5 minutes. Remove skillet from heat.
4. Add grated garlic, whole-grain mustard, honey, Worcestershire sauce, and juice of 2 of the charred lemon halves (about 1 tablespoon) to reserved drippings in bowl, and whisk to combine. Return charred lemon halves (including squeezed lemon halves) to skillet with vegetables. Place chicken, skin sides up, on top. Pour the drippings mixture evenly over chicken.
5. Place skillet in preheated oven, and bake until vegetables are tender and a thermometer inserted in thickest portion of chicken registers 160°F, 15 to 18 minutes. Remove from oven, and let stand 10 minutes (chicken temperature should rise to 165°F). Sprinkle with chopped rosemary and remaining ½ teaspoon pepper. Garnish with rosemary sprigs.

ROSEMARY CHICKEN
THIGHS AND VEGETABLES

PROTEIN PICK
Choose small chicken thighs, which tend to be juicier and more flavorful than large ones.

CHEESY BEEF-AND-
SPINACH RAVIOLI

SIMPLE SWAPS
Substitute ground
turkey or chicken for
the beef, or replace the
spinach with Swiss
chard leaves.

Cheesy Beef-and-Spinach Ravioli

ACTIVE 30 MIN. - TOTAL 35 MIN.
SERVES 6

- 1   lb. 85%-lean ground beef
- 1   Tbsp. olive oil
- 1   medium-size red onion, thinly sliced (about 3 cups)
- 2   tsp. finely chopped garlic (from 3 medium garlic cloves)
- 1   (28-oz.) can crushed tomatoes
- 1   cup chicken stock
- 1   tsp. dried Italian seasoning
- 1   tsp. kosher salt
- ¼   tsp. black pepper
- 1   (20-oz.) pkg. refrigerated four-cheese ravioli (such as Buitoni)
- 1   (5-oz.) pkg. baby spinach
- 4   oz. pre-shredded low-moisture, part-skim mozzarella (about 1 cup)
- 2   oz. grated Parmesan cheese (about ½ cup)
- ¼   cup torn fresh basil leaves

1. Preheat oven to broil with rack 9 inches from heat. Place a 12-inch cast-iron skillet on stove-top over medium-high. Add beef; cook, stirring often, until browned, 8 to 10 minutes. Remove beef; drain and set aside. Wipe skillet clean.
2. Heat oil in skillet over medium-high; add onion, and cook, stirring occasionally, until tender, 8 to 10 minutes. Add garlic to skillet; cook, stirring constantly, until fragrant, about 1 minute. Stir in crushed tomatoes, stock, Italian seasoning, salt, pepper, and ravioli. Bring to a boil; reduce heat to medium. Cover and simmer until ravioli are tender, about 8 minutes. Uncover and return cooked beef to skillet. Stir in half of spinach, and cook just until wilted. Repeat with remaining spinach. Top with mozzarella and Parmesan.
3. Broil in preheated oven until cheese is melted and golden, about 6 minutes. Remove from oven, and garnish with fresh basil.

Leek-and-Mushroom Grits Frittata

ACTIVE 20 MIN. - TOTAL 35 MIN.
SERVES 6

- 3   cups chicken stock
- ¾   cup uncooked regular grits
- 3   Tbsp. unsalted butter
- 6   oz. cream cheese

TIME-SAVER
Prepare the grits a day in advance, and refrigerate. Let them come to room temperature before adding to the egg mixture.

LEEK-AND-MUSHROOM GRITS FRITTATA

- 2   oz. Parmesan cheese, finely shredded (about ¾ cup), divided
- ¾   tsp. kosher salt, divided
- ½   lb. smoked sausage, chopped
- 12 oz. fresh cremini mushrooms, sliced
- 1   large leek, white and light green parts only, chopped (1 cup chopped)
- 3   large eggs
- ⅓   cup whole milk
     Fresh thyme leaves

1. Preheat oven to 425°F with oven rack in middle of oven. Bring stock to a boil in a medium saucepan over medium-high. Whisk in grits, and reduce heat to medium-low. Cook, covered, until grits are thickened and tender, 8 to 10 minutes. Uncover and stir in butter, cream cheese, 1½ ounces of the Parmesan, and ¼ teaspoon of the salt until butter and cheese are melted (mixture will be thick). Remove from heat; let stand at room temperature until ready to use.

2. Cook sausage in a 10-inch nonstick skillet over medium-high until browned and crisp on all sides, 5 to 6 minutes. Transfer to a plate lined with paper towels, reserving 1 tablespoon drippings in skillet. Add mushrooms to skillet, and cook, stirring occasionally, until mushrooms begin releasing liquid, 5 to 6 minutes. Add leek, and cook, stirring often, until tender and liquid has been absorbed, about 6 minutes. Sprinkle vegetables with ¼ teaspoon of the salt, and transfer to a medium bowl. Wipe skillet clean.
3. Whisk together eggs, milk, and remaining ¼ teaspoon salt in a large bowl. Stir in grits mixture, vegetables, and sausage. Pour grits-vegetable-sausage mixture into skillet.
4. Bake in preheated oven until almost set, 15 to 20 minutes. Increase oven temperature to broil. Sprinkle evenly with remaining ½ ounce Parmesan, and broil until top of frittata is slightly golden, 3 to 4 minutes. Remove from oven, and garnish frittata with thyme before serving.

A Quick Shrimp Supper

This simple pasta is tossed with seasonal veggies and a bright, tangy dressing

Spring Shrimp-and-Orzo Salad with Lemon Dressing

ACTIVE 30 MIN. - TOTAL 30 MIN.
SERVES 4

- ¼ cup extra-virgin olive oil
- 1 tsp. lemon zest plus 3 Tbsp. fresh juice (from 1 large lemon)
- 1½ tsp. kosher salt
- ½ tsp. black pepper
- 1 cup uncooked orzo
- 8 oz. fresh asparagus, trimmed and diagonally sliced into 1-inch pieces (about 1 cup)
- 4 oz. fresh sugar snap peas, trimmed (about 1 cup)
- 1 cup fresh or frozen English peas (thawed if frozen)
- 12 oz. medium peeled, deveined raw shrimp
- ¼ cup coarsely chopped fresh chives
- ¼ cup coarsely chopped fresh flat-leaf parsley
- ¼ cup coarsely chopped fresh tarragon

1. Whisk together oil, zest, juice, salt, and pepper in a small bowl. Set aside.
2. Prepare orzo according to package directions, omitting salt and fat; drain. Transfer orzo to a bowl, and cool to room temperature, about 10 minutes.
3. While orzo cooks, bring a large saucepan of water to a boil over high. Add asparagus and sugar snap peas to boiling water. Cook until bright green and tender-crisp, about 2 minutes. Add English peas, and stir until softened, about 30 seconds. Using a slotted spoon, transfer vegetables to an ice bath, reserving boiling water in saucepan.
4. Add shrimp to boiling water. Cook until opaque, about 3 minutes, and then drain. Transfer shrimp to ice bath with vegetables. Let stand until chilled, about 3 minutes; drain.
5. Toss together shrimp-vegetable mixture with orzo; drizzle with dressing. Add chives, parsley, and tarragon, and toss to combine. Serve at room temperature or chilled.

Nutritional Information: Calories: 411;
Protein: 22g; Carbs: 46g; Fiber: 5g; Fat: 16g

MIX IT UP
You'll need 3 cups of vegetables for this dish, but you can adjust the amounts of asparagus, sugar snap peas, and English peas.

Hot Potato

This cheesy soup feeds a crowd and freezes well too

Creamy Cheddar-Potato Soup with Bacon

ACTIVE 55 MIN. - TOTAL 55 MIN.
SERVES 8

- 1 bunch scallions
- 1 (12-oz.) pkg. bacon, roughly chopped
- 3 lb. russet potatoes, peeled and cut into ¼-inch pieces (7 to 8 cups)
- 2 cups chopped yellow onion (from 1 large onion)
- 3 Tbsp. butter
- 3 small garlic cloves, chopped
- ¼ cup all-purpose flour
- 1 tsp. kosher salt
- ½ tsp. black pepper
- 6 cups chicken broth
- 8 oz. white Cheddar cheese, shredded (about 2 cups)
- ½ cup heavy cream
- 2 oz. yellow Cheddar cheese, shredded (about ½ cup), for topping

1. Chop scallions, separating green and white parts. Set aside.
2. Cook bacon in a large Dutch oven over medium, stirring occasionally, until crispy, 10 to 15 minutes. Using a slotted spoon, transfer to a plate lined with paper towels, leaving 2 tablespoons of bacon drippings in Dutch oven.
3. Add potatoes, onion, butter, garlic, and white scallion pieces to Dutch oven, and cook over medium until onions are slightly softened, 5 to 6 minutes. Add flour, salt, and pepper, and stir until all ingredients are coated. Cook, stirring constantly, 1 minute. Stir in broth until combined. Bring mixture to a boil. Then reduce heat to medium-low, and simmer until potatoes are tender, about 12 minutes.
4. Using a potato masher, lightly mash mixture, leaving some whole pieces of potato. Add white Cheddar and cream, stirring until cheese melts. Keep warm.
5. Ladle soup into bowls. Top servings with bacon, green scallion pieces, and yellow Cheddar.

EXTRA CHEESY
Melted yellow Cheddar makes a great finishing touch. If you prefer to buy only one type of cheese, then add extra white Cheddar.

Party Perfect

A fluted tart pan makes this store-bought crust extra special

Asparagus-and-Goat Cheese Quiche

ACTIVE 20 MIN. - TOTAL 1 HOUR, 50 MIN.
SERVES 8

- ½ (15-oz.) pkg. refrigerated pie dough (such as Pillsbury)
- 12 oz. fresh asparagus spears, ends trimmed
- 2 Tbsp. unsalted butter
- 1 large leek, thinly sliced (about 1½ cups)
- 8 large eggs
- 1 cup heavy cream
- 2 Tbsp. chopped fresh flat-leaf parsley
- 1½ tsp. kosher salt
- ¼ tsp. black pepper
- 2 oz. crumbled goat cheese
  Fresh flat-leaf parsley leaves, for garnish

1. Preheat oven to 400°F.

2. Prepare the crust: Roll the pie dough to ⅛-inch thickness, and transfer to a 9-inch tart pan with a removable bottom. Press dough into bottom and up sides of pan, and trim excess dough around edges. Line bottom of dough with aluminum foil (or parchment paper), and fill with pie weights or dried beans. Bake 5 minutes. Remove pie weights and foil, and prick bottom of pastry evenly with a fork. Return to oven; bake until pastry is light golden brown, an additional 8 to 10 minutes. Transfer pan to a wire rack; cool crust completely, about 20 minutes. Reduce oven temperature to 350°F.

3. Meanwhile, prepare the filling: Set aside 6 or 7 whole asparagus spears, and cut remaining asparagus into ½-inch pieces. Melt butter in a skillet over medium-high. Add leek, and cook, stirring often, until tender, about 5 minutes. Stir in asparagus pieces, and cook, stirring often, until bright green, about 1 minute. Remove skillet from heat; cool vegetable mixture 5 minutes.

4. Whisk together eggs, cream, chopped parsley, salt, and pepper in a medium bowl until well combined. Transfer cooled crust to a baking sheet. Spoon vegetable mixture over the bottom of the crust, and sprinkle evenly with crumbled goat cheese. Pour the egg mixture over the vegetable-goat cheese mixture. Arrange the reserved whole asparagus spears on top.

5. Bake quiche at 350°F until center is just set, 50 to 55 minutes, shielding crust with aluminum foil after 10 minutes, if needed, to prevent excess browning. Transfer to a wire rack, and cool at least 15 minutes. Remove quiche from pan, and garnish with parsley leaves before serving.

MAKE IT AHEAD

You can prepare the quiche up to two days in advance. Store it, covered, in the refrigerator. Let it come to room temperature before serving.

PRODUCE POINTER

Medium-size asparagus spears (not too thick or thin) work best in the quiche filling.

COOKING (SL) SCHOOL

KNOW-HOW

Stickproof Your Skillet

Prevent food from getting caked on cast-iron, nonstick, and stainless-steel pans

"To quickly reseason a cast-iron skillet, rub the clean pan with a thin layer of canola oil and then place it in a hot oven for one hour."

—Robby Melvin
Test Kitchen Director

A
LET MEAT REST

Cold meat is more likely to stick to a hot pan. Let it stand at room temperature for 30 minutes before cooking. Blot off excess moisture from meat prior to adding it to the pan.

B
PREHEAT THE PAN

Make sure the skillet is nice and hot before you add food to it (unless it is a nonstick pan, which should not be heated above medium). Add the oil to the skillet as it preheats.

C
DON'T OVERFLIP

Place the meat in the hot pan; then let it sit undisturbed. Flip when it is evenly seared on one side or the breading is golden brown. If you turn it any sooner, it may stick.

GREAT GEAR

The Right Stuff

Best for Nonstick
For scratch-free flipping: GIR Mini Flip, $12; amazon.com

Best for Stainless Steel
For shining dingy pans: Bar Keepers Friend, $2; target.com

Best for Cast-Iron
For grabbing heated skillets: Lodge Hot Handle Holders, $9 for two; amazon.com

IN SEASON

Spring Fling

How to savor and share sugar snap peas

1

SAVE FOR LATER
Keep them in a plastic bag in the fridge up to three days. To store in the freezer, blanch them, pat completely dry, and then place in freezer bags.

2

PULL STRINGS
Stringless types of sugar snap peas are available, but if yours have strings, snap and pull off the stems.

3

SERVE YOURSELF
Quickly sauté them in butter, and garnish with herbs for a simple side dish; pickle them for a tangy snack; or slice raw ones to toss into salads for crunchy sweetness.

April

76   **Virginia's Sweet Spot** Horticulturist Diane Burns brings a delightful French strawberry to root at famed Pippin Hill Farm & Vineyards

81   **Back to Your Roots** Roasted, sauteed, or boiled—turn fresh vegetables into spectacular sides

84   **Easter Brunch for a Bunch** Five easy, crowd-pleasing dishes that will be a hit at your holiday celebration

89   **Pretty Tasty Pot Pie** Treat the family to a classic dish reinvented in a skillet

90   **Speedy Sheet Pan Salmon** A tangy honey-mustard sauce gives this fish a flavorful kick

91   **Fabulous and Flourless** Layer crisp meringues and coconut cream to make a gorgeous Passover dessert

92   **SL Cooking School** Our Test Kitchen professionals share the technique for giving piecrust a braided edge

HAZELNUT FINANCIERS
WITH STRAWBERRY
JAM AND LEMON PUREE
(PAGE 79)

Virginia's Sweet Spot

Horticulturist Diane Burns brings a delightful French strawberry to root at famed Pippin Hill Farm & Vineyards

On warm spring days, the heady scent of ripe strawberries drifts over the garden paths of Virginia's Pippin Hill Farm & Vineyards. The fragrance comes from the tiny but mighty Mara des Bois, a woodland-style French selection that bears fruit for months and imparts a deep, lasting sweetness on the tongue. "When I take people on tours of the garden, I encourage them to taste them," says Pippin Hill horticulturist Diane Burns. "It's almost like eating a Jolly Rancher candy."

Burns learned about the Mara des Bois from the previous gardener at Pippin Hill, who'd heard good things about the berry but had not yet attempted to grow that kind. So two years ago, Burns ordered some bare-root Mara des Bois online and planted the first crop. Because Pippin Hill is both a vineyard and a restaurant, everything she grows—including heirloom tomatoes, apples, figs, gooseeberries, and yellow-green Kieffer pears—ends up in the kitchen.

Luckily, Burns' experiment worked. The diminutive berry thrived in the climate and soil of the foothills southwest of Charlottesville, and their flavor and visual appeal thrilled Pippin Hill's executive chef, Ian Rynecki, who started using them in everything from salads to desserts. "They're about twice the size of blueberries and are the best strawberries you've ever tasted," he says.

And because the plant is everbearing, the Mara des Bois enlivens Pippin Hill menus from June all the way through the first hard frost of November. The berries also appear in the tasting room, where Burns likes to leave bowlfuls of freshly picked Mara des Bois to complement the vineyards' rosé.

Nurturing strawberries and other produce amid Virginia's grassy meadows is a big change from Burns' earlier career as a security officer for the U.S. State Department. "I tell people that I used to pack a pistol," she says, "and now I'm packing pruners instead."

Burns was born and raised in Northern Virginia and switched to horticulture when she settled in Charlottesville with her husband and young children over 20 years ago to slow down. "I enjoy being outside," she says. "I love the connection to the earth and working with the cycles of the seasons right alongside the birds and bees."

Once she picks a ripe Mara des Bois strawberry, it will not last more than two or three days in a cool pantry. "This strawberry is such a contrast to the grocery store type, which can be kind of dry and pithy and hollow," Burns says. "Mara des Bois is a really delicious berry, and you don't need many of them because they are just so flavorful."

STRAWBERRY GELATO
WITH ALMOND
SHORTBREAD AND
ELDERFLOWER CRÈME

Strawberry Gelato with Almond Shortbread and Elderflower Crème

ACTIVE 1 HOUR - TOTAL 4 HOURS (PLUS
4 HOURS FREEZING)
SERVES 4

STRAWBERRY GELATO
- ¾ cup halved (quartered, if large) fresh strawberries (about ⅓ lb.)
- ⅛ tsp. white balsamic vinegar
- 7 Tbsp. granulated sugar, divided
- 1¾ cups half-and-half
- 2½ Tbsp. heavy cream
- 1 Tbsp. fat-free powdered milk
- ¼ tsp. kosher salt
- ½ tsp. vanilla extract

ALMOND SHORTBREAD
- 10 Tbsp. unsalted butter, softened
- ⅓ cup granulated sugar
- ¾ tsp. kosher salt
- ½ tsp. almond extract
- 1½ cups all-purpose flour

ELDERFLOWER CRÈME
- 1 cup heavy cream
- 3 Tbsp. powdered sugar
- 1½ Tbsp. (¾ oz.) elderflower liqueur (such as St-Germain)

1. Prepare the Strawberry Gelato: Combine strawberries, vinegar, and 2 tablespoons of the granulated sugar in a saucepan. Cook over medium-low, stirring occasionally, until berries are very soft, 20 minutes. Mash with a potato masher; cool completely, 30 minutes.

2. Combine half-and-half, heavy cream, powdered milk, salt, vanilla, remaining 5 tablespoons granulated sugar, and cooled strawberry mixture in a large bowl. Process with an immersion blender until sugar is dissolved and ingredients are dispersed throughout, about 2 minutes. Cover, and refrigerate until well chilled, about 2 hours.

3. Pour strawberry mixture into frozen freezer bowl of a 1-quart electric ice-cream maker, and proceed according to manufacturer's instructions. Transfer to a freezer-safe container; cover, and freeze until firm, about 4 hours.

4. Prepare the Almond Shortbread: Place butter in the bowl of a heavy-duty stand mixer fitted with paddle attachment; beat on medium speed until fluffy, about 2 minutes. Add granulated sugar, salt, and almond extract; beat on low speed just until incorporated. Gradually add flour, beating on low speed just until blended after each addition. Shape dough into a

4½-inch square about 1 inch thick. Wrap in plastic wrap, and chill until firm, 1 to 2 hours.

5. Preheat oven to 325°F. Position rack in upper third of oven. Line a baking sheet with parchment paper. Roll dough between 2 sheets of plastic wrap into a 6-inch square (about ½ inch thick). Remove plastic wrap; cut dough into 4 (3-inch) squares. Transfer squares to prepared baking sheet, leaving 2 inches of space between each. Bake until shortbread is light golden brown, 17 to 19 minutes. Cool on baking sheet 5 minutes; transfer to a wire rack to cool completely, about 20 minutes.

6. Prepare the Elderflower Crème: Beat all 3 ingredients on high speed with an electric mixer until stiff peaks form, about 1 minute. Serve Gelato with Shortbread; top with Elderflower Crème.

Hazelnut Financiers with Strawberry Jam and Lemon Puree

Hazelnut meal and almond flour give these little cakes a lovely nutty flavor and chewy-crunchy texture. Blanched almond flour (made from skinless almonds) is lighter in color than regular almond meal, but the two products can be used interchangeably. (Photo, page 76)

ACTIVE 1 HOUR, 5 MIN. - TOTAL 4 HOURS (PLUS
3 HOURS CHILLING)
SERVES 12

HAZELNUT FINANCIERS
- ½ cup unsalted butter, plus more for greasing pan
- 1¼ cups powdered sugar
- ½ cup hazelnut meal (such as Bob's Red Mill)
- ¼ cup blanched almond flour (such as Bob's Red Mill)
- ¼ cup all-purpose flour
- 1 tsp. baking powder
- ¼ tsp. kosher salt
- 4 large egg whites, at room temperature

STRAWBERRY JAM
- 1 lb. fresh strawberries, hulled
- 1 cup cane sugar
- 1 Tbsp. fresh lemon juice

LEMON PUREE
- 3 cups granulated sugar
- 2 lemons
- ⅛ tsp. kosher salt

TOPPINGS
- Powdered sugar
- Sliced fresh strawberries

1. Prepare the Hazelnut Financiers: Cook butter in a small saucepan over low, stirring occasionally, until it just begins to brown, about 10 minutes. (It can burn quickly, so remove pan from heat when foam subsides and browning process begins.) Cool to room temperature, about 30 minutes.

2. Whisk together powdered sugar, hazelnut meal, almond flour, all-purpose flour, baking powder, and salt in a medium bowl. Add egg whites, 1 at a time, whisking just to combine. (Do not overwork batter.) Gradually whisk butter into flour mixture. Cover with plastic wrap; chill 3 hours.

3. Meanwhile, prepare the Strawberry Jam: Bring strawberries, cane sugar, and lemon juice to a boil in a medium saucepan over medium-high, stirring occasionally. Reduce heat to medium-low, and simmer, stirring often, until strawberry mixture thickens, about 30 minutes. Mash berry mixture with a potato masher to break up fruit. Transfer jam to a small bowl; cool to room temperature, about 1 hour.

4. Prepare the Lemon Puree: Bring granulated sugar and 3 cups water to a boil in a small saucepan over high. Reduce heat to medium-low; add whole lemons. Simmer until lemons are completely tender, 1 hour. Remove lemons, reserving cooking liquid. Cool lemons and liquid 10 minutes.

5. Place lemons and 1 cup of the reserved cooking liquid in a blender; process on high until mixture is the consistency of applesauce, about 1 minute, adding more reserved cooking liquid as needed. Pour lemon mixture through a fine wire-mesh strainer into a medium bowl, discarding solids. Stir salt into lemon mixture.

6. Preheat oven to 375°F. Coat a standard 12-cup muffin pan with baking spray. Spoon chilled batter into a ziplock plastic freezer bag; snip a ½-inch hole in 1 corner. Pipe batter into cavities of pan, filling each halfway full. Bake in preheated oven until golden brown, 16 to 18 minutes. Cool in pan on a wire rack, about 30 minutes.

7. Top financiers with powdered sugar and sliced strawberries. Serve with Strawberry Jam and Lemon Puree.

Note: Financiers can be made in an 8-cup (15¾- by 11-inch) mini loaf pan. Coat pan with baking spray, and fill 6 of the 8 cavities halfway with batter. Bake at 375°F until golden brown, 14 to 16 minutes.

Strawberry-Rhubarb Crisps with Sweet-and-Savory Granola

The crunchy, lightly spiced granola topping takes a bit of time to make, but it's the star of this dish and can be made in advance in stages. Store the prepared, cooled quinoa and almonds in airtight containers at room temperature up to three days.

ACTIVE 25 MIN. - TOTAL 1 HOUR, 15 MIN.
SERVES 12

- 1½ lb. fresh rhubarb stalks, cut into ¾-inch pieces
- 1 lb. fresh strawberries, hulled and quartered
- 1 cup plus 3 Tbsp. granulated sugar
- 2 Tbsp. tapioca flour or starch
- ¾ tsp. kosher salt, divided
- 10 Tbsp. unsalted butter
- ¾ cup packed dark brown sugar
- 1 cup uncooked old-fashioned rolled oats
- ¾ cup all-purpose flour
- 1 tsp. ground cinnamon
- 1 cup Five-Spice Almonds (recipe follows), crushed
- ½ cup Fried Red Quinoa (recipe follows)
- ¼ cup roasted salted sunflower seeds

1. Preheat oven to 350°F. Combine rhubarb, strawberries, granulated sugar, tapioca flour, and ½ teaspoon of the salt in a saucepan. Cook over medium-low, stirring occasionally, until juices begin to thicken, 10 minutes.
2. Meanwhile, combine butter, brown sugar, oats, all-purpose flour, cinnamon, crushed Five-Spice Almonds, Fried Red Quinoa, sunflower seeds, and remaining ¼ teaspoon salt in the bowl of a heavy-duty stand mixer fitted with paddle attachment. Beat on medium-low speed until combined, about 1 minute.
3. Coat 12 (3-inch) 6- to 8-ounce ramekins with cooking spray. Spoon warm fruit mixture into ramekins, filling each halfway full (about ⅓ cup per ramekin). Top evenly with oat mixture (about ⅓ cup per ramekin), making sure fruit is covered. Place on a rimmed baking sheet. Bake in preheated oven until fruit is bubbling and topping is golden brown, about 20 minutes. Cool at least 30 minutes before serving.

Five-Spice Almonds

ACTIVE 15 MIN. - TOTAL 2 HOURS
MAKES 1½ CUPS

Preheat oven to 300°F. Bring 1½ quart **water** and ½ cup **granulated sugar** to a boil in a saucepan over high. Reduce heat to medium; add ½ pound **raw almonds with skins** (1½ cups). Cook until skins begin to soften, about 5 minutes. Drain almonds; transfer to a large bowl. Toss with ¼ teaspoon **Chinese five-spice powder**, ¼ teaspoon **kosher salt**, a pinch of **cayenne pepper**, and ¼ cup **granulated sugar**. Add more five-spice powder to taste. Spread in an even layer on a rimmed baking sheet. Bake until sugar crystallizes, about 1 hour and 15 minutes, stirring occasionally. Remove from oven. Cool completely, about 30 minutes.

Fried Red Quinoa

ACTIVE 15 MIN. - TOTAL 1 HOUR, 30 MIN.
MAKES 1½ CUPS

Cook ½ cup uncooked **red quinoa** according to package directions; drain. Spread in an even layer on a rimmed baking sheet lined with 2 layers of paper towels. Let stand until completely cool and dry, 1 hour. Pour 1 quart **neutral cooking oil** (such as canola or vegetable) into a large skillet; heat over medium-high to 350°F. Fry quinoa, in batches, until big bubbles stop forming (there will still be some small bubbles), about 1 minute. Drain on a second baking sheet lined with paper towels; sprinkle with a pinch of **kosher salt**.

STRAWBERRY-RHUBARB CRISPS WITH SWEET-AND-SAVORY GRANOLA

Back to Your Roots

Roasted, sauteed, or boiled—turn fresh vegetables into spectacular sides

Lemony Potato-and-Beet Salad with Dill

ACTIVE 15 MIN. - TOTAL 1 HOUR, 15 MIN.
SERVES 4

- 1 lb. baby golden beets (5 to 6 small beets or 2 medium), trimmed
- 1 lb. baby red potatoes, quartered
- 2 garlic cloves, peeled and smashed
- 4 thyme sprigs
- 1 Tbsp. plus 1 tsp. kosher salt, divided
- 2 Tbsp. plain whole-milk yogurt
- 2 Tbsp. sour cream
- 1 tsp. lemon zest plus 1 Tbsp. fresh juice (from 1 lemon)
- 1 tsp. white wine vinegar
- ½ tsp. black pepper
- 1½ Tbsp. chopped fresh dill, divided

1. Place beets in a medium saucepan with water to cover. Bring to a boil over high. Reduce heat to medium, and simmer, uncovered, until fork-tender, about 20 minutes. Drain; cool 10 minutes. Peel beets, and cut into quarters (or cut into eighths if using larger beets). Place in a large mixing bowl.

2. While beets are cooking and cooling, place potatoes, garlic, thyme, and 1 tablespoon of the salt in a medium saucepan. Add water to cover, and bring to a boil over high. Reduce heat to medium, and simmer, uncovered, until potatoes are fork-tender, about 10 minutes. Drain, discarding garlic and thyme; cool about 20 minutes. Add potatoes to cooled beets in bowl; refrigerate until thoroughly chilled, about 30 minutes.

3. Whisk together yogurt, sour cream, lemon zest and juice, vinegar, pepper, 1 tablespoon of the dill, and remaining 1 teaspoon salt in a small bowl until smooth and combined. Add to chilled potato-beet mixture, and toss to coat. Transfer to a serving bowl. Sprinkle with remaining ½ tablespoon dill, and serve immediately.

LEMONY POTATO-AND-BEET SALAD WITH DILL

ROASTED CARROTS WITH
SPICED PECANS AND
SORGHUM

SAUTÉED RADISHES
WITH BACON AND
CILANTRO

ROASTED BABY
TURNIPS WITH TURNIP
GREEN PESTO

PEPPER JELLY-GLAZED
BABY TURNIPS

Roasted Carrots with Spiced Pecans and Sorghum

ACTIVE 15 MIN. - TOTAL 1 HOUR, 10 MIN.
SERVES 6

- ½ cup pecan halves
- 1 Tbsp. unsalted butter, melted
- ¼ tsp. smoked paprika
- ⅛ tsp. cayenne pepper
- 3 lb. small carrots with tops
- 2 Tbsp. olive oil
- 1 tsp. kosher salt
- ¼ tsp. black pepper
- 1 Tbsp. apple cider vinegar
- 2 Tbsp. sorghum syrup
- 1 Tbsp. thinly sliced fresh chives

1. Preheat oven to 350°F. Toss together pecans, butter, paprika, and cayenne on a rimmed baking sheet. Bake until lightly browned and toasted, about 8 minutes. Remove from oven; cool completely on pan, about 15 minutes. Coarsely chop pecans; set aside.
2. Increase oven to 450°F. Peel carrots; trim carrot tops to 1 inch. (Discard the trimmed greens, or reserve for another use.) Toss together trimmed carrots, oil, salt, and pepper in a bowl; spread in a single layer on a rimmed baking sheet. Roast, stirring once, until browned and tender, 30 to 35 minutes. Remove from oven; immediately drizzle hot carrots with vinegar, and toss to coat.
3. Arrange carrots on a serving platter. Drizzle with sorghum syrup; sprinkle with pecans and chives.

Sauteed Radishes with Bacon and Cilantro

ACTIVE 20 MIN. - TOTAL 20 MIN.
SERVES 4

- 4 thick-cut bacon slices, chopped
- 1 lb. radishes, cut in half lengthwise (quartered if large)
- 1 Tbsp. apple cider vinegar
- ½ tsp. honey
- ½ tsp. kosher salt
- ¼ tsp. black pepper
- ⅓ cup packed fresh cilantro leaves

1. Place bacon in a large nonstick skillet; cook over medium, stirring occasionally, until just starting to brown, about 4 minutes.
2. Add radishes to skillet; cook, stirring occasionally, until radishes are tender and bacon is crispy, about 12 minutes.

3. Push radishes and bacon to 1 side of skillet using a spatula. Carefully tilt skillet to drain drippings. Discard bacon drippings, reserving 1 tablespoon drippings in skillet. Add vinegar, honey, salt, and pepper to skillet; stir until well incorporated. Stir in cilantro, and serve immediately.

Roasted Baby Turnips with Turnip Green Pesto

ACTIVE 20 MIN. - TOTAL 40 MIN.
SERVES 4

- 4 (9 oz.) bunches baby turnips
- ¼ cup plus 2 Tbsp. olive oil, divided
- 1¼ tsp. kosher salt, divided
- ¾ tsp. black pepper, divided
- 2 Tbsp. chopped toasted pecans
- 1 small garlic clove
- 1 Tbsp. fresh lemon juice
- 2 Tbsp. plus 2 tsp. grated Parmesan cheese
- 1½ tsp. honey

1. Preheat oven to 425°F; place a rimmed baking sheet in oven 5 minutes while preheating. Trim turnip stems to 1 inch. Cut trimmed turnips in half lengthwise to measure 6 cups. Chop turnip greens to measure 4 cups. (Reserve remaining turnips and greens for another use.)
2. Toss together halved turnips, 2 tablespoons of the oil, ¾ teaspoon of the salt, and ½ teaspoon of the pepper in a bowl; spread in one even layer on warmed baking sheet. Roast in preheated oven until tender and golden brown, about 18 minutes.
3. While turnips roast, place 2 quarts water in a large saucepan, and bring to a boil over high. Add chopped greens; cook about 30 seconds. Fill a large bowl with ice water. Drain boiled greens, submerge in ice water, and stir once. Let stand until cold, about 1 minute. Remove greens, and squeeze out excess water. Transfer to a food processor.
4. Add pecans and garlic to the greens in the food processor, and process until a paste forms, stopping to scrape down sides as needed, about 1 minute. With processor running, pour lemon juice and remaining ¼ cup oil through food chute in a steady stream, processing until smooth, about 1 minute. Add Parmesan, honey, and remaining ½ teaspoon salt and ¼ teaspoon pepper, and process until blended, about 10 seconds. Set pesto aside until ready to serve.

5. Transfer roasted turnips to a serving platter; drizzle with pesto.

Shaved Carrot, Asparagus, and Apple Salad

(Photo, page 13)

ACTIVE 25 MIN. - TOTAL 25 MIN.
SERVES 4

- ⅓ cup olive oil
- ¼ cup red wine vinegar
- 2 Tbsp. honey
- 1 tsp. kosher salt
- ¼ tsp. black pepper
- 1 cup chopped fresh basil
- 3 large carrots, peeled
- 1 lb. fresh asparagus, trimmed
- 3 cups angel hair cabbage
- 1 large Granny Smith apple, unpeeled and thinly sliced (1⅓ cups)
- 1 bunch scallions, thinly sliced (1 cup)

1. Whisk together first five ingredients in a bowl until smooth. Stir in basil. Set aside.
2. Cut trimmed carrots and asparagus into thin ribbonlike strips using a vegetable peeler; place in a large bowl. Add cabbage, apple, scallions, and oil-vinegar mixture; toss to coat. Serve immediately.

Pepper Jelly-Glazed Baby Turnips

ACTIVE 20 MIN. - TOTAL 25 MIN.
SERVES 4

- 4 (9-oz.) bunches baby turnips
- 2 Tbsp. unsalted butter
- 1¼ tsp. kosher salt
- ⅓ cup red pepper jelly (from 1 [12-oz.] jar)
- 1 Tbsp. chopped fresh mint

1. Trim greens from turnips. Cut trimmed turnips into uniform ¾-inch pieces to measure 6 cups. (Discard trimmed greens and excess turnips, or reserve for another use.) Place in a large skillet, and stir in ¼ cup water, butter, and salt. Bring to a low simmer over medium. Cover and cook, undisturbed, 5 minutes.
2. Uncover skillet; stir in jelly. Cook, uncovered, stirring often, until turnips are tender and liquid is syrupy, 10 to 12 minutes. (If jelly separates from butter sauce while turnips cook, stir in additional water, 2 tablespoons at a time, to incorporate jelly back into sauce.)
3. Stir in mint; serve immediately.

Easter Brunch for a Bunch

Five easy, crowd-pleasing dishes that will be a hit at your holiday celebration

TRY TOSTADAS
Unlike tortillas, crisp corn tostadas will soften during baking but still maintain a good texture.

Huevos Rancheros Bake

ACTIVE 20 MIN. - TOTAL 45 MIN.
SERVES 6

18	corn tostadas (from 1 [12.3-oz.] pkg.)
2	(8-oz.) pkg. red enchilada sauce (such as Frontera)
1	(15-oz.) can refried beans, warmed
8	oz. Colby Jack cheese, shredded (about 2 cups)
4	oz. queso blanco, crumbled (about 1 cup)
1½	tsp. olive oil
6	large eggs, at room temperature
½	tsp. kosher salt
¼	tsp. black pepper
1	medium avocado, diced (1½ cups)
½	cup sour cream
¼	cup packed fresh cilantro leaves, chopped
1	medium jalapeño chile, seeded and finely chopped (1½ tsp.)

1. Preheat oven to 375°F. Arrange 6 of the tostadas evenly in a large cast-iron skillet, breaking into pieces as needed to cover bottom of skillet. Top evenly with ⅔ cup of the enchilada sauce, ½ cup of the beans, ⅔ cup of the Colby Jack cheese, and ⅓ cup of the queso blanco. Repeat layers 2 times. Bake until mixture bubbles, 20 to 25 minutes.
2. During final 5 minutes of baking, heat a large nonstick skillet over medium. Add oil; crack eggs into skillet. Cook until whites are set, 4 minutes.
3. Arrange cooked eggs on baked tostada mixture. Sprinkle with salt and pepper. Top with avocado, sour cream, cilantro, and jalapeño.

Orange-Vanilla French Toast Casserole with Bourbon-Maple Syrup

Spirited Syrup: A splash of bourbon enhances the maple syrup's caramel sweetness, but you can omit the alcohol if you prefer. Whether you add bourbon or not, be sure to choose the good stuff: 100%-pure maple syrup.

ACTIVE 15 MIN. - TOTAL 1 HOUR, PLUS 8 HOURS CHILLING

SERVES 6

- 1 cup packed light brown sugar
- 6 Tbsp. butter, melted
- 1 cup pure maple syrup, divided
- 1 cup chopped toasted pecans, divided
- 12 (1-inch-thick) baguette slices (from 1 baguette, ends discarded)
- 5 large eggs, lightly beaten
- 1¼ cups whole milk
- 2 Tbsp. granulated sugar
- 1 tsp. orange zest plus 1 Tbsp. fresh juice (from 1 orange)
- ½ tsp. ground cinnamon
- 1¼ tsp. vanilla extract, divided
- 2 Tbsp. (1 oz.) bourbon
  Powdered sugar, for serving

1. Stir together brown sugar, melted butter, and ¼ cup of the maple syrup. Spread mixture into a 13- x 9-inch baking dish lightly coated with cooking spray. Sprinkle with ¾ cup of the pecans. Arrange baguette slices evenly on top.

2. Whisk together next 5 ingredients and 1 teaspoon of the vanilla. Pour over baguette slices. Cover; chill 8 hours.

3. Preheat oven to 350°F. Remove baking dish from refrigerator; let stand at room temperature 10 minutes. Bake, uncovered, until golden brown and set, about 35 minutes.

4. During final 10 minutes of baking, combine bourbon and remaining ¾ cup maple syrup and ¼ teaspoon vanilla in a saucepan. Cook over low, stirring, until warm, 2 minutes. Remove from heat; cover pan.

5. Sprinkle casserole with powdered sugar and remaining ¼ cup pecans. Serve with Bourbon-Maple Syrup.

Company Quiche

ACTIVE 30 MIN. - TOTAL 2 HOURS, 45 MIN.
SERVES 8

- 1 large egg white, lightly beaten
- 1 (14.1-oz.) pkg. refrigerated piecrusts
- 1 Tbsp. butter
- ¾ cup thinly sliced spring onions
- 4 oz. asparagus, trimmed and cut into 1-inch pieces (about 1 cup)
- 1½ tsp. kosher salt, divided
- 4 oz. Gouda cheese, shredded (about 1 cup)
- 4 large eggs
- 1¾ cups half-and-half
- 2½ tsp. chopped fresh tarragon, divided
- ½ tsp. black pepper
- 1 Tbsp. chopped fresh chives

1. Whisk together egg white and 2 teaspoons water. Unroll 1 piecrust; fit inside a 9-inch pie plate. Trim excess dough around edge. Brush dough edge with some of the egg-water mixture.

2. Unroll remaining piecrust; cut into ½-inch-wide strips. Pinch the 3 longest strips (from the center) together at 1 end to seal; braid. Repeat process twice, with 3 strips each from left and right of center, making 3 braids total, each about 7 inches long. (Discard remaining dough.)

3. Preheat oven to 425°F. Press braids gently onto the dough edge. Brush braided dough with remaining egg-water mixture. Freeze 20 minutes. Place parchment paper over frozen piecrust, and top with pie weights. Bake until crust is lightly golden and set, about 10 minutes. Remove weights and parchment; continue baking until crust is fully dry, about 5 minutes. Cool on a wire rack, about 30 minutes.

4. Reduce oven temperature to 350°F. Melt butter in a large skillet over medium-high. Add spring onions, asparagus, and ½ teaspoon of the salt. Cook, stirring often, until very soft, about 8 minutes. Remove from heat; cool 5 minutes.

5. Spoon onion-asparagus mixture into cooled piecrust; sprinkle with cheese. Whisk together eggs, half-and-half, 2 teaspoons tarragon, pepper, chives, and remaining 1 teaspoon salt. Pour over vegetable mixture. Bake at 350°F until middle is nearly set, about 40 minutes. Cool 30 minutes. Sprinkle with remaining ½ teaspoon tarragon.

PASTRY POINTER
Blind-baking the crust (prebaking without the filling) with pie weights helps hold its shape. If you do not have pie weights, line the dough with parchment paper as directed, and use dried beans, rice, or popcorn kernels.

Sausage-Hash Brown Casserole

ACTIVE 30 MIN. - TOTAL 1 HOUR
SERVES 8

1 lb. pkg. ground pork sausage with sage (such as Jimmy Dean)
1 lb. pkg. hot ground pork sausage
1 (30-oz.) pkg. frozen shredded hash browns
2 tsp. kosher salt, divided
1 tsp. black pepper, divided
6 oz. sharp Cheddar cheese, shredded (about 1½ cups), divided
6 large eggs, lightly beaten
1 cup whole milk
1 Tbsp. chopped fresh flat-leaf parsley
1 Tbsp. chopped fresh chives

1. Preheat oven to 350°F. Coat a 13- x 9-inch baking dish with cooking spray. Cook ground sage sausage and ground hot sausage in a large skillet over medium-high, stirring often, until they are crumbled and browned, about 10 minutes. Remove from heat; drain well on paper towels.
2. Working in batches, cook hash browns in a large nonstick skillet according to package directions; omit salt if called for on package. Sprinkle with 1 teaspoon of the salt and ½ teaspoon of the pepper.
3. Stir together sausage, hash browns, and 1 cup of the cheese in a bowl. Spoon into prepared baking dish. Whisk together eggs, milk, and remaining 1 teaspoon salt and ½ teaspoon pepper in a medium bowl. Pour over sausage mixture. Sprinkle with remaining ½ cup cheese. Bake in preheated oven until set, about 30 minutes. Sprinkle with parsley and chives.

DOUBLE THE SAUSAGE TRICK
Two types of pork sausage make this casserole extra flavorful and hearty.

Shrimp and Grits Casserole

ACTIVE 25 MIN. - TOTAL 1 HOUR
SERVES 6

- 2 cups whole milk
- 2¼ cups heavy cream, divided
- 1 cup uncooked quick-cooking grits
- ¼ cup butter
- 1 large egg, lightly beaten
- 8 oz. sharp Cheddar cheese, shredded (about 2 cups)
- 1½ tsp. kosher salt, divided
- 5 thick-cut bacon slices, chopped (about 1 cup)
- ½ cup finely chopped red onion (from 1 small onion)
- ½ cup finely chopped red bell pepper (from 1 small bell pepper)
- 2 garlic cloves, minced (about 1 Tbsp.)
- ⅓ cup all-purpose flour
- 1 lb. medium peeled, deveined raw shrimp
- ½ cup (4 oz.) dry white wine
- 1 cup chicken broth
- 1 Tbsp. chopped fresh flat-leaf parsley
- 2 tsp. fresh thyme leaves
- ½ tsp. black pepper
- ⅛ tsp. cayenne pepper
- ¼ cup sliced scallions

1. Preheat oven to 350°F. Coat an 11- x 7-inch baking dish with cooking spray. Bring milk and 2 cups of the heavy cream to a boil in a medium saucepan over medium-high. Stir in grits and butter; let mixture return to a boil, whisking often. Reduce heat to medium; cook, whisking constantly, until grits are tender, 5 to 7 minutes. Remove from heat; stir in egg, cheese, and 1 teaspoon of the salt. Spoon mixture into prepared baking dish. Cover; bake until mixture is set, 35 to 40 minutes.

2. Meanwhile, cook bacon in a large saucepan over medium-high, stirring occasionally, until crisp, about 8 minutes. Drain on paper towels, reserving 3 tablespoons drippings in pan. Add onion and bell pepper to pan. Cook over medium-high, stirring often, until softened, about 3 minutes. Add garlic; cook, stirring constantly, 30 seconds. Add flour; cook, stirring constantly, 1 minute. Add shrimp; cook, stirring constantly, until shrimp are pink, about 3 minutes. Add wine; cook, stirring constantly, until thickened, 2 minutes. Stir in broth, parsley, thyme, black pepper, cayenne pepper, and remaining ¼ cup heavy cream and ½ teaspoon salt.

3. Spoon shrimp mixture over baked grits casserole using a slotted spoon; sprinkle with scallions and cooked bacon. Pour shrimp gravy from pan into a serving bowl; serve alongside casserole.

Pretty Tasty Pot Pie

Treat the family to a classic dish reinvented in a skillet

Skillet Pot Pie with Chicken and Spring Vegetables

ACTIVE 20 MIN. - TOTAL 1 HOUR, 10 MIN.
SERVES 6

- ½ cup butter
- 2 cups thinly sliced leek (from 1 large leek)
- 1 cup chopped carrots (from 3 medium carrots)
- ½ cup all-purpose flour, plus more for work surface
- 2 cups lower-sodium chicken broth
- 4 cups shredded rotisserie chicken
- 1 cup frozen petite sweet peas, thawed
- ¼ cup heavy cream
- 2 tsp. finely chopped fresh thyme
- 1½ tsp. kosher salt
- ½ tsp. black pepper
- 1 large egg
- ½ (17.3-oz.) pkg. frozen puff pastry sheets, thawed

1. Preheat oven to 400°F with rack in lower third of oven. Melt butter in a deep 10-inch ovenproof skillet over medium-high. Add leek and carrots. Cook, stirring often, until softened, about 6 minutes. Sprinkle with flour; cook, stirring constantly, 1 minute. Stir in broth; let mixture come to a simmer. Simmer, stirring constantly, until mixture thickens, 1 to 2 minutes. Stir in shredded chicken, peas, cream, thyme, salt, and pepper. Remove from heat; let cool 10 minutes.
2. Whisk together egg and 1 tablespoon water in a small bowl. Roll pastry sheet into a 12-inch square on a lightly floured surface. Cut into 16 (3-inch) squares. Arrange squares on top of chicken mixture in skillet, brushing each square with egg mixture and slightly overlapping squares to cover surface of chicken mixture. Place skillet on a rimmed baking sheet.
3. Transfer baking sheet with skillet to preheated oven. Bake until top is browned and filling is bubbly, about 30 minutes. Let stand 10 minutes, and serve.

PREP TIP
To save time, shred the chicken and chop the carrots and leek up to two days ahead. Cover and store in the refrigerator.

Speedy Sheet Pan Salmon

A tangy honey-mustard sauce gives this fish a flavorful kick

Honey–Mustard Salmon and Vegetables

ACTIVE 15 MIN. - TOTAL 30 MIN.
SERVES 4

Preheat oven to 425°F. Toss together 1 pound **baby red potatoes**, halved (3 cups); 3 **shallots**, quartered lengthwise (about 1 cup); 1 tablespoon **olive oil**; and ¼ teaspoon **kosher salt** on a large rimmed baking sheet. Arrange in an even layer, with potatoes cut sides down. Roast until almost tender, about 15 minutes. Remove from oven. Meanwhile, combine 3 tablespoons **whole-grain mustard**, ¼ teaspoon **kosher salt**, and 1 teaspoon **honey** in a bowl. Stir together ½ cup **panko breadcrumbs**, 2 teaspoons chopped **fresh thyme**, 1 tablespoon **olive oil**, and ¼ teaspoon **kosher salt** in a separate bowl. Arrange 4 (5-oz.) **skin-on salmon fillets**, skin sides down, on a plate. Spread mustard mixture evenly over tops of salmon fillets. Sprinkle tops evenly with panko mixture, pressing to adhere. Stir potato mixture on baking sheet, pushing it toward edges of sheet with a spatula. Place salmon fillets, skin sides down, in center of baking sheet, and scatter 3 cups trimmed **fresh sugar snap peas** evenly around salmon. Return baking sheet to oven. Bake at 425°F until salmon is cooked to medium doneness (turns flaky and opaque) and potatoes are tender, about 10 minutes. Meanwhile, whisk together 2 teaspoons **red wine vinegar**, 1 teaspoon grated **garlic**, ¼ teaspoon **smoked paprika**, 2 tablespoons **olive oil**, ¼ teaspoon **kosher salt**, 2 teaspoons **whole-grain mustard**, and ½ teaspoon **honey**. Divide salmon fillets and vegetables among 4 plates, and drizzle with honey-mustard mixture.

Nutritional information: Calories: 495; Protein: 33g; Carbs: 38g; Fiber: 6g; Fat: 23g

Fabulous and Flourless

Layer crisp meringues and coconut cream to make a gorgeous Passover dessert

Chocolate–Coconut Pavlova Cake

ACTIVE 30 MIN. · TOTAL 7 HOURS, 30 MIN.
SERVES 12

- 1½ Tbsp. potato starch (or cornstarch)
- 1½ cups plus 3 Tbsp. granulated sugar, divided
- 6 large egg whites, at room temperature
- ½ tsp. fresh lemon juice
- ⅛ tsp. kosher salt
- ¼ tsp. vanilla extract
- 1½ tsp. unsweetened cocoa
- 2 (14-oz.) cans unsweetened coconut cream, chilled 24 hours
- Chocolate shavings

1. Preheat oven to 225°F. Line 2 large baking sheets with parchment paper, and draw 2 (7-inch) circles on 1 parchment paper sheet. Draw 1 (7-inch) circle on second sheet. Turn sheets over, writing sides down.
2. Whisk together potato starch and 1½ cups of the sugar in a bowl; set aside. Beat egg whites with a heavy-duty stand mixer fitted with whisk attachment on medium-high speed for 1 minute. Add lemon juice and kosher salt, and beat until blended, about 30 seconds. With mixer running on high, gradually add sugar mixture (2 tablespoons at a time), beating just until glossy, stiff peaks form and sugar is almost dissolved, about 2 minutes. (Do not overbeat.) Reduce speed to low, and beat in vanilla.
3. Gently spoon egg white mixture evenly onto parchment paper circles. Sift ½ teaspoon cocoa over each. Using back of a spoon, spread egg white mixture to cover each circle.
4. Bake in preheated oven until meringues have formed a crust, about 3 hours; rotate baking sheets between top and bottom racks halfway through baking. Turn oven off, and let meringues stand in oven with door closed at least 4 hours or up to overnight.
5. Chill bowl of stand mixer and whisk attachment 30 minutes. Pour chilled coconut cream into chilled bowl. Add remaining 3 tablespoons sugar. Beat on medium speed, 1 minute. Increase speed to medium-high; beat until fluffy, 3 to 4 minutes.
6. Place 1 meringue on a serving plate; top with 1 to 1½ cups whipped coconut cream. Repeat with 2 remaining meringues and cream, ending with cream. Garnish with chocolate shavings.

COOKING (SL) SCHOOL

KNOW-HOW

Twirl Up a Piecrust

Use refrigerated dough to give any quiche or pie a braided edge

1

Cut a piecrust-dough circle into ½-inch-wide strips using a paring knife.

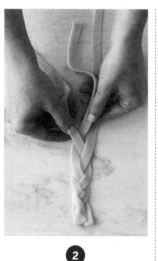

2

Pinch the 3 longest strips together at 1 end to seal; braid. Repeat process with remaining strips to make 3 braids total.

3

Place bottom crust into a pie plate. Press dough braids gently onto the outer edge around pie plate, creating a braided circle.

"When making scrambled eggs, pull the pan off the heat when the eggs are softly set but not runny. Rest them in the pan 1 minute so they firm up without becoming tough."

-Robby Melvin
Test Kitchen Director

EGGS 101

Crack the Size Code

Bigger isn't always better

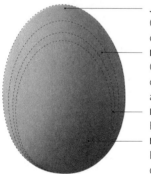

JUMBO
Great for oversize omelets and egg salad

EXTRA LARGE
Can be used in place of large eggs in small amounts (1 or 2 eggs)

LARGE
Best for baking

MEDIUM
Perfect choice for deviled eggs

COOKING TIPS

Secrets to Silky Quiche Fillings

**CHOOSE
THE RIGHT DAIRY**
A quiche filling is a custard, so full-fat dairy is necessary. We prefer half-and-half, though whole milk and heavy cream work well too.

**REMEMBER
THE RATIO**
To keep the filling from being rubbery or too soft, aim for about ½ cup of dairy for each egg used.

**DON'T
OVERBAKE**
Remove the quiche from the oven while the center still has a slight "wobble."

May

94   **The House That Mama Built**   Mama Dip's cooking legacy lives on through her daughters and granddaughters

98   **Eat Your Peas**   Discover a world of fresh and flavorful field peas this season

102   **Hooked on Shrimp**   Ready-in-a-flash suppers, from stir-fry to scampi

107   **A New Spin on Chicken Spaghetti**   Enjoy this lightened-up classic for Sunday supper when the entire family is together

108   **Pork Perfection**   Skip the usual breaded cutlets—this quick-cooking dish is better for you and just as flavorful

109   **It's Shortcake Season**   Whip up a sweet dessert with juicy strawberries and homemade biscuits and cream

110   **SL Cooking School**   Our Test Kitchen professionals give ideas for fabulous, up-scale shortcakes

Mama
in
the kitch

Home
cooking's
always on
the menu
at Dip's

By BRIDGETTE
Staff writer

The House That Mama Built

Mama Dip's cooking legacy lives on through her daughters and granddaughters

Mildred Council may have been known to the world by her childhood nickname, Dip (inspired by her long arms), but her reach has been so much longer.

A year after her death at age 89, her children, grandchildren, and even great-grandchildren still work at the restaurant she built, Mama Dip's Kitchen in Chapel Hill, North Carolina. And the Council family food businesses, all started with her encouragement and passion, are likely to continue for years to come.

One granddaughter sells biscuits that are so good she named her business Bomb Biscuits. Another granddaughter makes crispy baked meringue cookies that shatter on your tongue with a lingering sweetness. One daughter creates cake mixes that bake into red velvet or pound cake. More daughters and two sons run the restaurant and sell the Mama Dip's product line—salad dressing, barbecue sauces, and cornbread mix.

"It's a lot of history there, right?" says Erika Council, one of Mildred's granddaughters, who works in software engineering in Atlanta and serves her Bomb Biscuits at pop-ups at restaurants like B's Cracklin' Barbeque and at special events. "One thing we all say on the Council side is that it's definitely in our blood," she adds.

The popular story of Mildred Council and her renowned restaurant, Mama Dip's, is that she started it on a meager $64 set aside from what she earned as a cook and maid at Chapel Hill's wealthy homes and fraternity houses—and that's true. The food story goes back a lot further, though. The youngest daughter of seven children, Mildred "Dip" Cotton was such a good cook that her father let her take over the role at age 9, after her mother died. Then in 1947, she married Joe Council, whose family started a small restaurant, Bill's Bar-B-Que.

Mildred quickly found a place in the Council family restaurant, developing her recipe for fried chicken and working alongside Joe. Before they divorced in the 1970s, they had eight children: Norma, Geary (called Yea-Yea), Joe, Julia (Bon), William, Sandra (Lane), Annette (Neecy), and Anita (Spring). Yes, nicknames are a tradition in this family.

Food was at the center of their childhood: helping at Bill's, driving their father's food truck around to construction sites, and hanging out in the kitchen (elbows on the table) while their mother worked and talked. "People cooked back then," says her youngest daughter, Anita Council, who runs the restaurant with her sisters Annette and Sandra and her brothers Geary and Joe. "That's where the food really started for us."

Anita was 12 when she began helping behind the counter at Bill's Bar-B-Que, cooking burgers and hot dogs and learning to add figures in her head quickly. As a girl, she always had pocket money, but it didn't mean she got to spend her time having fun with it. Work always came first in the Council family. All of the children and grandchildren have memories of Mildred keeping busy. Anita's daughter, Tonya Council, remembers that even sitting in front of the TV at night, her grandmother would shell pecans for the next day's pies.

Tonya began waitressing at her grandmother's original restaurant, Dip's Country Kitchen, when she was 15 or 16, but her time there started a lot earlier. "I know I was in the way when I was 4, 5, 6," she says. "People ask where I grew up, and I say, '405 West Rosemary Street,'" the location of the original restaurant, an 18-seat diner. Tonya's side business, Tonya's Cookies, started out as a kitchen project when she got annoyed seeing an empty bakery case at the front of the restaurant. She decided to create a cookie that was as good as her grandmother's pecan pie. She tried

and tried, getting on everyone's nerves in the kitchen while she made batch after batch. Finally, she experimented with a fateful new recipe. She was going to throw the cookies out until her grandmother tried one and told her she'd done it.

Mildred gave Tonya permission to use the kitchen at the old location, a pink building across the street from the expanded restaurant the family built in 1999. She also offered her advice on packaging and suggested Tonya take samples to the local gourmet store, Southern Season, which became her first customer. Tonya still works at the restaurant nine months of the year, stepping out to run her cookie company from October (when the N.C. State Fair opens) through Christmas.

Tonya's aunt Annette is called Neecy, from an old Southern phrase, "knee baby," for the next-to-youngest child. She launched her cake-mix business, Sweet Neecy, after customers at the restaurant told them they couldn't bake good cakes. At first, she made them for people, but it took a lot of time. So she came up with easy mixes they could use instead. Whenever her mother was baking, the children were always in the kitchen. "We were waiting to lick the bowls," she says, laughing.

Tonya calls her cousin Erika Council "the biscuit whisperer." Erika says her influence in cooking came from both sides of her family: Her other grandmother, Geraldine Dortch, made food to raise money to support the Civil Rights Movement. "That story was super impactful for me," she adds.

While the Council daughters and granddaughters are resourceful about their businesses, they also inherited a creative streak. Besides Mildred's two cookbooks, both Erika and Anita have blogs, and Annette wrote a book about her family's history, *The Recipe: Have a Seat at Our Table*, in 2006.

They all credit Mildred for that trait. While she called herself a "dump cook" who kept her dishes simple and traditional, she always had magazines around the house. When she hosted

parties for her friends, the table was decorated just so. Annette says her younger sister, Anita, has the same touch. "Spring gets the classy in Southern food," she teases her.

Mildred always let the kids stay in the kitchen with her, Erika recalls. And she believed in the principle of "pull as you climb," helping others to be successful. "She was the embodiment of that," Erika says. "If you have the ability to let someone in and help them, use what you have to do that." She and her husband donate some of the proceeds from their biscuit sales to help underprivileged kids in Atlanta learn about science, technology, engineering, and mathematics.

In this family, everything has come back to the business. Mildred was there every day until the last two years of her life. Tonya says she still expects to see her in the kitchen in the chair where she would always sit, watching everything and talking to each friend who walked through the door. "The wisdom and advice is what I miss," she adds.

Now that Mildred is gone, her children and grandchildren have no doubt that the restaurant and the family food businesses will continue. That was what she wanted—a legacy that would go on long after she was gone. Tonya points out the Old Well, the most beloved landmark on the campus of The University of North Carolina at Chapel Hill, a few blocks from the restaurant. "My dream is to keep this place going as long as the Old Well stands on campus," she says.

Mama's Rum Cake

This rich, spirited Bundt is a Council family favorite. A double dose of rum makes this cake extra moist and fragrant.

ACTIVE 25 MIN. - TOTAL 1 HOUR, 55 MIN.
SERVES 14

CAKE

- 3 cups all-purpose flour
- 2 tsp. baking powder
- ½ tsp. baking soda
- ⅛ tsp. salt
- 1½ cups unsalted butter, softened
- 1½ cups granulated sugar
- 2 tsp. vanilla extract
- 3 large eggs
- 1 large egg yolk
- ¾ cup (6 oz.) gold rum (such as Bacardí Gold)
- ¾ cup heavy cream

RUM SYRUP

- ½ cup unsalted butter
- 1 cup granulated sugar
- ½ cup (4 oz.) gold rum (such as Bacardí Gold)
- ½ tsp. vanilla extract

1. Prepare the Cake: Preheat oven to 350°F. Generously coat a 10-inch (10- to 15-cup) Bundt pan with cooking spray; set aside. Stir together flour, baking powder, baking soda, and salt in a bowl; set aside.
2. Beat butter, sugar, and vanilla in a stand mixer fitted with a paddle attachment on medium speed until light and fluffy, about 4 minutes. Add eggs, 1 at a time, and egg yolk, beating well after each addition. Reduce mixer speed to low; gradually beat in rum. Add flour mixture to egg mixture in thirds, alternately with heavy cream, beginning and ending with flour mixture, beating on low after each addition.
3. Transfer batter to prepared Bundt pan, smoothing the top. Bake in preheated oven until golden brown and a wooden pick inserted in center comes out clean, 50 to 55 minutes (cover loosely with aluminum foil after 30 minutes to prevent excess browning if needed). Remove from oven.
4. During final 10 minutes of bake time, prepare the Rum Syrup: Melt butter in a saucepan over medium. Add sugar and ¼ cup water; let mixture come to a boil. Boil, stirring occasionally, until syrupy, about 5 minutes. Carefully add rum and vanilla. (Mixture will bubble.) Boil, stirring often, 1 minute. Remove from heat.
5. Using a wooden skewer, poke warm Cake in pan all over. Spoon ¾ cup of the Rum Syrup evenly over Cake. Let stand 10 minutes. Invert onto a cake stand. Spoon remaining Rum Syrup (about ½ cup) evenly over top. Let cool at least 20 minutes or up to 8 hours before serving.

Eat Your Peas

Discover a world of fresh and flavorful field peas this season

Field peas are the South's most varied legume, but many cooks never venture past black-eyed peas and might not realize there are other choices. We should, however. Although black-eyed peas are good, they are the Red Delicious apples of the field pea universe: the most well-known and widespread but a bit generic and not necessarily the tastiest or most interesting.

So what are field peas? They are technically beans and have little in common with green English peas. Field peas are cowpeas, so named because they were grown as a rotational crop in the fields instead of in kitchen gardens. Dozens of different types—what we now call heirloom selections—were grown in Southern communities that valued them for their flavor and ability to flourish in local conditions. Families and neighbors often saved the seeds and passed them down through the generations. We still have heirloom types in the South with charming, descriptive names such as Whippoorwill, Dimpled Brown Crowder, Turkey Craw, Washday, Red Ripper, and Old Timer.

Freshly harvested peas often stick close to home, unlike dried black-eyed peas that are shipped far and wide. The best sources for them are farmers' markets, family gardens, and hometown grocery stores. A single shopping trip can reveal the tastiest treasures. As with summer tomatoes, locally grown, peak-of-season peas are hard to beat. The good news is to preserve the harvest, fresh field peas freeze and keep well.

Some markets sell field peas still in their colorful pods, but most do the shelling for us. Fresh peas cook quickly compared to dried peas and beans that must be soaked. Their flavor and texture range from delicate and vegetal to earthy and meaty, but they are usually lighter

FIELD PEAS IN HERBED BROTH

PICKING POINTER
Each kind has its own qualities, but if you can't find a specific pea mentioned in a recipe, enjoy what you can find locally. Most types of field peas are interchangeable.

and less murky than dried black-eyed peas. (When dried is the only option, we can turn to one of the excellent Southern types, such as the iconic Sea Island red pea, the original used in hoppin' John.)

Many of us eat field peas for luck on January 1, but to limit them to a single winter day (or use only the ubiquitous black-eyed kind) is to miss out on their delightful versatility. All sorts of field peas are easy to find and love in the South. Lucky us.

Field Peas in Herbed Broth

ACTIVE 15 MIN. - TOTAL 50 MIN.
SERVES 6

- 3 cups shelled fresh or thawed frozen field peas (1 lb.), rinsed
- 2 small yellow onions, quartered
- 1 medium carrot, cut into chunks
- 1 medium celery stalk, cut into chunks
- 2 medium garlic cloves, smashed
- 2 small bay leaves
- 6 flat-leaf parsley sprigs
- 2 tsp. kosher salt
- 4 cups chicken stock or vegetable broth, or amount needed
- 2 Tbsp. unsalted butter
- 1 Tbsp. fresh thyme leaves
- ¼ tsp. black pepper

1. Stir together peas, onions, carrot, celery, garlic, bay leaves, parsley, and salt in a medium saucepan. Add stock to cover by a depth of 1 inch. Bring to a boil over high, skimming foam that rises to the top. Reduce heat to medium. Partially cover; simmer until tender, 15 to 25 minutes. Remove pan from heat; let stand 15 minutes.

2. Remove and discard onions, carrot, celery, garlic, bay leaves, and parsley. Do not drain peas. (To make ahead, transfer cooked peas and liquid to an airtight container; cover and refrigerate up to 3 days.) Stir in butter, thyme, and pepper. Serve warm.

Field Pea Cakes with Tomato–Ginger Jam

ACTIVE 30 MIN. - TOTAL 45 MIN.
SERVES 6

- 3 cups shelled fresh or thawed frozen field peas (1 lb.), rinsed
- 2 tsp. kosher salt, divided
- 2 Tbsp. peanut oil or canola oil, plus more for frying
- ½ cup finely chopped yellow onion (from 1 small onion)
- ½ cup finely chopped red bell pepper (from 1 small bell pepper)
- 1 tsp. curry powder or garam masala
- 2 cups panko breadcrumbs, divided
- ½ cup all-purpose flour
- 2 large eggs
  Tomato-Ginger Jam (recipe follows)
  Sliced scallions for topping

1. Stir together peas and 1 teaspoon of the salt in a medium saucepan. Add water to cover by a depth of 1 inch. Bring to a boil over high, skimming foam that rises to the top. Reduce heat to medium; partially cover, and simmer until tender, 15 to 25 minutes. Drain and set aside.

2. Heat oil in a large skillet over medium-high. Stir in onion and bell pepper; cook, stirring occasionally, until tender, about 5 minutes. Stir in curry powder; cook, stirring constantly, 1 minute. Transfer mixture to a food processor. Add 2 cups of cooked peas and remaining 1 teaspoon salt. Pulse until mixture forms a coarse paste, 5 to 6 times. Transfer mixture to a medium bowl. Fold in ½ cup of the panko and remaining 1 cup cooked peas. Form into 12 (3-inch) cakes.

3. Place flour in a shallow bowl. Lightly beat eggs in a separate shallow bowl. Place remaining 1½ cups panko in a third shallow bowl. Working with 1 cake at a time, dredge in flour, dip in eggs, and then dredge in panko, pressing gently to adhere.

4. Pour oil into a large skillet to a depth of ¼ inch; heat over medium-high. Working in batches, add cakes to hot oil; cook until browned and crisp, about 2 minutes per side, flipping once. Drain on paper towels. (Skim and discard panko bits between batches to prevent burning.) Serve warm with Tomato-Ginger Jam; top with scallions.

Tomato–Ginger Jam

ACTIVE 20 MIN. - TOTAL 40 MIN.
MAKES ABOUT 1¼ CUPS

- 1 cup canned crushed tomatoes in puree
- ¼ cup packed light brown sugar
- 2 Tbsp. sherry vinegar
- 2 Tbsp. very finely chopped fresh ginger (from 1 [1-inch] piece ginger)
- ½ tsp. kosher salt
- ½ tsp. curry powder or garam masala
- ½ tsp. yellow mustard seeds
- ¼ tsp. ground cinnamon
- ¼ tsp. cayenne pepper

Stir together all ingredients in a saucepan. Bring to simmer over medium-high, stirring to dissolve sugar. Reduce heat to low; simmer, stirring occasionally, until slightly thickened, about 15 minutes. Cool 20 minutes. Transfer to an airtight container; cover and chill up to 2 weeks. Serve slightly chilled.

FIELD PEA CAKES WITH TOMATO-GINGER JAM

FIELD PEA-TOMATO SALAD
WITH LEMON VINAIGRETTE

Field Pea-Tomato Salad with Lemon Vinaigrette

ACTIVE 20 MIN. - TOTAL 35 MIN.
SERVES 6

VINAIGRETTE
- 1 medium shallot, finely chopped
- 1 Tbsp. grated lemon zest plus ¼ cup fresh juice (from 2 lemons)
- 2 medium garlic cloves, finely chopped (2¼ tsp.)
- ½ tsp. kosher salt
- ¼ tsp. black pepper
- 1 Tbsp. honey
- 1 tsp. whole-grain Dijon mustard
- ½ cup extra-virgin olive oil

SALAD
- 2 cups shelled fresh field peas (10 oz.), rinsed
- 1¼ tsp. kosher salt, divided
- 2 cups cherry tomatoes or grape tomatoes, halved lengthwise
- 3 Tbsp. chopped fresh lemon balm, lemon verbena, or mint
- 2 Tbsp. chopped fresh flat-leaf parsley

- 2½ lb. large heirloom tomatoes (2 or 3 tomatoes), cored and sliced
- ¼ tsp. black pepper

1. Stir together shallot, lemon zest, lemon juice, garlic, salt, and pepper in a medium bowl; let stand 5 minutes. Whisk in honey and mustard. Add oil in a slow, steady stream, whisking constantly. Set aside.
2. Stir together peas and 1 teaspoon of the salt in a medium saucepan. Add water to cover by a depth of 1 inch. Bring to a boil over medium-high, skimming foam that rises to the top. Reduce heat to medium-low. Partially cover; simmer until tender, 15 to 25 minutes. Drain; transfer peas to Vinaigrette in bowl. Let mixture stand, stirring occasionally, until cool, about 10 minutes.
3. Stir cherry tomatoes, lemon balm, parsley, and remaining ¼ teaspoon salt into cooled pea mixture. Arrange sliced heirloom tomatoes on a serving platter. Top with pea mixture; sprinkle with pepper. Serve immediately.

Field Peas, Corn, and Okra in Country-Ham Cream

ACTIVE 25 MIN. - TOTAL 1 HOUR, 15 MIN.
SERVES 6

- 3–4 ears fresh corn, husks removed
- 3 cups shelled fresh or thawed frozen field peas (1 lb.), rinsed
- 1 tsp. kosher salt
- 5 oz. sliced country ham, cut into thin strips (from 1 [10-oz.] pkg.)
- ¾ cup heavy cream
- ¼ cup tomato paste
- 3 Tbsp. unsalted butter
- 1 small red onion, halved and thinly sliced
- 1 cup fresh okra, cut into thin rounds
- 1–2 Tbsp. hot sauce, to taste
- ¼ tsp. black pepper
- ½ cup fresh basil leaves

1. Cut off corn kernels from ears; scrape corn from cobs to yield about 2 cups total. Set aside kernels and scraped corn; discard cobs.

FIELD PEAS, CORN, AND OKRA IN COUNTRY-HAM CREAM

SMOKY FIELD PEA-AND-GREENS DIP

2. Stir together peas and salt in a medium saucepan. Add water to cover by a depth of 1 inch. Bring to a boil over high, skimming foam that rises to the top. Reduce heat to medium, and partially cover. Simmer until tender, 15 to 25 minutes. Drain; set aside.

3. While peas simmer, cook ham in a small saucepan over medium, stirring often, until slightly browned, about 5 minutes. Add cream and tomato paste, stirring to loosen browned glaze from bottom of pan. Reduce heat to medium, and bring to a simmer; remove from heat. Set aside.

4. Melt butter in a large skillet over medium-high. Add onion; cook, stirring occasionally, until onion starts to soften, about 5 minutes. Stir in corn, peas, and okra. Reduce heat to medium-low; cover and cook, undisturbed, 5 minutes. (Let okra cook a few minutes before stirring to reduce stringiness.)

5. Uncover skillet. Stir in reserved ham-cream mixture, and cook, stirring occasionally, until vegetables are tender and sauce thickens slightly, 10 minutes. Stir in hot sauce and pepper. Stir in basil; serve immediately.

Smoky Field Pea-and-Greens Dip

ACTIVE 25 MIN. - TOTAL 1 HOUR, 20 MIN.
SERVES 8

- 3 cups shelled fresh or thawed frozen field peas (1 lb.), rinsed
- 1½ tsp. kosher salt, divided
- 3 thick-cut bacon slices, diced
- 1 cup chopped yellow onion (from 1 small onion)
- 8 cups baby spinach or kale, coarsely chopped (about 8 oz.)
- 8 oz. Italian cheese blend, shredded (about 2 cups)
- 8 oz. cream cheese, at room temperature
- ½ cup mayonnaise
- 1 tsp. smoked paprika
- ½ tsp. garlic powder
- ¼ tsp. cayenne pepper
- 1½ oz. Parmesan cheese, shredded (about ⅔ cup)
  Baguette slices, for serving

1. Stir together peas and 1 teaspoon of the salt in a medium saucepan. Add water to cover by a depth of 1 inch. Bring to a boil over high, skimming foam that rises to the top. Reduce heat to medium. Partially cover, and simmer until tender, 15 to 25 minutes. Drain; transfer to a bowl. Set aside.

2. Preheat oven to 350°F. Cook bacon in a large skillet over medium, stirring occasionally, until crisp, 10 minutes. Transfer to paper towels to drain; reserve drippings in pan. Stir in onion; cook, stirring occasionally, until tender, about 5 minutes. Add spinach in large handfuls. Cook, tossing with tongs to wilt before adding more, until wilted, 3 minutes. Stir mixture into peas in bowl.

3. Stir together Italian cheese blend, cream cheese, mayonnaise, paprika, garlic powder, cayenne, and remaining ½ teaspoon salt in a large bowl. Stir in spinach-pea mixture. Transfer to a medium ovenproof skillet or 1½-quart baking dish, and smooth top. Sprinkle with Parmesan.

4. Bake in preheated oven until browned, 30 minutes. Let stand 15 minutes. Sprinkle with reserved bacon. Serve warm with baguette slices.

Hooked on Shrimp

Ready-in-a-flash suppers, from stir-fry to scampi

SHRIMP-AND-BACON
STIR-FRY

Shrimp-and-Bacon Stir-Fry

ACTIVE 25 MIN. - TOTAL 30 MIN.
SERVES 4

- ¼ cup sweet chili sauce
- 2 Tbsp. fresh lime juice (from 1 lime)
- 4 tsp. soy sauce
- 2 tsp. fish sauce (optional)
- 6 oz. (4 slices) thick-cut bacon, cut into 1-inch pieces
- 12 oz. large peeled, deveined raw shrimp
- 1 Tbsp. toasted sesame oil
- 1 small red bell pepper, sliced (about 1 cup)
- 1 small yellow or orange bell pepper, sliced (about 1 cup)
- ¼ tsp. kosher salt
- 1 Tbsp. finely chopped fresh ginger (from a 1-inch piece)
- 2 garlic cloves, chopped (about 2 tsp.)
- 2 (8.5-oz.) pkg. precooked microwavable jasmine rice (such as Uncle Ben's Ready Rice)
  Cilantro leaves
  Lime wedges, for serving

1. Stir together sweet chili sauce, lime juice, soy sauce, and, if desired, fish sauce in a small bowl.
2. Heat a wok or large skillet over medium. Add bacon; cook, stirring occasionally, until crisp, 8 to 10 minutes. Using a slotted spoon, remove bacon to a plate lined with paper towels, reserving 1 tablespoon bacon drippings in wok. Increase heat to high. Add shrimp; cook, stirring occasionally, until opaque and cooked through, 2 to 3 minutes. Transfer to plate with bacon.
3. Add sesame oil, bell peppers, and salt to wok. Cook, stirring often, until peppers are tender-crisp, about 4 minutes. Add ginger and garlic, and cook, stirring constantly, until fragrant and peppers are lightly charred, about 2 minutes. Add chili sauce mixture, shrimp, and bacon. Cook, stirring constantly, until heated through and well coated, about 20 seconds. Transfer to a medium bowl.
4. Heat rice according to package directions. Divide rice evenly among 4 shallow bowls, and top with shrimp mixture. Garnish with cilantro, and serve with lime wedges.

SHRIMP CAKES WITH
SMOKY HORSERADISH
SAUCE

Shrimp Cakes with Smoky Horseradish Sauce

ACTIVE 25 MIN. - TOTAL 35 MIN.
SERVES 4

- 1 lb. large peeled, deveined raw shrimp, cut into ½-inch pieces
- 3 Tbsp. unsalted butter, melted
- 2 large eggs, beaten
- 2 minced scallions (about ⅓ cup), plus more, sliced, for garnish
- ½ tsp. lemon zest, plus 1½ Tbsp. fresh juice, divided
- 1½ cups panko breadcrumbs, divided
- 2¼ tsp. kosher salt, divided
- ¾ tsp. smoked paprika, divided
- ½ cup mayonnaise
- 2 tsp. refrigerated prepared horseradish
- 4 Tbsp. canola oil
  Lemon wedges, for serving

1. Combine shrimp, butter, eggs, scallions, lemon zest, ¾ cup of the panko, 1 tablespoon of the lemon juice, 1½ teaspoons of the salt, and ½ teaspoon of the paprika in a bowl. Shape into 8 (3-inch) cakes. Sprinkle remaining ¾ cup panko on a large plate; gently transfer cakes to plate, pressing both sides in panko. Place cakes on a parchment paper-lined baking sheet. Cover; chill 15 minutes.
2. Combine mayonnaise, horseradish, ½ teaspoon of the salt, and remaining ½ tablespoon lemon juice and ¼ teaspoon paprika. Set aside.
3. Heat 2 tablespoons of the oil in a large nonstick skillet over medium. Cook 4 cakes 4 to 5 minutes per side. Transfer to a plate lined with paper towels; sprinkle with ⅛ teaspoon of the salt. Wipe skillet; repeat with remaining 2 tablespoons oil, 4 cakes, and ⅛ teaspoon salt. Top with sliced scallions and sauce. Serve with lemon wedges.

Basil Shrimp Scampi

ACTIVE 15 MIN. - TOTAL 25 MIN.

SERVES 4

- ¼ cup, plus 1½ tsp. kosher salt, divided
- 12 oz. uncooked linguine
- ⅓ cup olive oil
- 1 lb. large peeled, deveined raw shrimp
- ¼ tsp. black pepper, plus more for topping
- ¼ cup dry white wine
- 3 garlic cloves, chopped (about 1 Tbsp.)
- ¼ cup unsalted butter, cut into ½-inch pieces
- 2 Tbsp. fresh lemon juice (from 1 lemon)
- ⅓ cup fresh torn basil leaves
  Lemon peel strips
  Small fresh basil leaves

1. Place 4 quarts water in a stockpot; bring to a boil over high. Add ¼ cup of the salt, and stir until dissolved. Add pasta, and cook until al dente, about 9 minutes. Drain. Reserve 1 cup cooking water; set aside with pasta.
2. Heat oil in a large skillet over medium-high. Add shrimp; sprinkle with pepper and ½ teaspoon of the salt. Cook, stirring occasionally, until shrimp are partially opaque, about 30 seconds. Add wine and garlic; continue cooking, stirring occasionally, until shrimp are mostly cooked through, about 1½ minutes.
3. Add pasta and ¼ cup of the cooking water; bring to a simmer. Add butter, lemon juice, and remaining 1 teaspoon salt. Cook, stirring constantly, until sauce thickens and coats pasta, about 1 minute, adding more cooking water, ¼ cup at a time, if needed. Remove from heat. Stir in torn basil. Top with lemon peel strips, basil leaves, and black pepper.

THE SECRET TO THE SAUCE

Remember to reserve a cup of pasta cooking water before you drain the cooked linguine. The starchy, salty liquid brings the wine, butter, and lemon juice together into a bright and silky sauce.

Jambalaya Skewers

ACTIVE 20 MIN. - TOTAL 20 MIN.
SERVES 4

- 8 oz. large peeled, deveined raw shrimp (about 16)
- 6 oz. smoked sausage (such as Conecuh), cut into ½-inch rounds (about 1 cup)
- 1 small sweet onion, cut into 1-inch pieces (about 1 cup)
- 1 small red bell pepper, cut into 1-inch pieces (about ¾ cup)
- 16 cherry tomatoes (about ½ pint)
- 3 Tbsp. olive oil
- 2 tsp. Cajun seasoning (such as Slap Ya Mama)
- 1 tsp. chopped fresh thyme
- ½ tsp. chopped fresh oregano
- 2 Tbsp. chopped fresh flat-leaf parsley

1. Preheat grill to high (450°F to 500°F), or heat a grill pan over high. Combine shrimp, sausage, onion, bell pepper, tomatoes, olive oil, Cajun seasoning, thyme, and oregano in a large bowl, and toss to coat. Thread mixture onto 8 (10-inch) skewers, alternating ingredients.
2. Place skewers on oiled grates, and grill, uncovered, until vegetables and sausage are lightly charred and shrimp is cooked through, about 2 minutes per side. Transfer skewers to a serving plate, and sprinkle with parsley.

SAVE 30 MINUTES!
Normally, wooden skewers should be soaked in water for 30 minutes before they go on a hot grill, but the cook time for these kebabs is so short—just two minutes per side—that you can use the skewers without soaking.

Quick Shrimp-and-Corn Chowder

ACTIVE 20 MIN. - TOTAL 35 MIN.
SERVES 4

- 3 medium (1 lb., 5 oz. total) ears fresh shucked yellow corn
- 2 Tbsp. unsalted butter
- ½ cup chopped yellow onion (from 1 small onion)
- 2 garlic cloves, chopped (about 2 tsp.)
- 1¾ cups lower-sodium chicken broth
- 10 oz. (6 medium) baby red potatoes, cut into ½-inch pieces
- 1 tsp. kosher salt
- ¼ tsp. black pepper
- 8 oz. medium-size peeled, deveined raw shrimp
- 2 Tbsp. heavy cream
- 2 Tbsp. sliced fresh chives

1. Cut kernels from corncobs (about 2¼ cups); place in a bowl. Using the large holes on a box grater, scrape pulp and liquid (about ½ cup) from cobs into bowl with kernels. Discard cobs.

2. Heat butter in a large saucepan over medium-high. Add onion and garlic; cook, stirring occasionally, until softened, 3 to 4 minutes. Stir in chicken broth, potatoes, salt, and pepper. Bring to a boil. Reduce heat to medium-low; cook, stirring occasionally, until potatoes are just tender, 12 to 15 minutes. Add corn mixture; stir until well combined.

3. Transfer 1 cup of the chowder to a blender. Secure lid on blender, and remove center piece to allow steam to escape. Place a clean towel over opening. Process until smooth, about 15 seconds. Stir mixture back into remaining chowder. Bring to a simmer over medium. Add shrimp, and cook, stirring occasionally, until opaque and cooked through, about 3 minutes. Stir in heavy cream. Ladle into 4 bowls. Sprinkle each serving with chives.

A New Spin on Chicken Spaghetti

Enjoy this lightened-up classic for Sunday supper when the entire family is together

Creamy Chicken Spaghetti

ACTIVE 30 MIN. - TOTAL 1 HOUR, 35 MIN.
SERVES 10

- 6 cups unsalted chicken stock
- 1 (14-oz.) bone-in, skin-on chicken breast, skin removed
- 3 (7-oz.) bone-in, skin-on chicken thighs, skin removed
- 12 oz. uncooked spaghetti
- 1 (5-oz.) can evaporated milk
- 2 Tbsp. all-purpose flour
- 1 Tbsp. lower-sodium Worcestershire sauce
- 2 tsp. hot sauce
- 2 tsp. kosher salt
- 2 Tbsp. unsalted butter
- 1½ cups chopped yellow onion (about 1 medium onion)
- 1½ cups chopped red bell pepper (about 1 large pepper)
- 2 cups chopped tomatoes (about 3 medium tomatoes)
- 4 oz. sharp white Cheddar cheese, shredded (about 1 cup)

1. Preheat oven to 400°F. Bring stock to a boil in a Dutch oven over high. Add chicken to stock. Cover; reduce heat to medium. Cook until a thermometer inserted in thickest piece of chicken registers 160°F, about 25 minutes. Remove chicken; let stand until ready to use. (Inner temperature of chicken will rise as it stands.)

2. Return stock to a boil over high. Add pasta to Dutch oven, and cook until just tender, about 9 minutes. Transfer pasta to a medium bowl (reserving stock). Return stock to a boil over high; boil until liquid is reduced to about 2½ cups, about 1 minute. Whisk together evaporated milk and flour in a small bowl. Stir into stock; boil until slightly thickened, 2 minutes. Remove from heat; stir in Worcestershire sauce, hot sauce, and salt. Pour stock mixture over pasta.

3. Return Dutch oven to medium-high heat. Add butter, onion, and bell pepper. Cook, stirring often, until tender, 5 to 6 minutes. Remove from heat; add pasta mixture back to Dutch oven. Shred chicken, discarding bones. (You should have about 4½ cups meat.) Add chicken and tomatoes to Dutch oven; toss to coat. Pour mixture into a 13- x 9-inch baking dish coated with cooking spray. Top with cheese. Lightly coat aluminum foil with cooking spray. Cover with foil; bake until cheese is melted, 25 to 30 minutes.

GIVE IT A TWIRL
Instead of pouring the pasta mixture from the pot into the baking dish, use tongs and a large spoon to twirl the noodles into nests.

Pork Perfection

Skip the usual breaded cutlets—this quick-cooking dish is better for you and just as flavorful

Pork Paillards with Lemony Squash Salad

ACTIVE 25 MIN. · TOTAL 25 MIN.
SERVES 4

  2 Tbsp. fresh lemon juice
  2 Tbsp. finely chopped shallot
      (from 1 small shallot)
  1 Tbsp. chopped fresh thyme
1½ tsp. Dijon mustard
1¼ tsp. kosher salt, divided
  ¾ tsp. black pepper, divided
  6 Tbsp. olive oil, divided
1¼ lb. pork tenderloin, trimmed
  ½ cup all-purpose flour
  6 cups spring mix lettuces
  3 cups shaved yellow squash
      (from 1 [12-oz.] squash)
  2 cups halved cherry tomatoes
  ½ cup torn fresh basil leaves

1. Whisk together first 4 ingredients,
½ teaspoon of the salt, and ¼ teaspoon
of the pepper; let stand 5 minutes. Slowly
whisk in ¼ cup of the oil; set aside.
2. Cut pork into 8 (1½-inch-thick) slices.
Place slices in 1 layer, cut sides up,
between 2 sheets of plastic wrap. Flatten
to ¼-inch thickness, using flat side of a
meat mallet. Place flour in a shallow dish.
Dredge slices, 1 at a time, in flour, shaking
off excess.
3. Heat 1 tablespoon of the oil in a large
nonstick skillet over medium-high. Cook
4 pork paillards in hot oil until browned
on 1 side, 2 minutes. Flip, and cook 1 more
minute. Remove from skillet; cover to
keep warm. Repeat with remaining oil and
pork. Sprinkle with remaining ¾ teaspoon
salt and ½ teaspoon pepper.
4. Combine lettuces, squash, tomatoes,
and basil in a large bowl. Whisk dressing
to combine. Add to salad; toss gently to
coat. Serve salad alongside pork.

Nutritional information: Calories: 391; Protein: 33g;
Carbs: 13g; Fiber: 4g; Fat: 24g

MAKE IT YOUR WAY
This recipe is surprisingly
flexible—use boneless
chicken instead of pork,
swap in zucchini for the
yellow squash, or
substitute arugula for the
spring mix.

It's Shortcake Season

Whip up a sweet dessert with juicy strawberries and homemade biscuits and cream

Favorite Strawberry Shortcakes

ACTIVE 25 MIN. - TOTAL 1 HOUR, 45 MIN.
SERVES 12

- 4 cups fresh strawberries, hulled and quartered
- 1 Tbsp. lemon zest plus 2 Tbsp. fresh juice (from 1 lemon)
- ½ cup, plus 2 Tbsp. granulated sugar, divided
- 4 cups all-purpose flour, plus more for work surface and kneading
- 1 Tbsp. baking powder
- 1 tsp. baking soda
- 1½ tsp. kosher salt
- 1¼ cups cold unsalted butter, cut into small pieces
- 1½ cups whole buttermilk
- 2 cups, plus 2 Tbsp. cold heavy cream, divided
- 1 Tbsp. sanding sugar (or coarse sugar)
- ½ cup powdered sugar
- 1 vanilla bean pod, split

1. Stir together strawberries, lemon zest, lemon juice, and ½ cup of the granulated sugar in a medium bowl. Cover; refrigerate at least 30 minutes or up to 1 hour.
2. Preheat oven to 425°F. Whisk together flour, baking powder, baking soda, salt, and remaining 2 tablespoons granulated sugar in a large bowl. Cut in butter with a pastry blender (or use fingertips) until mixture resembles peas. Add buttermilk, and stir gently with a spatula or wooden spoon until well combined and shaggy. Turn out dough onto a lightly floured surface, and knead gently until dough just comes together, 2 or 3 times. Pat dough with lightly floured palms to 1½-inch thickness (do not use a rolling pin).

Cut out biscuits using a 2½-inch round cutter, gathering and patting scraps once more to make 12 biscuits.
3. Place biscuits about 2 inches apart on a parchment paper-lined baking sheet. Refrigerate 30 minutes. Brush tops of biscuits with 2 tablespoons of the heavy cream; sprinkle with sanding sugar. Bake in preheated oven until golden brown, 18 to 20 minutes. Cool on baking sheet 10 minutes.
4. Place powdered sugar in bowl of an electric stand mixer fitted with whisk attachment. Scrape vanilla bean seeds into powdered sugar; add remaining 2 cups heavy cream. Beat on medium speed until soft peaks form, 4 to 5 minutes. Split biscuits; place on plates or a large platter. Spoon strawberry mixture onto bottom halves of biscuits. Dollop with whipped cream; cover with biscuit tops.

KEEP IT REAL
Pure vanilla makes the whipped cream extra rich. Scrape the seeds from a vanilla bean pod, or use 1 teaspoon pure (not imitation) vanilla extract or vanilla bean paste.

COOKING (SL) SCHOOL

FRESH IDEAS

Not Your Average Shortcake

Hold the strawberries, and try one of these creative combos

BANANA NUT
Sliced bananas + toasted coconut + chopped pecans

RASPBERRY TRUFFLE
Raspberries + hot fudge + chocolate shavings

TIPSY PEACH
Bourbon-soaked sliced peaches + dulce de leche

ZESTY BLACKBERRY
Blackberries + lemon curd + fresh basil

TEST KITCHEN TIPS

Shrimp Made Simple

Shopping smarts and storage pointers

Robby Melvin
Test Kitchen Director

Buying:
Most "fresh" shrimp have simply been thawed. Buy individually frozen, unpeeled shrimp so you'll know when they were defrosted.

Thawing:
Let frozen shrimp thaw in the refrigerator up to one day. Or put them in a colander under cold running water.

Storing:
Keep thawed shrimp very cold. Place drained shrimp in a bowl with a plastic bag full of ice on top. Refrigerate up to two days.

HOW-TO

Pound a Paillard

Master this fancy-sounding technique for meat that cooks in minutes

SLICE IT
Start with a boneless, skinless protein (chicken, beef, or pork) about 1½ to 2 inches thick. If it is bigger, slice lengthwise or into sections. Place between two pieces of plastic wrap.

POUND IT
Using the flat side of a meat mallet, strike the meat evenly until the entire piece is about ⅛ to ¼ inch thick. Remove and discard the plastic wrap. Season with salt and pepper on both sides, and cook in a hot oiled skillet.

June

112 **Veggie Delights** Canning, pickling, preserving. You know them; you love them. But think outside the jar, and turn that bumper crop of produce into decadent desserts

116 **Fresh in a Flash** Turn your farmers' market haul into a tasty supper in 30 minutes or less

120 **Steak Salad with a Kick** A coffee-and-chile rub adds bold flavor without extra calories

121 **Sunrise Sliders** Nothing beats a simple breakfast sandwich made for weekend crowds

122 **SL Cooking School** Our Test Kitchen professionals share delicious and even unexpected ideas for using fresh basil

GREEN TOMATO
SKILLET PIE

112

Veggie Delights

Canning, pickling, preserving. You know them; you love them. But think outside the jar, and turn that bumper crop of produce into decadent desserts

Green Tomato Skillet Pie

Unripe green tomatoes take on fruity notes (similar to Granny Smith apples or rhubarb) when baked with warm spices, such as cinnamon and cloves.

ACTIVE 25 MIN. - TOTAL 4 HOURS
SERVES 8

CRUST
- 3 cups all-purpose flour, plus more for work surface
- 1 Tbsp. granulated sugar
- 1 Tbsp. kosher salt
- ½ cup cold unsalted butter, cubed
- ½ cup bacon drippings, cold

FILLING
- 1½ cups granulated sugar
- ½ cup golden raisins
- ⅓ cup all-purpose flour
- 1 tsp. ground cinnamon
- ½ tsp. orange zest (from 1 orange)
- ⅛ tsp. ground cloves
- Pinch of kosher salt
- 5 medium-size green tomatoes (about 1 lb., 12 oz. total), thinly sliced into half-moons (5 cups)
- 1 Tbsp. apple cider vinegar

ADDITIONAL INGREDIENTS
- 1 Tbsp. unsalted butter, cubed
- 1 large egg, lightly beaten
- 2 tsp. turbinado sugar

1. Prepare the Crust: Place flour, sugar, and salt in a food processor; pulse to combine, about 3 times. Add butter and drippings; pulse until mixture resembles coarse crumbs, about 10 times. Gradually add ½ cup cold water, pulsing until mixture forms a dough, about 5 times. Turn out onto a lightly floured surface. Divide dough in half; shape into 2 disks. Cover disks tightly in plastic wrap. Chill until firm, up to 1 day.
2. Prepare the Filling: Preheat oven to 350°F. Stir together granulated sugar, raisins, flour, cinnamon, zest, cloves, and salt in a large bowl. Add tomatoes and vinegar. Toss to coat; set aside.
3. Unwrap 1 dough disk. Place on a lightly floured surface; sprinkle dough with flour.

Roll into a 14-inch circle. Fit into a 10-inch cast-iron skillet. Unwrap remaining disk. Roll into a 12-inch circle; cut into 1-inch-wide strips.
4. Pour tomato mixture into dough in skillet; dot with butter. Arrange strips in a lattice design over Filling. Trim and discard excess dough; crimp edges of Crust. Freeze, uncovered, 10 minutes.
5. Brush chilled pie with beaten egg; sprinkle with turbinado sugar. Bake in preheated oven until Crust is golden brown, about 1 hour. Cool 2 hours before serving.

Yellow Squash Bundt Cake

Yellow squash makes this lemony cake extra tender while boosting its golden hue.

ACTIVE 25 MIN. - TOTAL 2 HOURS, 20 MIN.
SERVES 12

YELLOW SQUASH BUNDT CAKE
- 2 cups all-purpose flour
- 1 tsp. baking powder
- ½ tsp. baking soda
- ½ tsp. salt
- 3 large eggs, at room temperature
- 1½ cups granulated sugar
- 1 cup canola oil
- 2 cups grated yellow squash (from 2 medium [6½ oz. each] squash)
- 1 Tbsp. lemon zest plus 2 Tbsp. fresh juice (from 1 lemon)

LEMON-BUTTERMILK GLAZE
- 2 cups unsifted powdered sugar
- 2 Tbsp. whole buttermilk
- 1 tsp. lemon zest plus 1 Tbsp. fresh juice (from 1 lemon)

1. Prepare the Cake: Preheat oven to 350°F. Coat a 10-cup Bundt pan with baking spray. Stir together flour, baking powder, baking soda, and salt in a bowl. Place eggs, sugar, and oil in bowl of a stand mixer fitted with a paddle attachment. Beat on medium-high speed until light and airy, about 3 minutes, stopping to scrape down sides as needed. Stir in squash, lemon zest, and juice. Gradually add flour mixture, beating on low speed until just combined, about 45 seconds. Pour batter into prepared pan.
2. Bake in preheated oven until a wooden pick inserted in center comes out clean, 50 to 55 minutes. Cool in pan 10 minutes. Invert onto a wire rack; cool 1 hour.
3. Prepare the Glaze: Whisk together all ingredients in a bowl until smooth. Drizzle over cooled cake.

YELLOW SQUASH BUNDT CAKE

Chocolate-Zucchini Cake

This impressive yet easy to make cake got rave reviews in our Test Kitchen. It's packed with plenty of green stuff (two medium zucchini), but you'll be too distracted by the chocolate flavor and the nutty brown butter frosting to notice. For optimal texture, shred the zucchini on the large holes of a box grater.

ACTIVE 35 MIN. - TOTAL 3 HOURS, 20 MIN.
SERVES 12

CHOCOLATE-ZUCCHINI CAKE
- 2 cups granulated sugar
- ½ cup unsalted butter, softened
- ½ cup canola oil
- 1 tsp. vanilla extract
- 2 large eggs, at room temperature
- 2½ cups all-purpose flour
- ¾ cup unsweetened cocoa powder
- 1 tsp. baking powder
- ½ tsp. baking soda
- ½ tsp. kosher salt
- ½ cup sour cream
- 2½ cups grated zucchini (from 2 medium [6 oz. each] zucchini)
- 1 cup semisweet chocolate chips

BROWN BUTTER-PISTACHIO FROSTING
- ½ cup unsalted butter
- 1 (8-oz.) pkg. cream cheese, at room temperature
- 4 cups unsifted powdered sugar
- 1 tsp. vanilla extract
- ¼ tsp. kosher salt
- 8 Tbsp. roasted salted pistachios, finely chopped, divided

1. Prepare the Cake: Preheat oven to 325°F. Spray a 13- x 9-inch baking pan with baking spray. Beat sugar, butter, oil, and vanilla with an electric mixer on high speed until fluffy, about 2 minutes. Add eggs; beat until incorporated, about 15 seconds.

2. Stir together flour, cocoa powder, baking powder, baking soda, and salt in a bowl. Add flour mixture to butter mixture alternately with sour cream, beginning and ending with flour mixture, beating well on low speed after each addition. Stir in zucchini and chocolate chips. Pour into prepared pan; smooth top with a spatula.

3. Bake in preheated oven until a wooden pick inserted in center comes out clean, 45 to 50 minutes. Remove from oven; cool completely in pan, about 1 hour.

4. Prepare the Frosting: Melt butter in a small saucepan over medium-high. Cook, stirring occasionally, until butter begins to brown, about 10 minutes. Remove from heat; pour into a heatproof glass bowl. Chill 1 hour.

5. Transfer solidified brown butter to bowl of a heavy-duty stand mixer fitted with a paddle attachment; beat on medium-high speed until creamy, about 30 seconds. Add cream cheese; beat on high speed until smooth, about 20 seconds. Reduce speed to low; gradually beat in powdered sugar, vanilla, and salt. Increase speed to high, and beat until fluffy, 2 minutes. Stir in 5 tablespoons of the pistachios.

6. Spread frosting over cake. Sprinkle with remaining 3 tablespoons pistachios.

Corn Custards with Berry Compote

Sweet summer corn adds its signature flavor to these creamy custards, and yellow cornmeal thickens while enhancing the color and flavor. Don't be tempted to use frozen kernels here—you want the pure, milky, robust flavor found only in fresh.

ACTIVE 45 MIN. - TOTAL 3 HOURS
SERVES 8

CORN CUSTARDS
- 4 cups fresh corn kernels (from 5 ears)
- 1 cup heavy cream
- 1 cup whole milk
- 3 large eggs
- 2 large egg yolks
- 1 cup granulated sugar
- 6 Tbsp. unsalted butter, melted
- 2 Tbsp. plain yellow cornmeal
- 1 Tbsp. fresh lemon juice (from 1 lemon)
- ½ tsp. kosher salt

BERRY COMPOTE
- 1 cup fresh blackberries
- 2 Tbsp. granulated sugar
- 2 tsp. fresh lemon juice (from 1 lemon)
- 1½ tsp. cornstarch
- 1 cup fresh strawberries, sliced

1. Prepare the Custards: Preheat oven to 300°F. Place 8 (6- to 8-ounce) ramekins in a large roasting pan; spray ramekins with cooking spray. Stir together corn, cream, and milk in a saucepan; bring to a boil over medium-high. Reduce heat to low; simmer 5 minutes. Remove from heat. Cover; steep 15 minutes.

2. Transfer mixture to a blender; process until smooth, 1 minute. Pour through a fine wire-mesh sieve into a bowl; discard solids.

3. Stir together eggs, egg yolks, sugar, melted butter, cornmeal, lemon juice, and salt in a large bowl. Stir in strained corn mixture. Pour into prepared ramekins.

4. Place roasting pan in preheated oven. Add hot water to pan to a depth of 1 inch up the sides of ramekins. Bake until centers are wobbly, 50 minutes to 1 hour. Remove from oven; cool 1 hour.

5. Prepare the Compote: Stir first 4 ingredients together in a saucepan over medium-high. Bring to a boil; cook, stirring occasionally, until thickened, 3 minutes. Stir in strawberries. Remove from heat; cool 20 minutes. Spoon Compote over Custards.

CHOCOLATE-ZUCCHINI CAKE

CORN CUSTARDS WITH
BERRY COMPOTE

Fresh in a Flash

Turn your farmers' market haul into a tasty supper in 30 minutes (or less!)

PICO DE GALLO
PORK CHOPS

DON'T TOSS THAT TOMATO
Got overripe tomatoes? Put them to good use in this zesty pico de gallo. The salsa can be made with any type or combination of tomatoes except for grape or cherry, which are too small to seed.

Pico de Gallo Pork Chops

ACTIVE 25 MIN. - TOTAL 30 MIN.
SERVES 4

- ½ tsp. black pepper
- ½ tsp. ground cumin
- ¼ tsp. chili powder
- 1½ tsp. kosher salt, divided
- 4 (8-oz., 1-inch-thick) bone-in center-cut pork chops
- 2 Tbsp. olive oil, divided
- 1 lb. tomatoes, seeded and diced (about 2 cups)
- ⅓ cup chopped fresh cilantro
- ¼ cup finely chopped white onion (from 1 small onion)
- 1 medium-size fresh serrano chile, seeded and finely chopped
- 1 medium garlic clove, minced
- 1 tsp. lime zest, plus 3 Tbsp. fresh juice (from 2 limes)
- 2 cups hot cooked white rice

1. Preheat grill to medium-high (400°F to 450°F). Stir together black pepper, cumin, chili powder, and ½ teaspoon of the salt in a small bowl. Brush pork chops with 1 tablespoon of the oil; rub with black pepper mixture. Set aside.
2. Stir together tomatoes, cilantro, onion, serrano, garlic, lime zest, lime juice, and remaining 1 tablespoon oil and 1 teaspoon salt in a bowl.
3. Place pork chops on oiled grates. Grill, covered, turning occasionally, until a thermometer inserted in thickest portion of meat registers 145°F, about 6 minutes. Remove from grill; let rest 5 minutes. Serve over rice with pico de gallo.

BASIL FRIED RICE WITH BUTTER PEAS

Basil Fried Rice with Butter Peas

ACTIVE 20 MIN. - TOTAL 20 MIN.
SERVES 4

- 3 large scallions
- 3 Tbsp. vegetable oil
- ½ cup chopped red bell pepper (from 1 small bell pepper)
- ½ cup chopped green bell pepper (from 1 small bell pepper)
- 2 medium garlic cloves, minced
- 1 tsp. minced fresh ginger
- 4 cups cooked long-grain white rice, cooled
- 1 tsp. kosher salt
- 3 large eggs, lightly beaten
- 1 cup cooked butter peas
- ½ cup chopped, plus 1 Tbsp. thinly sliced fresh basil, divided
- 3 Tbsp. soy sauce
- 1 Tbsp. toasted sesame oil

1. Slice white and green parts of scallions, keeping parts separate. (You should have about ¼ cup each of white and green parts.)
2. Heat vegetable oil in a wok or large cast-iron skillet over high. Add red and green bell peppers, garlic, ginger, and white parts of scallions. Cook, stirring constantly, until vegetables are just tender, about 1 minute. Add rice and salt, stirring to break up clumps. Cook, stirring occasionally, until rice begins to crisp, about 4 minutes.
3. Push rice mixture to 1 side of wok; add eggs to other side. Cook, stirring eggs often, until eggs are scrambled and cooked through, about 1 minute. Stir eggs into rice mixture. Add butter peas, chopped basil, soy sauce, and sesame oil. Cook, stirring constantly, until just combined and heated through, about 1 minute. Sprinkle with green parts of scallions and sliced basil.

Grilled Chicken with Quick-Pickled Squash Salad

ACTIVE 25 MIN. - TOTAL 30 MIN.
SERVES 4

- ½ cup red wine vinegar
- 3 Tbsp. fresh lemon juice (from 1 lemon)
- 1 Tbsp. minced shallot
- 1½ Tbsp. chopped fresh basil
- 1 medium garlic clove, minced
- ¾ cup, plus 1 Tbsp. olive oil, divided
- 1¾ tsp. kosher salt, divided
- 1 tsp. black pepper, divided
- 3 medium zucchini, diced (about 4 cups)
- 3 medium-size yellow squash, diced (about 4 cups)
- 4 (6-oz.) boneless, skinless chicken breasts
- 4 oz. feta cheese, crumbled
- ½ cup mixed herb leaves (such as parsley, basil, and dill)

1. Preheat grill to medium-high (400°F to 450°F). Whisk together first 5 ingredients, ¾ cup of the oil, 1 teaspoon of the salt, and ½ teaspoon of the pepper. Place zucchini and squash in a bowl; stir in half of the vinaigrette. (Set aside remaining half.) Let stand 20 minutes.
2. Brush chicken with remaining 1 tablespoon oil; sprinkle with remaining ¾ teaspoon salt and ½ teaspoon pepper. Grill, covered, turning occasionally, until a thermometer inserted in middle of chicken registers 165°F, 6 minutes. Remove from grill; let rest 5 minutes.
3. Sprinkle squash mixture with feta and mixed herbs; serve with chicken and remaining vinaigrette.

GRILLED CHICKEN WITH QUICK-PICKLED SQUASH SALAD

SWITCH UP YOUR SQUASH
We like the mix of yellow and green types in this salad, but you can use any kind that's in season, from round pattypan to bicolored Zephyr. Just avoid large squash, which tend to be watery and have more seeds.

Shrimp-and-Sausage Skillet Corn

ACTIVE 30 MIN. - TOTAL 30 MIN.
SERVES 4

- 3 Tbsp. unsalted butter
- 6 cups fresh corn kernels (from about 8 large ears)
- 1 cup chopped sweet onion (from 1 small onion)
- 4 oz. cream cheese, softened
- ½ cup half-and-half
- 1 tsp. black pepper
- 1¾ tsp. kosher salt, divided
- 2 Tbsp. chopped fresh chives, plus more for garnish
- 1 tsp. olive oil
- 8 oz. hickory-smoked sausage, cut into ¼-inch slices
- 1 lb. medium-size peeled, deveined raw shrimp
- 1 Tbsp. chopped fresh flat-leaf parsley

1. Melt butter in a large skillet over medium-high. Add corn and onion; cook, stirring occasionally, until tender, 8 minutes. Stir in cream cheese, half-and-half, pepper, and 1 teaspoon of the salt. Cook, stirring constantly, until cream cheese melts, 2 minutes. Stir in chives. Remove pan from heat; cover to keep warm.
2. Heat oil in a separate large skillet over medium-high. Add sausage; cook, stirring occasionally, until browned, 6 minutes. Drain on paper towels, reserving drippings in pan. Sprinkle shrimp with remaining ¾ teaspoon salt. Add to pan; cook over medium-high, stirring occasionally, until shrimp turn pink, 3 minutes.
3. Serve corn topped with sausage, shrimp, chives, and parsley.

Pasta with Summer Beans and Bacon

ACTIVE 25 MIN. - TOTAL 25 MIN.
SERVES 4

- 12 oz. uncooked cavatappi pasta
- 8 oz. thick-cut bacon slices, chopped
- 2 garlic cloves, smashed
- 12 oz. fresh green and yellow wax beans, trimmed and cut into 3-inch pieces
- ¼ tsp. kosher salt
- ¼ tsp. black pepper
- 3 Tbsp. butter, softened
- 1 Tbsp. fresh lemon juice (from 1 lemon)
- 1 cup Parmesan cheese, grated, divided
- 1 Tbsp. chopped fresh chives
- 1 Tbsp. fresh flat-leaf parsley leaves

1. Cook pasta in salted water according to package directions; drain, reserving 1 cup cooking water.
2. Meanwhile, cook bacon in a large nonstick skillet over medium-high, until crispy, 8 minutes. Drain on paper towels, reserving 2 tablespoons drippings in pan.
3. Add garlic to pan; cook over medium, stirring constantly, 1 minute. Stir in beans, salt, and pepper. Cook until tender-crisp, 4 minutes. Stir in butter, pasta, and ½ cup of the reserved cooking water. Add lemon juice, ¾ cup of the cheese, and remaining ½ cup cooking water. Cook, stirring constantly, 1 minute. Stir in bacon. Sprinkle with chives, parsley, and remaining ¼ cup cheese.

SHRIMP-AND-SAUSAGE SKILLET CORN

PASTA WITH SUMMER BEANS AND BACON

Steak Salad with a Kick

A coffee-and-chile rub adds bold flavor without extra calories

Grilled Steak Salad with Potatoes and Pickled Red Onion

ACTIVE 30 MIN. - TOTAL 30 MIN.
SERVES 4

- ⅔ cup apple cider vinegar
- 2 tsp. granulated sugar
- 2 tsp. kosher salt, divided
- ½ cup vertically sliced red onion (from 1 small onion)
- 1 Tbsp. finely ground coffee beans
- 1 tsp. chipotle chile powder
- 12 oz. hanger steak (1 inch thick)
- 12 oz. baby Yukon Gold potatoes
- ¼ cup extra-virgin olive oil
- 1 tsp. Dijon mustard
- 5 cups mixed baby greens

1. Stir together vinegar, sugar, ¼ cup water, and 1 teaspoon of the salt in a small saucepan; bring to a boil over high. Stir in onion; remove from heat. Let stand 15 minutes. Drain, reserving onion and 3 tablespoons pickling liquid.

2. Meanwhile, preheat grill to high (450°F to 500°F), or heat a grill pan over medium-high. Stir together ground coffee, chile powder, and remaining 1 teaspoon salt in a small bowl; rub evenly over steak. Place steak on oiled grates. Grill, uncovered, until a thermometer inserted in thickest portion of meat registers 130°F to 135°F for medium-rare, 4 to 5 minutes per side. Remove from grill; let rest 5 minutes. Slice against the grain into ¼-inch-thick strips.

3. Place potatoes and 1 tablespoon water in a microwavable bowl. Cover with plastic wrap; microwave on HIGH until tender, about 5 minutes. Cut potatoes in half lengthwise. (Discard water in bowl.)

4. Whisk together oil, mustard, and reserved pickling liquid in a large bowl. Add greens and halved potatoes; toss gently to coat. Arrange mixture on a large platter; top with sliced steak and pickled onion.

Nutritional information: Calories: 333; Protein: 20g; Carbs: 17g; Fiber: 3g; Fat: 20g

WATCH THAT GRILL
Hanger steak cooks quickly (4 to 5 minutes per side) and is best served medium-rare. Remove the meat from the grill when it reaches 130°F to 135°F.

Sunrise Sliders

Nothing beats a simple breakfast sandwich made for weekend crowds

Sausage, Egg, and Cheddar Biscuit Sandwiches

ACTIVE 10 MIN. - TOTAL 45 MIN.
MAKES 16 MINI SANDWICHES

- 1 Tbsp. canola oil
- ½ lb. hickory-smoked sausage, cut into 3- to 4-inch links
- 12 large eggs
- ¼ cup heavy cream
- ½ cup minced roasted red bell peppers (from 1 [12-oz.] jar), patted dry
- 3 Tbsp. finely chopped fresh chives
- ½ tsp. kosher salt
- ¼ tsp. black pepper
- 8 oz. sharp Cheddar cheese, shredded (about 2 cups), divided
- 16 mini biscuits, split and warmed
  - Spicy mustard
  - Baby arugula leaves
  - Thinly sliced avocado
  - Hot sauce

1. Preheat oven to 400°F. Place a small rimmed baking sheet (about 17 x 12 inches) in oven 5 minutes. Remove pan from oven; brush with oil. Return to oven 2 additional minutes. Remove from oven, and arrange sausages on hot pan (making sure links do not touch). Bake until browned, about 15 minutes, turning sausages after 8 minutes. Transfer to a plate lined with paper towels; cool slightly, 5 minutes. Reserve 1 tablespoon drippings on pan. Reduce oven temperature to 325°F.

2. Chop sausages. Whisk together eggs and cream in a large bowl; stir in peppers, chives, salt, pepper, chopped sausages, and half of the cheese. Pour into pan with drippings; sprinkle with remaining 1 cup cheese.

3. Bake at 325°F until eggs are just set, 14 to 16 minutes. Cut into 32 squares. Spread mustard on bottom half of each biscuit, and then add 2 egg squares, arugula, sliced avocado, hot sauce, and biscuit top.

THE RIGHT WAY TO REHEAT

Refrigerate leftover eggs up to 1 day. Reheat in the oven (not in the microwave) at 325°F for 5 minutes to keep them from drying out.

WASTE NOT

4 Brilliant Uses for Basil

Turn an abundance of this herb into delicious pantry staples

BASIL SIMPLE SYRUP

Stir 1 cup water and ½ cup **sugar** in a saucepan over high. Add ¾ cup **basil;** simmer 3 minutes. Strain; discard solids. Refrigerate up to 2 weeks.

BASIL BUTTER

Whip ½ cup softened **butter** and ½ cup **basil** in a food processor, 20 seconds. Refrigerate, covered, up to 1 day.

BASIL OIL

Blend 4 cups blanched **basil**, 1 cup **olive oil**, and ¼ tsp. **kosher salt** in a blender on high, 1 minute. Strain; discard solids. Store up to 3 days.

BASIL SUGAR

Pulse 1 cup **sugar,** ½ cup **basil,** and ¼ tsp. **lemon zest** in a food processor, about 30 seconds. Refrigerate, covered, up to 2 weeks.

COOKING TIP

Get Stir Crazy

More tasty combos for our sheet pan eggs (recipe, page 121)

Diced cooked ham
+

Chopped steamed broccoli
+

Cheddar cheese

OTHER OPTIONS
▼

Roasted tomatoes **+** feta cheese **+** basil pesto

Caramelized onions **+** Gruyère cheese **+** fresh thyme

Diced canned green chiles **+** queso fresco **+** fresh cilantro

"Blanch fresh basil leaves to preserve their bright color in sauces like pesto. Place the leaves in boiling water for 10 seconds; then transfer them to an ice bath. Gently squeeze dry." **—Robby Melvin,** Test Kitchen Director

July

124   **The Bradford Melon**   Sumter, South Carolina, farmer Nat Bradford mounts a delightful comeback for this sweet heirloom crop

130   **Gather Round the Grill**   Seasonal menus for outdoor get-togethers

136   **Time for Tomato Pie!**   Slices of peak-season tomatoes shine in this savory summertime staple

138   **Heavenly Corn**   Smoky, savory, or sweet? Four tasty ways to take this grilled veggie up a notch

140   **Tortellini with a Twist**   This pasta salad with chicken and fresh veggies is great for dinner and even better for lunch

141   **Berry Delicious**   With a press-in cracker crust, this beautiful tart is a snap to make

142   **SL Cooking School**   Our Test Kitchen professionals share ideas for making the most of your outdoor grill

MARINATED WATERMELON-
AND-TOMATO SALAD
(PAGE 126)

The Bradford Melon

Sumter, South Carolina, farmer Nat Bradford mounts a delightful comeback for this sweet heirloom crop

It was just 7:36 on a Sunday night at Motor Supply Company Bistro in Columbia, South Carolina, but the Bradford Watermelon Salad with shaved fennel, arugula, and toasted hazelnuts had already sold out.

"It's so good," whispered a diner at the bar, who'd snagged the last plate. But she didn't mean to brag. She just couldn't help marveling at the watermelon's sweetness, its delicate texture, and edible rind like a cucumber.

Meanwhile, the run on specials prompted the bartender to regale customers with the tale of the Bradford melon. His story involved a prisoner of the Revolutionary War named John Franklin Lawson, who scored a wedge of watermelon as a water source on a pirate ship bound for the West Indies. It tasted so good that he saved the seeds for his eventual return to the States. Around 1840, Nathaniel Napoleon Bradford crossed the Lawson watermelon with the Mountain Sweet, and the Bradford was born.

"How many people do you get to believe that?" a customer asked, teasing the bartender.

Sure enough, the Bradford watermelon's epic history could have faded into obscurity. The melon's thin skin kept it from being shipped, so it fell out of favor with commercial growers, who preferred types with sturdier rinds.

Then along came Nat Bradford, the great-great-great-grandson of that watermelon's developer.

Today, visitors to Bradford's farmhouse in Sumter, South Carolina, a sleepy town about 45 miles from Columbia, have to step over watermelons covering the front porch. It's all melons all the time in late harvest as he decides which ones to save seeds from and which ones to process as pickled rinds or red molasses (an old-fashioned recipe that took him two years to perfect). Every year before harvest, he allots just about 500 melons that get snatched up during presale.

He might also deliver some of the watermelons to restaurants within a few hours' drive. But otherwise, these fruits can't be shipped, their elusive nature making them even more special.

"Last year, the first folks who showed up drove down from Long Island, New York, loaded up 15 melons, took a few pictures, turned around, and drove back," Bradford says. "I'm not sure what they did with them. They wanted to be part of the story, which is humbling."

Growing up, Bradford remembers his family planting just a small patch in the front yard and saving watermelon seeds in Mason jars. His father worked as a dermatologist and was the first generation to deviate from the farming business.

Bradford thought about farming after high school in the early 1990s, but he didn't know about many career possibilities in heirloom or organic agriculture at the time, so he went into landscape architecture instead.

> "It was important to do, and people expected it,"
> he says of reviving the family melon,
> "but I needed some soul behind it."

Then in 1997, he discovered an 1850s book heralding the Bradford watermelon as one of the finest. "Could that be our melon?" he wondered. The thought floated in the back of his mind until 2012, when David Shields, a food historian and professor at the University of South Carolina, confirmed that fact. Bradford knew he had to return the melons to market.

Living in Seneca at the time—and running his landscape business—he just needed a little encouragement to return to the family land. Shields introduced him to heritage-grain guru Glenn Roberts, through whom he met acclaimed chef Sean Brock. The staff at one of Brock's restaurants at the time, McCrady's, helped process the first batch of watermelon pickles. "I don't even know these people," Bradford recalls thinking. "This is a whole different world."

He also added a charitable arm, Watermelons for Water, to his first growing season, donating proceeds from that harvest to fund hand-dug wells for small farmers in Bolivia. "It was important to do, and people expected it," he says of reviving the family melon, "but I needed some soul behind it."

These days, Bradford also grows heirloom greens and okra, but in late summer it's watermelon that he slices at his dining room table, causing his five children to thunder down the stairs for a taste. They help in the fields when they're not in school. And they haven't yet tired of eating the fruits of their labor, which have a cotton candy texture, intense sweetness, and white seeds.

Gesturing to one of his sons, Bradford says, "When he gets out on his own someday and eats his first store-bought watermelon, he's gonna say, 'Gosh, I want that old melon back.' " And Bradford hopes that memory will send his children home to carry on the family legacy.

Taste of Summer

Three recipes to make with your favorite melon

Marinated Watermelon-and-Tomato Salad

(Photo, page 124)

ACTIVE 20 MIN. - TOTAL 20 MIN., PLUS 30 MIN. CHILLING

SERVES 8

5	Tbsp. fresh lime juice (from 3 large limes)
1½	Tbsp. honey
1	Tbsp. finely chopped fresh mint
1	Tbsp. grated fresh ginger (from 1 [4-inch] piece)
½	tsp. dried mint
1½	tsp. kosher salt, divided
⅓	cup olive oil
6	cups 1-inch watermelon cubes (from 1 [7-lb.] seedless watermelon)
3	cups cherry tomatoes, halved
2	medium shallots, thinly sliced (about 1 cup)
½	cup roughly torn fresh basil leaves
½	cup roughly torn fresh mint leaves
4	oz. goat cheese, crumbled (1 cup)

1. Whisk together lime juice, honey, fresh mint, ginger, dried mint, and ½ teaspoon of the salt in a small bowl. Drizzle in oil, whisking, until blended. Place watermelon and tomatoes in a large ziplock plastic bag. Pour in lime dressing, squeeze air out of bag, and seal. Chill 30 minutes.
2. Transfer watermelon and tomatoes to a large bowl, reserving marinade in bag. Toss watermelon mixture with shallots, ¼ cup of the reserved marinade, and remaining 1 teaspoon salt. Gently toss in basil and mint. Transfer to a large platter, and sprinkle with crumbled goat cheese. Serve remaining marinade on the side as a dressing.

Watermelon-Ginger Mojitos

ACTIVE 20 MIN. · TOTAL 20 MIN., PLUS 1 HOUR,
15 MIN. CHILLING

SERVES 10

½ cup granulated sugar
5 large fresh mint sprigs, plus more
   for garnish
8 cups seedless watermelon cubes
   (from 1 [7½-lb.] seedless
   watermelon)
3 cups (24 oz.) light rum (such as
   Bacardí Superior), chilled
1 (12-oz.) bottle ginger beer, chilled

½ cup fresh lime juice (from 4 limes)
   Ice cubes
   Small watermelon wedges, for
   garnish

1. Bring ½ cup water and sugar to a
simmer in a small saucepan over high.
Simmer, stirring often, until sugar
dissolves, 1 to 2 minutes. Remove from
heat; add mint, and stir until submerged.
Refrigerate until mixture is completely
cool, 1 hour. Pour mint mixture through a
fine wire-mesh strainer into a bowl; discard
solids. Chill mint syrup until ready to use.

2. While syrup cools, place watermelon
in a blender, and process until smooth,
about 20 seconds. Pour through a fine
wire-mesh strainer into a large measuring
cup, pressing gently to squeeze out juice.
Discard solids, and refrigerate 15 minutes.
Repeat straining procedure. (You should
have about 4 cups juice.)

3. Stir together mint syrup, watermelon
juice, rum, ginger beer, and lime juice in a
large pitcher.

4. Pour evenly into 10 highball glasses
filled with ice; garnish each with a mint
sprig and small watermelon wedge cut to
sit on rim of glass.

Watermelon Chiffon Pie

ACTIVE 35 MIN. - TOTAL 55 MIN, PLUS 2 HOURS, 30 MIN. CHILLING
SERVES 8

- 2½ cups crumbled crisp gourmet cookies (such as Biscoff; from 1 [8.8-oz.] pkg.)
- ½ tsp. kosher salt
- ½ cup, plus 2 Tbsp. granulated sugar, divided
- 6 Tbsp. unsalted butter, melted
- 1 (7½-lb.) seedless watermelon
- ½ cup uncooked quick-cooking tapioca
- 1 Tbsp. lemon zest plus 1 Tbsp. fresh juice (from 1 lemon)
- 1–2 drops red food coloring gel (optional)
- 2 cups heavy cream, divided
- 1 (8-oz.) container mascarpone cheese, divided
- ½ cup, plus ⅓ cup powdered sugar, divided

1. Heavily coat a 9-inch pie plate with cooking spray; set aside. Place crumbled cookies, salt, and 2 tablespoons of the granulated sugar in a food processor, and process until finely ground, 10 to 15 seconds. Add melted butter; process until mixture is moist and clumps together easily, about 5 seconds. Press crumb mixture evenly on bottom and up sides of greased pie plate. Refrigerate until set, about 30 minutes.

2. Cut part of the watermelon into cubes to equal 3 cups (about 16 oz.). Cover remaining watermelon with plastic wrap, and refrigerate until ready to use. Place cubed watermelon in a blender, and process until smooth, about 20 seconds. Pour through a fine wire-mesh strainer into a large measuring cup, pressing gently to squeeze out juice; discard solids. (You should have about 1½ cups of watermelon juice.)

3. Place tapioca in a spice grinder or coffee grinder; process until finely ground, about 40 seconds. Sift ground tapioca through a fine wire-mesh strainer into a small bowl. Set aside 2 tablespoons plus 1 teaspoon of the tapioca powder. (Reserve remaining tapioca powder for another use.)

4. Stir together watermelon juice, 2 tablespoons plus 1 teaspoon tapioca powder, and remaining ½ cup granulated sugar in a small saucepan; let stand 5 minutes. Bring to a boil over high, and cook, whisking often, until tapioca dissolves, 5 to 6 minutes. Immediately remove watermelon mixture from heat. Let stand, stirring occasionally, until thickened, about 20 minutes. Stir in lemon zest, lemon juice, and (if desired) 1 or 2 drops food coloring gel.

5. While watermelon mixture stands, beat 1 cup of the heavy cream and ¼ cup of the mascarpone with an electric mixer fitted with whisk attachment on high speed until soft peaks form, about 50 seconds. Gradually add ½ cup of the powdered sugar, beating until stiff peaks form, about 10 seconds. Working in batches, gently fold watermelon mixture into whipped cream mixture until smooth and blended. Spoon watermelon mixture into prepared pie plate. Refrigerate until firm, about 2 hours.

6. Scoop out flesh of remaining watermelon with a sharp 1-inch melon baller, making about 10 (1-inch) balls. Cut watermelon balls in half, and place, cut sides down, on a plate lined with paper towels; set aside.

7. Gently stir together remaining mascarpone cheese and ⅓ cup powdered sugar in a large bowl just until combined. Beat remaining 1 cup heavy cream in a medium bowl on medium speed until stiff peaks form. Gently fold whipped cream into mascarpone mixture.

8. Dollop mascarpone-whipped cream topping on top of pie, leaving a 1-inch border. Place watermelon-ball halves, cut sides down, along edges of whipped cream topping. Serve immediately.

WATERMELON CHIFFON PIE

Gather Round the Grill

Seasonal menus for outdoor get-togethers

BBQ-GLAZED CEDAR-
PLANK SALMON
(PAGE 135)

CHARRED POTATO-
OKRA SALAD
(PAGE 135)

PEACH-RICOTTA-
PROSCIUTTO TOASTS
(PAGE 135)

SUNDAY NIGHT CHICKEN SUPPER

Dry-Brined Beer-Can Chickens

Rub the chickens with the spice mixture, and refrigerate up to a day in advance. Keep them uncovered so the skin dries out and crisps up on the grill.

ACTIVE 30 MIN. - TOTAL 2 HOURS, 30 MIN., PLUS 8 HOURS BRINING
SERVES 8

- ¼ cup kosher salt
- 1 Tbsp. light brown sugar
- 1 Tbsp. ground cumin
- 2 tsp. ground coriander
- 2 tsp. smoked paprika
- 1 tsp. black pepper
- 2 (3½- to 4-lb.) whole chickens
- 2 (12-oz.) cans beer (such as Modelo Especial)

1. Stir together salt, brown sugar, cumin, coriander, paprika, and pepper in a small bowl. (If necessary, remove giblets from chickens, and discard or reserve for another use.) Sprinkle skin and cavities of chickens with salt mixture. Chill, uncovered, at least 8 hours or up to 24 hours.
2. Preheat a gas grill to medium (350°F to 400°F) on 1 side. Open beer cans; pour out ½ cup beer from each can. (Drink the poured-out beer, or reserve for another use.) Working with 1 chicken at a time, hold chicken upright with cavity facing down, and insert 1 opened beer can into cavity. Pull legs forward to form a tripod, allowing chicken to stand upright.
3. Place chickens upright on unoiled grates over unlit side of grill. Grill, covered with grill lid, until the skin is crispy and a thermometer inserted in thickest portion of thighs registers 165°F, about 1 hour, 40 minutes. Remove from grill; rest 10 minutes. Carefully remove cans; cut chickens into quarters.

Grilled Sweet Potato Fries

ACTIVE 20 MIN. - TOTAL 35 MIN.
SERVES 6

Cut 3 large unpeeled **sweet potatoes** (about 2½ lb.) into 8 wedges each; toss with 1½ Tbsp. **olive oil** in a microwavable

bowl. Cover with plastic wrap; microwave on HIGH until tender when pierced with a knife, about 8 minutes, tossing and re-covering after 4 minutes. Cool 15 minutes. Add 1 Tbsp. **olive oil**, 1 tsp. **chili powder**, 1 tsp. **kosher salt**, and ¼ tsp. **black pepper**; toss to coat. Place potatoes, cut sides down, on oiled grill grates over medium heat (350°F to 400°F). Grill, uncovered, until charred and tender, 2 to 3 minutes per cut side. Remove from grill. Drizzle evenly with 1 Tbsp. **honey**; sprinkle with 1 oz. crumbled **queso fresco** (about ¼ cup) and 1 Tbsp. chopped **fresh chives**.

Spicy Pepper Jelly Coleslaw

ACTIVE 20 MIN. - TOTAL 20 MIN.
SERVES 6

Toss together 4 cups shredded **napa cabbage** (from 1 head cabbage), 1 cup thinly sliced **red bell pepper** (from 1 bell pepper), 1 cup thinly sliced **yellow bell pepper** (from 1 bell pepper), ½ cup thinly sliced **red onion** (from 1 onion), and ½ cup chopped **fresh cilantro** in a bowl. Whisk together ¼ cup **red pepper jelly**, 3 Tbsp. **olive oil**, 2 Tbsp. **fresh lime juice**, 1½ tsp. **kosher salt**, and ¼ tsp. each **cayenne pepper** and **black pepper** in a bowl. Add to cabbage mixture; toss until well coated.

BACKYARD PIZZA PARTY

Sausage-and-Shrimp Pizzas with Spinach-Basil Pesto

Medium shrimp (43 to 50 typically come in a pound) are best for this pizza because they won't overcook or undercook.

ACTIVE 1 HOUR, 20 MIN. - TOTAL 1 HOUR, 20 MIN.
SERVES 8

- 2 cups packed baby spinach
- 1 cup packed fresh basil leaves
- ½ cup chopped toasted pecans
- 2 oz. Parmesan cheese, grated on smallest holes of box grater (about ½ cup)
- 2 medium garlic cloves, crushed
- 1 tsp. lemon zest plus 1 Tbsp. fresh juice (from 1 lemon)
- ½ tsp. black pepper
- 8 Tbsp. extra-virgin olive oil, divided
- 1½ tsp. kosher salt, divided
- 8 oz. hot Italian sausage, casings removed
- 1 lb. medium-size peeled, deveined raw shrimp
- ¼ cup fine yellow cornmeal
- 2 (1-lb.) fresh prepared pizza doughs, at room temperature
- 8 oz. fresh mozzarella cheese, torn into small pieces, divided

1. Process spinach, basil, pecans, Parmesan, garlic, lemon zest and juice, pepper, 7 tablespoons of the oil, and 1 teaspoon of the salt in a food processor until almost smooth, 30 seconds, stopping to scrape down sides of bowl as needed. Set pesto aside.

2. Preheat a gas grill to medium-high (400°F to 450°F) on 1 side; preheat other side to low (250°F to 300°F). Place a large grill-safe skillet on unoiled grates over medium-high heat. Add remaining 1 tablespoon oil to skillet. Add sausage; cook, breaking up into small pieces, 5 minutes. Add shrimp and remaining ½ teaspoon salt; cook, stirring occasionally, 3 minutes. (Shrimp will not be cooked through.) Remove skillet from grill; set aside.

3. Sprinkle cornmeal evenly over a large rimless baking sheet. Shape 1 of the pizza doughs into a 14-inch circle; place on prepared baking sheet. Spray the grill grates over medium-high heat with cooking spray; slide dough off baking sheet and onto grates. Grill, covered, until grill marks appear, 2 to 3 minutes.

Remove from grill. Flip over, and spread grilled side of crust with half of the pesto, leaving a ¾-inch border. Sprinkle evenly with half of the sausage-shrimp mixture and half of the mozzarella cheese. Return pizza to grill grates over low heat. Grill, covered, until cheese melts, 10 to 12 minutes. Remove from grill; cut into 8 slices. Repeat with remaining pizza dough, pesto, sausage-shrimp mixture, and mozzarella cheese.

Chopped Salad with Buttermilk Dressing

ACTIVE 15 MIN. - TOTAL 15 MIN.
SERVES 8

Toss together 8 cups chopped **assorted lettuces**, 1¾ cups halved **cherry tomatoes**, and 1 cup chopped **avocado** (from 1 large avocado) in a large bowl. Whisk together ¾ cup **whole-milk buttermilk**, ½ cup **mayonnaise**, 2 Tbsp. chopped **fresh chives**, 1 Tbsp. **fresh lemon juice**, 1 pressed medium **garlic clove**, ¾ tsp. **kosher salt**, and ½ tsp. **black pepper** in a separate bowl until combined. Drizzle over salad.

Oven-Fried Zucchini Sticks

ACTIVE 25 MIN. - TOTAL 50 MIN.
SERVES 8

Stir together 1 cup **panko breadcrumbs**, 3 oz. grated **Parmigiano-Reggiano cheese** (about ¾ cup), ½ tsp. **kosher salt**, ¼ tsp. **black pepper**, and ¼ tsp. **garlic powder** in a shallow dish. Stir together ½ cup **all-purpose flour** and ½ tsp. **kosher salt** in a separate shallow dish. Whisk together 2 large **eggs** and 3 Tbsp. **whole milk** in a third shallow dish. Cut 4 small **zucchini** (about 1½ lb. total) into 3- to 4-inch x ½-inch sticks. Working in batches, dredge sticks in flour mixture, dip in egg mixture, and dredge in panko mixture, pressing to coat. Arrange sticks in an even layer on a generously greased (with **cooking spray**) wire rack set on a baking sheet. Bake at 425°F until lightly browned and tender, about 25 minutes. Serve with warmed **jarred marinara sauce**.

BEACH HOUSE CLAMBAKE

Foil-Pack Clams with White Wine and Herbs

If littlenecks aren't available, try steamer, Manila, or cherrystone clams. Avoid chowder clams, which are too big for this recipe.

ACTIVE 20 MIN. - TOTAL 30 MIN.
SERVES 6

- 1½ cups unsalted butter, softened
- ¼ cup finely chopped shallot (from 1 medium shallot)
- 2 Tbsp. chopped fresh flat-leaf parsley
- 1 Tbsp. chopped fresh tarragon
- 1 Tbsp. chopped fresh chives
- 1½ tsp. lime zest (from 1 lime)
- 1½ tsp. kosher salt
- ¼ tsp. crushed red pepper
- 60 littleneck clams (about 3½ lb.), with shells scrubbed clean
- 3 lemons, quartered lengthwise
- 6 thyme sprigs
- ¾ cup (6 oz.) dry white wine

1. Stir together first 8 ingredients in a bowl until well blended.
2. Preheat a grill to medium-high (400°F to 450°F). Cut 12 (12-inch) squares of heavy-duty aluminum foil. Place 6 of the foil squares in a single layer on work surface, and set aside remaining 6 squares. Place 10 clams on each of the 6 foil squares on work surface. Top each clam mound with 2 lemon wedges, 1 thyme sprig, and ¼ cup of the butter mixture. Carefully pour 2 tablespoons wine over each mound. Top each with 1 of the remaining 6 foil squares; tightly crimp all sides.
3. Place sealed foil packets on unoiled grates. Grill, covered, until clams open, about 10 minutes, rotating halfway through grilling time. Discard any clams that do not open.

Grilled Garlic Bread

ACTIVE 15 MIN. - TOTAL 15 MIN.
SERVES 6

Split 1 (12-oz.) **baguette** horizontally; cut each piece in half crosswise. Cook 6 Tbsp. **unsalted butter**, 4 minced medium **garlic cloves** (1½ Tbsp.), 1 tsp. **kosher salt**, and ¼ tsp. **black pepper** in a small skillet over medium, stirring occasionally, 5 minutes. Stir in ¼ cup chopped **fresh flat-leaf parsley**. Reduce heat to low; cover to keep warm. Place bread pieces, split sides down, on unoiled grill grates over medium heat (350°F to 400°F). Grill, uncovered, until slightly charred and crisp, 1 minute. Flip bread, and grill 1 minute. Remove from grill. Brush cut sides of bread with warm butter mixture. Cut each into thirds.

Mixed Herb-and-Tomato Salad

ACTIVE 15 MIN. - TOTAL 25 MIN.
SERVES 6

Place 2 lb. **heirloom tomatoes** (cut into assorted slices and wedges) and 1 pt. halved **multicolored cherry tomatoes** in a large bowl. Add ½ cup **extra-virgin olive oil**, ¼ cup **red wine vinegar**, 3 smashed medium **garlic cloves**, 1½ tsp. **kosher salt**, and ½ tsp. **black pepper**; gently stir to coat. Let stand 10 minutes. Stir in 1 cup packed torn **mixed fresh herbs** (such as basil, flat-leaf parsley, and chives). Serve immediately.

CHEESEBURGERS FOR A CROWD

Smashed Bacon Cheeseburgers

These burger patties are pressed down on a hot griddle to make them thin with crispy edges. You'll need a flat spatula without holes to smash them properly.

ACTIVE 45 MIN. - TOTAL 1 HOUR, 45 MIN.
SERVES 8

- 8 oz. thick-cut hickory-smoked bacon, coarsely chopped
- 2 lb. 85/15 lean ground beef
- 1 tsp. kosher salt
- 1 tsp. black pepper
- 8 medium Cheddar cheese slices (about 1 oz. each)
- 8 hamburger buns, split
- 3 Tbsp. butter, melted
   Spicy-Sweet Refrigerator Pickles (recipe follows)
   Optional toppings: sliced tomatoes, lettuce, mayonnaise

1. Arrange bacon in an even layer on a small baking sheet; place in freezer until frozen, about 1 hour. Transfer bacon to a food processor; pulse until finely ground, 5 to 10 times. Transfer bacon to a large bowl. Add beef, salt, and pepper; combine using hands until fully incorporated. Gently shape into 8 even balls.

2. Place a griddle or large cast-iron skillet on unoiled grates of a gas grill, and preheat grill to high (450°F to 500°F) until griddle smokes, about 10 minutes.
3. Working in 2 batches, coat hot griddle with cooking spray; arrange burger balls on griddle. Using a large, flat metal spatula, press balls firmly to flatten to about ¾-inch-thick patties. Cover grill; cook patties 2 minutes. Turn patties over; cover grill, and cook 1 minute. Place 1 cheese slice on each patty. Cover grill; cook until cheese melts, 1 minute. Transfer to a plate; cover loosely with aluminum foil. Repeat with remaining patties and cheese.
4. Brush cut sides of buns with melted butter. Place buns, cut sides down, on unoiled grates of hot grill. Grill until toasted, about 1 minute per side.
5. Place 1 patty on each bun bottom; top with Spicy-Sweet Refrigerator Pickles, desired toppings, and bun tops.

Spicy-Sweet Refrigerator Pickles

ACTIVE 15 MIN. - TOTAL 1 HOUR, 20 MIN.
SERVES 8

Thinly slice 6 oz. **sweet mini peppers**, 1 small **red onion**, and 1 large unseeded **jalapeño chile**. Pack vegetables into a 1-pt. heatproof jar; add 1 sliced medium **garlic clove**, 2 thin **lemon** slices, and 2 **thyme sprigs**. Bring 1 cup **rice vinegar**, ⅔ cup **sugar**, and 1½ tsp. **kosher salt** to a boil in a saucepan over high, stirring until sugar dissolves. Pour mixture over vegetables in jar. Let stand until completely cool, 1 hour. Seal jar; refrigerate up to 2 weeks.

Charred Onion Dip

ACTIVE 15 MIN. - TOTAL 25 MIN.
SERVES 8

Slice 1 medium-size **sweet onion** crosswise into ½-inch-thick rings. Brush onion rings evenly with 1 Tbsp. **olive oil**. Grill on unoiled grates over medium-high heat (400°F to 450°F) until grill marks appear, about 5 minutes per side. Remove from grill. Cool 10 minutes, and chop. Stir together chopped onion, 16 oz. **sour cream**, 2 oz. grated **Parmesan cheese** (about ½ cup), 1 tsp. **kosher salt**, ½ tsp. **black pepper**, and ½ tsp. **hot sauce** in a bowl. Sprinkle with ¼ cup chopped **fresh chives**. Serve with **chips**.

DINNER ON THE PATIO

BBQ-Glazed Cedar-Plank Salmon

The salmon and the potato-okra salad should be served hot off the grill, so set out a platter of Peach-Ricotta-Prosciutto Toasts for guests to enjoy while you finish up dinner.

ACTIVE 10 MIN. - TOTAL 1 HOUR, 25 MIN.
SERVES 6

- ¾ cup bottled chili sauce
- 3 Tbsp. rice vinegar
- 2½ Tbsp. light brown sugar
- 2 Tbsp. whole-grain mustard
- 1½ Tbsp. Worcestershire sauce
- 1½ tsp. kosher salt, divided
- ¾ tsp. black pepper, divided
- 6 (6-oz.) skin-on salmon fillets

1. Soak 2 (11- x 5- x ¼-inch) cedar grilling planks in water 1 hour. Drain; set aside.

2. Stir together chili sauce, vinegar, brown sugar, mustard, Worcestershire sauce, ½ teaspoon of the salt, and ¼ teaspoon of the pepper in a small saucepan. Bring to a boil over medium-high; boil, stirring constantly, 1 minute. Remove from heat. Pour half of the mixture into a small heatproof bowl, and reserve for serving. Set aside remaining mixture in saucepan.
3. Preheat a gas grill to medium (350°F to 400°F). Place grilling planks on unoiled grates; let stand until planks are charred on bottoms, about 3 minutes. Flip planks. Place 3 salmon fillets, skin sides down, on each plank. Sprinkle salmon evenly with remaining 1 teaspoon salt and ½ teaspoon pepper; brush with chili sauce mixture in saucepan. (Discard remaining mixture in saucepan.) Grill, covered, until desired degree of doneness, about 20 minutes for medium-rare. Serve with reserved chili sauce mixture in bowl.

Charred Potato-Okra Salad

ACTIVE 15 MIN. - TOTAL 25 MIN.
SERVES 6

Cut 1 lb. unpeeled **baby red potatoes** into 1-inch pieces. Place potatoes and 2 Tbsp. **water** in a 1-qt. microwavable dish; cover tightly with plastic wrap. Microwave on HIGH until tender, about 7 minutes. Drain. Toss together potatoes, 1 Tbsp. **olive oil**, 1 tsp. **kosher salt**, and ¼ tsp. **black pepper** in a bowl. Toss together 1 lb. **fresh okra**, 1 Tbsp. **olive oil**, 1 tsp. **kosher salt**, and ¼ tsp. **black pepper** in a separate bowl. Place potatoes on oiled grill grates over medium-high heat (400°F to 450°F). Grill, covered, turning occasionally, until charred and tender on all sides, 4 to 6 minutes. Transfer to a large heatproof bowl; set aside. Place okra on oiled grates. Grill, covered, until charred and tender, about 4 minutes, turning once halfway through cook time. Transfer to a cutting board; cut in half lengthwise. Add to potatoes in bowl. Stir in ½ cup thinly sliced **scallions**, 2 Tbsp. **fresh lemon juice** (from 1 lemon), 1 Tbsp. **olive oil**, and 1 tsp. chopped **fresh thyme**.

Peach-Ricotta-Prosciutto Toasts

ACTIVE 10 MIN. - TOTAL 10 MIN.
SERVES 6

Cut 1 (12-oz.) **baguette** into 18 (½-inch-thick) slices. Place slices on unoiled grill grates over medium-high heat (400°F to 450°F). Grill, uncovered, until charred on both sides, about 1 minute per side. Stir together 1¾ cups **whole-milk ricotta cheese**, 1 Tbsp. **olive oil**, 1 tsp. **lemon zest**, and ¼ tsp. **black pepper** in a bowl. Spread mixture over toasts. Top with 36 (¼-inch-thick) **peach** slices (from 3 unpeeled fresh peaches), 4 **prosciutto** slices (torn into ½-inch pieces), and ¼ cup torn **fresh basil**; sprinkle with ¼ tsp. **black pepper**.

Time for Tomato Pie!

Slices of peak-season tomatoes shine in this savory summertime staple

Heirloom Tomato Pie with Parmesan-Buttermilk Crust

Beyond the requisite tomatoes, cheese, and mayonnaise, it doesn't matter so much what you put in your tomato pie as long as you make one before summer passes you by.

ACTIVE 30 MIN. - TOTAL 2 HOURS, 50 MIN., PLUS 1 HOUR STANDING
SERVES 8

- 3 lb. assorted medium to large heirloom tomatoes
- 1 tsp. kosher salt, divided
- 6 thick-cut bacon slices, diced
- 2 large shallots, chopped
- 2 garlic cloves, finely chopped (2 tsp.)
- 6 oz. aged extra-sharp white Cheddar cheese, grated (about 1½ cups)
- ½ cup mayonnaise
- ½ cup chopped fresh basil
- ¼ cup thinly sliced fresh chives
- 1 Tbsp. Dijon mustard
- 1 large egg
- ¼ tsp. black pepper
  Parmesan-Buttermilk Crust (recipe follows)
  Fresh basil leaves
  Minced fresh chives

1. Preheat oven to 400°F. Cut tomatoes into ½-inch-thick slices. Place about 7 or 8 slices (enough to cover top of pie) on a baking sheet lined with paper towels, and sprinkle with ¼ teaspoon of the salt. Cover with additional paper towels, and reserve.
2. Arrange remaining tomatoes in a single layer on a lightly greased wire rack set on a large baking sheet. Sprinkle with ½ teaspoon of the salt. Bake in preheated oven until wilted and slightly dried out, 40 to 45 minutes. Cool completely, about 1 hour.

3. Meanwhile, cook bacon in a skillet over medium-high until fat is beginning to render, 4 to 5 minutes. Add chopped shallots, and cook until bacon is crisp and shallots are caramelized, 6 to 7 more minutes. Stir in garlic; cook until fragrant, about 1 minute. Using a slotted spoon, transfer bacon mixture to a plate lined with paper towels to drain. Cool 20 minutes.
4. Stir together cheese, mayonnaise, basil, chives, Dijon, and egg until combined. Sprinkle with pepper and remaining ¼ teaspoon salt. Fold in bacon mixture.
5. Gently spread a third of cheese mixture onto Parmesan-Buttermilk Crust; layer with half of the roasted tomato slices in slightly overlapping pattern. Spread another third of cheese mixture on top of tomato slices. Repeat with remaining roasted tomato slices and cheese mixture. Top with reserved sliced fresh tomatoes, pressing filling gently into crust. Shield edges of pie with aluminum foil.
6. Bake in preheated oven until filling is set, 40 to 45 minutes. Transfer to a wire rack, and let stand 1 hour before serving. Sprinkle with basil and chives.

LET'S TALK TOMATOES

Raw tomatoes are naturally full of water, which tends to leach out as the pie cooks, giving it a runny texture—one of the most common conundrums when making this recipe. Luckily, the fix is easy: Roast most of the tomatoes before the pie goes into the oven. Not only does this simple step keep the filling from being too wet, but it also caramelizes the tomatoes, intensifying their flavor. You can even roast them up to a day in advance. When they have cooled, store them in an airtight container in the refrigerator.

Parmesan-Buttermilk Crust

Whether using store-bought or homemade dough, don't forget to blind-bake the crust (bake it a bit on its own) before adding the filling. This extra step will keep the crust from turning soggy as the pie bakes.

ACTIVE 30 MIN. - TOTAL 2 HOURS, PLUS 2 HOURS CHILLING
MAKES 1 DEEP-DISH PIECRUST

Pulse 2½ cups **all-purpose flour**, 3 oz. finely shredded **Parmigiano-Reggiano cheese** (about 1 packed cup), ½ tsp. **kosher salt**, and ¼ tsp. **black pepper** in food processor until combined, about 3 times. Add ¾ cup cubed cold **unsalted butter** and ¼ cup cubed cold **solid vegetable shortening**; pulse until butter and shortening are pea-size pieces, about 5 times. Drizzle in 6 Tbsp. **whole-milk buttermilk**; process until dough just begins to come together. Lightly knead dough into a ball on a large piece of plastic wrap. Flatten into a disk, and wrap tightly. Chill at least 2 hours or up to 2 days. Preheat oven to 400°F. Roll dough out on a floured surface into a 15- to 16-inch circle, about ⅓ inch thick. Transfer to a 9-inch deep-dish pie plate. Trim edges, leaving a 1-inch overhang. Fold edges under and crimp. Freeze dough 20 minutes. Line piecrust with parchment paper, and fill with pie weights or dried beans. Bake crust 20 minutes. Remove parchment and weights; bake until edges are golden and bottom of crust is set, about 8 minutes. Cool completely, about 30 minutes.

Heavenly Corn

Smoky, savory, or sweet? Four tasty ways to take this grilled veggie up a notch

Classic Grilled Corn

ACTIVE 40 MIN. - TOTAL 40 MIN.
SERVES 6

- 6 large ears yellow or white corn with husks (about 5 lb.)
- ¼ cup butter, cut evenly into 12 pieces
- ¾ tsp. kosher salt
- ¼ tsp. black pepper

1. Preheat a gas grill to medium-high (400°F to 450°F) on 1 side, or push hot coals to 1 side of a charcoal grill.
2. Working with 1 ear at a time, grab silks at top of corn with half the silks in each hand. Slowly peel silks down, 1 side at a time, peeling back all silks and husks in 1 motion. Discard silks; pull husks together to form a ponytail-like handle. Tear off 1 small husk piece; use it to tie a knot around husks to secure.
3. Coat corn with cooking spray; place on unoiled grates on lit side of grill. Grill, uncovered, turning occasionally, until charred in spots, 15 to 18 minutes. Hang husks over edge of grill to prevent burning.
4. Remove corn from grill. Wrap individually in aluminum foil, excluding husks, placing 2 butter pieces on each ear. Put wrapped corn on unlit side of grill. Cover grill to keep warm until ready to serve, at least 5 minutes or up to 30 minutes. Unwrap corn; sprinkle with salt and pepper.

Basil Butter with Parmesan

ACTIVE 10 MIN. - TOTAL 10 MIN.
SERVES 6

Process ½ cup packed fresh **basil leaves**, ½ cup softened **butter**, 2 tsp. fresh **lemon juice**, and ¼ tsp. **kosher salt** in a food processor until smooth, 1 minute. Arrange Classic Grilled Corn on a platter. Rub corn with butter mixture; sprinkle evenly with ½ cup finely grated **Parmigiano-Reggiano**.

Bacon with Ranch Drizzle

ACTIVE 20 MIN. - TOTAL 20 MIN.
SERVES 6

Cook 6 **bacon slices** in a large skillet over medium-high, turning occasionally, until very crisp, about 8 minutes. Transfer to a plate lined with paper towels, and let stand 5 minutes. Meanwhile, measure 2 Tbsp. drippings from skillet into a heatproof bowl. Add 3 Tbsp. each of **mayonnaise**, **sour cream**, and **whole-milk buttermilk** to bowl, whisking until combined. Add 2 tsp. each finely chopped **fresh flat-leaf parsley**, **fresh dill**, and **fresh chives**; 1 tsp. fresh **lemon juice**; ½ tsp. **kosher salt**; and ¼ tsp. **onion powder**, stirring to combine. Finely chop bacon. Arrange Classic Grilled Corn on a platter, and drizzle with ranch mixture. Sprinkle evenly with chopped bacon.

Honey-Chipotle Glaze

ACTIVE 15 MIN. - TOTAL 15 MIN.
SERVES 6

Process 3 Tbsp. **honey**, 2 Tbsp. chopped **scallion** (white and light green parts only), 1½ Tbsp. **apple cider vinegar**, 1 Tbsp. **chipotle chile in adobo sauce** (from 1 [7-oz.] can), 1 minced large **garlic clove**, and ½ tsp. **kosher salt** in a food processor until smooth, 1 minute. Brush mixture evenly over Classic Grilled Corn. Return corn to lit side of grill. Grill, uncovered, until glaze is warmed through and adheres to corn, 4 to 5 minutes. Arrange grilled corn on a platter, and sprinkle evenly with ¼ cup finely chopped **fresh chives**.

Smoky Barbecue Rub

ACTIVE 10 MIN. - TOTAL 15 MIN.
SERVES 6

Stir together 2 Tbsp. **dark brown sugar**; 1 Tbsp. **smoked paprika**; 1 tsp. fresh **lime zest**; and ½ tsp. each of **ancho chile powder**, **kosher salt**, **black pepper**, and **garlic powder** in a small bowl. Sprinkle mixture evenly over Classic Grilled Corn. Return corn to lit side of grill. Grill, uncovered, turning occasionally, until sugar is melted, 4 to 5 minutes. Arrange grilled corn on a platter, and serve with lime wedges.

Tortellini with a Twist

This pasta salad with chicken and fresh veggies is great for dinner and even better for lunch

Chicken-Tortellini Salad with Basil Vinaigrette

Prep this recipe a day in advance. Make and refrigerate the vinaigrette. Mix the salad ingredients (except for the arugula and pecans) in a large bowl; cover and refrigerate. Before eating, dress the tortellini mixture, stir in the arugula, and top with pecans.

ACTIVE 20 MIN. - TOTAL 20 MIN.
SERVES 6

- ¼ cup white balsamic vinegar
- ⅛ tsp. black pepper
- ¾ tsp. kosher salt, divided
- ⅓ cup extra-virgin olive oil
- 2 Tbsp. chopped fresh basil
- 2 (9-oz.) pkg. refrigerated cheese-filled tortellini, cooked according to pkg. directions, rinsed in cool water, and drained
- 2 cups shredded rotisserie chicken
- 1 cup halved cherry tomatoes
- ½ cup drained and rinsed black-eyed peas (from 1 [15½-oz.] can)
- ½ cup fresh corn kernels (from 1 ear)
- 1 cup baby arugula
- 3 Tbsp. chopped toasted pecans

1. Whisk together balsamic vinegar, pepper, and ½ teaspoon of the kosher salt in a small bowl until combined. Gradually add olive oil in a slow, steady stream, whisking constantly until smooth. Stir in basil, and set aside.

2. Gently toss together cooked tortellini, chicken, tomatoes, peas, corn, and remaining ¼ teaspoon kosher salt in a large bowl. Gently stir in basil vinaigrette, and fold in arugula. Sprinkle with pecans.

Nutritional information: Calories: 499; Protein: 29g; Carbs: 45g; Fiber: 5g; Fat; 24g

Berry Delicious

With a press-in cracker crust, this beautiful tart is a snap to make

Black-and-Blue Buttermilk Tart

ACTIVE 25 MIN. - TOTAL 55 MIN., PLUS 8 HOURS CHILLING

SERVES 8 TO 10

- 56 round buttery crackers (such as Ritz; from 2 sleeves)
- 1 large egg white
- ¼ cup unsalted butter, melted
- ½ cup, plus 3 Tbsp. granulated sugar, divided
- ¾ cup heavy cream
- 1 large vanilla bean pod
- 1¼ tsp. unflavored gelatin (from 1 [¼-oz.] envelope)
- 1½ (8-oz.) pkg. cream cheese, softened
- ¾ cup whole buttermilk
- ¼ tsp. kosher salt
- 1½ cups fresh blackberries
- 1½ cups fresh blueberries
  Small fresh basil leaves

1. Preheat oven to 350°F. Pulse crackers in a food processor until finely ground, 6 to 8 times. Add egg white, butter, and 3 tablespoons of the sugar. Pulse until well combined, about 4 times.

2. Scatter crumb mixture evenly on bottom of a 9- or 10-inch tart pan with removable bottom. Using a straight-sided glass or dry measuring cup, firmly press crumbs on bottom and against sides of pan.

3. Bake crust in preheated oven until golden brown around the edges, 12 to 14 minutes. Cool completely on a wire rack, about 30 minutes.

4. Meanwhile, pour cream into a small saucepan. Using a small knife, split the vanilla bean lengthwise. Using back of knife, scrape seeds from bean into cream; discard pod. Sprinkle gelatin evenly over cream. Let stand 5 minutes. Stir in remaining ½ cup sugar. Cook over medium-low, stirring constantly, until gelatin and sugar are dissolved, 4 to 5 minutes.

PICK YOUR PAN

If you don't have a tart pan, use a 9-inch pie plate. The crust will be a bit shallower but will still look and taste great.

5. Transfer cream mixture to food processor. Pinch cream cheese into 1- to 2-inch pieces, and place in food processor. Add buttermilk and salt. Process mixture until smooth, 20 to 30 seconds; pour into cooled tart crust. Chill until set, 8 hours or up to 1 day. Before serving, scatter berries over top; garnish with basil leaves.

FAST & FRESH

Perfect Summer Party Dip

A cross between salsa verde and guacamole that's almost as easy as opening a jar

Charred Tomatillo–Avocado Salsa

ACTIVE 10 MIN. - TOTAL 15 MIN.
MAKES 1 CUP

Place 2 unpeeled medium **garlic cloves** on unoiled grill grates over medium-high heat (400°F to 450°F). Grill, covered, until charred and softened, about 2 minutes. Remove from grill. Place 1 lb. husked fresh **tomatillos;** 1 medium-size ripe **avocado,** halved lengthwise; 1 small **white onion,** cut into 4 wedges; and 1 medium **jalapeño chile** on unoiled grates. Grill, covered, until charred and tender, about 4 minutes. Remove from grill; cool 5 minutes. Remove and discard garlic skins and jalapeño seeds. Transfer all ingredients to a blender. Add 1 cup fresh **cilantro** leaves, 2 Tbsp. fresh **lime juice,** 1¾ tsp. **kosher salt,** 1 tsp. ground **cumin,** and ¼ tsp. **black pepper.** Process until nearly smooth, about 30 seconds.

HOW-TO

Master the Plank

Four steps for infusing seafood, meat, and veggies with wood-fired flavor

SOAK
Place the plank in a baking dish filled with water. Top with a heavy glass to keep it submerged. Soak 1 hour.

CHAR
Set the saturated plank on a hot unoiled grill. Allow the plank to char on 1 side, about 3 minutes. Flip it, and then place the food on the charred side.

GRILL
Close the grill lid, and let the food cook, covered, as directed. Don't touch or flip once it is on the plank.

CLEAN
Use a scouring pad and hot water to scrub off any food residue. Do not use soap. Allow the plank to dry completely before reusing it.

GRILLING GEAR

Holy Smoke!

An eco-friendly new charcoal

Athens, Georgia-based Fire & Flavor makes all-natural charcoal that's sustainably harvested from almond and olive trees. Both give a woodsy aroma to grilled and smoked foods, with no added chemicals.

Lump Charcoals, Almond or Olive Wood, $35 for an 8-pound bag; fireandflavor.com

August

144   **Just Add Fizz**   Southern bakers know that soft drinks have long been the key to some of our most beloved cake recipes

150   **5-Ingredient Suppers**   Produce fresh from the farmers' market plus a few pantry staples prove less really is more

155   **Berry Good Breakfast**   Raspberry, blueberry, blackberry—whip up these cornmeal muffins with any combination you have on hand

156   **Fresh from the Garden**   Late-summer tomatoes and basil add vibrant flavor to this one-pan dinner

157   **Break Out the Broccoli**   A satisfying salad that's simple to make, giving you more family time

158   **Peaches and Cream**   Layers of ice cream, pound cake, and fruit hit the spot on a hot day

159   **SL Cooking School**   Our Test Kitchen professionals show how pantry items add great flavor and save prep time

WARM IT UP
For an extra-moist cake, make sure the cola is hot when you add it to the batter.

COCA-COLA LAYER CAKE WITH FUDGY COLA FROSTING (RECIPE, PAGE 146)

Just Add Fizz

Southern bakers know that soft drinks have long been the key to some of our most beloved cake recipes. Author Toni Tipton-Martin delves into the history behind this sweet tradition

With the exception of 7UP and RC Cola cakes, few recipes for baking with soft drinks were part of my childhood in Southern California. I wondered why, and after examining more than 375 black-authored cookbooks for my book, *The Jemima Code: Two Centuries of African American Cookbooks*, I now know that cakes made with bubbly soft drinks are totems of Southern cooking. They rely, for the most part, on beverages invented and manufactured in this region: Coca-Cola (Georgia), Dr Pepper (Texas), 7UP (Missouri), Nehi (Georgia), and Cheerwine (North Carolina). Most African-American cookbooks that came into print during the soft drink industry's heyday did so in the North and West.

Baking from scratch wasn't always the "piece of cake" it is today. Before the advent of baking powder, it was a nuanced and temperamental art. Victorian cooks leavened cakes with a variety of agents—pearl ash, made of hardwood ashes; saleratus, which predated baking soda; large quantities of beaten eggs; or a chemist's formula for baking powder (mixing baking soda and cream of tartar). All of that required knowledge, thoughtful measuring and combining, and astute observation skills—not to mention strong muscles. Room-temperature butter had to be "rubbed to a cream" in an "earthen" bowl and the remaining batter ingredients beaten until soft and creamy using a wooden cake spoon with slits, a silver spoon, or a wooden paddle.

Baking with carbonated beverages offered several handy shortcuts. Whether invented by home cooks in response to wartime sugar rationing, fierce marketing by manufacturers, or abstinence from alcohol, adding soft drinks to desserts intensifies sweetness and creates airiness without chemical leavening—a labor-saving measure.

Mid-20th-century food manufacturers capitalized upon this history, selling effort-saving ingredients, such as cake mix, condensed milk, marshmallows, wafer cookies, and soft drinks to housewives. Companies distributed "back of the box" recipes, booklets, and brochures and pushed stories in women's magazines that replaced cooking liquids in familiar dishes with effervescent beverages. Sometimes the substitution—as in cola barbecue sauce—was obvious. In other cases, like baked goods, it was less so.

When I was food editor at *The Plain Dealer* in Cleveland, Ohio, I purchased a divine slice of pound cake at a church bake sale and saved a small piece to share with my husband, Bruce. When I got home, the napkin cradling the cake was saturated with sweet butter. He begged me to find the woman who had baked that incredibly moist treat. I couldn't, so instead, I spent the next several years trying to duplicate its puddinglike center and crisp crust. To ease my frustration, a cousin offered up her instructions for classic 7UP cake, which came very close. Eventually, I remembered a pound cake recipe my grandmother had scribbled years earlier on one of those little sample cards that department store clerks spray with perfume. I combined the two recipes, and today, that 7UP cake keeps my husband whooping and hollering like a spirit-filled preacher.

7UP BUNDT CAKE
(RECIPE, PAGE 146)

7UP Bundt Cake

Baked goods made with soft drinks can be traced back to the 1930s and 1940s, according to food expert Lynne Olver. On her website, Food Timeline, she cited early recipes like Ginger Ale Icebox Cake and Raisin Cake Made with Pepsi-Cola. Soda has popped up in all sorts of recipes, with 7UP cake being one of the most famous. The effervescence of 7UP produces a lighter crumb in pound cakes made from scratch and gives packaged cake mix a mild lemon flavor. Some may disagree, but I'm one of those purists who reject suggestions to substitute any other brand of lemon-lime soda. Photo, page 145

ACTIVE 45 MIN. - TOTAL 4 HOURS
SERVES 12

> Vegetable shortening, for greasing pan
> 3 cups all-purpose flour, plus more for pan
> 1½ cups butter, softened
> 2½ cups granulated sugar
> 5 large eggs
> 1 Tbsp. lemon zest plus 1 Tbsp. fresh juice (from 2 lemons)
> 1 Tbsp. lime zest (from 3 limes)
> 1 tsp. vanilla extract
> 1 cup lemon-lime soft drink (such as 7UP)
> Lemon-Lime Cream Cheese Frosting (recipe follows)
> Sugared Lemon-Lime Zest (recipe follows)

1. Preheat oven to 350°F. Grease and flour a 14- to 16-cup Bundt pan. Beat butter in a stand mixer fitted with a paddle attachment on medium speed until creamy, about 2 minutes. Gradually add sugar, beating on medium speed until light and fluffy, 3 to 5 minutes. Add eggs, 1 at a time, beating until just blended after each addition. Add lemon zest, lemon juice, lime zest, and vanilla; beat on low speed until just blended, about 30 seconds. Add flour to butter mixture alternately with soft drink, beginning and ending with flour, beating until just blended after each addition.

2. Pour batter into prepared pan. Bake in preheated oven until a wooden pick inserted in center of cake comes out clean, 1 hour to 1 hour and 15 minutes, loosely tenting pan with aluminum foil after about 45 minutes to prevent excessive browning.

3. Cool cake in pan on a wire rack 10 minutes. Remove from pan. Transfer to wire rack, and let cool completely, 2 hours.

4. Spoon Lemon-Lime Cream Cheese Frosting into a piping bag or heavy-duty ziplock plastic bag. Cut a 1-inch hole in corner of bag, and pipe frosting in a roped pattern over top and sides of cake. Top cake with Sugared Lemon-Lime Zest.

Lemon-Lime Cream Cheese Frosting

ACTIVE 10 MIN. - TOTAL 10 MIN.
MAKES ABOUT 2 CUPS

Beat 6 oz. softened **cream cheese** and 6 Tbsp. softened **butter** with an electric mixer on medium speed until fluffy, about 2 minutes. Gradually add 3 cups sifted **powdered sugar**, beating on low speed until combined, 1 minute. Add 1½ tsp. **fresh lime juice** (from 1 lime), 1 tsp. **lemon zest**, and 1½ tsp. **fresh lemon juice** (from 1 lemon), beating until combined, about 30 seconds.

Sugared Lemon-Lime Zest

ACTIVE 15 MIN. - TOTAL 1 HOUR
MAKES ABOUT 1 CUP

Bring ½ cup **lemon-lime soft drink (such as 7UP)** and ¼ cup **granulated sugar** to a boil in a small saucepan over medium-high. Boil, undisturbed, until reduced by half, 5 to 7 minutes. Remove from heat; cool completely, about 20 minutes. Meanwhile, zest 2 **large lemons** and 2 **large limes** using a channel knife (or citrus zester if larger pieces are desired); reserve fruit for another use. Dip zest into cooled soft drink syrup using a small fine-mesh strainer, letting excess syrup drain from zest. Place 1½ cups **sanding sugar** in a bowl; toss dipped zest into sanding sugar (a few at a time). Transfer sugared zest to parchment paper in a single layer. Let stand until dry, about 30 minutes.

Coca-Cola Layer Cake with Fudgy Cola Frosting

Coca-Cola cake was a favorite at family reunions during the 1950s. It resembles Mississippi mud cake, a chocolate sheet cake studded with marshmallows that are sprinkled on the top before baking or immediately after while the cake is still hot. In Mama's Tea Cakes: 101 Delicious Soul Food Desserts, chef and author Wilbert Jones stirred the marshmallows into the batter before putting his version of the cake in the oven. If that wasn't decadent enough, in 1997, the Cracker Barrel restaurant chain used twice the cocoa, intensifying the taste. Their rendition was called Double Chocolate Fudge Coca-Cola Cake. Photo, page 144

ACTIVE 35 MIN. - TOTAL 2 HOURS, 10 MIN.
SERVES 12

> 2 cups all-purpose flour, plus more for pans
> 1½ cups (9 oz.) semisweet chocolate chips
> 1 cup granulated sugar
> 1 cup packed light brown sugar
> ½ cup butter, softened
> 3 large eggs
> 1 tsp. baking soda
> ½ tsp. salt
> 1 (8-oz.) container sour cream
> 1 cup cola soft drink (such as Coca-Cola)
> 1 tsp. vanilla extract
> Fudgy Cola Frosting (recipe follows)
> Assorted sizes of white sugar pearls

1. Preheat oven to 350°F. Coat 2 (9-inch) round baking pans with cooking spray; dust with flour. Microwave chocolate chips in a microwavable bowl on MEDIUM (50%) until melted and smooth, about 2 minutes, stopping to stir every 30 seconds.

2. Beat granulated sugar, brown sugar, and butter with a stand mixer fitted with a paddle attachment on medium speed until well blended, about 4 minutes. Add eggs, 1 at a time, beating until just blended after each addition. Add melted chocolate, beating until just blended.

3. Sift together flour, baking soda, and salt in a bowl; gradually add to butter mixture alternately with sour cream, beginning and ending with flour mixture, beating on low speed until just blended after each addition.

4. Place cola in a microwavable cup; microwave on HIGH until hot, about 45 seconds. Gradually add cola to flour-butter mixture in a slow, steady stream, beating on low speed until just blended. Beat in vanilla. Pour batter evenly into prepared pans.

5. Bake in preheated oven until a wooden pick inserted in centers of cakes comes out clean, 33 to 36 minutes. Cool in pans on wire racks 10 minutes. Remove cakes from pans. Transfer to wire racks, and cool completely, about 1 hour.

6. Spread Fudgy Cola Frosting between cake layers and on top and sides of cake. Garnish with sugar pearls.

Fudgy Cola Frosting

ACTIVE 15 MIN. - TOTAL 15 MIN.
MAKES ABOUT 3½ CUPS

Beat 1 cup softened **butter** with an electric mixer on medium speed until creamy, about 2 minutes. Sift together 6 cups **powdered sugar**, ⅓ cup **unsweetened cocoa**, and ¼ tsp. **salt** in a bowl. Stir together 1 tsp. **vanilla extract** and 5 tablespoons **cola soft drink (such as Coca-Cola)** in a small bowl. Add powdered sugar mixture to butter alternately with vanilla mixture, beginning and ending with powdered sugar mixture, beating on low speed until just blended after each addition. If needed, beat in 1 additional tablespoon **cola**, 1 teaspoon at a time, until desired consistency is reached.

Dr Pepper Texas Sheet Cake

Chocolate sheet cakes were popular among early 20th-century cooks from Kentucky to California. Dr Pepper cake takes its cues from those recipes. Fragrant with spices like ground cinnamon, cloves, and nutmeg and topped with a chocolate frosting that's speckled with pecans, it may remind some of Texas sheet cake. For nearly 20 years, I baked a version of this sweet treat to celebrate the birthday of a friend and neighbor from Wichita Falls, Texas, who was haunted (in a good way) by her childhood memories of the delicious dessert.

ACTIVE 20 MIN. - TOTAL 2 HOURS, 5 MIN.
SERVES 16

DR PEPPER TEXAS
SHEET CAKE

SHEET CAKE
- 1½ cups spicy, fruity cola soft drink (such as Dr Pepper)
- 1 cup butter
- ½ cup unsweetened cocoa
- 2 cups all-purpose flour
- 2 cups granulated sugar
- 1½ tsp. baking soda
- 1 tsp. ground cinnamon
- ½ tsp. salt
- 2 large eggs, lightly beaten
- ½ cup whole buttermilk
- 2 tsp. vanilla extract

RICH FUDGE ICING
- ½ cup butter
- ¼ cup unsweetened cocoa
- ¼ cup spicy, fruity cola soft drink (such as Dr Pepper)
- 2 Tbsp. whole milk
- 4 cups powdered sugar, sifted
- 1 tsp. vanilla extract

ADDITIONAL INGREDIENT
- 1½ cups coarsely chopped toasted pecans

1. Prepare the Sheet Cake: Preheat oven to 350°F. Coat a 17½- x 12½-inch rimmed baking sheet with cooking spray. Bring cola, butter, and unsweetened cocoa to a boil in a medium saucepan over medium-high, stirring often. Remove from heat.

2. Whisk together flour, sugar, baking soda, cinnamon, and salt in a large bowl. Add cola mixture; whisk until blended. Whisk in eggs, buttermilk, and vanilla. Pour batter into prepared baking sheet. Bake in preheated oven until a wooden pick inserted in center of cake comes out clean, 16 to 20 minutes. Remove from oven.

3. Prepare the Rich Fudge Icing: Cook butter and cocoa in a medium saucepan over medium-low, whisking often, until butter melts and mixture is smooth, about 1 minute. Reduce heat to low; whisk in cola and milk until blended. Gradually add powdered sugar, whisking constantly until blended. Whisk in vanilla.

4. Pour warm icing over warm cake; gently spread in an even layer. Sprinkle with pecans. Cool completely in baking sheet on a wire rack, about 1 hour.

NEHI ORANGE
POKE CAKE

Nehi Orange Poke Cake

Orange flavor turns up often in African-American cookbooks, whether the cook enlivens biscuits with a bit of sweet citrus juice or uses it to make pecan pie extra special. Mildred "Mama Dip" Council included two recipes for orange-flavored cake in Mama Dip's Family Cookbook, *her collection of recipes and reminiscences. One is a rich butter cake laced with fresh juice and grated zest. The other relies on an orange cake mix that's "doctored up" with Mountain Dew. The poke cake featured here, inspired by the latter, is filled with a tangy citrus curd made with Nehi orange-flavored soda.*

ACTIVE 40 MIN. - TOTAL 2 HOURS, 30 MIN.
SERVES 16

SHEET CAKE
Vegetable shortening,
for greasing pan
All-purpose flour, for pan
2 large eggs
1 (15¼-oz.) pkg. white cake mix

1 (8-oz.) container sour cream
¼ cup salted butter, melted
1 tsp. vanilla extract
NEHI ORANGE CURD
1¾ cups granulated sugar
½ cup butter, softened
4 large eggs
2 large egg yolks
¾ cup orange soft drink (such as Nehi)
¼ cup fresh lemon juice (from 2 lemons)
1 Tbsp. orange zest (from 1 orange)
3 or 4 drops orange food coloring gel
MASCARPONE-WHIPPED CREAM FROSTING
1 (8-oz.) container mascarpone cheese
½ cup unsifted powdered sugar
2 tsp. vanilla extract
2 cups heavy cream, divided
GARNISH
Orange slices

1. Prepare the Sheet Cake: Preheat oven to 350°F. Grease and flour a 9- x 13-inch baking pan. Beat eggs, cake mix, sour cream, melted butter, and vanilla extract with a stand mixer fitted with a paddle attachment on low speed until dry ingredients are just moistened, about 1 minute. Increase speed to medium. Beat until batter is smooth, about 2 minutes, stopping to scrape down bottom and sides of bowl as needed. Spoon batter into prepared pan; spread into an even layer. Bake in preheated oven until a wooden pick inserted in center comes out clean, 20 to 22 minutes. Cool in pan on a wire rack 20 minutes.

2. Meanwhile, prepare the Nehi Orange Curd: Beat sugar and butter with an electric mixer on medium speed until blended, about 1 minute. Add eggs and egg yolks, 1 at a time, beating until just blended after each addition. Gradually add soft drink and lemon juice to butter mixture, beating on low speed until just blended; stir in orange zest. (Mixture will look curdled.) Transfer mixture to a heavy 4-quart saucepan. Cook over medium-low, whisking constantly, until mixture thickens and coats the back of a spoon, 14 to 16 minutes. Remove from heat; stir in food coloring gel. (Use while mixture is still hot or very warm.)

3. Using a wooden dowel or round handle of a wooden spoon, poke holes over entire cake surface (spaced 1 to 2 inches apart), being careful not to poke all the way to the bottom. Pour warm curd mixture over cake, being sure to fill all holes and smoothing excess curd mixture evenly over surface. Let stand 30 minutes. Transfer to refrigerator; chill until completely cool, about 1 hour.

4. Prepare the Mascarpone-Whipped Cream Frosting: Whisk together mascarpone cheese, sugar, vanilla, and ¼ cup of the heavy cream in a large bowl until just blended. (Don't overmix.) Beat remaining 1¾ cups heavy cream with an electric mixer on medium-high speed until stiff peaks form, about 1 minute. Gently fold whipped cream into mascarpone mixture.

5. Spread frosting evenly over chilled cake; chill until ready to serve. Garnish with orange slices just before serving.

Cheerwine Cherry Cupcakes with Cherry-Swirl Frosting

Cheerwine is a cherry-flavored soda invented in North Carolina in 1917. Whether you combine the bubbly drink with a recipe for homemade white cake or pound cake or a packaged cake mix, the result is a pale pink crumb that tastes of almond extract and mild cherry. This regional drink is so popular that the Apple Baking Company of Salisbury, North Carolina (known for its packaged pound cake slices and "Ugly" glazed pastries), experimented with a cake flavored with Cheerwine syrup and soda, which it sold in 2009. The following year, doughnuts filled with Cheerwine-flavored cream debuted at Krispy Kreme in North Carolina.

ACTIVE 30 MIN. - TOTAL 2 HOURS, 15 MIN.
MAKES 24

- 1 (15¼-oz.) pkg. white cake mix
- ½ cup all-purpose flour
- ¼ cup granulated sugar
- 1 Tbsp. cherry-flavored gelatin (from 1 [3-oz.] envelope)
- 4 large eggs
- ¾ cup liquid coconut oil (such as LouAna)
- ½ cup cherry soft drink (such as Cheerwine)
- ½ cup finely chopped stemmed maraschino cherries, patted dry
- Cherry-Swirl Frosting (recipe follows)
- Pink food coloring gel
- Maraschino cherries, stems removed

1. Preheat oven to 350°F. Line 2 (12-cup) muffin pans with paper baking cups; coat with cooking spray. Whisk together cake mix, flour, sugar, and gelatin in a bowl; transfer mixture to bowl of a heavy-duty stand mixer fitted with a paddle attachment. Add eggs, coconut oil, and soft drink; beat on low speed 1 minute. Stop to scrape down sides. Beat on medium speed an additional 2 minutes, stopping to scrape down sides as needed. Stir in chopped maraschino cherries by hand until fully incorporated. Spoon batter evenly into prepared baking cups, filling each cup about two-thirds full.
2. Bake in preheated oven until a wooden pick inserted in centers of cupcakes comes out clean, 22 to 25 minutes. Cool in pans on wire racks 10 minutes. Remove cupcakes from pans. Transfer to wire racks, and cool completely, about 1 hour.
3. Divide Cherry-Swirl Frosting evenly between 2 bowls. Stir 1 or 2 drops food coloring gel into 1 frosting bowl until incorporated. Fit a large pastry bag with a large star tip (Wilton #2110). Spoon pink-tinted frosting into half of bag; spoon untinted frosting into remaining half of bag. Pipe frosting onto cupcakes, and top each with 1 maraschino cherry.

Cherry-Swirl Frosting

ACTIVE 10 MIN. - TOTAL 10 MIN.
MAKES ABOUT 3 CUPS

Beat 1 cup softened **butter** with a heavy-duty stand mixer fitted with a paddle attachment on medium speed until creamy, about 2 minutes. Gradually add 6 cups sifted **powdered sugar**, 3 Tbsp. **cherry soft drink (such as Cheerwine)**, and ¼ tsp. **salt**, beating until blended, about 3 minutes. Beat in 1 to 3 tsp. **whole milk**, ½ teaspoon at a time, until desired consistency is reached.

GIVE IT A SWIRL
Combine two frosting colors in one piping bag for a fancy look.

CHEERWINE CHERRY CUPCAKES WITH CHERRY-SWIRL FROSTING

5-Ingredient Suppers

Produce fresh from the farmers' market plus a few pantry staples prove less really is more

GRILLED SALMON
PANZANELLA SALAD

Grilled Salmon Panzanella Salad

ACTIVE 30 MIN. - TOTAL 30 MIN.
SERVES 6

- 6 Tbsp. sherry vinegar
- 6 Tbsp. extra-virgin olive oil
- 1 tsp. kosher salt, divided
- ½ tsp. black pepper, divided
- 4 (6-oz.) skin-on salmon fillets
- 5 (2-oz.) day-old rustic bread loaf slices (about 1 inch thick)
- 2 pt. multicolored cherry tomatoes, halved
- 4 cups loosely packed fresh baby spinach

1. Whisk together vinegar, oil, ½ teaspoon of the salt, and ¼ teaspoon of the pepper in a small bowl. Reserve 2 tablespoons vinegar mixture in a separate small bowl.
2. Heat a grill pan over medium-high. Brush salmon fillets evenly with reserved 2 tablespoons vinegar mixture. Add salmon, skin sides down, to grill pan; cook 5 minutes. Flip salmon, and cook 2 to 3 minutes or to desired degree of doneness. Transfer salmon to a plate; remove and discard skin.
3. Add bread slices to grill pan; cook until toasted and grill marks appear, 2 to 3 minutes per side. Transfer bread to a cutting board; cut into 1-inch cubes.
4. Stir together bread cubes, tomatoes, and remaining vinegar mixture, ½ teaspoon salt, and ¼ teaspoon pepper in a bowl until combined. Break salmon into bite-size pieces. Gently fold salmon and spinach into bread mixture. Serve at room temperature.

Easy Steak Fajitas

ACTIVE 30 MIN. - TOTAL 1 HOUR, 35 MIN.
SERVES 6

- 2½ tsp. fajita seasoning
- 1 tsp. lime zest plus 3 Tbsp. fresh juice (from 2 limes)
- ¼ tsp. black pepper
- ¼ cup, plus 2 Tbsp. olive oil, divided
- 1 tsp. kosher salt, divided
- 1 (1½-lb.) flank steak (1½ to 2 inches thick), trimmed
- 1 (14-oz.) container sliced fresh onion-and-bell pepper mix

EASY STEAK FAJITAS

TOP YOUR OWN
Let everyone customize their fajitas by setting out an assortment of toppings such as fresh cilantro, guacamole, salsa, and sour cream.

- 12 (5- to 6-inch) corn tortillas, warmed

1. Stir together fajita seasoning, lime zest and juice, black pepper, ¼ cup of the oil, and ½ teaspoon of the salt in a small bowl. Reserve 2 tablespoons fajita marinade in a separate bowl, and set aside. Place steak in a 1-gallon ziplock plastic bag. Pour in remaining fajita marinade, and seal bag. Marinate in refrigerator at least 1 hour or up to 4 hours, turning and massaging marinade into meat in sealed bag occasionally.
2. Heat 1 tablespoon of the oil in a large cast-iron skillet over high. Add onion-and-bell pepper mix; cook, stirring often, until slightly softened and caramelized, about 6 minutes. Sprinkle with remaining ½ teaspoon salt; stir in reserved 2 tablespoons fajita marinade. Cook, stirring constantly, 1 minute. Transfer onion mixture to a plate; cover with aluminum foil to keep warm. Wipe skillet clean.
3. Add remaining 1 tablespoon oil to skillet; heat over high. Remove steak from marinade, allowing any excess to drip off; discard marinade. Add steak to skillet; cook to desired degree of doneness, 5 to 6 minutes per side for medium-rare. Transfer to a cutting board. Tent with aluminum foil, and let rest 5 minutes.
4. Thinly slice steak across the grain, and arrange on a platter. Place onion mixture alongside steak. Serve with warm tortillas.

Smoky Grilled BLTs

ACTIVE 25 MIN. - TOTAL 25 MIN.
SERVES 4

- 8 thick-cut hickory-smoked bacon slices
- 8 5-grain bread slices (about 1 inch thick)
- 3 small (5- to 6-oz.) tomatoes, cut into ½-inch-thick slices
- 5 Tbsp. plus 1 tsp. mayonnaise
- 8 butter lettuce leaves (from 1 head)
- ½ tsp. kosher salt
- ½ tsp. black pepper

1. Preheat grill to medium-high (400°F to 450°F). Place a 12-inch cast-iron skillet or grill pan on grill grates. Working in 2 batches, add bacon to skillet. Cook, turning occasionally, until crisp, 7 to 8 minutes per batch. Transfer bacon to a plate lined with paper towels; let cool 2 minutes. Break each bacon slice in half. Remove skillet from grill; reserve 4 tablespoons drippings.
2. Brush reserved drippings evenly onto 1 side of bread slices. Place bread, greased sides down, on unoiled grates. Grill, uncovered, until lightly toasted, 2 to 3 minutes. Transfer bread to a plate; cover with aluminum foil to keep warm.
3. Place tomato slices on oiled grates. Grill, uncovered, until warmed and faint grill marks appear, about 30 seconds per side. Remove from grill.
4. Spread mayonnaise evenly onto the ungrilled sides of bread slices. Top 4 bread slices evenly (mayonnaise sides up) with bacon pieces, tomato slices, and lettuce. Sprinkle evenly with salt and pepper. Top with remaining 4 bread slices, mayonnaise sides down.

BUILD THE BEST BLT
How do you improve on the classic sandwich? Grill it. Cook the bacon outside, char the tomatoes, and toast the bread.

Creamy Pesto-and-Shrimp Penne with Peas

ACTIVE 25 MIN. - TOTAL 25 MIN.
SERVES 6

- 12 oz. uncooked penne
- 1 lb. medium-size peeled, deveined raw shrimp
- 1 cup frozen sweet peas
- 1 (7-oz.) container refrigerated basil pesto
- ¼ tsp. kosher salt
- ¼ tsp. black pepper
- 1 oz. Parmesan cheese, shaved (about ½ cup)

1. Prepare pasta according to package directions in a pot of salted boiling water, adding shrimp and peas to water during final 2 minutes of cook time. Drain pasta mixture, reserving ½ cup cooking water in a small heatproof bowl. Return pasta mixture to pot.
2. Add pesto, salt, and pepper to pasta mixture; stir to combine. Stir in reserved cooking water as needed, ¼ cup at a time, until desired consistency is reached. Transfer pasta mixture to a serving bowl; sprinkle with Parmesan. Serve immediately.

PICK THE RIGHT PREPARED PESTO
Instead of buying the jarred, shelf-stable version, choose the kind found in the refrigerator case. It tastes fresher and more like homemade.

Chicken Salad–Stuffed Tomatoes

ACTIVE 15 MIN. - TOTAL 15 MIN.
SERVES 6

- 6 large beefsteak tomatoes, (½ to ¾ lb. each)
- 4 cups chopped rotisserie chicken
- 1½ cups chopped tricolor bell pepper mix (from 1 [8-oz.] container)
- ¾ cup mayonnaise
- 2 Tbsp. fresh lemon juice (from 1 lemon)
- 1 tsp. kosher salt
- ½ tsp. black pepper

1. Remove and discard tops of tomatoes; then core and seed them.
2. Stir together next 6 ingredients in a bowl until combined. Spoon about ½ cup mixture into each cored tomato. (Cover and refrigerate leftover chicken salad up to 5 days.)

Berry Good Breakfast

Raspberry, blueberry, blackberry—whip up these cornmeal muffins with any combination you have on hand

"Any-Berry" Muffins with Cornmeal Streusel

ACTIVE 15 MIN. - TOTAL 50 MIN.
MAKES 1 DOZEN

- 1½ tsp. baking powder
- ½ tsp. salt
- 1⅔ cups all-purpose flour, divided
- ⅓ cup, plus 2 Tbsp. plain yellow cornmeal, divided
- 1 cup granulated sugar, divided
- ½ cup unsalted butter, melted and divided
- ½ cup whole-milk buttermilk
- 1 large egg
- 1 large egg yolk
- 1½ tsp. vanilla extract
- 1⅓ cups fresh berries (such as strawberries, blueberries, raspberries, or blackberries)

1. Preheat oven to 425°F. Line a 12-cup muffin pan with 12 paper cupcake liners. Whisk together baking powder, salt, 1⅓ cups of the flour, and ⅓ cup of the cornmeal in a medium bowl; set aside.
2. Stir together ¼ cup of the sugar, 3 tablespoons of the melted butter, and remaining ⅓ cup flour and 2 tablespoons cornmeal in a separate bowl until crumbly; reserve for streusel topping.
3. Whisk together buttermilk, egg and yolk, vanilla, and remaining ¾ cup sugar in a medium bowl until well combined. Make a well in center of flour mixture. Slowly pour buttermilk mixture into flour mixture, stirring with a spatula until just combined (it will be lumpy). Fold in berries and remaining 5 tablespoons melted butter.

4. Scoop batter into prepared pan until each cup is three-fourths full (about 3 tablespoons each). Top each with about 1 tablespoon reserved streusel topping. Bake in preheated oven until a wooden pick inserted in centers comes out clean, about 18 minutes. Remove from oven; cool in pan 5 minutes. Cool muffins on a wire rack, about 10 minutes.

BIGGER ISN'T BETTER

Small berries can be added to the batter whole, but skip or chop the larger ones so the fruit is evenly distributed throughout the muffins.

Fresh from the Garden

Late-summer tomatoes and basil add vibrant flavor to this one-pan dinner

Tomato–Basil Couscous with Chicken and Smoked Sausage

ACTIVE 15 MIN. - TOTAL 25 MIN.
SERVES 4

- 1 Tbsp. olive oil
- 4 (5-oz.) skinless, boneless chicken breasts
- 1¼ tsp. kosher salt, divided
- 1 tsp. black pepper, divided
- 4 oz. smoked turkey sausage, cut into ½-inch-thick slices
- 1½ cups chopped yellow onion (from 1 large onion)
- 5 garlic cloves, chopped
- 1 cup uncooked Israeli couscous
- 1 lb. large cherry tomatoes, halved
- 1¼ cups unsalted chicken stock
- 1 Tbsp. chopped fresh thyme
- 1 cup small fresh basil leaves, divided

1. Heat oil in a large, high-sided skillet with a tight-fitting lid over medium-high. Sprinkle chicken with ¼ teaspoon salt and ½ teaspoon pepper. Add chicken and sausage to skillet; cook until lightly browned on both sides, 5 minutes. Transfer to a plate. (Do not wipe out skillet.)
2. Add onion to skillet; cook, stirring occasionally, until onion is translucent, 3 minutes. Add garlic; stir constantly, 1 minute. Add couscous; stir often until it is toasted, 2 minutes. Return chicken and sausage to skillet; add tomatoes, stock, thyme, ¾ cup of the basil, ¾ teaspoon of the salt, and remaining ½ teaspoon pepper. Cover and bring to a boil over high. Reduce heat to medium; simmer until a thermometer inserted in thickest part of chicken registers 165°F, liquid is absorbed, and couscous is tender, 10 to 12 minutes.
3. Remove chicken from skillet, and let stand 5 minutes. Thinly slice chicken. Stir remaining ¼ teaspoon salt into couscous mixture. Spoon into shallow bowls; top with chicken and remaining ¼ cup basil.

Nutritional information: Calories 496; Protein 46g; Carbs 53g; Fiber 5g; Fat 11g

PEARLS OF WISDOM
Israeli couscous (also called pearl couscous) is best for this dish because the round, toothsome grains take the same amount of time to cook as the chicken, unlike Moroccan couscous, which is much smaller.

Break Out the Broccoli

A satisfying salad that's simple to make, giving you more family time

Crispy Chicken-and-Broccoli Salad

ACTIVE 15 MIN. - TOTAL 15 MIN., PLUS 2 HOURS CHILLING

SERVES 4 TO 6

- 2 Tbsp. honey
- 2 Tbsp. apple cider vinegar
- 1 Tbsp. Dijon mustard
- 1 tsp. kosher salt
- ½ tsp. black pepper
- ⅔ cup olive oil
- 5 cups broccoli florets
- 1½ cups seedless grapes, halved
- 4 oz. sharp Cheddar cheese, grated (about 1 cup)
- ¾ cup sliced almonds, toasted
- ½ cup thinly sliced red onion (from 1 small red onion)
- 5 fried chicken tenders, coarsely chopped (about 4 cups)

Whisk together honey, vinegar, mustard, salt, and pepper in a large bowl until blended and smooth. Drizzle in oil, whisking until emulsified, 30 seconds. Stir in broccoli, grapes, cheese, almonds, and onion. Cover; chill at least 2 hours or up to overnight. Stir in chicken before serving.

SAVE THE STEMS

Broccoli stems are as tasty as the florets. Trim off and discard the bottom 2 inches, and then slice the rest into thin coins.

Peaches and Cream

Layers of ice cream, pound cake, and fruit hit the spot on a hot day

Creamy Peach Icebox Cake

ACTIVE 20 MIN. - TOTAL 20 MIN., PLUS 8 HOURS
FREEZING
SERVES 8

2	(10¾-oz.) frozen pound cakes, thawed
1	(10-oz.) jar peach preserves, divided
1	qt. vanilla ice cream, slightly softened
1	cup heavy cream
½	tsp. vanilla extract
3	Tbsp. powdered sugar
1	cup peeled fresh peach slices

1. Trim brown crusts from pound cakes using a serrated knife. Discard crusts. Cut each cake into ½-inch-thick slices. (You will have 18 to 24 slices.) Line bottom and sides of a 9- x 5-inch loaf pan with plastic wrap, allowing a 4-inch overhang on sides. Place 1 tablespoon of the preserves in a microwavable bowl; chill until ready to use.

2. Arrange 6 to 8 cake slices, side by side, to cover bottom of pan in 1 layer (trimming slices, if needed, to fully cover bottom). Spread 2 cups ice cream over cake layer to edges of pan. Spread half of the remaining preserves (about ⅓ cup) evenly over ice cream layer. Repeat process with 6 to 8 remaining cake slices (trimming if needed) and remaining ice cream and preserves. Arrange last 6 to 8 cake slices over preserves layer. Pull plastic wrap overhang up and tightly over cake. Freeze 8 hours.

3. Beat cream and vanilla extract with an electric mixer on high speed until foamy, 30 seconds. Gradually add powdered sugar, beating until stiff peaks form, 1 to 2 minutes.

4. Remove cake from freezer. Holding the plastic wrap overhang, lift cake from pan; invert onto a platter. (Discard plastic wrap.) Spread whipped cream over cake.

5. Heat reserved 1 tablespoon preserves on HIGH until just melted and smooth, 10 to 15 seconds; mash large lumps with a spoon. Gently stir in peach slices to coat. Spoon mixture over cake; serve immediately.

SLICING SECRET
For clean, neat cuts, run hot water over the knife's blade and wipe it with a moist towel every time you make a slice.

COOKING ⟨SL⟩ SCHOOL

TIPS AND TRICKS FROM THE SOUTH'S MOST TRUSTED KITCHEN

Store-Bought Shortcuts

Meals in minutes? Our pros share their in-a-pinch picks

1
TRADER JOE'S ONION SALT

"I sprinkle this stuff on everything. It's the easiest way to spice up plain proteins like skillet pork chops, baked chicken, or even scrambled eggs."

—Karen Rankin

2
ALDI SPECIALLY SELECTED PREMIUM MARINARA

"Homemade marinara is best but not always possible on a weeknight. For about $3, you can't beat the robust flavor of this jarred pasta sauce."

—Paige Grandjean

3
MARZETTI SIMPLY DRESSED CAESAR DRESSING

"This makes a fantastic Caesar salad, but I use it in coleslaw and pasta salads too. If you're grilling, you can also brush the dressing over shrimp or chicken."

—Pam Lolley

4
NEAR EAST ORIGINAL PLAIN COUSCOUS

"I keep at least one box of this tiny pasta in my pantry at all times because there's no faster way to get a starch on everyone's dinner plate. And it tastes great with anything."

—Robby Melvin

The Best Smoked Sausage

Three grocery store options that made the cut

BEST TURKEY: Hillshire Farm Turkey Smoked Sausage
WHY WE LOVE IT: This heat-and-eat sausage is a good addition to red beans or pasta if you're avoiding pork.

BEST PORK: Conecuh Hickory Smoked Sausage
WHY WE LOVE IT: Deep smoky flavor and snappy natural casing make this a Test Kitchen favorite.

BEST CHICKEN: Al Fresco Roasted Pepper & Asiago Chicken Sausage
WHY WE LOVE IT: It's low in fat and sodium, but bold spices keep it from being bland.

Preserving Summer

Upgrade our simple brine recipe with a colorful array of produce

START HERE

Master Pickling Brine

ACTIVE 10 MIN. - TOTAL 20 MIN., PLUS
2 DAYS PICKLING

MAKES 4 CUPS

- ⅔ cup rice vinegar
- ⅔ cup apple cider vinegar
- ⅓ cup granulated sugar
- 2 Tbsp. kosher salt

Stir together 1 cup water and all ingredients in a medium saucepan. Bring to a boil over high, stirring until sugar dissolves. Remove from heat; cool 10 minutes. Pour over vegetables or fruits. Cover with a tight-fitting lid; chill 2 days. Store, covered, in refrigerator up to 2 months.

TURMERIC-DILL CUCUMBERS

Slice 1 lb. **Persian cucumbers** crosswise into ¼-inch-thick rounds. Divide cucumbers and 2 **dill sprigs** between 2 (16-oz.) Mason jars. Prepare **Master Pickling Brine**, adding 1 Tbsp. each **yellow mustard seeds, dill seeds,** and **black peppercorns** plus ½ tsp. **ground turmeric** to brine mixture before bringing to a boil.

TUSCAN CHERRY TOMATOES

Remove and discard stem ends from 1 lb. **red and yellow cherry tomatoes.** Divide tomatoes and 2 small **rosemary sprigs** between 2 (16-oz.) Mason jars. Prepare **Master Pickling Brine**, adding 1 Tbsp. **black peppercorns** and 3 **garlic cloves** to brine mixture before bringing to a boil.

ZESTY OKRA

Divide 10 oz. trimmed **fresh okra** and 2 **mint sprigs** between 2 (16-oz.) Mason jars. Prepare **Master Pickling Brine**, adding ¼ cup thinly sliced **shallot** (from 1 small shallot) and ¼ tsp. **crushed red pepper** to brine mixture before bringing to a boil.

ALL-PURPOSE RED ONIONS

Divide 1 thinly sliced large **red onion** between 2 (16-oz.) Mason jars. Prepare **Master Pickling Brine**, adding 2 **bay leaves** and 1 Tbsp. **caraway seeds** to brine mixture before bringing to a boil.

SPICY GREEN AND YELLOW BEANS

Divide 10 oz. trimmed **fresh green and yellow beans,** 1 (1-oz.) halved and seeded **jalapeño chile,** and 2 **tarragon sprigs** between 2 (16-oz.) Mason jars. Prepare **Master Pickling Brine**, adding 1 Tbsp. **fennel seeds** to brine mixture before bringing to a boil.

FIELD PEA CAKES WITH
TOMATO-GINGER JAM
(PAGE 99)

FIELD PEA-
TOMATO SALAD
WITH LEMON
VINAIGRETTE
(PAGE 100)

SMOKY FIELD PEA-AND-
GREENS DIP (PAGE 101)

163

CLOCKWISE FROM TOP LEFT:

• FIELD PEAS, CORN, AND OKRA IN COUNTRY-HAM CREAM (PAGE 100)

• QUICK SHRIMP-AND-CORN CHOWDER (PAGE 106)

• SHRIMP-AND-BACON STIR-FRY (PAGE 103)

• SHRIMP CAKES WITH SMOKY HORSERADISH SAUCE (PAGE 103)

CREAMY CHICKEN
SPAGHETTI (PAGE 107)

JAMBALAYA SKEWERS
(PAGE 105)

CLOCKWISE FROM TOP LEFT:

• BASIL FRIED RICE WITH BUTTER PEAS (PAGE 117)

• PORK PAILLARDS WITH LEMONY SQUASH SALAD (PAGE 108)

• FAVORITE STRAWBERRY SHORTCAKES (PAGE 109)

GREEN TOMATO SKILLET
PIE (PAGE 113)

YELLOW SQUASH BUNDT
CAKE (PAGE 113)

169

CHOCOLATE-ZUCCHINI
CAKE (PAGE 114)

CORN CUSTARDS WITH
BERRY COMPOTE (PAGE 114)

CLOCKWISE FROM TOP LEFT:

- PICO DE GALLO PORK CHOPS
(PAGE 117)

- GRILLED CHICKEN
WITH QUICK-PICKLED
SQUASH SALAD (PAGE 118)

- SHRIMP-AND-SAUSAGE
SKILLET CORN (PAGE 119)

- PASTA WITH SUMMER BEANS
AND BACON (PAGE 119)

WATERMELON-GINGER MOJITOS
(PAGE 127)

WATERMELON CHIFFON
PIE (PAGE 128)

CHOPPED SALAD WITH
BUTTERMILK DRESSING
(PAGE 132)

OVEN-FRIED ZUCCHINI
STICKS (PAGE 132)

SAUSAGE-AND-SHRIMP
PIZZAS WITH SPINACH-
BASIL PESTO (PAGE 132)

MIXED HERB-AND-
TOMATO SALAD
(PAGE 133)

FOIL-PACK CLAMS WITH
WHITE WINE AND HERBS
(PAGE 133)

GRILLED
GARLIC BREAD
(PAGE 133)

HEIRLOOM TOMATO
PIE WITH PARMESAN-
BUTTERMILK CRUST
(PAGE 136)

CLASSIC GRILLED CORN
(PAGE 139)

BLACK-AND-BLUE
BUTTERMILK TART
(PAGE 141)

COCA-COLA LAYER
CAKE WITH FUDGY COLA
FROSTING (PAGE 146)

7UP BUNDT CAKE
(PAGE 146)

CHEERWINE CHERRY
CUPCAKES WITH
CHERRY-SWIRL FROSTING
(PAGE 149)

DR PEPPER TEXAS SHEET
CAKE (PAGE 147)

CLOCKWISE FROM TOP LEFT:

• GRILLED SALMON
PANZANELLA SALAD
(PAGE 151)

• SMOKY GRILLED BLTS
(PAGE 152)

• CREAMY PESTO-AND-SHRIMP
PENNE WITH PEAS (PAGE 153)

• CHICKEN SALAD-
STUFFED TOMATOES
(PAGE 154)

EASY STEAK FAJITAS
(PAGE 151)

185

CREAMY PEACH ICEBOX
CAKE (PAGE 158)

GINGERY CARROTS
WITH PISTACHIOS AND
COCONUT-BUTTERMILK
SAUCE (PAGE 199)

CLOCKWISE FROM TOP LEFT:

• CURRIED CHICKEN POT PIE
(PAGE 208)

• GREEK STUFFED PEPPERS
(PAGE 208)

• GREEN CHILE-CHICKEN SOUP
(PAGE 207)

• SHRIMP FAJITA BOWLS
(PAGE 207)

SMOKY KIMCHI PIMIENTO
CHEESE (PAGE 202)

BAKED CHICKEN WINGS
WITH PEPPER JELLY GLAZE
(PAGE 204)

BACON-CHEDDAR DUTCH
BABY (PAGE 211)

OLD-FASHIONED APPLE PIE
(PAGE 195)

Apple Pie
•Preheat oven to 425°
•cut (after peeling, coring) about 9/10 appls-
thinly sliced is best 1/8 inch is awesome! Tart
appls- McIntosh is my personal favorite
-mix: 1/2 c. sugar
1/4 c. flour
1 t. cin

Debbie
Hedberg

September

194   **For the Love of Apple Pie**   A Virginia woman set out to find her grandmother's lost recipe and, along the way, discovered so much more than a list of ingredients

196   **Finding Her Groove**   Chef and musician Cheetie Kumar soulfully blends her past with the present at Raleigh, North Carolina's Garland restaurant

202   **Game Day Snack Trays**   Four fun and creative supper ideas for when everyone's hungry and glued to the game

205   **Kickin' Chicken**   A honey-chile sauce makes this dish sing

206   **Fix & Freeze**   Take the pressure off weeknights with five suppers that go from the freezer to the table with ease

210   **Easy, Cheesy Meatballs**   Tender ground turkey lightens up this flavorful one-pan supper

211   **Going Dutch**   Impress your brunch crowd with a savory skillet pancake

212   **SL Cooking School**   Our Test Kitchen professionals suggest frozen products to use in quick weeknight dinners

For the Love of Apple Pie

A Virginia woman set out to find her grandmother's lost recipe and, along the way,
discovered so much more than a list of ingredients

It all started with a memory. Two years ago, Courtney Page Ferrell was contemplating what she would take to her family's annual Thanksgiving dinner in Montpelier, Virginia, and couldn't get an image out of her head. "I had the clearest picture of my grandmother's old pie safe," says Ferrell. "When my sister and I stayed at her house as children, she would wake us up for midnight snacks." The trio would sneak downstairs to the pie safe, a three-shelved wooden cabinet with a glass front and two swinging doors used for storing pies. "Sometimes it was homemade peach or chocolate, but my favorite was her apple. She'd cut a thick slice and top it with PET vanilla ice

cream, and I thought there was no better treat in the whole world," she recalls.

Her grandmother, Madge Wickham Page, was a country woman who was soft to hug and easy with a laugh. She could shell a pea and milk a cow better than most and spent her time in the dairy barn or volunteering at the hospital. Determined to honor her grandmother by bringing her apple pie to the holiday dinner, Ferrell sent out requests to family members, hoping one of them would uncover a timeworn recipe card "from the kitchen of Madge Page," bearing her unmistakable handwriting. But no one had it.

One fall afternoon, she spotted a "Lost Dog" sign on a telephone pole

in her neighborhood and had an idea. "You can't see a 'Lost Dog' sign and not want to help bring that pet home where it belongs," says Ferrell, a creative consultant and sought-after speaker who champions the power of human connections. "I went home, made 'Lost Pie' signs, and began hanging them all over Richmond. I thought there was a chance someone in town knew my grandmother, or someone of her generation might have shared a similar recipe. I would know it when I tasted it."

The signs, which read: "Lost: My Grandmother's Apple Pie Recipe," solicited strangers to send their grandmothers' renditions. When Ferrell traveled for work, she posted signs in other cities across the South, from Dallas to New Orleans. Slowly, the letters (addressed to "Apple Pie") trickled in, and Ferrell's walk to the mailbox became one of sweet anticipation.

Each night, she would open the envelopes with her husband, Wortie, and three children, Giles (13), Rosewell (10), and McGill (7), who took turns reading the mail. Ferrell was touched by the number of people who took the time to handwrite their grandmothers' recipes—she received more than 50—but what surprised her most were the stories attached to each of them.

Many shared happy childhood memories, like a Richmond woman who described leafing through her grandmother's 1943 edition of *Joy of Cooking*. The book had recipe cards tucked into its pages between sheets of wax paper, including one for a double-crust apple pie that was covered with food stains. "Every time Grandma would make pie, with a homemaker's economy, she would press tin animal-shaped cookie cutters into the spare dough, creating small 'cookies' that she would dust with cinnamon and sugar and bake for just a few minutes," she wrote.

Other stories went deeper. A woman from Dallas wrote about a grandmother who escaped Germany during World War II, leaving behind everything but a pie recipe tucked in her handbag. It survived a decade of food rations and two transatlantic voyages before the grandmother could afford to buy the necessary ingredients. Ferrell recalls, "This woman wrote that when she bakes the pie, she thinks about the moment when her grandmother could finally make it for her mother and what a treat it must have been to savor. Now she tastes what they tasted, and she's connected to two generations of women who came before her."

The letters pointed Ferrell to her own kitchen, where she worked her way through the stack of recipes. "Every

weekend throughout the fall, my family baked pies," she says. Together, they would peel and core apples, reading each story as they rolled out dough and created buttery cocoons or cinnamon-crumb blankets for piles of sugarcoated apples. The Ferrells even cleared out a kitchen cabinet to make their own version of Madge's pie safe.

One afternoon, while Ferrell watched her children weaving lattice crusts and sneaking peeks through the oven door as pies bubbled and baked, she had a revelation. "I might never find my grandmother's exact pie, but what I discovered was even better. We were creating new memories of apple pie that I hope will remain with us forever."

Old-Fashioned Apple Pie

ACTIVE 30 MIN. - TOTAL 1 HOUR, 40 MIN., PLUS 2 HOURS CHILLING AND 1 HOUR COOLING

SERVES 8

CRUST

- 2 cups all-purpose flour, plus more for work surface
- 1 cup cold unsalted butter or cold vegetable shortening, cut into small pieces
- 1 tsp. kosher salt

FILLING

- 9 or 10 tart apples such as Granny Smith or McIntosh (about 4 lb. total), peeled and thinly sliced
- ½ cup granulated sugar
- ¼ cup all-purpose flour
- 1 tsp. ground cinnamon
- Dash of kosher salt
- 2 Tbsp. unsalted butter, cut into small pieces

1. Prepare the Crust: Using your fingers, mix together flour, butter, and salt in a large bowl until butter is well incorporated. Gradually sprinkle 2 to 4 tablespoons very cold water into mixture, kneading as you add water, until dough just comes together. (You may not need to add all the water.) Turn dough out onto a lightly floured work surface; knead until it forms a smooth ball, 2 to 3 times. Divide dough in half, and shape into 2 disks. Wrap each disk in plastic wrap; chill at least 2 hours or up to overnight.
2. Unwrap 1 chilled dough disk, and place on a lightly floured work surface. Let

stand at room temperature until slightly softened, about 5 minutes. Sprinkle with flour; roll into a 12-inch circle. Carefully fit dough round into a 9-inch deep-dish glass pie plate, leaving a 1½-inch overhang around edges. Refrigerate until ready to use.
3. Prepare the Filling: Preheat oven to 425°F with oven rack in lowest position. Stir together apples, sugar, flour, cinnamon, and salt in a large bowl until apples are evenly coated. Spoon mixture into prepared piecrust; sprinkle mixture with butter.
4. Unwrap remaining chilled pie dough disk, and place on a lightly floured work surface. Let stand at room temperature until slightly softened, about 5 minutes. Sprinkle with flour; roll into a 12-inch circle. Cut into 12 (¾-inch-wide) strips. (Discard remaining dough scraps, or use for another purpose.) Arrange strips in a lattice design over Filling; trim strips as needed to meet the bottom Crust overhang. Fold dough edges under, and crimp using your fingers or a fork.
5. Place assembled pie on a rimmed baking sheet. Bake in preheated oven 15 minutes. Reduce oven temperature to 350°F (leaving pie in oven); continue baking 45 minutes. Cover loosely with aluminum foil to prevent excessive browning; continue baking until juices are thick and bubbly, Crust is golden brown, and apples are tender when pierced with a long wooden pick, about 30 minutes. Transfer pie to a wire rack, and cool at least 1 hour.

RAJMA (PUNJABI RED
BEANS) (PAGE 198)

PICKLED
ONIONS
(PAGE 201)

Finding Her Groove

Chef and musician Cheetie Kumar soulfully blends her past with the present at Raleigh, North Carolina's Garland restaurant

Cheetie Kumar delights in change. "I love transitions in general, in life and seasons," says the chef behind Garland in Raleigh. "I'm excited by the vast array of things that might be possible. It forces you to evaluate the decisions you've made and figure out what's still relevant and what's not."

Born to Indian parents in Pennsylvania, Kumar and her family moved to Chandigarh, India, when she was just 6 months old. For years, she listened to her parents talk about returning to the U.S. " 'When we move to America...,' 'In America, this...,' 'In America, that...,' " she recalls. Kumar was 8 when they finally settled in New York, but the reality of life there didn't match her expectations. "It was not the America we'd talked about," she says. "No shining, gleaming streets. No suburban house and carpeting or Hoover vacuum cleaners or spaghetti in pretty jars." Her family's first three years back in the States were riddled with anxiety as her parents, both biochemists, worked to secure permanent resident status.

Uncertainty was a constant, but dinner together was too. "Every single day, my mother cooked us a meal from scratch," Kumar says of Adarsh, who passed away in 2016. She made simple dishes that Kumar says "sparkled," such as Punjabi-style black lentils with kidney beans. "It's like an all-day chili. It was vegetarian, but it had a meatiness to it."

Food became the language Kumar shared with her mother, who'd lost her own parents in the bloody Partition of India as a child. "I think I knew how sad my mom was," she says. "I had this unspoken understanding that, if I 'got' food, I could be closer to her. I could have a vocabulary with her that was beyond words, which she wasn't very good at."

If cooking was how Kumar connected with her mother, music was where she found herself. After college, she moved to Raleigh to pursue a career in music management (she still plays guitar in the rock band Birds of Avalon). But touring the South with her band only intensified her relationship with food—she found a taste of home in the restaurants they frequented on the road.

"I loved going to a meat 'n' three and naturally 'getting it,' " she says. "That's the way Indian people eat too. It's a thali—a vegetable plate! You've got a bean, a vegetable; you may have some pickled cucumbers. It's the exact same."

Other parts of the region's culinary identity also felt familiar. Many ingredients found in Southern dishes, okra, for instance, belonged to Indian (and African) cuisine first. She says, "There's a direct line between Indian and Southern fare (mind you, with a layover of a couple hundred years), but there was so much cross-pollination."

Beyond the shared ingredients, there were other commonalities between the two cultures. "That sense of

communal cooking, using everything that's available to you, the importance of the matriarch in the kitchen, and her ability to spend several hours making something that's labor-intensive or simmers on low for a long time–those things are so much a part of both of our traditions," she says.

The self-taught chef has orchestrated an artful and ever-evolving menu at Garland, where Indian and Pan-Asian flavors mingle with their Southern surrounds: Fried chicken thighs are drizzled in turmeric-yogurt sauce, and fresh North Carolina produce is the star of her pakoras (fried fritters) served with chutney. It may seem like an unexpected combination, but it's one that she says shouldn't surprise us.

When Kumar opened Garland in 2013, she brought all the pieces together–the broader cultural context; the seasonality of the ingredients; and her mother, the woman who taught her everything that she knows. "I feel her [at the restaurant] all the time," she adds. "The patience in the cooking is hers. You can't rush a good masala. You have to cook the onions slowly and can't compromise that."

Her meticulous approach extends to every facet of the restaurant, from its curated playlist of what she calls "experimental global-feeling music" to the long communal table, which is designed to foster shared experiences–and food.

With a third James Beard Award semifinalist honor under her belt, it would be easy for the celebrated chef to rest on her laurels, but complacency is not in her DNA. "I'm hoping to continue what we do but do it better, be more creative," Kumar says. And she won't take any shortcuts. "Slow and steady. That was my mom's motto, so that is what I'm going with."

Rajma (Punjabi Red Beans)

Masala Memories: "My mother kept a batch of the 'masala base' (spice mixture) divided up in the fridge or freezer and made beans in the pressure cooker for instant dinners. After we moved to the U.S., the beans simmered in the slow cooker all day while she was at work and we were at school. When we got home, she quickly refried the masala and stirred it into the beans, and dinner was ready after I prepared the rice," Kumar recalls.

ACTIVE 1 HOUR · TOTAL 2 HOURS, 30 MIN., PLUS 8 HOURS SOAKING

SERVES 4

- ½ lb. dried red kidney beans (such as Camellia brand), rinsed
- 2 tsp. ground turmeric, divided
- 2¾ tsp. kosher salt, divided
- 4 Tbsp. ghee (or 2 Tbsp. canola oil plus 2 Tbsp. unsalted butter), plus more for serving
- 1 cup chopped yellow onion
- 1 black cardamom pod (optional)
- 2 Tbsp. minced fresh ginger (from 1 [2-inch] piece)
- 1 serrano chile, halved lengthwise and seeded
- 1 Tbsp. finely chopped garlic (from 3 garlic cloves)
- 1½ tsp. cumin seeds
- 2 tsp. ground coriander
- 1 Tbsp., plus 1 tsp. garam masala (such as MDH), divided
- 1½ cups canned crushed tomatoes (from 1 [15-oz.] can)
- ½ tsp. coarsely ground black pepper
- ⅛ tsp. cayenne pepper (optional)
- ½ cup chopped fresh cilantro
- 2 tsp. fresh lemon juice (from 1 lemon)
- Cooked basmati rice, warm

1. Place beans in a medium bowl or saucepan; add cold water as needed to cover 2 inches above beans. Cover and refrigerate 8 hours or overnight. Drain.
2. Bring drained beans, 8 cups water, and 1 teaspoon of the turmeric to a boil in a large saucepan over high. Reduce heat to medium; simmer, stirring occasionally, until beans are tender but still hold their shape, 1 hour, 15 minutes to 1 hour, 30 minutes, stirring 2 teaspoons of the salt into bean mixture during final 30 minutes of cook time.
3. While beans cook, heat 3 tablespoons of the ghee in a large heavy-bottomed saucepan over medium until very fragrant, about 3 minutes. Add onion, ½ teaspoon of the salt, and (if using) black cardamom pod; stir to coat. Reduce heat to medium-low. Cook, stirring occasionally, until onion just begins to turn golden brown in spots, about 10 minutes. Reduce heat to low; add ginger, serrano chile, and remaining 1 tablespoon ghee. Cook, scraping bottom of pan to loosen browned bits, until onion is caramelized and crisped in spots, 10 to 14 minutes. Add garlic; cook, stirring often, until slightly softened, about 2 minutes.
4. Add ½ cup water to onion mixture, scraping bottom of pan to loosen browned bits. Cook over low, stirring occasionally, until water evaporates and onion starts to sizzle in remaining pan drippings, 5 to 15 minutes. Repeat process using additional ½ cup water.
5. Push onion mixture to 1 side of pan, and tilt pan so that any remaining drippings slide to empty side of pan. Add cumin seeds to drippings in empty side of pan. Cook over low, stirring just the cumin often, until cumin sizzles vigorously, about 1 minute. Add coriander, 1 tablespoon of the garam masala, and remaining 1 teaspoon turmeric to cumin; stir just the cumin mixture together. Stir cumin mixture into onion mixture. Add tomatoes, black pepper, and (if using) cayenne pepper. Cook, stirring often, until mixture is dry and slightly reduced, about 5 minutes. Remove from heat; set aside, uncovered, until beans are finished cooking.
6. Pour cooked bean mixture (do not drain beans) into onion mixture; add remaining 1 teaspoon garam masala. Bring to a simmer over medium. Reduce heat to medium-low. Simmer gently, stirring occasionally, until mixture has a stewlike consistency, about 15 minutes. Remove from heat; stir in cilantro, lemon juice, and remaining ¼ teaspoon salt. Serve over warm rice, and add more ghee to taste.

Gingery Carrots with Pistachios and Coconut-Buttermilk Sauce

The secret sauce: "A tangy coconut-buttermilk sauce rounds out the sweetness in the carrots and adds some needed richness," Kumar says. "If you want to simplify this dish, the carrots are just as good served with plain Greek yogurt with a little salt and olive oil stirred in."

ACTIVE 1 HOUR, 5 MIN. - TOTAL 1 HOUR, 5 MIN.
SERVES 6

- 2 lb. small carrots with tops
- 1¼ tsp. cumin seeds
- 3½ Tbsp. canola oil or grapeseed oil, divided
- 1 tsp. kosher salt
- 4 (3-inch) orange peel strips plus 1 cup fresh juice (from 4 [8-oz.] oranges)
- ½ tsp. ancho chile powder
- 1-2 tsp. honey
- 2 Tbsp. minced fresh ginger (from 1 [3-inch] piece)
- 1½ tsp. ground coriander
- 1 tsp. finely chopped serrano chile with seeds and ribs removed (optional)
- Coconut-Buttermilk Sauce (recipe follows)
- 2 Tbsp. finely chopped toasted pistachios
- Roughly torn fresh mint leaves

GINGERY CARROTS WITH PISTACHIOS AND COCONUT-BUTTERMILK SAUCE

1. Remove and discard tops from carrots; peel carrots. (If some are thick, cut in half lengthwise so all are roughly the same size.) Heat cumin seeds and 1½ tablespoons of the oil in a high-sided 13- to 14-inch skillet over medium until cumin seeds begin to sizzle, about 3 minutes. Add carrots and salt; stir to coat carrots. Increase heat to medium-high; cook carrots, turning occasionally, until lightly browned in spots, 6 to 9 minutes. Stir in orange peel strips, orange juice, ⅔ cup of water, and ancho chile powder. Increase heat to high; bring to a boil. Reduce heat to medium; simmer, turning carrots occasionally, until they are tender-crisp when pierced with a paring knife, 15 to 18 minutes. Remove from heat; gently transfer carrots to a large plate, reserving liquid in skillet.
2. Return skillet to medium heat; continue to cook liquid, stirring often, until slightly reduced, about 3 minutes. Pour sauce through a fine-mesh strainer into a small bowl; discard solids. Stir in desired amount of honey; set aside.
3. Heat remaining 2 tablespoons oil in a separate large skillet over medium until shimmering. Add ginger, coriander, and, if desired, chile. Cook, stirring constantly, until fragrant and ginger is slightly softened, 1 minute. Return carrots to skillet. Cook, stirring often, until warmed through, 2 minutes. Remove skillet from heat. Add orange sauce; stir to coat carrots. Gently transfer carrots to a large serving platter; spoon orange sauce on top. Drizzle 4 tablespoons Coconut-Buttermilk Sauce evenly over carrots; sprinkle evenly with pistachios and mint. Serve with remaining Coconut-Buttermilk Sauce.

Coconut-Buttermilk Sauce

ACTIVE 5 MIN. - TOTAL 5 MIN.
MAKES ¾ CUP

Remove ¼ cup of the solidified cream from the top of 1 (5.4-oz.) can **unsweetened coconut cream** (such as Native Forest). Reserve remaining coconut cream for another use. Whisk together ½ cup **whole-milk buttermilk**, 2 tsp. **extra-virgin olive oil**, ½ tsp. **lemon zest** plus 1 tsp. **juice** (from 1 lemon), ¼ tsp. **kosher salt**, and ¼ cup solidified coconut cream in a medium bowl until smooth.

PAN-ROASTED
OKRA AND
SWEET ONIONS
WITH LEMONY
MASALA

SIMPLE
RAITA

PICKLED
ONIONS

Pan-Roasted Okra and Sweet Onions with Lemony Masala

A Twist on Tradition: "Mom would cut slits lengthwise in okra, stuff each pod with a lemony masala paste, then pan-roast them, finishing the dish with sweet onions. She was a patient woman," Kumar says. "My lazier version relies on whole okra roasted and tossed with onions and spices while scalding hot. It's not as special as hers, but it's delicious and much easier."

ACTIVE 30 MIN. - TOTAL 1 HOUR, 30 MIN.
SERVES 4 TO 6

MASALA
- 2 Tbsp. cumin seeds
- ¼ cup coriander seeds
- 1 tsp. fennel seeds
- 1 tsp. ajowan seeds
- 1 Tbsp. dried mint flakes (optional)
- 2 Tbsp. amchoor powder (such as Pure Indian Foods)
- ½ tsp. finely ground black salt or kosher salt
- ⅛ tsp. cayenne pepper

ROASTED OKRA
- 6 Tbsp. grapeseed oil or canola oil
- ¼ tsp. ground turmeric or 1 tsp. grated fresh turmeric
- 2 lb. fresh okra (about 14 cups)
- 2 medium sweet onions, cut into ½-inch-thick strips (about 3½ cups)
- ⅓ cup fresh lemon juice (from 3 lemons)
- 1 tsp. kosher salt

1. Prepare the Masala: Heat cumin seeds in a small skillet over low, stirring occasionally, until very fragrant, about 2 minutes. Transfer to a large plate. Repeat procedure with coriander seeds, fennel seeds, and ajowan seeds, toasting each spice separately and adding to cumin seeds. Let spices cool 10 minutes. In 2 batches, process cumin mixture and, if desired, mint in a spice grinder until finely ground, about 15 seconds per batch. Transfer to an airtight container; stir in amchoor powder, black salt, and cayenne; set aside.

2. Prepare the Roasted Okra: Place 1 oven rack 6 inches from heat; place second rack in lower third of oven. Place a large rimmed baking sheet on each rack. Preheat broiler to high. (Do not remove baking sheets while oven preheats.)

3. Stir together grapeseed oil and turmeric in a large bowl. Add okra and onions, tossing to coat. Remove pan from top rack of oven. Spread half of the okra mixture (about 8 cups) in a single layer in hot pan, and return to top oven rack. Broil on high until okra is tender and charred in spots, about 10 minutes. Transfer to a large bowl. Spread remaining okra mixture in a single layer on second hot sheet pan, broiling on top rack as directed.

4. Gently toss cooked okra mixture with lemon juice, salt, and 4 teaspoons of the Masala. Transfer to a large serving platter.

Basmati Rice

Even if you've cooked rice countless times, you should try Kumar's way. Her method produces tender, aromatic, nicely defined grains that "stand tall on their own, shoulder to shoulder with their compatriots," she adds. This recipe works well for most types of long-grain white rice.

ACTIVE 20 MIN. - TOTAL 40 MIN., PLUS 30 MIN. CHILLING
MAKES 7 CUPS

Place 2 cups uncooked **aged basmati rice (such as Iberia)** in a medium bowl. Fill bowl with cold **water**; while adding water, agitate rice using your hands. Pour rice mixture through a fine-mesh strainer, discarding liquid. Repeat process until water runs clear, 3 or 4 times. Place drained rice and 2 tsp. **kosher salt** in a medium bowl. Cover with cold water, and gently stir for about 5 seconds. Refrigerate, uncovered, 30 to 40 minutes; drain. Bring ¼ tsp. crushed **black peppercorns** and/or ¼ tsp. crushed **green cardamom seeds** and 2¾ cups water to a boil in a large heavy-bottomed saucepan over high. Stir in drained rice; return to a boil. Reduce heat to low; cover, and simmer 13 minutes. Remove from heat. Let stand, covered, until rice is cooked through, about 5 minutes. Transfer rice to a large bowl; add 2 Tbsp. **unsalted butter**, if desired. Fluff with a fork.

Top It Off

Indian condiments are just as lively as the dishes. Look for jarred chutneys or achar (pickles) at the supermarket or pureindianfoods.com. Try these homemade recipes as well.

Simple Raita

ACTIVE 5 MIN. - TOTAL 5 MIN.
MAKES 2 CUPS

Stir together 2 cups **plain whole-milk yogurt**, 1 tsp. **kosher salt**, ½ tsp. each coarsely ground **black pepper** and coarsely ground **cumin seeds**, and (if desired) ¼ cup chopped **fresh cilantro** in a small bowl until thoroughly blended.

Pickled Onions

ACTIVE 10 MIN. - TOTAL 10 MIN., PLUS 2 HOURS MARINATING
MAKES 1½ CUPS

Peel 1 (2-inch) piece of **fresh ginger**; slice into ⅛-inch-thick rounds. Cut 1 **serrano chile** in half lengthwise. Place sliced ginger and serrano chile halves on a double layer of cheesecloth. Gather edges of cheesecloth together, and tie securely. Toss together 3 cups thinly sliced **red onion** (from 1 [12-oz.] onion) and 2 tsp. **kosher salt** in a medium bowl; transfer to a ziplock plastic bag. Add ginger, serrano chile, ½ cup fresh **lemon juice** (from 4 lemons), and 2 tablespoons **red wine vinegar**. Seal bag, removing as much air as possible, and turn to coat. Lay bag flat on a work surface; let stand at room temperature 2 to 3 hours, turning occasionally. Drain onion mixture; discard chile and ginger. Use onions immediately, or refrigerate in an airtight container up to 2 days.

Game Day Snack Trays

Four fun and creative supper ideas for when everyone's hungry and glued to the game

It's an hour before kickoff, and I haven't figured out what to serve for dinner. I know that the kids and the hub want to watch the game, so we need something snacky that we can eat in front of the television. I peer inside the fridge to see what I can pull together. There's a small nub of cheese, a few pickled okra pods, and a handful of sugar snap peas. That's not enough to feed the family. But wait! I also have eggs, bacon, and all kinds of condiments. I can whip together some deviled eggs and arrange the other bits around them.

And just like that, a quick fridge clean out led to one of my family's favorite traditions. My boys named these grab-bag meals "snack dinners." They've become a mainstay on fall Saturdays, when we're watching SEC football on TV and don't want to leave our posts on the couch.

The secret to a great snack supper is to include one main recipe and let all the accompanying foods orbit around it in support. Here, the star dishes are crispy oven-baked chicken wings, bacon-infused deviled eggs, a killer take on pimiento cheese, and garlicky sautéed shrimp. I like to incorporate fresh vegetables for color and crunch, something pickled for balance, a creamy dip or cheese for richness, and bread or crackers so everyone's appetite is satisfied.

A sheet pan is the best way to serve these meals: It's the largest tray I own, the raised sides hold everything in nicely, and it's easy to transport. I also find delight in the challenge of filling up the pan with vibrant, beautiful, delicious food.

Smoky Kimchi Pimiento Cheese

Many Southern cooks have their own special riffs on pimiento cheese. I am half Korean, and so is this recipe, which blends a little kimchi into the mix.

Suggested accompaniments: hard salami, baked frozen waffle fries, boiled peanuts, crackers, mini sweet peppers, radishes, cucumbers, carrots

ACTIVE 15 MIN. - TOTAL 15 MIN., PLUS 15 MIN. IF SMOKING PEPPER
SERVES 8

- ½ small red bell pepper
- 1 medium shallot
- 1 (8-oz.) block sharp Cheddar cheese
- ½ cup mayonnaise (such as Duke's)
- ¼ cup finely chopped drained kimchi
- 2 Tbsp. chopped fresh chives

- ½ tsp. black pepper
- ½ tsp. smoked paprika (optional)
- ¼ cup applewood chips or hickory wood chips
- ¼ tsp. kosher salt (optional)

1. Preheat broiler to high. Place bell pepper half, skin side up, on an aluminum foil-lined baking sheet; flatten with hand. Broil in preheated oven until blackened, 8 to 10 minutes. Fold foil around pepper to seal tightly; let stand 10 minutes.

2. Meanwhile, grate shallot onto paper towels using small holes of a box grater. Transfer grated shallot to a large bowl. Finely shred half of cheese using the small holes of box grater; shred remaining cheese using large holes. Add shredded cheese to bowl with shallot. Stir in mayonnaise, kimchi, chives, and black pepper.

3. Unwrap foil around bell pepper; peel and discard skin. (Note: If you want to skip Step 4, finely chop pepper, and stir into cheese mixture with smoked paprika instead.)

4. Place an 8-inch square or 11- x 7-inch disposable foil pan upside down on a cutting board. Pierce 6 to 10 holes at 1 end of bottom of pan, near edge, using a knife. Turn pan right side up. Place dry wood chips in one layer over holes in pan. Place bell pepper on other side of pan; cover pan tightly with foil. Turn on vent hood. Set pan over a gas or electric burner so holes come in contact with heat. Turn burner on high; let pan sit on burner until smoke begins to seep from foil, about 30 seconds. Reduce heat to medium-low; smoke 4 minutes. Remove pan from burner; carefully uncover. (If needed, spritz wood with water to prevent burning.) Transfer pepper to a cutting board. Finely chop; stir into cheese mixture.

5. Taste for seasoning; if desired, add salt. Store in refrigerator up to 2 weeks.

Garlic-Butter Shrimp

The shrimp are coated in a glossy, buttery sauce made with a touch of dry sherry for a rich, nutty flavor.

Suggested accompaniments: sugar snap peas, grilled corn, grilled artichoke hearts, Marcona almonds, olives, grilled baguette slices, soppressata

ACTIVE 15 MIN. - TOTAL 15 MIN.
SERVES 4

- 1 lb. large peeled, deveined raw shrimp, tail-on
- 1 Tbsp. olive oil
- 1 tsp. granulated sugar
- ¾ tsp. kosher salt
- ¼ cup unsalted butter, divided
- ¼ tsp. crushed red pepper
- 2 large garlic cloves, grated on a Microplane grater
- ¼ cup dry sherry
- 1 tsp. sherry vinegar or apple cider vinegar
- 2 Tbsp. finely chopped fresh flat-leaf parsley

1. Combine shrimp, oil, sugar, and salt in a medium bowl, tossing well to coat.

2. Heat a large stainless-steel skillet over high. Add 1 tablespoon of the butter; swirl pan until butter melts, about 30 seconds. Add shrimp mixture; cook, stirring occasionally, until shrimp are almost done, 2 to 3 minutes. Remove shrimp from skillet with a slotted spoon.

3. Add 1 tablespoon of the butter to skillet; swirl pan until butter melts, about 30 seconds. Add red pepper and garlic; cook, stirring constantly, 30 seconds. Add sherry and vinegar, stirring and scraping bottom of skillet to loosen browned bits; cook until liquid reduces by about half, about 2 minutes. Add remaining 2 tablespoons butter, stirring until butter melts. Return shrimp to skillet; cook until cooked through, about 2 minutes. Stir in parsley.

Baked Chicken Wings with Pepper Jelly Glaze

This is my favorite way to make crispy, you'd-swear-they-were-fried chicken wings in the oven. (Photo, page 190)

Suggested accompaniments: celery, carrots, cherry tomatoes, blue cheese dressing, potato chips, pickled pepperoncini

ACTIVE 10 MIN. - TOTAL 1 HOUR
SERVES 4

- 1¾ lb. chicken wings, separated into drumettes and flats
- 2 tsp. kosher salt
- 1½ tsp. baking powder
- 1 tsp. ground coriander
- ½ tsp. ground ginger
- ½ cup red pepper jelly (such as Braswell's)
- 1 Tbsp. apple cider vinegar
- 1 Tbsp. unsalted butter

1. Preheat oven to 450°F. Pat chicken very dry with paper towels; place in a large bowl. Stir together salt, baking powder, coriander, and ginger in a small bowl. Sprinkle spice mixture over chicken; toss well to coat. Arrange chicken, fatty sides down, in a single layer on a rimmed baking sheet lined with parchment paper (or lined with aluminum foil and then parchment paper if you don't want to wash the baking sheet).
2. Bake in preheated oven 25 minutes. Turn chicken over; bake until well browned and crispy, 17 to 20 minutes. Remove baking sheet from oven. Drain chicken on paper towels; let stand 5 minutes.
3. Stir together jelly and vinegar in a large skillet; bring to a boil over high. Cook, stirring occasionally, until jelly melts, about 2 minutes. Add butter, and stir until butter melts, 30 seconds. Add chicken; toss well to coat, and remove from heat.

Bacon Deviled Eggs

I like deviled eggs with a well-seasoned, firm filling. There's so much bacon in these that you can't pipe the filling!

Suggested accompaniments: prosciutto-wrapped pickled okra, hummus, cheese straws, pickled Peppadew peppers (stuffed with herbed goat cheese), carrots, cheddar cheese, breadsticks, radicchio, cornichons

ACTIVE 15 MIN. - TOTAL 30 MIN.
MAKES 12

- 6 large eggs
- 3 Tbsp. mayonnaise (such as Duke's)
- 1 tsp. Dijon mustard
- ¼ tsp. black pepper
- ¼ tsp. garlic powder
- ⅛ tsp. cayenne pepper
- 2 Tbsp. thinly sliced scallions
- 3 thick-cut bacon slices, cooked and crumbled
- Thinly sliced pickled okra
- 2 tsp. chopped fresh chives

1. Fill a medium saucepan with 1 inch of water; fit with a steamer basket. Bring to a boil over high. Add eggs to basket; cover and steam until eggs are hard-cooked, about 13 minutes. Transfer eggs to an ice bath, and let sit until chilled, about 6 minutes. Crack eggs all over; peel and discard shells.
2. Cut eggs in half lengthwise. Carefully scoop yolks into a medium bowl, leaving whites intact. Mash yolks with a fork until very smooth. Add mayonnaise, mustard, black pepper, garlic powder, and cayenne; mash until very smooth. Stir in scallions and bacon. Divide filling evenly among egg whites. Top each with a slice of pickled okra; sprinkle with chives.

Kickin' Chicken

A honey-chile sauce makes this dish sing

One-Pan Hot Honey Chicken and Rice

ACTIVE 20 MIN. - TOTAL 45 MIN.
SERVES 4

- 1 Tbsp. olive oil
- 4 (7-oz.) bone-in, skin-on chicken thighs
- 3 tsp. kosher salt, divided
- 1 (5-oz.) bunch scallions
- 2 Tbsp. honey
- 2 tsp. Asian chile-garlic sauce
- 1 tsp. lower-sodium soy sauce
- 1 large baby bok choy, thinly sliced (about 1½ cups)
- 1 medium-size red bell pepper, chopped (1 cup)
- 2 Tbsp. minced fresh ginger (from 1 [2-inch] piece)
- 3 medium garlic cloves, finely chopped (about 1 Tbsp.)
- 1 cup uncooked jasmine rice

1. Preheat oven to 375°F with rack in upper third position. Heat oil in a deep 4-quart 11-inch skillet over medium-high until shimmering. Sprinkle chicken evenly with 1 teaspoon of the salt. Place chicken, skin sides down, in hot oil. Cook, undisturbed, until skin is golden brown, 8 to 10 minutes. Transfer to a plate. Reserve 1 tablespoon drippings in skillet.

2. While chicken cooks, thinly slice scallions; reserve ¼ cup sliced green scallions for garnish. Stir together honey, chile-garlic sauce, and soy sauce; set aside.

3. Reduce heat under skillet to medium. Add bok choy, bell pepper, and remaining sliced scallions. Cook, stirring often, until tender-crisp, about 3 minutes. Add ginger and garlic. Cook, stirring often, until fragrant, 1 minute. Stir in 1¼ cups water, rice, and remaining 2 teaspoons salt. Nestle chicken, skin sides up, in rice mixture; bring to a boil over high. Cover skillet, and transfer to preheated oven. Bake until a thermometer inserted in thickest portion of chicken thighs registers 165°F and rice is just tender, about 20 minutes.

4. Increase oven temperature to low broil. Uncover skillet; broil until chicken skin is crisp, about 5 minutes. Remove from oven; spoon honey mixture over chicken. Garnish with reserved sliced scallions.

Fix & Freeze

Take the pressure off weeknights with five suppers that go from the freezer to the table with ease

FASTER FAJITAS
Prep the shrimp, onions, peppers, and seasonings, and freeze them in the same bag so you can pull together dinner in minutes on busy nights.

SHRIMP FAJITA
BOWLS

Shrimp Fajita Bowls

ACTIVE 15 MIN. - TOTAL 15 MIN. (IF FREEZING,
ADD AT LEAST 1 HOUR THAWING.)
SERVES 4

- 1½ lb. medium-size peeled, deveined raw shrimp
- 3 cups thinly sliced bell peppers
- 1 cup thinly sliced red onion
- 1 medium jalapeño chile, seeded and thinly sliced lengthwise
- 2½ tsp. ground cumin
- 1 tsp. ancho chile powder
- ½ tsp. garlic powder
- 2 Tbsp. olive oil
- ½ cup chopped fresh cilantro, plus leaves for garnish
- ¾ tsp. kosher salt
- ¼ tsp. black pepper
- 1 Tbsp. fresh lime juice
  Hot cooked rice, diced avocado, pico de gallo, and lime wedges

Toss together shrimp, bell peppers, onion, jalapeño, cumin, chile powder, and garlic powder in a large bowl.

To cook now: Preheat oven to high broil with rack positioned 6 inches from heat source. Arrange mixture on a rimmed baking sheet; drizzle with oil. Broil in preheated oven until shrimp is cooked through and mixture is tender and slightly browned, 7 to 9 minutes, stirring every 3 minutes to cook evenly. Sprinkle with chopped cilantro, salt, and black pepper; drizzle with lime juice. Serve in bowls on top of rice with avocado, pico de gallo, lime wedges, and cilantro leaves for garnish.

To freeze for later: Place mixture in a large ziplock plastic freezer bag. Flatten, seal, and freeze up to 3 months.

To thaw and cook: Thaw overnight in refrigerator or at room temperature 1 hour. Preheat oven to high broil with rack positioned 6 inches from heat source. Break up any clumps of thawed shrimp mixture (some pieces may still be slightly frozen). Arrange mixture on a rimmed baking sheet; drizzle with oil. Broil in preheated oven until shrimp is cooked through and mixture is tender and slightly browned, 9 to 11 minutes, stirring every 4 minutes to cook evenly. Sprinkle with chopped cilantro, salt, and black pepper; drizzle with lime juice. Serve in bowls on top of rice with avocado, pico de gallo, lime wedges, and cilantro leaves for garnish.

Green Chile–Chicken Soup

ACTIVE 20 MIN. - TOTAL 1 HOUR (IF FREEZING,
ADD 30 MIN. COOLING AND 1 HOUR REHEATING.)
SERVES 8

- 2 Tbsp. olive oil
- 2¼ lb. bone-in, skinless chicken thighs (about 6 thighs)
- 2 tsp. kosher salt, divided
- 1½ cups chopped white onion
- 1½ cups chopped poblano chiles
- 8 fresh tomatillos, husked and chopped
- 1 Tbsp. minced garlic
- 1 Tbsp. ground cumin
- 2 tsp. dried thyme
- 4 cups chicken broth
- 2 (15-oz.) cans white hominy, drained and rinsed
  Sliced radishes, fresh cilantro, hot sauce, and sour cream for topping

1. Heat oil in a large Dutch oven over medium-high. Sprinkle chicken with 1 teaspoon of the salt. Cook until browned, 4 minutes per side. Transfer to a plate; reserve drippings in pan. Add onion, poblanos, and tomatillos to hot drippings. Cook, stirring, until softened, 3 minutes. Stir in garlic, cumin, and thyme; cook 1 minute. Stir in broth and remaining 1 teaspoon salt.

2. Add chicken; cover and cook over medium-low until tender, about 40 minutes. Remove from heat. Transfer chicken to a cutting board; cool 5 minutes. Remove and discard bones. Chop chicken; return to Dutch oven.

To serve now: Stir in hominy. Top soup as desired.

To freeze for later: Cool completely, 30 minutes. Transfer to ziplock plastic freezer bags. Freeze up to 3 months.

To reheat and serve: Thaw bags of soup slightly in warm water. Peel off and discard bags as you place soup in a saucepan; add hominy. Cover; cook over medium-low 1 hour. Top as desired.

GREEK STUFFED PEPPERS

Greek Stuffed Peppers

ACTIVE 25 MIN. - TOTAL 55 MIN. (IF FREEZING, ADD 24 HOURS THAWING AND 15 MIN. BAKING.)
SERVES 4

- 4 medium bell peppers with stems
- 1 Tbsp. olive oil
- 1 lb. 85/15 lean ground beef
- 1 cup chopped red onion
- 2 tsp. minced garlic
- 1 (15-oz.) can diced fire-roasted tomatoes, drained
- 1 cup cooked long-grain white rice
- 1 Tbsp. red wine vinegar
- 1 Tbsp. chopped fresh oregano, plus more for garnish
- 1½ tsp. kosher salt
- ½ tsp. black pepper
- 4 oz. feta cheese, crumbled (1 cup)

1. Cut peppers in half through the stems. Remove seeds and membranes; discard.
2. Heat oil in a large skillet over medium-high. Add beef; cook, stirring to crumble, until mostly browned, about 6 minutes. Add onion and garlic; cook, stirring, until beef is cooked and onion is tender, about 4 minutes. Stir in next 6 ingredients. Cook,

undisturbed, 1 minute. Remove from heat; cool 5 minutes.
3. Divide mixture evenly among bell pepper halves (about ½ cup each). Arrange in a 9- x 13-inch baking dish.
To cook now: Preheat oven to 350°F. Bake 10 minutes. Sprinkle cheese on peppers; bake until heated through, 20 to 35 minutes. Sprinkle with oregano.
To freeze for later: Wrap dish tightly in 2 layers of plastic wrap. Wrap in heavy-duty aluminum foil. Freeze up to 1 month.
To thaw and cook: Thaw in refrigerator 24 hours. Preheat oven to 350°F; place unwrapped dish on counter while oven preheats. Bake 20 minutes. Sprinkle cheese on peppers; bake 25 to 30 minutes. Sprinkle with oregano.

Curried Chicken Pot Pie

ACTIVE 25 MIN. - TOTAL 2 HOURS (IF FREEZING, ADD 24 HOURS THAWING AND 20 MIN. BAKING.)
SERVES 6

- 3 Tbsp. butter
- 1 cup chopped carrots
- 1 cup chopped shallots

- 2 medium garlic cloves, minced
- 2 Tbsp. red curry paste
- 1 tsp. kosher salt
- 3 Tbsp. all-purpose flour
- 2 cups chicken broth
- 2 cups chopped rotisserie chicken breast
- ¾ cup frozen sweet peas, thawed
- 2 Tbsp. heavy cream
- 1 (14.1-oz.) pkg. refrigerated piecrusts, divided
- 1 large egg, lightly beaten

1. Melt butter in a medium skillet over medium. Add carrots and shallots. Cook, stirring occasionally, until tender, about 5 minutes. Add garlic, curry paste, and salt. Cook, stirring occasionally, until fragrant, about 2 minutes. Stir in flour; cook, stirring constantly, until vegetables are coated, about 1 minute. Add broth; let mixture come to a boil, stirring constantly. Continue boiling, stirring constantly, until thickened, about 2 minutes. Stir in chicken, peas, and cream. Remove from heat; let cool completely, about 20 minutes.
2. Unroll 1 of the piecrusts, and fit inside a 9-inch pie plate. Spoon chicken

SMOKED-PORK-
-STUFFED SHELLS

CURRIED CHICKEN
POT PIE

mixture into piecrust in plate. Cut remaining piecrust in half. Cut 1 half into 3 (1½-inch-wide) strips. Cut remaining half into 7 (½-inch-wide) strips. Arrange the 1½-inch-wide strips vertically over filling. Weave the ½-inch-wide strips perpendicularly into the wider strips to form a lattice pattern. Press ends of lattice strips to edge of bottom piecrust to seal. Trim excess dough; crimp edges.

To cook now: Place a baking sheet in oven; preheat oven to 375°F. Brush crust with egg. Place pie on baking sheet; bake in oven until crust is browned and filling is bubbly, about 55 minutes to 1 hour. Let stand 20 minutes before serving.

To freeze for later: Wrap entire pie with plastic wrap. Wrap with heavy-duty aluminum foil. Freeze at least 24 hours (up to 1 month).

To thaw and cook: Remove pie from freezer; thaw in refrigerator 24 hours. Remove pie from refrigerator, and unwrap. Place a baking sheet in oven; preheat oven to 375°F. Brush crust with egg. Place pie on preheated baking sheet; bake in oven until crust is browned and filling is bubbly, about 1 hour, 15 minutes. Let stand 20 minutes before serving.

Smoked-Pork-Stuffed Shells

ACTIVE 20 MIN. - TOTAL 1 HOUR, 10 MIN.
(IF FREEZING, ADD 24 HOURS THAWING AND 20 MIN. BAKING.)
SERVES 6

24	uncooked jumbo pasta shells
1	lb. chopped smoked pork
1¼	cups ricotta cheese (about 10 oz.)
¾	cup panko breadcrumbs
1	Tbsp. minced garlic
1	tsp. kosher salt
½	tsp. black pepper
¼	tsp. crushed red pepper
2	cups shredded mozzarella cheese (about 8 oz.), divided
¼	cup, plus 2 Tbsp. chopped fresh flat-leaf parsley, divided
1	(24-oz.) jar marinara sauce
¾	cup bottled barbecue sauce

1. Cook pasta in heavily salted boiling water until al dente, about 9 minutes. Drain, and transfer to a baking sheet. Cool 15 minutes.

2. Meanwhile, stir together next 7 ingredients, 1 cup of the mozzarella, and ¼ cup of the parsley in a large bowl. Stir together marinara and barbecue sauce in a bowl. Spread 1¾ cups of the marinara mixture in bottom of a 9- x 13-inch baking dish.

3. Fill each cooled shell with 2 heaping tablespoons pork mixture, and arrange in prepared baking dish. Pour remaining 2 cups marinara mixture over shells.

To cook now: Preheat oven to 375°F. Sprinkle with remaining 1 cup mozzarella. Cover with aluminum foil. Bake until heated through, 20 to 25 minutes. Uncover; bake until bubbly, about 20 minutes. Sprinkle with remaining 2 tablespoons parsley.

To freeze for later: Wrap tightly in 2 layers of plastic wrap. Freeze up to 3 months.

To thaw and cook: Thaw in refrigerator 24 hours. Preheat oven to 375°F; place unwrapped dish on counter while oven preheats. Sprinkle with remaining 1 cup mozzarella. Cover with aluminum foil. Bake until heated through, 40 to 45 minutes. Uncover, and bake until bubbly, about 20 minutes. Sprinkle with remaining 2 tablespoons parsley.

Easy, Cheesy Meatballs

Tender ground turkey lightens up this flavorful one-pan supper

Skillet Turkey Meatballs

ACTIVE 30 MIN. - TOTAL 30 MIN.
SERVES 4

- ½ cup dry breadcrumbs
- 3 Tbsp. whole milk
- 1 large egg, lightly beaten
- ½ cup grated yellow onion (from 1 small onion)
- 3 Tbsp. grated Parmesan cheese
- 1 Tbsp. red wine vinegar
- ½ tsp. kosher salt
- ½ tsp. black pepper
- 1 lb. ground turkey
- 1½ Tbsp. olive oil
- 1 (24-oz.) jar lower-sodium marinara sauce
- 6 oz. fresh baby spinach (6 cups)
- 3 oz. shredded low-moisture part-skim mozzarella cheese (about ¾ cup)
- 2 Tbsp. sliced fresh basil

1. Stir together breadcrumbs and milk in a large bowl; soak 5 minutes. Add egg, onion, Parmesan, vinegar, salt, and pepper; stir to combine. Add turkey, stirring gently until just combined. Using your hands, gently shape mixture into 16 (1½-inch) balls.

2. Heat oil in a large nonstick skillet over medium-high. Add meatballs; cook, turning often, until browned on all sides, 8 to 10 minutes. Transfer to a plate.

3. Reduce heat under skillet to medium-low; add marinara and spinach. Increase heat to medium, and bring to a simmer. Simmer until spinach just begins to wilt, 2 to 3 minutes. Return meatballs to sauce in skillet; sprinkle with mozzarella. Cover and cook until meatballs are cooked through, 4 to 6 minutes. Sprinkle with basil; serve immediately.

Nutritional information: Calories: 459; Protein: 36g; Carbs: 30g; Fiber: 5g; Fat: 22g

DON'T SQUEEZE, PLEASE
Form your fingers into a rigid claw, and gently shape the meatballs in your hand. Squeezing will make them chewy.

Going Dutch

Impress your brunch crowd with a savory skillet pancake

Bacon-Cheddar Dutch Baby

ACTIVE 15 MIN. - TOTAL 35 MIN.
SERVES 4

- 4 thick-cut bacon slices (about 6 oz.), chopped
- 3 large eggs, at room temperature
- ½ cup whole milk, at room temperature
- ½ cup all-purpose flour
- 1 Tbsp. unsalted butter, melted and slightly cooled
- ½ tsp. kosher salt
- ¼ tsp. black pepper
- 3 oz. sharp Cheddar cheese, shredded (about ¾ cup)
- 1 Tbsp. finely chopped fresh chives

1. Preheat oven to 425°F. Cook bacon in a 10-inch cast-iron skillet over medium, turning occasionally, until bacon is crisp and fat has rendered, about 10 minutes. Remove from heat; transfer bacon to a plate lined with paper towels. Reserve 1½ tablespoons drippings in skillet.
2. While bacon cooks, process eggs, milk, flour, melted butter, salt, and pepper in a blender on medium speed until completely smooth, about 30 seconds, stopping to scrape down sides as needed.
3. Return skillet to medium heat; let heat 1 minute. Remove skillet from heat, and pour batter into skillet. Immediately transfer skillet to preheated oven. Bake until Dutch baby is puffed and golden brown, about 18 minutes. Do not open oven while cooking.
4. Remove Dutch baby from oven; immediately sprinkle with cheese. Return to oven; bake at 425°F until cheese melts, 1 to 2 minutes. Sprinkle with bacon and chives; serve immediately.

RISE AND SHINE
A Dutch baby puffs up dramatically as it bakes. Using room-temperature ingredients and keeping the oven door shut will help it rise in the pan.

TEST KITCHEN TIPS

Suppers on the Fly

Three products our pros stock up on for speedy weeknight dinners

CAULIFLOWER RICE

"I swap this in for white rice to make a fast and healthy cauliflower fried rice for my two sons." –Robby Melvin
Riced Veggies Cauliflower; greengiant.com

CHEESE TORTELLONI

"I keep a bag of refrigerated cheese-filled tortelloni (or smaller tortellini) on hand to pop in chicken soup in place of noodles or to stir into a marinara sauce for a family-favorite pasta night." –Pam Lolley
Cheese Lovers Tortelloni; giovanniranausa.com

HASH BROWNS

"For an easy shepherd's pie, fill a dish with browned ground beef, carrots, onions, peas, and gravy. Before throwing it in the oven, top it off with frozen hash browns." –Karen Rankin
Yukon Select Hashed Browns; alexiafoods.com

> "Never take a glass dish out of the freezer and put it directly in a hot oven. Let it sit on the counter as the oven preheats."
>
> **—Robby Melvin**
> Test Kitchen Director

HOW-TO

Freeze with Ease

Flash freezing keeps produce and proteins from sticking together so you can thaw what you need

1
PREP
Cut the ingredients, and assemble on a parchment-lined pan so they don't touch.

2
FREEZE
Place the uncovered pan in the freezer until ingredients are solid, at least 1 hour.

3
STORE
Transfer the frozen food from pan to a ziplock plastic freezer bag. Store in the freezer.

October

214   **Boiled-Peanut Perfection**   Master this roadside staple at home

216   **The Oyster Feast**   Chef Steven Satterfield's ideal day on Georgia's Tybee Island starts with wild oyster harvesting and ends with plenty of food, friends, and fun

221   **Pumpkin Picking Time!**   Saturdays at Gentry's Farm in Franklin, Tennessee, are a fall tradition for entertaining expert Katie Jacobs and her family

224   **Bring Out the Beef**   Four fast and delicious supper ideas from soup to stir-fry

227   **Falling for Persimmons**   Enjoy this rich, spiced, cakelike dessert

228   **Sweet on Shortbread**   Easy, buttery slice-and-bake cookies topped with pecan halves

229   **The Instant Pot Roast**   Ranch seasoning gives this old-school family favorite a delicious new spin

230   **Mushrooms Make It Better**   Two types of 'shrooms give this chicken dish a savory flavor

231   **Not Your Ordinary Oatmeal**   Wake up to a make-ahead breakfast loaded with spices, fruits, and nuts

232   **SL Cooking School**   Our Test Kitchen professionals share four flavorful mushrooms to spice up fall dishes

Boiled-Peanut Perfection

Master this roadside staple at home

KNOW YOUR NUTS
Raw peanuts have been air-dried to reduce their moisture content, making them shelf-stable and available year-round. Green peanuts are freshly dug from the field and should be used within a few days of their harvest.

As strange as boiled peanuts may sound to anyone living outside the South, raw (unroasted) peanuts boiled in a seasoned brine have been enjoyed for centuries throughout Asia, South America, and Africa. And while the peanut plant (*Arachis hypogaea*, native to South America) was brought to North American shores during the transatlantic slave trade, research shows that boiled peanuts in the eastern United States have been primarily a delicacy of African-

American foodways that crossed over into other cultures of the South in the early part of the 20th century. Nowadays, they inspire an intense cultural loyalty across lines of class and race.

We grew up in the 1980s in Charleston, South Carolina, and loved them so much that when we moved away to colleges in Massachusetts, we started a mail-order business selling them and other pantry staples that we missed from home. We called it The Lee

Bros. Boiled Peanuts Catalogue, and it's still going strong.

In the South, this snack is associated with leisure time outdoors and can be purchased by the side of the road from vendors set up in vacant lots and sandy strips on the way to the beach, the ballpark, or the fairgrounds. They're prepared in homes as well but rarely in restaurant settings. (However, that seems to be changing; they can be found at The Glass Onion in Charleston and

are even served with Cajun spices and country ham broth out West at JuneBaby in Seattle, Washington.)

Our grandmother's landlady, Elizabeth Jenkins Young, once remarked to us that the smell of our recipe boiling on Gran's stove reminded her of a "sweet potato gone sour." Not that she didn't like them: She proudly displayed her "I BRAKE FOR BOILED PEANUTS" bumper sticker in the back window of her blue Volkswagen Rabbit. But the

earthy quality of the nut (which grows underground and is full of protein and minerals) and the sweetness of it do in fact suggest the heartiness—and the roots—of a sweet potato.

To the uninitiated, wet peanuts may present several obstacles to their enjoyment. Not everyone goes for their unique beany flavor—a world of difference from the roasted kind—or the wetness as you pick them apart. But we believe they are divine.

Classic Boiled Peanuts

ACTIVE 10 MIN. - TOTAL 5 HOURS, 10 MIN., PLUS 8 HOURS SOAKING AND 1 HOUR COOLING
SERVES 12

- 1½ cups kosher salt, divided, plus more to taste
- 2 lb. raw peanuts in the shell or 3 lb. green peanuts

1. Place 2 gallons of water in a 10- to 12-quart stockpot. Add ½ cup of the salt to water; stir until salt dissolves. Add raw peanuts. (Skip this step if you are using green peanuts.) Use a large dinner plate to help submerge the floating peanuts. Soak peanuts 8 hours or overnight. (This step saves a little time boiling, but if you don't have the luxury of soaking time, you can skip it.)

2. Drain soaking water; add 2 gallons water and 1 cup salt to peanuts. (Note level of water on side of pot.) Bring to a boil over high. Reduce heat to low. Simmer, covered, until peanuts are as soft as roasted chestnuts or softer, 5 to 8 hours (2 to 3 hours for green peanuts), keeping water in pot within an inch or so of its original level with regular additions of water. After peanuts have boiled 3 hours (1 hour for green peanuts), sample them to check their texture and salinity. Remove a peanut, and wait until it is cool enough to handle. Open the shell, and give the peanut a chew, slurping some brine with it. If it crunches, cook it more. If the brine lacks salt, add more by ¼-cup amounts. If it is too salty, remove some of the water, and replace with the same volume of fresh water. Allow an hour for the salinity to equalize before testing again. Sample peanuts every hour until they are pleasantly yielding and as salty and appetizing as a good pickle.
3. When peanuts are cooked, remove from heat, and let them cool in the pot 1 hour (20 minutes for green peanuts). When cool enough to handle, drain and eat. Or store in the shell, in a sealed container, in the refrigerator 7 to 10 days or in the freezer several months.

Choose your peanut adventure

They're delicious plain, but also try them paired with boldly flavored ingredients—from barbecue sauce to Old Bay seasoning.

BEER AND OLD BAY

In Step 2, reduce kosher salt to ¾ cup and water to 1 gallon. Stir 6 (12-oz.) cans beer, 6 Tbsp. Old Bay seasoning, and 2 halved lemons into brine. Bring to a boil, and continue with recipe as directed.

SMOKY BARBECUE

In Step 2, stir 2 cups barbecue sauce, 2 Tbsp. smoked paprika, 1 halved head of garlic, and 4 bay leaves into cooking liquid with kosher salt. Bring to a boil, and continue with recipe as directed.

SOY AND SPICE

In Step 2, reduce kosher salt to ¾ cup. Stir 2½ cups soy sauce, 2 (5-inch) cinnamon sticks, 3 star anise, ¼ cup coriander seeds, and 1½ tsp. garlic powder into brine. Bring to a boil, and continue with recipe as directed.

The Oyster Feast

Chef Steven Satterfield's ideal day on Georgia's Tybee Island starts with wild oyster harvesting and ends with plenty of food, friends, and fun

At low tide, the wild oyster reefs along this Georgia barrier island's marshy shore stand out like gnarled stalagmites in a vast cave. One misstep, and the flinty clusters of shell can cause serious injury. So chef Steven Satterfield comes prepared: rubber boots; thick gloves; and a knee-length, waterproof trench coat. Below his salt-and-pepper beard, not an inch of skin is showing.

Armed with a weathered roofing hammer, he climbs the craggy buttes of Chatham County's Oyster Creek. Calcium dust chokes the air as he chisels out the choicest oysters and pitches them into a notched metal bucket. After an hour, he can barely budge the teetering mound, so his friend Seth Solomon, a Tybee Island firefighter, helps him hoist it into their boat, anchored just off the Georgia tributary.

"Growing up in Savannah, we'd come down here every winter and build a fire, roast oysters, and set out all kinds of sauces. It was this big event we'd look forward to all year long," says Satterfield. "Now I get to share that with my closest friends."

With two bushels in tow, Satterfield and Solomon race back to Solomon's dock, now adorned with buoys and string lights for the night's festivities. Tybee Island Social Club chef Kurtis Schumm is already busy building the firepit using granite cobblestones that once lined the downtown streets.

While Solomon cleans and shapes the oysters in a cement mixer, Satterfield flips over a fishing skiff and uses the bottom surface to prep a haul of produce from Canewater Farm—a purveyor beloved at his restaurant, Miller Union, in Atlanta's Westside neighborhood.

With the fire kindled and more friends arriving to lend a hand, Satterfield takes a moment to change out of his mud-spattered clothes to focus on a pot of oyster stew already bubbling inside. Chef Mashama Bailey and her business partner, Johno Morisano, of The Grey restaurant in Savannah, take happy hour into their own hands, raiding the citrus trees surrounding Solomon's property for a batch of whiskey sours made with fresh clementines and amaro.

"If you want a drink, you have to grab a shucking knife," says Bailey as conversation resumes over a pile of newly polished oysters that have been dumped onto a picnic table. At the grill, Satterfield is doling out the first round of steamed half shells as a kind of briny amuse-bouche alongside johnnycakes, a salad of wood-fired carrots and turnips, and a variety of mignonettes.

At sunset, everyone gathers in Solomon's dockside gazebo, helping themselves to steaming bowls of oyster stew and a buttermilk trifle made with two types of oranges. Popping a bottle of bubbly, Satterfield concedes that today was "far nicer than the oyster roasts of my youth. It was magical," he says, raising a toast. "Here's to new traditions."

1. Place firewood and/or natural lump charcoal in base of grill, and ignite. Once fire has burned down and coals are glowing orange and white and have reached medium-high (400°F to 450°F), place 3 to 4 dozen oysters, cupped sides down, on grill grate. Grill, covered, until oysters just begin to open at the wide end, 8 to 10 minutes. Discard any that do not open.

2. Use tongs to carefully transfer hot oysters to a serving platter, retaining as much liquid as possible. Let stand until cool enough to handle with a towel, 10 minutes. Using an oyster or paring knife, pry open oysters, discard top shells, and place the half shells on the platter. Serve immediately. Repeat with remaining oysters.

Hot Pepper Vinegar

ACTIVE 5 MIN. - TOTAL 15 MIN.,
PLUS 8 HOURS CHILLING
MAKES ABOUT 2 CUPS

Place 6 halved, stemmed, and seeded jalapeño chiles in a medium bowl or jar. Whisk together 2 cups apple cider vinegar and 2 Tbsp. kosher salt in a small saucepan over medium. Bring to a boil. Remove from heat; immediately pour vinegar mixture over chiles. Let cool completely. Store, covered, in refrigerator at least 8 hours or overnight. (For best flavor, make several days in advance.) When ready to serve with oysters, thinly slice a few of the chiles, and place slices in a serving bowl. Add some of the vinegar, and stir in 1 Tbsp. chopped fresh cilantro before serving with oysters.

Meyer Lemon–Ginger Mignonette

ACTIVE 10 MIN. - TOTAL 10 MIN.,
PLUS 30 MIN. STANDING
MAKES ABOUT 2 CUPS

Combine ½ cup champagne vinegar, 1½ Tbsp. fresh Meyer lemon zest and 6 Tbsp. juice (from 1 Meyer lemon), 1 minced shallot (about 6 Tbsp.), 2 Tbsp. peeled and minced fresh ginger (from a 1-inch piece), 1 tsp. black pepper, and ½ tsp. fine sea salt in a bowl. Stir well; let stand 30 minutes before serving with oysters.

Clementine Whiskey Sour

(Photo, page 306)

ACTIVE 5 MIN. - TOTAL 5 MIN.
SERVES 1

6 Tbsp. (3 oz.) bourbon
 (such as Jim Beam)
2 Tbsp. fresh clementine juice
 (from 1 clementine)
2 Tbsp. fresh lemon juice
 (from 1 lemon)
1 Tbsp. (½ oz.) Fernet-Branca
1 Tbsp. simple syrup
2 dashes of Angostura bitters
 Clementine slices and leaves

Combine bourbon, clementine juice, lemon juice, Fernet-Branca, and simple syrup in a cocktail shaker filled with ice. Shake until shaker feels very cold, 1 minute. Strain into a rocks glass filled with ice. Finish with bitters; do not stir. Garnish with clementine slices and leaves.

Grilled Oysters

Unlike a traditional Lowcountry oyster roast (which requires cooking them under a layer of wet burlap on a large metal slab, usually with help from several people), this simplified version is much easier to pull off.

ACTIVE 40 MIN. - TOTAL 2 HOURS, 40 MIN.
SERVES 16

8 **dozen oysters in the shell,
 scrubbed and dried**

Johnnycakes with Leeks and Collard Greens

(Photo, page 307)

ACTIVE 20 MIN. - TOTAL 20 MIN.
SERVES 8

- ½ cup whole milk
- ½ cup unsalted butter
- 2 cups fine cornmeal
- 1 cup baby collard greens or turnip greens, stemmed and thinly sliced
- 1 leek, trimmed and thinly sliced (about 1 cup)
- 2 tsp. kosher salt
- 1½ cups boiling water
  Whipped butter, for serving

1. Combine milk and ½ cup unsalted butter in a small saucepan over medium. Cook, stirring occasionally, until butter is melted. Set aside.
2. Stir together cornmeal, greens, leek, and salt in a large heatproof bowl. Whisk in boiling water. Add warm milk-and-butter mixture. Whisk to combine.
3. Heat an ungreased cast-iron skillet or griddle over medium-high. Drop ¼ cup of the batter, per cake, onto hot surface. Cook until lightly browned and crisp, 2 to 3 minutes. Flip, and cook other side until browned, 2 to 3 minutes. Serve hot with whipped butter.

Wood-Fired Root Vegetables with Charred Scallion Aïoli

(Photo, page 306)

ACTIVE 35 MIN. - TOTAL 35 MIN.
SERVES 12

VEGETABLES
- 2 bunches carrots (about 2 lb.)
- 2 bunches Hakurei turnips (about 2 lb.)
- ½ cup olive oil
- 1½ tsp. kosher salt
- ¾ tsp. black pepper
  Chopped parsley, for topping

AÏOLI
- 1 bunch scallions (8 large)
- 3 garlic cloves, grated
- 1 tsp. kosher salt
- 2 tsp. lemon zest plus 3 Tbsp. fresh juice (from 1 lemon)
- 2 large egg yolks (pasteurized, if desired)
- ¾ cup extra-virgin olive oil
- ¾ cup pure olive oil

1. Preheat a grill to medium-high (400°F to 450°F). Trim carrots and turnips, and rub dry with a kitchen towel. Remove and discard tops.
2. Toss together carrots, turnips, olive oil, salt, and pepper in a large bowl. Place carrots and turnips directly on grates of a hot grill. Grill, uncovered, turning often, until just tender, charring slightly, 7 to 8 minutes for carrots and 11 to 13 minutes for turnips. Remove from grill, and let cool completely.
3. Meanwhile, prepare the Aïoli: Char scallions on hot grill, 5 to 6 minutes; set aside to cool. Transfer scallions to a cutting board, and thinly slice crosswise.
4. Process sliced scallions, garlic, salt, lemon zest, and juice in a food processor until smooth. While machine is running, add egg yolks, processing until combined. Slowly drizzle olive oils into mixture, processing until it thickens and emulsifies. Taste for seasoning, and adjust as needed.
5. Slice carrots and turnips into bite-size pieces. Sprinkle with parsley, and serve with Aïoli.

Oyster Stew

(Photo, page 306)

ACTIVE 30 MIN. - TOTAL 40 MIN.
SERVES 6

- 2 dozen fresh shucked oysters in liquid
- 1 lb. russet potatoes, peeled, cut into ¼-inch pieces (about 2½ cups)
- 3 tsp. kosher salt, divided
- 8 collard stems, sliced crosswise into ¼-inch pieces
- 3 cups whole milk
- 1 cup heavy cream
- ¼ cup unsalted butter
- 1 large yellow onion, finely diced (about 2 cups)
- 3 celery stalks, finely diced (about 1 cup)
- ¼ cup all-purpose unbleached flour
- ½ lb. bacon, cut into ¼-inch pieces and cooked, reserving bacon drippings
  Freshly ground black pepper
- ⅛ tsp. cayenne pepper
  Roughly chopped fresh flat-leaf parsley and celery leaves

1. Place a fine-mesh strainer over a medium bowl, and drain oysters, reserving ⅓ cup oyster liquor.
2. Place potatoes and 1 teaspoon of the salt in a pot of water over high, and bring to a boil. Add collard stems. Boil 1 minute. Drain in a colander, and rinse under cold water.
3. Warm milk and cream in a medium saucepan over medium; cook until just beginning to boil. Remove from heat, and cover with a lid to keep warm.
4. Melt butter in a large Dutch oven over medium until foamy. Add onion, celery, potatoes, collard stems, and 1 teaspoon of the salt. Cook, stirring often, until onion is tender and translucent, 6 to 8 minutes. Sprinkle flour over vegetable mixture, and cook, stirring often, until thickened, about 2 minutes.
5. Slowly whisk in warm milk and heavy cream. Bring mixture to a boil, stirring often to keep mixture from sticking. Stir reserved oyster liquor into Dutch oven, and cook until all vegetables are tender, about 2 minutes.
6. Warm reserved bacon drippings in a large skillet over medium. Add drained oysters in a single layer. Sprinkle with a few grinds of pepper and remaining 1 teaspoon salt. Cook just until oysters begin to curl around the edges. Immediately transfer oysters to Dutch oven; stir to combine. Remove from heat. Cover; let stand 10 minutes.
7. When ready to serve, ladle hot stew into bowls, and sprinkle each evenly with cayenne and a few grinds of pepper. Top with cooked bacon, parsley, and celery leaves
Note: The liquid that naturally occurs inside of an oyster is referred to as "liquor" because of its rich flavor.

Orange-Buttermilk Trifle

ACTIVE 40 MIN. - TOTAL 40 MIN., PLUS
8 HOURS CHILLING

SERVES 12 TO 16

- 1 cup granulated sugar
- ½ cup cornstarch
- ½ tsp. kosher salt
- 4 large eggs
- 4 cups whole milk
- ½ cup unsalted butter
- 1 tsp. vanilla extract
- 1 cup whole buttermilk
  White Chocolate-Buttermilk Cake
    (recipe follows)
- 2 cups orange marmalade
- 4 blood oranges, zested, then peeled
    and cut into wedges, divided
- 4 navel oranges, peeled and cut into
    wedges
  Whipped cream, for topping

1. Whisk together sugar, cornstarch, salt, and eggs in a medium bowl until smooth, and set aside. Bring milk to a low boil in a medium-size heavy-bottomed saucepan over medium; remove from heat.
2. Temper eggs by slowly whisking one-third of the hot milk into sugar mixture until combined. Slowly add tempered egg mixture back to saucepan with hot milk, and whisk to combine. Cook over medium-low, whisking constantly, until mixture is thickened and just begins to bubble, 12 to 15 minutes.
3. Remove from heat; whisk in butter and vanilla. Transfer to a large bowl; place plastic wrap directly on warm custard to keep a film from forming. Refrigerate until chilled, at least 8 hours.
4. Whisk together chilled custard and buttermilk until smooth. Set aside.
5. Cut White Chocolate-Buttermilk Cake into 1½-inch pieces, and arrange half of the cake pieces in bottom of an 18- to 20-cup serving dish. Spread half of the marmalade over cake pieces. Spoon half of the custard (about 3 cups) over marmalade. Layer sliced oranges in alternating colors tightly across top of custard. Repeat layers twice. Top with whipped cream; sprinkle with blood orange zest.

ORANGE-
BUTTERMILK
TRIFLE

White Chocolate–Buttermilk Cake

ACTIVE 20 MIN. - TOTAL 1 HOUR,
PLUS 1 HOUR COOLING

MAKES 1 CAKE

- 2 cups bleached cake flour
- 1 tsp. baking powder
- ½ tsp. baking soda
- ½ tsp. fine sea salt
- 2 oz. white chocolate
- ¾ cup unsalted butter, at room
    temperature
- 1¾ cups granulated sugar, divided
- 4 large eggs, separated
- 2 tsp. vanilla extract
- 1 cup whole buttermilk

1. Preheat oven to 325°F. Sift together flour, baking powder, baking soda, and salt; set aside.
2. Place white chocolate in a microwavable bowl, and microwave on 50% power until melted, 1 to 1½ minutes, stirring every 30 seconds; set aside.
3. Beat together butter and 1½ cups of the sugar in the bowl of a heavy-duty stand mixer on medium speed until light and fluffy, 4 to 5 minutes. Add melted white chocolate to butter mixture; beat on medium speed until incorporated.
4. With mixer on low speed, add egg yolks, 1 at a time, beating just until incorporated after each addition; add vanilla extract. Add flour mixture to egg yolk mixture alternately with buttermilk, beginning and ending with flour mixture.
5. Whisk egg whites in a separate bowl until frothy. Gradually add remaining ¼ cup sugar, whisking until meringue is stiff but glossy. Gently fold meringue mixture into batter until incorporated. Transfer cake batter to a heavily greased and floured 13- x 9-inch cake pan. Bake in preheated oven until a wooden pick inserted in the middle comes out clean, 40 to 45 minutes. Cool cake completely on a wire rack before removing from pan, about 1 hour.

Pumpkin Picking Time!

Saturdays at Gentry's Farm in Franklin, Tennessee, are a fall tradition
for entertaining expert Katie Jacobs and her family

Crisp air, changing leaves, and football games start the buzz around Franklin: "We've got to get out to Gentry's." Fall has finally arrived.

I made my first trip to the 400-acre farm when I was in first grade. I remember swinging on a tire that hung from the massive oak tree beside the old barn, and now I watch my daughters (Emmaline, 4, and Joey Kate, 1) play in that exact spot. The property has been in the Gentry family since 1848, but nearly 30 years ago, they opened their gates to the community, offering summer day camps; educational programs for school groups; and a fall harvest celebration with pick-your-own pumpkins, hayrides, corn mazes, and friendly farm animals—like Elvis the goat.

Maybe it's the simple act of disconnecting and getting my hands dirty, but returning to the farm each year takes me back in time—to the way things used to be. This land's roots run deep, and as our small town of Franklin continues to grow, it only takes one fall Saturday in a pumpkin patch to make us all feel like kids again. –Katie Jacobs

Katie's Tailgate Tips

Easy ideas for a harvest picnic

Doughnuts made with fall ingredients like pecans, pumpkin, and pure maple syrup are a sure hit. Plus, minis are just the right size for dunking in Hot Spiced Tea.

- -

I love handing guests a special cocktail when they arrive at the party. Keep it simple: Think big batch and ready to serve.

- -

Satisfy cravings with a sweet, salty snack: Fill waffle cones with a combination of cereal squares, pretzels, cheese crackers, marshmallows, and Reese's Pieces.

- -

Personalized picnic bags are easy to prep in advance and will help you cater to specific food allergies and individual tastes.

- -

Sparkling Caramel–
Apple Sangría

(Photo, page 309)

ACTIVE 5 MIN. - TOTAL 5 MIN.,
PLUS 30 MIN. CHILLING
SERVES 12

- 1 (750-ml) bottle pecan-flavored vodka (such as Cathead)
- 4 cups fresh apple cider
- 5–6 (3-inch) cinnamon sticks
- 4–5 small whole apples
- 2 (750-ml) bottles sparkling wine, chilled
- 12 caramel-dipped apple slices

1. Stir together vodka, cider, cinnamon, and whole apples in a drink dispenser. Chill 30 minutes.
2. Pour mixture evenly into 12 glasses; top with sparkling wine. Garnish glasses with caramel-dipped apple slices.

Hot Spiced Tea

ACTIVE 5 MIN. - TOTAL 25 MIN.
SERVES 16

- 6 regular-size cinnamon-spice or chai tea bags
- 1 cup granulated sugar
- 2 Tbsp. whole cloves or mulling spices
- 2 (3-inch) cinnamon sticks
- 1 cup pineapple juice (not from concentrate)
- 1 cup refrigerated orange juice (such as Simply Orange)
- ½ cup fresh lemon juice (from 3 lemons)

1. Bring 4 cups water to a boil over high in a large pot. Remove from heat; add tea bags. Cover pot; let tea steep according to package directions. Remove and discard tea bags.
2. Stir sugar, cloves, cinnamon sticks, and 8 cups additional water into tea in pot. Bring mixture to a boil over high. Reduce heat to medium. Simmer, stirring occasionally, until sugar dissolves and mixture is fragrant, about 5 minutes. Remove spices using a small handheld fine-mesh strainer, and discard.
3. Stir pineapple juice, orange juice, and lemon juice into tea mixture in pot. Remove from heat. Serve immediately or chilled. Store, covered, in refrigerator up to 1 week.

Sweet-and-Salty Autumn
Snack Mix

(Photo, page 309)

ACTIVE 10 MIN. - TOTAL 40 MIN.,
PLUS 30 MIN. COOLING
SERVES 12

- 3 cups corn cereal squares (such as Corn Chex)
- 2 cups bite-size pretzels
- 2 cups bite-size Cheddar cheese crackers (such as Cheez-It)
- 2 cups rice cereal squares (such as Rice Chex)
- 1 cup crisp wheat cereal squares (such as Wheat Chex)
- ½ cup unsalted butter, melted
- ½ cup packed light brown sugar
- 2 Tbsp. honey
- 1 tsp. kosher salt
- 2 cups miniature marshmallows
- 1 cup candy-coated peanut butter pieces (such as Reese's Pieces)

1. Preheat oven to 300°F. Line a rimmed baking sheet with parchment paper. Stir together corn cereal, pretzels, cheese crackers, rice cereal, and wheat cereal in a large bowl. Whisk together butter, brown

BAKED MINI PUMPKIN-
PECAN DOUGHNUTS
AND HOT SPICED TEA

sugar, honey, and salt in a small bowl until smooth. Pour butter mixture over cereal mixture; stir to thoroughly coat. Spread mixture in an even layer on prepared baking sheet.

2. Bake in preheated oven until mixture is light golden brown and toasted, about 30 minutes, stirring every 10 minutes. Remove from oven. Let cool completely, about 30 minutes, stirring occasionally and breaking up clumps with your hands. Stir in marshmallows and candy-coated peanut butter pieces. Store in an airtight container at room temperature up to 1 week.

Salted Caramel–Apple Hand Pies

(Photo, page 308)

ACTIVE 20 MIN. - TOTAL 35 MIN.,
PLUS 30 MIN. COOLING
MAKES 16

- 2 Granny Smith apples, peeled and cut into small cubes (2 cups)
- ¼ cup granulated sugar
- 2 tsp. all-purpose flour, plus more for work surface
- 2 tsp. fresh lemon juice (from 1 lemon)
- ½ tsp. ground cinnamon
- ¼ tsp. kosher salt
- 2 (14.1-oz.) pkg. refrigerated piecrusts (4 piecrusts total)
- 8 soft caramel candies, roughly chopped
   Pinch of flaky sea salt
- 1 large egg
   Sanding sugar (optional)

1. Preheat oven to 375°F. Line a baking sheet with parchment paper. Stir together apples, granulated sugar, flour, lemon juice, cinnamon, and kosher salt in a bowl until combined.

2. Unroll 1 of the piecrusts on a lightly floured surface, and cut out 8 circles using a 3-inch cookie cutter. (Discard dough scraps, or reserve for another use.) Repeat process with remaining 3 piecrusts.

3. Arrange 16 of the dough rounds on prepared baking sheet. Spoon 1 heaping tablespoon of the apple filling mixture onto center of each of the 16 rounds, leaving a ¼-inch border around filling. (Reserve remaining filling for another use.) Sprinkle chopped caramel candies evenly onto filling mounds, and sprinkle with sea salt.

4. Whisk together egg and 1 tablespoon water in a small bowl, and brush some of the mixture over edges of the 16 filled dough rounds. Top filled dough rounds with remaining 16 dough rounds. Crimp together top and bottom dough-round edges using a fork, sealing each pie. Brush pie tops with remaining egg mixture. Cut small slits (about ½ inch long) into each pie top. Sprinkle pies with sanding sugar, if desired.

5. Bake in preheated oven until pies are golden brown, 15 to 20 minutes. Let cool completely on baking sheet, about 30 minutes.

Baked Mini Pumpkin–Pecan Doughnuts

ACTIVE 20 MIN. - TOTAL 1 HOUR, 15 MIN.
MAKES 4 DOZEN

- 2 large eggs
- 8 oz. (about 1 cup) canned pumpkin
- 1½ cups granulated sugar
- ½ cup vegetable oil
- 1 tsp. baking soda
- ¾ tsp. kosher salt
- ½ tsp. ground cinnamon
- ½ tsp. ground nutmeg
- ⅛ tsp. ground cloves
- 1¾ cups all-purpose flour
- 2 cups powdered sugar
- 2 Tbsp. pure maple syrup
- ½ cup chopped toasted pecans

1. Preheat oven to 350°F. Whisk together first 9 ingredients and ⅓ cup water in a large bowl until just combined. Add flour; stir until just combined. Lightly coat 2 (12-count) nonstick mini doughnut pans with cooking spray.

2. Spoon batter into a large piping bag. (Alternatively, spoon into a large ziplock plastic bag, and snip a ½-inch hole in 1 corner.) Pipe half of the batter evenly into rings of pans, filling each ring halfway. Bake in preheated oven until tops spring back when touched, 7 to 9 minutes. Cool in pans 10 minutes on a wire rack; turn out onto wire rack to cool completely, about 20 minutes. Meanwhile, wipe pans clean, and repeat process with remaining batter.

3. Whisk together powdered sugar and maple syrup in a bowl. Whisk in 2 to 3 tablespoons water, 1 teaspoon at a time, until icing is creamy. Dip doughnut tops into icing; transfer to wire rack, and immediately sprinkle with pecans. Let glaze set about 10 minutes.

TURKEY, BRIE, AND FIG
PRESSED SANDWICHES

Turkey, Brie, and Fig Pressed Sandwiches

ACTIVE 15 MIN. - TOTAL 15 MIN., PLUS
6 HOURS CHILLING
SERVES 6

- ¼ cup butter, softened
- 2 (10-oz.) ciabatta baguettes (about 12 inches long), each split in half horizontally
- 6 oz. fig jam (heaping ½ cup)
- 12 oz. deli turkey slices
- 8 oz. Brie cheese, cut into ¼-inch-thick slices
- 2 Tbsp. balsamic vinegar
- 4 oz. arugula (4 cups)

1. Spread butter evenly over cut sides of baguette halves. Spread jam evenly over cut sides of top baguette halves. Arrange turkey slices evenly over cut sides of bottom baguette halves. Top with cheese slices, drizzle with vinegar, and top with arugula. Replace top baguette halves. (You will have 2 assembled baguette sandwiches.)

2. Wrap each sandwich tightly with plastic wrap; place on a platter or baking sheet. Top each sandwich with a heavy skillet or baking sheet weighted down with cans. Place in refrigerator; chill at least 6 hours or overnight.

3. Remove plastic wrap from sandwiches. Cut each pressed sandwich crosswise into thirds (about 4-inch-long pieces).

Bring Out the Beef

Four fast and delicious supper ideas from soup to stir-fry

Speedy Skillet Beef and Broccoli

ACTIVE 20 MIN. - TOTAL 20 MIN.
SERVES 4

- 1 Tbsp. canola oil
- 1 lb. ground chuck
- 2 large heads broccoli, cut into florets, stems peeled, and sliced (about 6 cups)
- 2 large garlic cloves, finely chopped (about 1 Tbsp.)
- 3 cups cold cooked long-grain rice
- 1 large (11-oz.) red bell pepper, sliced
- 3 Tbsp. lower-sodium soy sauce
- 2 Tbsp. rice wine vinegar
- 1 Tbsp. toasted sesame oil
- 2 tsp. light brown sugar
- 4 scallions, thinly sliced (about ½ cup)
- 1 tsp. kosher salt
- ¼ tsp. crushed red pepper

1. Heat oil in a large skillet over high. Add beef, and press into a thin layer covering bottom of skillet. Cook, stirring once, until browned, about 6 minutes. Add broccoli and garlic. Cook, stirring occasionally, until broccoli begins to soften, about 6 minutes. Add rice and bell pepper. Cook, stirring often, until heated through and beginning to brown, about 6 minutes.
2. Stir together soy sauce, vinegar, sesame oil, and brown sugar in a small bowl. Pour soy mixture over rice mixture, stirring to combine.
3. Remove from heat; sprinkle with scallions, salt, and crushed red pepper.

SPEEDY SKILLET BEEF AND BROCCOLI

CHOOSE CHUCK
Ground chuck has more fat than ground sirloin. It cooks up extra crispy in this stir-fry without drying out, and the tasty juices are soaked up by the rice. Spread the beef in an even layer in the pan to create a nice sear.

BEEFY BUTTERNUT
SQUASH PASTA

BEEF-AND-VEGETABLE
SOUP WITH GNOCCHI

Beefy Butternut Squash Pasta

ACTIVE 15 MIN. - TOTAL 35 MIN.
SERVES 4

- 1 Tbsp. olive oil
- 1 lb. ground sirloin
- 1 medium-size yellow onion, chopped (about 1½ cups)
- 2 garlic cloves, finely chopped (about 2 tsp.)
- 1 tsp. chili powder
- 1 Tbsp. all-purpose flour
- 3 cups lower-sodium chicken broth
- 12 oz. cubed, peeled butternut squash (about 2½ cups)
- 8 oz. uncooked large shell pasta
- 2 tsp. kosher salt
- ⅛ tsp. black pepper
- 3 cups chopped, stemmed collard greens
- 3 oz. Parmesan cheese, grated (about ¾ cup)

1. Heat oil in a large skillet over high. Add beef, and cook, stirring often, until browned, about 8 minutes. Add onion, garlic, and chili powder, and cook until onion is just softened, about 3 minutes.
2. Stir in flour; cook, stirring often, 1 minute. Stir in broth, squash, pasta, salt, and pepper. Bring to a boil over high; reduce heat to medium-low. Cover, and cook until pasta is al dente, about 8 minutes. Remove from heat.
3. Stir in collards. Cover, and let stand until collards have wilted, about 10 minutes. Uncover, and stir in Parmesan.

Beef-and-Vegetable Soup with Gnocchi

ACTIVE 15 MIN. - TOTAL 30 MIN.
SERVES 6

- 2 tsp. olive oil
- 1 lb. ground chuck
- 1 large yellow onion, chopped (about 3 cups)
- 4 celery stalks, thinly sliced (about 2 cups)
- 3 garlic cloves, finely chopped (about 4 tsp.)
- 1 (28-oz.) can whole, peeled plum tomatoes, drained
- 2 tsp. dried oregano
- 8 cups lower-sodium chicken broth
- 1 (12-oz.) pkg. refrigerated gnocchi
- 1 (6-oz.) pkg. fresh spinach
- 3 tsp. kosher salt
- ⅛ tsp. black pepper
  Grated Parmesan cheese, for serving

1. Heat oil in a large saucepan over high. Add beef, and cook, stirring occasionally, until browned, about 8 minutes. Add onion, celery, and garlic. Cook, stirring often, until vegetables are softened, about 8 minutes.
2. Stir in tomatoes and oregano, breaking up tomatoes with a wooden spoon. Stir in broth, and bring to a boil. Reduce heat to medium-low, and gently boil until vegetables are tender, about 8 minutes. Add gnocchi, and cook until just tender, about 3 minutes more. Remove from heat. Stir in spinach, salt, and pepper. Sprinkle each serving with grated Parmesan.

PATTY-MELT POINTERS
Sturdy, thick-cut bread such as sourdough can stand up to the meat and gooey cheeses in this diner classic. Use a cast-iron pan; it's a pro at handling the heat needed to cook the patties and toast the bread.

Diner-Style Patty Melts

ACTIVE 30 MIN. · TOTAL 30 MIN.
SERVES 4

- 4 Tbsp. canola oil, divided
- 1 large yellow onion, thinly sliced (about 4 cups)
- 1½ tsp. kosher salt, divided
- 1¼ lb. ground chuck
- ½ tsp. black pepper
- ¼ cup mayonnaise
- 1 Tbsp. Dijon mustard
- 1 Tbsp. barbecue sauce
- 1 Tbsp. ketchup
- 3 oz. sharp yellow Cheddar cheese, shredded (about ¾ cup)
- 8 (¾-inch-thick) sourdough bread slices
- 4 Swiss cheese slices
- 4 Tbsp. butter, divided

1. Heat 2 tablespoons of the oil in a medium skillet over medium. Add onion and ½ teaspoon of the salt. Cook, stirring often, until golden brown and soft, about 20 minutes. Set aside.

2. Meanwhile, divide ground beef into 4 portions. Press each into a flat, ¼-inch-thick patty. Sprinkle with pepper and remaining 1 teaspoon salt.

3. Heat remaining 2 tablespoons oil in a large cast-iron skillet over medium-high. Cook 2 patties at a time, pressing gently, until browned but still pink in the center, 2 minutes per side. Transfer to a plate.

4. Stir together mayonnaise, mustard, barbecue sauce, and ketchup in a small bowl until combined.

5. Wipe out cast-iron skillet; reduce heat to medium. Divide Cheddar among 4 of the bread slices; top each with a patty, caramelized onions, Swiss cheese slice, mayonnaise mixture, and remaining bread. Melt 2 tablespoons of the butter in skillet. Place 2 sandwiches in hot butter; cook (with another skillet on top of sandwiches to weight them down) until golden brown and cheeses are melted, about 3 minutes per side. Repeat with remaining 2 tablespoons butter and 2 sandwiches.

Falling for Persimmons

Enjoy this rich, spiced, cakelike dessert

I can't recall exactly when I first tasted persimmon pudding, but I do know the place: my grandmother's North Carolina dairy farm kitchen, where I spent many happy hours feasting on the simple, seasonal Southern dishes I still love to cook today.

Dense and sturdy enough to cut into squares like a brownie, Grandmother's recipe was spiced with cinnamon, nutmeg, allspice, and ginger. Its sweet flavor, moist texture, and deep brown hue pleased me greatly, even though it was rather plain compared to the monumental coconut layer cakes and decadent pies she baked for the holidays. Those were fancy prizes, while this was a quiet pleasure at the kitchen table on a cool autumn afternoon.

Fall is when persimmons come into season, and wild trees thrive throughout the South on the edges of cleared fields, from Maryland to Florida and from the North Carolina Piedmont to Texas and beyond. Their branches release yellowing leaves along with plump, orange-to-umber fruit, which dangle like Christmas tree ornaments. The sweet orbs drop to the earth from mid-August through late fall, which is also when you'll find conventionally grown types at your local grocery store.

Pudding is the best way to enjoy this fruit, and it's well represented in community cookbooks and family recipe boxes, though the dessert is far less popular today than it was when gardens, canning, and foraging were common and essential.

I fell in love with persimmon pudding again, two decades after enjoying it as a young girl, having moved back home to Greensboro after three years as a Peace Corps volunteer in Thailand. I had settled into daily life teaching middle school English and social studies, and (because I loved cooking) visiting the farmers' market was part of my weekly routine.

One day, I spotted it on a vendor's table, an old friend I'd nearly forgotten but recognized with pleasure even before I noticed the hand-lettered "Persimmon Pudding" sign. Rustic and deeply spiced, it tasted exactly like fall.

The vibrant and dazzling flavors of Thai cooking had expanded my sense of edible wonders, but this culinary reunion reminded me of what I'd missed during my years far from home.
—Nancie McDermott

Persimmon Pudding

Once the fruit is peeled, seeded, chopped, and pureed in a food processor, don't forget to press the mixture through a fine-mesh strainer.

ACTIVE 15 MIN. - TOTAL 1 HOUR, 15 MIN., PLUS 1 HOUR COOLING (OPTIONAL)
SERVES 12

- 4 cups all-purpose flour
- 1 cup granulated sugar
- 1 cup packed light brown sugar
- 2 tsp. baking powder
- 1 tsp. baking soda
- 1 tsp. kosher salt
- 1 tsp. ground cinnamon, plus more for garnish
- ½ tsp. ground ginger
- ½ tsp. ground nutmeg
- 4 large eggs
- 1 cup whole milk
- 1 cup half-and-half
- 1 Tbsp. orange zest (from 1 orange)
- 1 Tbsp. orange liqueur (optional)
- 2½ cups persimmon puree
- 1 cup chopped toasted pecans
- ½ cup butter, melted
  Cinnamon Whipped Cream (recipe follows)
  Fresh persimmon slices

1. Preheat oven to 300°F. Lightly grease a 13- x 9-inch baking dish with cooking spray; set aside. Whisk together first 9 ingredients in a large bowl. Whisk together eggs, milk, half-and-half, zest, and liqueur (if using) in a separate large bowl until well combined. Add flour mixture to milk mixture alternately with persimmon puree, beginning and ending with flour mixture. Stir in chopped toasted pecans until just combined. Gradually add melted butter, and stir until just combined. Pour mixture into prepared baking dish.

2. Bake in preheated oven until mixture is browned and a wooden pick inserted in center comes out clean, 1 hour to 1 hour and 10 minutes. Serve warm, or transfer to a wire rack to cool completely, about 1 hour. Serve with Cinnamon Whipped Cream. Sprinkle with cinnamon, and top with persimmon slices.

Cinnamon Whipped Cream

ACTIVE 5 MIN. - TOTAL 5 MIN.
MAKES ABOUT 1¾ CUPS

Beat together 1 cup heavy cream, 1 tsp. vanilla extract, and ⅛ tsp. ground cinnamon with an electric mixer on high speed until foamy, 1 minute. Gradually add 3 Tbsp. powdered sugar, beating at high speed until medium peaks form, about 2 minutes. Chill until ready to serve.

Sweet on Shortbread

Easy, buttery slice-and-bake cookies topped with pecan halves

Salted Butter-Pecan Shortbread Cookies

ACTIVE 15 MIN. · TOTAL 40 MIN., PLUS 4 HOURS CHILLING

MAKES 3 ½ DOZEN

- 1 cup butter, softened
- ¾ cup unsifted powdered sugar
- 1 cup chopped toasted pecans
- 1 tsp. vanilla extract
- 2 cups all-purpose flour
- ¼ tsp. baking powder
- 1 cup turbinado or Demerara sugar
- 1 large egg, lightly beaten
- 42 pecan halves (about 1 cup)

1. Beat butter in a stand mixer fitted with a paddle attachment on medium speed until creamy, about 1 minute. Gradually add powdered sugar, beating until mixture is smooth, about 1 minute. Stir in chopped toasted pecans and vanilla.

2. Whisk together flour and baking powder in a bowl. With mixer running on low speed, gradually add flour mixture to butter mixture until blended.

3. Transfer dough to a work surface; shape into 2 (7-inch) logs. Wrap logs separately in plastic wrap; refrigerate at least 4 hours or up to 2 days.

4. Preheat oven to 350°F. Line 2 baking sheets with parchment paper. Place turbinado sugar in a shallow dish. Unwrap logs, and brush evenly on all sides with egg. Roll each log in turbinado sugar. Cut logs into ⅓-inch-thick slices (you should have 42 cookies total), and place 1 inch apart on prepared baking sheets. Top each cookie with 1 pecan half, pressing lightly to adhere.

5. Bake in preheated oven until cookie edges are golden, 10 to 12 minutes. Let cool 5 minutes on baking sheets. Transfer cookies to a wire rack; cool 10 minutes.

ON THE EDGE
For extra crunch, evenly coat both dough logs with turbinado sugar before slicing them.

The Instant Pot Roast

Ranch seasoning gives this old-school family favorite a delicious new spin

Quick Mississippi Pot Roast

ACTIVE 20 MIN. - TOTAL 1 HOUR, 30 MIN.
SERVES 8

- 2 Tbsp. canola oil
- 3 lb. boneless chuck roast, trimmed
- 1½ tsp. kosher salt
- 1 tsp. black pepper
- 2 medium-size (10 oz. each) red onions, quartered
- 3 medium garlic cloves
- 1 cup jarred pepperoncini salad peppers, plus 2 Tbsp. liquid from jar, divided
- ¼ cup beef broth
- 2 Tbsp. unsalted butter
- 1 (1-oz.) envelope ranch dressing mix
- 1 Tbsp. chopped fresh dill
- 1 Tbsp. chopped fresh chives

1. Select "sauté" setting on a programmable pressure multicooker, such as Instant Pot. (Instructions, times, and settings may vary by brand or model.) Select "high" temperature setting; allow to preheat. Add oil to cooker. Pat roast dry; sprinkle all sides with salt and pepper. Add roast; cook, turning often, until browned, 10 minutes. Remove from cooker. Add onions and garlic to cooker. Cook, stirring often to scrape browned bits, until just softened, 2 minutes. Press "cancel." Add browned roast, peppers, broth, butter, and ranch dressing mix.
2. Cover cooker with lid, and lock in place. Turn steam release handle to "sealing" position. Select "manual/pressure cook" setting. Select "high" pressure for 55 minutes. (It will take 8 to 10 minutes to come up to pressure before cooking starts.)
3. Let the pressure release naturally. (This will take 10 to 12 minutes.) Remove lid; transfer roast to a deep serving platter. Stir pepper liquid into juices in cooker. Top roast with onion mixture; pour juices in cooker over mixture. Sprinkle with herbs. Slow-cooker method: Sear roast on the stove in a skillet over high. Place all ingredients in slow cooker. Cover; cook on low for 8 to 9 hours or on high 5 to 6 hours.

Mushrooms Make It Better

Two types of 'shrooms give this chicken dish a savory flavor

Chicken–Mushroom Skillet

ACTIVE 30 MIN. - TOTAL 30 MIN.
SERVES 4

- 4 (6-oz.) boneless, skinless chicken breasts
- ½ tsp. black pepper
- 1¼ tsp. kosher salt, divided
- 2 Tbsp. olive oil
- 1 Tbsp. unsalted butter
- 6 oz. cremini mushrooms, halved
- 6 oz. oyster mushrooms, torn
- 6 garlic cloves, smashed
- ½ cup (4 oz.) dry white wine
- ¼ cup unsalted chicken stock
- 1 Tbsp. fresh thyme leaves
- 1 Tbsp. chopped fresh flat-leaf parsley
- 1 (8.8-oz.) pkg. precooked microwavable brown-and-wild rice, prepared according to pkg. directions
  Lemon wedges

1. Sprinkle chicken evenly with pepper and ¾ teaspoon of the salt. Heat oil in a large skillet over medium-high. Add chicken. Cook until well browned, about 6 minutes per side. Transfer to a plate; set aside.

2. Melt butter in pan over medium-high. Add mushrooms. Cook, undisturbed, 3 minutes. Stir in garlic. Cook, stirring occasionally, 3 minutes. Sprinkle with remaining ½ teaspoon salt. Stir in wine and stock.

3. Return chicken to pan, and sprinkle with thyme. Cook, undisturbed, until a thermometer inserted in thickest portion registers 165°F, about 3 minutes. Sprinkle with parsley. Serve with rice and lemon wedges.

Nutritional information: Calories: 436; Protein: 44g; Carbs: 24g; Fiber: 2g; Fat: 16g

Not Your Ordinary Oatmeal

Wake up to a make-ahead breakfast loaded with spices, fruits, and nuts

Baked Apple-Cranberry-Pecan Oatmeal

ACTIVE 15 MIN. - TOTAL 1 HOUR, PLUS OVERNIGHT CHILLING

SERVES 6

2	large eggs
1¼	cups whole milk
2	tsp. vanilla extract
1	tsp. apple pie spice
¼	tsp. kosher salt
¾	cup packed light brown sugar, divided
8	Tbsp. butter, melted, divided
2	cups small cubed, peeled apple (about 1 large apple)
3½	cups uncooked old-fashioned regular rolled oats, divided
1	cup coarsely chopped pecans, divided
1	cup dried cranberries, divided

1. Lightly coat an 8-inch square (2-quart) baking dish with cooking spray. Whisk together eggs, milk, vanilla, apple pie spice, salt, ½ cup of the brown sugar, and 5 tablespoons of the melted butter in a large bowl. Add apple cubes, 3 cups of the oats, ½ cup of the pecans, and ½ cup of the cranberries; stir to combine. Pour mixture into prepared baking dish; cover with plastic wrap.

2. Stir together remaining ¼ cup brown sugar, 3 tablespoons melted butter, ½ cup oats, and ½ cup pecans in a medium bowl. Cover with plastic wrap. Place covered baking dish and covered bowl in refrigerator; chill 8 hours or overnight.

3. Preheat oven to 350°F. While oven preheats, remove baking dish and bowl from refrigerator; remove plastic wrap. Stir apple-oat mixture in baking dish to redistribute wet ingredients. Sprinkle top evenly with oat-pecan topping mixture.

4. Bake in preheated oven until mixture is set in the middle and topping is golden brown, about 35 minutes. Remove from oven, and sprinkle with remaining ½ cup dried cranberries. Cool 10 minutes. Serve warm.

APPLE PICKING

Choose a firm, sweet apple (such as a Fuji or Honeycrisp) that will retain its shape and a little texture after being baked.

COOKING ⦿SL SCHOOL

IN SEASON

Go Beyond the Button

Four flavorful mushrooms to spice up fall dishes

MAITAKE
These rich, savory mushrooms grow in large, ruffled clusters, which is why they are called "hen of the woods." Toss on the grill, or saute with pork or chicken.

SHIITAKE
Toadstool-shape shiitakes have a mild smoky flavor and a firm texture that holds up well in soups and noodle dishes. Trim off and discard the stems; they're too tough to eat.

OYSTER
Typically white or pale gray, oyster mushrooms can also be pink or yellow. The scalloped caps taste great in stir-fries and have a delicate nutty flavor.

CHANTERELLE
Picked in the wild, these pricey mushrooms are prized for their toothsome texture and an earthy, slightly fruity taste. Add to a dish where they will shine, like a risotto or pasta.

KNOW-HOW

Sear Smart

The best way to brown a roast before preparing it on the stove, in the oven, or in a multicooker

1
Let the beef come to room temperature. Pat dry with a paper towel; season with salt and pepper.

2
Coat the bottom of a large skillet with canola oil. Place the pan over high heat until the oil shimmers. Add beef, fat side down. Let it sit undisturbed in the pan until well browned on one side, about 5 minutes. Repeat on other side.

3
Use tongs to hold up the beef, and sear both ends until well browned, about 5 minutes on each side.

November

234 **A Texas-Size Thank-You** Chef Chris Shepherd prepares a feast of gratitude for local Houston firefighters

236 **Picture-Perfect Pies** One of our favorite food stylists shares her best-kept secrets for baking Instagram-worthy desserts

242 **Tastes like Home** Celebrate the holidays with some of the South's most storied recipes

254 **Roll Call** Warm, light, and fluffy, these extra-special buns will be the talk of the buffet line

255 **The Giving Tree** If you're lucky enough to live near pecan trees, they will bestow upon you a mighty precious—and delicious—bounty

260 **Thanksgiving Classics** Enjoy all the traditional crowd-pleasers, from green bean casserole to pumpkin chess pie

268 **SL Cooking School** Our Test Kitchen professionals have some tasty twists on the annual day-after turkey salad sandwich

A Texas-Size Thank-You

Chef Chris Shepherd prepares a feast of gratitude for local Houston firefighters

Shepherd serves local firefighters fried turkey with all the traditional trimmings.

Most of us bank on spending the holidays at home, but for firefighters and other public workers, being on the clock—while the rest of us are sitting around the table—is part of the job. Chris Shepherd thought about this rough justice in 2008. Then a chef at buzzy Spanish restaurant Catalan, he was already preparing his family's Thanksgiving feast in the ample space of an industrial kitchen. It would be easy, he figured, to knock out extra food for his local firehouse. "I remember thinking, 'I have the ability to do this; why wouldn't I?'" he says.

That initial gesture led to a tradition that the award-winning Houston chef has relished for over a decade. "It's one of my favorite days of the year," he says. Shepherd used to get up early to make everything himself. But now that his company, Underbelly Hospitality, offers to-go Thanksgiving Day meals (with dishes such as creamed collard greens, cornbread custard, and potato tot casserole), he makes the deliveries and handles the main event: fried turkey. Over the years, he's roasted and smoked birds, but he finds frying especially satisfying. In his recipe, a peppery apple cider vinegar mixture perfumed with garlic, bay leaves, and orange zest infuses the turkey with its first layer of flavor. After frying, the crispy skin gets a liberal dose of Creole seasoning.

Although Shepherd is well-known in culinary circles, the area firefighters don't always recognize the guy in glasses driving into the station, rolling down his window to ask, "Hey, what's up?" But that doesn't matter. "It feels good to look out for and take care of the people around us," he says. "I see them driving down the street and think, 'Those are our guys.'"

Understanding and appreciating Houston's diverse community is at the heart of all of Shepherd's projects. Inspired by the city's culinary melting pot, his new book, *Cook Like a Local*, shares recipes and wisdom learned from chefs at area Vietnamese and Indian restaurants, Korean grocery stores, and more.

In return for his holiday generosity, Shepherd has been recognized in different ways: He received an honorary patch from Houston Fire Station 7 and a firefighter coin (along with instructions to keep it in his pocket at all times). "It's kind of cool to feel inducted with them," he says.

Aaron Wallace, captain at Fire Station 16 in Houston's Montrose neighborhood, says that even after 24 years on the job, gestures of gratitude (large or small) never get old. He adds, "There's nothing more rewarding than to know that people out there genuinely appreciate you."

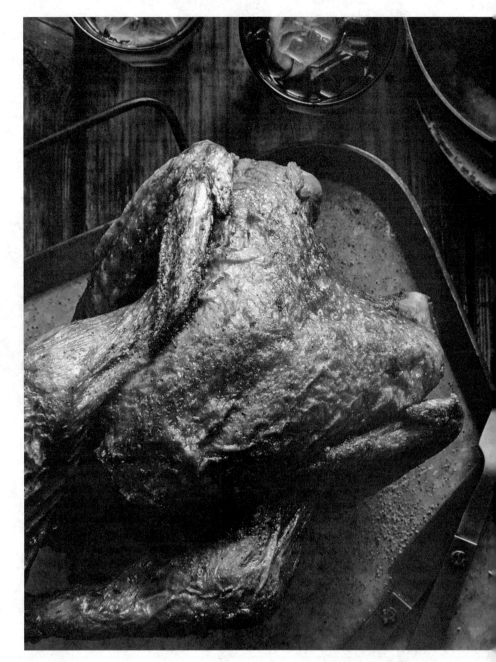

Crispy Fried Turkey with Creole Spices

ACTIVE 30 MIN. - TOTAL 1 HOUR, 30 MIN., PLUS 8 HOURS CHILLING
SERVES 10

- ¼ cup apple cider vinegar
- 3 Tbsp. light brown sugar
- 2 Tbsp. kosher salt
- 1 Tbsp. black pepper
- 1 Tbsp. ground bay leaves
- 1 Tbsp. garlic powder
- 1 Tbsp. orange zest (from 1 orange)
- 1 (10- to 12-lb.) frozen whole turkey, completely thawed, neck and giblets removed
- 3 gal. canola oil, for frying
- 3 Tbsp. Creole seasoning (such as Zatarain's)

1. Combine 1¼ cups of water, vinegar, brown sugar, salt, pepper, ground bay leaves, garlic powder, and orange zest in a small saucepan. Bring to a boil over high, stirring often. Reduce heat to medium-high; simmer, stirring constantly, 1 minute. Remove from heat, and cool completely, about 30 minutes. Pour through a fine-mesh strainer into a bowl; discard solids.
2. Pat turkey dry. Fill a meat injector with marinade mixture, and inject in turkey breasts, legs, and thighs. Repeat until the injector is empty. Place turkey on a large parchment paper-lined rimmed baking sheet. Chill, uncovered, at least 8 hours or up to 24 hours. Remove from refrigerator, and let stand at room temperature 20 minutes.
3. Meanwhile, pour oil in a deep propane turkey fryer. (The 3-gallon amount is below the recommended fill line, about 10 to 12 inches from top of fryer, which will help prevent hot oil from bubbling over once frying begins.) Heat oil to 350°F over a medium-low flame according to manufacturer's instructions. Using the turkey rod attachment, carefully lower turkey, neck down and legs up, into hot oil. (Hot oil may bubble over the rim of the pot, so pay close attention!) Fry turkey about 3 minutes per pound, until golden brown and an instant-read thermometer inserted in thickest part of thigh registers 155°F, about 30 minutes. Carefully lift turkey out of oil; transfer to a carving board.
4. Sprinkle hot turkey all over with Creole seasoning. Rest until thermometer registers 165°F, about 30 minutes. Carve turkey, and serve.

First-Time Frying Tips

Conquer your fears with easy-to-follow advice

Defrost the turkey, and pat it dry. Even a semi-frozen bird will cook unevenly and cause splattering.

Catch oil spills by placing a large piece of cardboard under the fryer; weight down the edges with bricks.

Keep children and pets away from the cooking area at all times. Never leave the fryer unattended.

PIECRUST TIP
Unlike most crusts, this dough should not be chilled before it's rolled out. Let it rest at room temperature so the coconut oil doesn't harden and the dough remains soft and pliable.

SPICED COCONUT-PUMPKIN PIE

Picture-Perfect Pies

One of our favorite food stylists shares her best-kept secrets for baking Instagram-worthy desserts

Marian Cooper Cairns travels for pie. Every summer, when magazines and cookbook publishers are planning for the holidays, the in-demand recipe developer and food stylist flies around the country to make bubbling, flaky creations worthy of glossy covers (like ours).

Over the past 12 years, she has developed a reputation for inventive fillings, basketlike lattices, and creative crimps. Her passion for baking started because of her late mother, Jane, who worked in our Test Kitchen for 10 years. Cairns followed in her footsteps, spending seven years here developing and styling recipes.

Although she has an artist's eye and baking is in her blood, she says the perfect pie is a result of practice and patience. "When I first started in the Test Kitchen, I was so intimidated. I couldn't even crimp a crust," she confesses. "But I had the best teachers, and I really worked at it."

Of course, when your job entails making two dozen pies for one magazine cover, you learn a few tricks along the way–like adding a touch of shortening to the pie dough. "It's more forgiving to work with when I'm braiding and cutting shapes," she says. She crumples parchment paper before placing it in a pie plate so it fits more snugly and uses a ruler to precisely measure dough strips. Cairns also prefers to blind-bake pies on a low oven rack for the crispiest bottom crust.

She even has a few time-saving tips. Use two rolls of refrigerated store-bought dough (she prefers the Trader Joe's and Publix brands), and let them stand for 10 minutes to soften before kneading them together and rolling the dough into a circle to fit your dish. "A single roll isn't enough for a pretty crimp or to fill a deep-dish pie plate," she says. "There's no shame in taking a shortcut–I do it, too, at home!"

Spiced Coconut-Pumpkin Pie

Coconut milk (choose the full-fat kind) adds richness and a hint of tropical sweetness to the fragrant spiced filling.

ACTIVE 45 MIN. - TOTAL 3 HOURS, 5 MIN., PLUS 3 HOURS COOLING
SERVES 10

COCONUT CRUST
- 3 cups all-purpose flour, plus more for work surface
- 2 Tbsp. granulated sugar
- ¾ tsp. kosher salt
- ½ cup plus 2 Tbsp. solid refined coconut oil (such as LouAna), at room temperature
- 8–11 Tbsp. ice-cold water
- 1 large egg

PUMPKIN FILLING
- 1 Tbsp. cornstarch
- ¾ cup granulated sugar
- 1 (15-oz.) can pumpkin (such as Libby's)
- 1 cup well-shaken and stirred canned coconut milk
- 1 tsp. vanilla extract
- ¾ tsp. ground cinnamon
- ¾ tsp. ground cardamom
- ½ tsp. ground ginger
- ¼ tsp. allspice
- Pinch of finely ground black pepper
- 3 large eggs
- ½ tsp. kosher salt
- Sweetened whipped cream

1. Prepare the crust: Combine flour, sugar, and salt in a food processor. Pulse until well blended, 6 to 7 times. Add oil in rounded tablespoonfuls. Pulse until oil is well blended, 6 to 7 times. While pulsing continually, add ice-cold water, 1 tablespoon at a time, processing until dough begins to clump and come together. Transfer to work surface. Pat dough together; divide in half. Shape into 1 flat disk and 1 flat rectangle. Wrap each in plastic wrap; let stand at room temperature 30 minutes.
2. Unwrap dough disk. Roll out on a floured surface into a 13-inch circle (about ⅛ inch thick). Fit into a 9-inch pie

plate. Trim edges with a sharp knife. Prick bottom of dough a few times with a fork; chill until ready to use. Unwrap dough rectangle, and roll out into a ⅛-inch-thick rectangle (about 14 x 8 inches). Using a sharp knife, cut 9 (⅓-inch-wide) strips from rectangle. Braid 3 strips at a time to create 3 braided ropes. Trim rough edges from braided ropes. Wrap the remaining scraps; let stand at room temperature.
3. Whisk together egg and 1 tablespoon water until well blended. Brush edges of dough with egg wash. Arrange braided strips along edges of pie, pinching to blend seams and pressing lightly to adhere. Brush tops of braids with egg wash. Chill 30 minutes.
4. Preheat oven to 375°F. Line dough with parchment paper; fill to the rim with pie weights or dried beans. Bake until pale golden around edges, about 15 minutes. Remove parchment and weights; continue baking until bottom of crust is set, 8 to 10 more minutes. Transfer to a wire rack. Cool completely, about 30 minutes.
5. Prepare the filling: Reduce oven temperature to 325°F. Whisk together cornstarch and sugar in a large bowl. Whisk in pumpkin, coconut milk, vanilla, cinnamon, cardamom, ginger, allspice, pepper, eggs, and salt until smooth. Pour into cooled crust. Bake until center is almost set, 45 to 50 minutes, shielding the edges with aluminum foil, if needed. Transfer to a wire rack to cool completely, about 2 hours.
6. While the pie cools, increase oven temperature to 350°F. Press scraps together, smoothing to ⅛-inch thickness on lightly floured surface. Cut dough using small assorted leaf-shaped cookie cutters. Brush tops lightly with egg wash. Arrange on a parchment paper-lined baking sheet. Bake until golden brown, 10 to 15 minutes. Transfer to a wire rack to cool completely, about 30 minutes. Before serving, arrange crust leaf shapes around 1 edge. Serve with whipped cream.

Pomegranate-Chess Tart

A layer of Pomegranate Gelée (a fancy word for gelatin) sits atop this tart's creamy chess filling. (Photo, page 312)

ACTIVE 40 MIN. - TOTAL 3 HOURS, 50 MIN., PLUS 5 HOURS, 30 MIN. CHILLING
SERVES 10

CREAM CHEESE-CORNMEAL CRUST
- 1 cup all-purpose flour, plus more for work surface
- ½ cup fine yellow cornmeal
- ½ tsp. kosher salt
- ½ cup unsalted butter, softened
- 4 oz. cream cheese, softened
- 1 large egg yolk

CITRUS CHESS FILLING
- 1 cup granulated sugar
- 1 Tbsp. all-purpose flour
- 1 Tbsp. fine yellow cornmeal
- ¼ cup unsalted butter, melted
- ¼ cup whole buttermilk
- 1 Tbsp. orange zest plus 3 Tbsp. fresh juice (from 1 orange)
- 2 Tbsp. fresh lemon juice (from 1 lemon)
- 3 large eggs, beaten

POMEGRANATE GELÉE
- 1¼ cups fresh pomegranate juice
- 2 Tbsp. granulated sugar
- 2½ tsp. unflavored gelatin (from 2 [¼-oz.] envelopes)
- 3 Tbsp. orange liqueur (such as Cointreau or Grand Marnier)
- ⅔ cup pomegranate arils (seeds)

1. Prepare the crust: Whisk together flour, cornmeal, and salt in a large bowl; set aside. Beat butter and cream cheese with an electric mixer fitted with paddle attachment on medium speed until creamy and well combined, 1 minute. Add egg yolk; beat on low speed until just combined. Add flour mixture; beat on low speed until dough begins to form. Shape into a flat disk. Wrap in plastic wrap; chill 2 hours or up to 2 days.
2. When ready to use, remove dough from refrigerator, and let sit at room temperature until soft to the touch and easy to roll, 20 to 30 minutes. Unwrap and roll out on a lightly floured surface into a 12- to 13-inch circle. Fit dough into a 10-inch tart pan with a removable bottom. Fold edges over. Press into pan, forming an even, thick edge along sides and bringing dough ¼ inch over top of pan. Prick bottom of dough with a fork a few times. Chill until firm, about 30 minutes.
3. Preheat oven to 375°F. Line dough with parchment paper; fill with pie weights or dried beans. Bake until pale golden around the edges, about 15 minutes. Remove the parchment and weights, and continue baking until bottom of crust is set, 8 to 10 more minutes. Transfer to a wire rack; cool completely, about 30 minutes.
4. Prepare the filling: Reduce oven temperature to 325°F. Whisk together sugar, flour, cornmeal, butter, buttermilk, orange zest, orange juice, and lemon juice until blended. Add eggs, and whisk until smooth. Pour mixture into prepared tart crust. Bake on the lowest oven rack until golden and set, 35 to 40 minutes. Cool completely on a wire rack, about 2 hours. Chill tart until cold, about 2 hours.
5. Prepare the gelée: Combine pomegranate juice and sugar in a saucepan. Sprinkle gelatin over mixture, and let stand 5 minutes. Cook over medium just until mixture is steaming and gelatin dissolves, about 5 minutes. Remove from heat; cool 20 minutes. Skim off foam, if needed. Stir in liqueur.
6. Gently and slowly pour pomegranate mixture over top of chilled tart until just below edge of crust, being careful not to overfill (you may have extra pomegranate mixture). Continue to chill tart until gelée sets, about 1 hour. Sprinkle with pomegranate arils just before serving.

Dulce de Leche-Cheesecake Pecan Pie

A caramel-flavored cheesecake pairs with a gooey, nutty filling in this twist on the usual pecan pie. (Photo, page 311)

ACTIVE 35 MIN. - TOTAL 4 HOURS, PLUS 3 HOURS COOLING
SERVES 10

CINNAMON-PECAN CRUST
- ⅓ cup chopped toasted pecans
- 1½ cups all-purpose flour, plus more for work surface
- 2 Tbsp. granulated sugar
- ½ tsp. ground cinnamon
- ½ tsp. kosher salt
- 6 Tbsp. cold unsalted butter, cubed
- 2 Tbsp. cold vegetable shortening, cubed
- 4 Tbsp. whole buttermilk

PECAN PIE FILLING
- 3½ cups pecan halves, divided
- 2 large eggs
- ½ cup dark corn syrup
- ¼ cup packed light brown sugar
- 2 tsp. vanilla extract
- 2 tsp. fine cornmeal
- ¾ tsp. kosher salt

DULCE DE LECHE-CHEESECAKE FILLING
- 6 oz. cream cheese, at room temperature (from 1 [8-oz.] pkg.)
- 1 large egg
- 1 tsp. vanilla extract
- ½ tsp. kosher salt
- ½ cup canned dulce de leche

1. Prepare the crust: Pulse pecans in a food processor until finely chopped. Add next 4 ingredients; pulse until well combined, 3 or 4 times. Add butter and shortening; pulse until mixture looks like coarse meal, 5 or 6 times. Drizzle buttermilk over mixture; pulse just until dough begins to come together. Shape into a flat disk. Wrap in plastic wrap; chill 2 hours or up to 2 days.
2. When ready to use, let dough sit at room temperature until soft to the touch, 20 to 30 minutes. Unwrap dough; roll out on a lightly floured surface into a 12- to 13-inch circle. Fit into a 9-inch pie plate. Fold edges under; crimp. Prick bottom of dough a few times with a fork; freeze 15 minutes.
3. Preheat oven to 375°F. Line dough with parchment paper; fill with pie weights or dried beans. Bake until edges are lightly golden and just set, about 15 minutes. Remove parchment and weights; continue baking until bottom of crust is set, 8 to

10 more minutes. Transfer to a wire rack; cool completely, about 30 minutes.

4. Prepare the Pecan Pie Filling: Reduce oven temperature to 350°F. Chop 2 cups of the pecan halves; reserve remaining 1½ cups pecan halves. Spread chopped pecans in a single layer on a baking sheet. Bake until lightly toasted, about 5 to 6 minutes. Cool completely, about 30 minutes.

5. Whisk eggs until smooth and well combined. Add corn syrup, brown sugar, vanilla, cornmeal, and salt; whisk until thickened and smooth. Set aside 3 tablespoons of mixture.

6. Prepare the Dulce de Leche-Cheesecake Filling: Beat cream cheese, egg, vanilla, and salt in a medium bowl with an electric mixer fitted with paddle attachment on medium speed until very creamy and smooth, 1 minute. Add dulce de leche; beat until well combined, 1 minute. Spoon into prepared crust. Sprinkle toasted chopped pecans over cream cheese mixture in crust. Gently spoon Pecan Pie Filling over chopped pecans.

7. Reduce oven temperature to 325°F. Toss reserved 1½ cups pecan halves with 3 tablespoons reserved Pecan Pie Filling. Arrange over top of pie in a spoke pattern, with halves slightly overlapping. Position oven rack 3 to 4 inches from bottom of oven; place pie on rack. Bake just until filling is slightly puffed and set in the middle and crust is golden brown, 40 to 45 minutes, shielding pie with aluminum foil halfway through baking time. Transfer to a wire rack. Cool completely, 2 to 3 hours.

Pear–Cranberry Pie with Ginger–Almond Streusel

A jammy filling, crumbly topping, and vanilla bean-flecked crust make this a surefire holiday winner. (Photo, page 313)

ACTIVE 35 MIN. · TOTAL 3 HOURS, 30 MIN., PLUS 2 HOURS, 20 MIN. COOLING
SERVES 10

BUTTERY VANILLA BEAN CRUST
- 1 large egg
- 1–3 Tbsp. ice-cold water
- 1¾ cups all-purpose flour, plus more for work surface
- 2 Tbsp. granulated sugar
- ¾ tsp. kosher salt
- 1 vanilla bean, split lengthwise
- 10 Tbsp. cold unsalted butter, cubed

GINGER-ALMOND STREUSEL
- 5 Tbsp. packed light brown sugar
- ¼ cup unsalted butter, melted
- ½ tsp. kosher salt
- ½ cup plus 1 Tbsp. all-purpose flour
- ⅓ cup coarsely chopped almonds
- 3 Tbsp. finely chopped crystallized ginger

PEAR-CRANBERRY FILLING
- 1 (10-oz.) pkg. fresh or frozen cranberries
- ½ cup plus 2 Tbsp. granulated sugar
- 2 tsp. orange zest plus 2 Tbsp. fresh orange juice (from 1 orange), divided
- 4 large (about 8 oz. each) firm ripe pears, peeled and chopped
- 2 Tbsp. cornstarch
- ¾ tsp. ground cinnamon
- ¼ tsp. ground nutmeg

1. Prepare the crust: Whisk together egg and 1 tablespoon ice-cold water in a small bowl until well blended. In a food processor, combine flour, sugar, and salt. Using the back of a small knife, scrape seeds from vanilla bean into food processor. Pulse until well blended, about 5 to 6 times. Add butter; pulse until mixture resembles coarse meal, 5 to 6 times. With processor running, gradually add egg mixture. Process until dough just begins to come together (adding more water, 1 tablespoon at a time, if needed). Shape into a flat disk. Wrap in plastic wrap; chill 2 hours or up to 2 days.

2. Prepare the streusel: Stir together brown sugar, butter, and salt in a bowl. Stir in flour, almonds, and ginger until evenly blended. Set aside.

3. Prepare the filling: Combine cranberries, sugar, and orange juice in a saucepan. Cook over medium, stirring often, until cranberries have just popped, 5 to 7 minutes. Remove from heat; pour mixture into a bowl. Cool 20 minutes, stirring occasionally. Fold zest, pears, cornstarch, cinnamon, and nutmeg into cranberry mixture.

4. Assemble pie: Unwrap dough disk, and roll out on a lightly floured surface into a 13-inch circle. Fit into a 9-inch deep-dish pie plate. Fold edges under. Use a small spoon to create a pattern around edges. Freeze 15 minutes.

5. Preheat oven to 375°F. Spoon filling into prepared pie plate. Crumble streusel in small and large pieces over filling. Bake on the lowest oven rack until top is golden brown and crust is golden (shielding edges, if needed, after 20 minutes), 40 to 45 minutes. Cool completely on a wire rack, 2 hours, before serving.

HOW-TO

Make a Spoon Crimp

Dip a teaspoon in flour. Press the tip of the spoon into the pie dough edge 3 times to make a scalloped pattern. Repeat, flouring the spoon each time, until the entire edge is crimped.

HOW-TO

Make a Wavy Crimp

Pinch your thumb and index finger together on the outer edge of the dough. Using your other thumb, press into the crimp to form a thick triangle. Repeat until the entire edge is crimped.

Although she has an artist's eye and baking is in her blood, she says the perfect pie is a result of practice and patience.

Roasted Granny Smith Apple Pie

Roasting the apples makes them tender and extra flavorful. You can prepare and chill the filling a day in advance.

ACTIVE 45 MIN. - TOTAL 5 HOURS, 45 MIN., PLUS 2 HOURS, 30 MIN. CHILLING
SERVES 10

CLASSIC CRUST
- 3 cups all-purpose flour, plus more for work surface
- ¾ cup cold unsalted butter, sliced
- 5½ Tbsp. cold vegetable shortening, sliced
- 1½ Tbsp. granulated sugar
- 1 tsp. kosher salt
- 6–8 Tbsp. ice-cold water

ROASTED APPLE FILLING
- 5 lb. Granny Smith apples, peeled, sliced into ½-inch wedges
- ¾ cup granulated sugar
- ¼ cup all-purpose flour, divided
- ½ cup packed light brown sugar
- 1 tsp. ground cinnamon
- ¼ tsp. ground nutmeg
- ½ tsp. kosher salt

ADDITIONAL INGREDIENTS
- 3 Tbsp. unsalted butter, cut into small pieces
- 1 large egg

1. Prepare the crust: Pulse first 5 ingredients in a food processor until mixture resembles coarse meal, 5 to 6 times. While pulsing, gradually add ice-cold water, 1 tablespoon at a time, pulsing just until dough begins to come together. Divide dough in half; shape into 2 flat disks. Wrap each in plastic wrap; chill 2 hours or up to 2 days.

2. Prepare the filling: Preheat oven to 375°F. Toss together apples, granulated sugar, and 2 tablespoons of the flour in a bowl until well coated. Divide apples between 2 large parchment paper-lined rimmed baking sheets. Bake until just tender, about 30 minutes, rotating baking sheets between top and bottom racks halfway through baking time. Cool 30 minutes. Transfer to a bowl. Fold in brown sugar, cinnamon, nutmeg, salt, and remaining 2 tablespoons flour until combined. Chill 1 hour.

3. Assemble pie: Unwrap 1 dough disk. Roll out on a lightly floured surface into a ¼- to ⅛-inch thickness. Fit into a lightly greased (with cooking spray) 9-inch deep-dish pie plate. Repeat rolling procedure with remaining disk. Cut 6 (1¼-inch-wide) strips, and set aside. Cut 3 (¾-inch-wide) strips from remaining dough. Braid thinner strips.

4. Spoon filling into prepared pie plate, smoothing to form an even surface; dot with butter. Arrange 1¼-inch-wide dough strips and the braid in a lattice design over filling. Trim excess dough from edges; fold dough under to create a clean edge. Chill pie 30 minutes.

5. Preheat oven to 375°F. Whisk together egg and 1 tablespoon water until well blended. Brush entire pie with egg wash. Bake on lowest oven rack until crust is golden and filling is bubbly, 1 hour to 1 hour and 20 minutes, shielding pie with aluminum foil after 50 minutes, if needed. Cool on a wire rack 2 hours before serving.

Add a Braid to a Lattice

STEP 1
Arrange 3 dough strips horizontally on the filled pie shell.

STEP 2
Fold back every other strip. Place 1 strip vertically across the strips. Repeat with remaining 2 strips, leaving final edge folded back.

STEP 3
Place the braid on the pie and unfold the folded strips over the top to complete the lattice.

Tastes like Home

Celebrate the holidays with some of the South's most storied recipes

The annual Thanksgiving parade of side dishes takes us on a familiar journey to places and people we know and love. Depending on what part of the South you're from or where you're gathering, that might mean a platter of Louisiana-style Shrimp-Stuffed Mirlitons, a skillet of Fried Arkansas Black Apples kissed with brown sugar and cinnamon, or a pan of spicy Texas cornbread dressing loaded with chorizo and peppers. We hope this collection will inspire you to add a new recipe to the sideboard this year, bring back an old-fashioned favorite, and—most of all—give thanks for the deliciously diverse dishes of the South.

Sweet on Squash

West Virginia is the only state located entirely within the Appalachian Mountains. With the brief May-to-September growing season there, sturdy crops are welcomed and cherished by cooks and gardeners, particularly produce selections that stand up to frost and keep well into the colder months.

In her award-winning book, *Victuals: An Appalachian Journey, with Recipes,* Ronni Lundy celebrates the foodways of the Mountain South, writing: "In the mountains, affection is keen for winter squash varieties not commonly found elsewhere." One particular kind worth seeking out is the orange-skinned Candy Roaster. Lundy describes its marvelous sweet taste and "creamy textured flesh that is more akin to a sweet potato than a pumpkin."

A simple stunner for your spread, this roasted squash is topped with two West Virginia staples: black walnuts and sorghum syrup. (The cranberries aren't native, but given the occasion, they add a vibrant and festive note.) Butternut squash makes an excellent substitute in this dish if the lovely Candy Roaster isn't an option.

Candy Roaster Squash with Sorghum, Black Walnuts, and Cranberries

ACTIVE 15 MIN. - TOTAL 45 MIN.
SERVES 6

- 1   2½- to 3-lb. Candy Roaster squash or butternut squash
- 2   Tbsp. olive oil
- ¾   tsp. black pepper
- 1¼ tsp. kosher salt, divided
- ¼   cup unsalted butter
- ½   cup sorghum syrup
- 1   cup toasted black walnuts
- ½   cup chopped dried cranberries

1. Preheat oven to 400°F. Line 2 large baking sheets with aluminum foil. Peel squash, halve lengthwise, and trim ends. Remove and discard seeds. Cut squash into about ¾-inch-thick wedges. Place in a large bowl; toss with oil, pepper, and 1 teaspoon of the salt. Arrange in a single layer on prepared baking sheets (do not overcrowd). Bake until golden and tender, about 35 minutes, gently turning squash halfway through cook time.
2. While squash bakes, melt butter in a small saucepan over medium until bubbly, swirling pan occasionally to help butter melt evenly. Once butter mostly stops bubbling and has started to brown, remove pan from heat. Whisk in sorghum and remaining ¼ teaspoon salt. Cover and set aside to keep warm.
3. Transfer squash to a serving platter. Pour half of the sorghum mixture over squash; pour remaining sorghum mixture into a small serving bowl or pitcher. Sprinkle squash with toasted walnuts and cranberries. Serve hot or warm alongside additional remaining sorghum mixture.

Eugene's Greens

Alabama was home to Eugene Walter, who spent his life observing Southern food and culture and wrote with passion about the cooks, recipes, and culinary traditions of his beloved region. A prolific artist, poet, novelist, editor, and bon vivant, he spent decades living in New York, Paris, and Rome before returning home to Mobile in 1979.

Walter's respect and affection for greens shines forth in his masterpiece, *American Cooking: Southern Style,* an essential volume in the Foods of the World series from Time-Life Books. In another classic cookbook, *The Happy Table of Eugene Walter: Southern Spirits in Food and Drink,* he offered two recipes: Wednesday Greens and Sunday Greens, one plain and the other fancy. He inspired our version with his mention of sippets, a British take on croutons. Sippets are tidbits of stale bread that are fried with cloves of garlic. Finish with a splash of red wine vinegar as well as Walter's beloved freshly ground pepper.

Collard Greens with Garlic and Sippets

ACTIVE 30 MIN. - TOTAL 30 MIN.
SERVES 6

- 1   Tbsp., plus 1 tsp. kosher salt, divided
- 1   (1-lb.) pkg. chopped fresh collard greens (about 8 cups)
- ⅔   cup pure olive oil
- ⅓   cup sliced garlic (from 1 large garlic head)
- 2   cups torn sourdough bread pieces (about 1 inch each, from 4 oz. bread)
- 1   Tbsp. red wine vinegar
- 1   tsp. black pepper

COLLARD GREENS
WITH GARLIC
AND SIPPETS

CANDY ROASTER
SQUASH WITH SORGHUM,
BLACK WALNUTS,
AND CRANBERRIES

1. Place 3 quarts water in a large stockpot; bring to a rolling boil over high, and add 1 tablespoon of the salt. Add collard greens. Cook, stirring occasionally, until greens are tender but still have a fresh green color, 10 to 12 minutes. Drain; return greens to stockpot.

2. While greens cook, heat oil in a medium-size heavy skillet over medium. Add 1 garlic slice to oil. Once it sizzles, add remaining garlic slices. Cook, stirring occasionally, until garlic is lightly and evenly browned and aromatic, 2 to 3 minutes. Remove from heat. Transfer garlic to a plate using a slotted spoon, and set aside; reserve garlic-infused oil in skillet.

3. Heat garlic-infused oil over medium-high. Add 1 bread piece to oil; once bread sizzles, add remaining bread in a single layer. (If needed, work in batches to avoid overcrowding the skillet.) Cook, undisturbed, until golden and crisp on 1 side, about 2 minutes. Turn bread pieces. Cook, undisturbed, until just golden brown on other side, about 1 minute. Using a slotted spoon, transfer bread to a plate lined with paper towels. Repeat process with remaining bread.

4. To serve, pour warm garlic-infused oil over greens in stockpot; toss to coat. Add vinegar, pepper, half of the reserved garlic slices (reserve the remaining slices for another use), bread pieces, and remaining 1 teaspoon salt; toss gently. Transfer to a serving platter; serve warm.

CREAMY BAKED MACARONI AND CHEESE WITH BACON

1 tsp. black pepper
1 tsp. dry mustard
3 cups whole milk
1 cup whole buttermilk
⅓ cup unsalted butter, plus more for greasing dish
12 oz. extra-sharp Cheddar cheese, shredded (about 3 cups)
4 oz. Monterey Jack, provolone, or mozzarella cheese, shredded (about 1 cup)
2 large eggs, well beaten

1. Preheat oven to 350°F. Bring 3 quarts water to a boil over high in a large stockpot. Stir in pasta and 1 tablespoon of the salt, and return to a boil. Cook, stirring occasionally, until pasta is tender but still firm, about 6 minutes. Reserve and set aside 2 cups cooking water, and then drain the pasta. Return pasta to pot, and remove from heat. Cover to keep warm.
2. Generously butter a 13- x 9-inch baking dish, and set aside. Toss together breadcrumbs; Parmesan cheese; and half of the cooked, crumbled bacon in a bowl, and set aside. Stir together flour, pepper, mustard, and remaining 1½ teaspoons salt in a small bowl. Heat milk and buttermilk in a medium saucepan over medium, undisturbed, until barely steaming but not boiling, 4 to 5 minutes. Set aside.
3. Melt butter in a large heavy saucepan over medium-high. Add flour mixture. Cook, whisking often, until mixture is smooth and thick and has a delicate golden color and toasted aroma, about 2 minutes. Slowly whisk in warm milk mixture. Bring to a boil over high. Cook, stirring often, until thickened to the texture of cream, about 3 minutes.
4. Stir shredded Cheddar and Monterey Jack cheeses into milk mixture, and remove from heat. Stir in beaten eggs until mixture forms a smooth sauce.
5. Uncover cooked pasta, and stir. (If pasta sticks together, stir in reserved warm cooking water, and drain again.) Stir cheese mixture and remaining bacon into drained pasta in stockpot.
6. Transfer pasta mixture to prepared baking dish, and sprinkle evenly with breadcrumb mixture. Bake in preheated oven until firm, puffed up, and lightly browned, 35 to 40 minutes. Serve hot or warm.

TENNESSEE

A Beacon for Bacon

Stove-top macaroni and cheese is an everyday pleasure, but at Southern Thanksgivings, we long for a big pan of the comforting baked version. This creamy casserole connects us to cooks and kitchens of the early 19th century. Their "macaroni pie" is a clear ancestor of the dish we love today.

Cheese, noodles, butter, and milk are musts, of course, but we wanted a little sizzle to make it a recipe to remember. "Sizzle" led to "bacon," and that one word turned our eyes toward Tennessee, home to Benton's Smoky Mountain Country Hams. At this legendary smokehouse in East Tennessee, Allan Benton and his team produce gloriously smoky bacon that they ship all over the country to chefs as well as home cooks.

To pay even more homage to the state, we added a tangy splash of buttermilk to the cheese sauce in honor of Knoxville's Cruze Farm, a family dairy that makes some of the best around.

Our take on this classic is familiar enough for the traditionalists but revved up just enough to please those eager for something unexpected.

Creamy Baked Macaroni and Cheese with Bacon

ACTIVE 30 MIN. - TOTAL 1 HOUR, 10 MIN.
SERVES 10

1 lb. uncooked large elbow macaroni
1 Tbsp., plus 1½ tsp. kosher salt, divided
¾ cup fresh breadcrumbs
2 oz. Parmesan cheese, shredded or grated (about ½ cup)
6 thick-cut bacon slices, cooked and crumbled, divided
⅓ cup all-purpose flour

Bring On the "bagars"

Rutabagas may not look like much, piled up in a heap at a farmers' market, but chef Vivian Howard knows they're worthy of a place on the Thanksgiving table. She includes this root vegetable among the two dozen Eastern North Carolina ingredients featured in her award-winning cookbook, *Deep Run Roots: Stories and Recipes from My Corner of the South.* It's an essential crop in Eastern North Carolina's coastal region for thriving in sandy soil, surviving freezing winters and sultry summers, and filling hungry stomachs during hard times.

Howard loves the flavor of "bagars," including their greens, but notes the challenge of preparing them—their tough, thick skin and dry texture can make them tricky to peel and chop. Inside, they're an autumnal yellow, but outside they range from various shades of purple to brown and may be coated in food-grade wax to protect them from their tendency to dry out during cold-weather storage.

We say it's worth the effort for their natural sweetness and the handsome color waiting inside. While Howard prefers rutabagas that are roughly mashed, in this version, we pair them with Yukon Gold potatoes for a creamier, smoother texture and spice things up with a little nutmeg.

Simple Mashed Rutabagas and Potatoes

(Photo, page 314)

ACTIVE 40 MIN. - TOTAL 40 MIN.
SERVES 8

- 2½ lb. rutabagas, trimmed, peeled, and cut into 2- to 3-inch pieces (about 6 cups)
- 1 Tbsp., plus 2½ tsp. kosher salt, divided
- ¾ cup heavy cream
- 1½ lb. Yukon Gold potatoes, peeled and cut into 2- to 3-inch pieces (about 4 cups)

- ½ cup butter, cut into small pieces, plus more for serving
- 1 tsp. freshly grated nutmeg
- 2 Tbsp. finely chopped fresh flat-leaf parsley

1. Place 3 quarts water, rutabagas, and 1 tablespoon of the salt in a large stockpot, and bring to a boil over high. Reduce heat to medium, and simmer until rutabagas are barely tender, about 10 minutes.
2. Meanwhile, heat cream in a small saucepan over medium, undisturbed, until steaming hot but not boiling. Remove from heat, and cover to keep warm.
3. Once rutabagas are tender, add potatoes to stockpot. Cook over medium until potatoes are tender, 20 to 25 minutes. Drain well, and return rutabagas and potatoes to stockpot. Add warm cream, butter, nutmeg, and remaining 2½ teaspoons salt. Mash well until a few tiny lumps remain.
4. Transfer mixture to a serving bowl or platter, and sprinkle with parsley. Serve hot or warm with butter.

Arkansas' Black Beauty

Fried apples add a sweet presence to the Thanksgiving table, where cranberry sauce sometimes carries the fruit flag all alone. The state's namesake apple, the Arkansas Black, dates back to 1870, when a Benton County farmer encountered an impressive seedling in his orchard. A descendant of the Winesap, it earned national acclaim through the 1920s for its beautiful color, tart flavor, round shape, and extraordinary keeping qualities.

With refrigeration making root cellars obsolete, the Arkansas Black's national star dimmed, but it has remained a treasure in its home state. Elizabeth and John Aselage of A & A Orchard in Green Forest grow 50 different types of apples, taking them to grateful customers at farmers' markets in Fayetteville, Eureka Springs, and Bentonville.

Even after 40 years in the apple-growing business, they are partial to the Arkansas Black. "It's the last apple we pick each October, and it's gorgeous—that deep, dark red color close to black," says John. "It's tart and dense, becoming sweeter and a bit softer over time."

Modern fried apple recipes tend to call for "firm and tart" types, specifically Granny Smiths. But old-timers fried up what they had on hand—from their own trees, a neighbor's orchard, or the store. If Arkansas Black apples are available in your area, this recipe is a great way to enjoy them. Or you can use a firm red apple, such as Red Delicious or Honeycrisp.

Since the process of frying them and the addition of brown sugar enhances any apple's flavor, look for smaller ones, which are prettier when sliced. Those cranberries needn't claim all the visual glory on the holiday table.

Fried Arkansas Black Apples

(Photo, page 315)

ACTIVE 15 MIN. - TOTAL 15 MIN.
SERVES 6

- ⅓ cup packed light brown sugar
- ½ tsp. kosher salt
- ¼ tsp. ground cinnamon, cloves, or allspice
- ¼ cup unsalted butter
- 5 cups unpeeled red apple slices (from 3 [1¾ lb. total] apples)
- 3 Tbsp. apple cider

1. Stir together brown sugar, salt, and cinnamon in a small bowl, and set aside.
2. Melt butter in a large cast-iron or nonstick skillet over medium. Add half of the apple slices in a single layer. (Don't overcrowd the pan.) Cook, turning once, until slightly softened but still quite firm, 2 to 3 minutes per side. Transfer to a plate using a slotted spoon. Repeat process with remaining apples.
3. Return cooked apple slices to hot skillet, and add cider and reserved brown sugar mixture. Cook over medium, gently turning occasionally, until apples are glazed, browned, and tender, 3 to 4 minutes. Transfer fried apples to a serving bowl or plate. Serve warm.

A Taste of the Islands

Made with two Lowcountry staples—freshly caught blue crab and long-grain rice—crab rice is a signature Gullah Geechee dish. It graces both everyday and celebration tables throughout the Sea Islands, where palmettos and pine trees tower over waters teeming with fish, crabs, shrimp, and oysters.

James Beard Award-winning Savannah chef Mashama Bailey includes it on her menu at The Grey, saying, "The Gullah Geechee people have lived on the barrier islands and along the coast from North Carolina to Florida for generations. During my time in this region, I've discovered that many of the foods I thought were indigenous to Savannah can also be found in the Charleston, South Carolina, area."

When Bailey wanted to put crab rice on the menu, she reached out to "the realest chef in the region," Charleston's BJ Dennis, who shared his traditional recipe. Dennis says crab rice is basic home cooking. "I grew up helping pick the crabmeat and learned how to cook it, to caramelize it just right," he says.

Crab rice is also a staple dish for Gullah cookbook author Sallie Ann Robinson, who grew up catching crabs off the docks on Daufuskie Island, near Savannah. Robinson included her mom's crab fried rice on catering menus and featured it in her first cookbook, *Gullah Home Cooking the Daufuskie Way.*

Her family recipe, adapted here, is easy to prepare and makes a wonderful counterpoint to the holiday classics.

Prepare the rice in advance, not only to save time on Thanksgiving morning but also because fried rice tastes best when made with cold cooked rice that's been broken up into individual grains.

Sea Island Crab Fried Rice

ACTIVE 30 MIN. · TOTAL 30 MIN.
SERVES 8

- 2 bacon slices, cut into 1-inch pieces
- 4 Tbsp. vegetable oil, divided
- 1 cup chopped yellow onion (from 1 medium onion)
- 1 cup chopped green bell pepper (from 1 large pepper)
- ¾ cup chopped celery (from 3 stalks)
- 1 Tbsp. chopped garlic (from 3 garlic cloves)
- ½ cup chopped scallions, white and green parts separated (from 1 bunch)
- 1 lb. fresh crabmeat, picked over
- 4 cups cooked long-grain white rice
- 1½ tsp. kosher salt
- ½ tsp. black pepper
- ¼ cup chopped fresh flat-leaf parsley

1. Cook bacon in a 12-inch skillet over medium-high, turning often, until nicely browned and crisp (adjusting heat as needed to prevent burning), about 8 minutes. Transfer bacon to a small bowl using a slotted spoon, and set aside. Reserve drippings in skillet.
2. Add 2 tablespoons of the oil to drippings in skillet. Add onion, bell pepper, celery, garlic, and white parts of scallions. Cook over medium-high, tossing often, until vegetables are fragrant and tender, 2 to 3 minutes.
3. Add crabmeat to skillet, and cook, tossing occasionally, until crabmeat is lightly browned, about 5 minutes. Add cooked rice, salt, black pepper, and remaining 2 tablespoons oil. Cook, tossing often, until rice is hot and all ingredients are combined evenly, about 4 minutes.
4. Add parsley, green parts of scallions, and reserved bacon to skillet, and toss well to combine. Transfer crab fried rice to a serving platter, and serve hot or warm.

SEA ISLAND CRAB FRIED RICE

Some Like It (Extra) Hot

Of all the side dishes to include on your November 28 menu, everyone can agree that dressing is essential. What goes into it–crawfish, pecans, sausage, oysters, cream of chicken soup–is another story. If you're a Texan, dressing probably starts with cornbread, and if you're Hugo Ortega, the James Beard Award-winning chef behind Houston's H Town Restaurant Group, it includes chorizo. Ortega says the spicy pork sausage, which he makes at his restaurants, is a must.

In addition to the widely known dark red chorizo, he makes two other varieties: green (which gets its signature color from leafy greens; serrano chile peppers; and bouquets of cilantro, epazote, and parsley) and Chorizo Istmeño (a specialty of his home region of Oaxaca in Mexico, which uses chintextle, a seasoning paste made of chiles, spices, and dried shrimp).

Like many families, Ortega and his wife, Tracy (who co-owns H Town), celebrate Thanksgiving twice. First, they join her relatives for a traditional feast with cornbread dressing (studded with bacon or chorizo), giblet gravy, pickled peaches, and beets. Then, they head to his mother's home, where his seven siblings enjoy tamales, posole, turkey in adobo, and a spread of desserts made by his brother Ruben, H Town's pastry chef.

Our hearty dressing takes its cues from Ortega and the state of Texas. We added plenty of fresh Mexican chorizo and chopped jalapeño for extra heat, plus green bell pepper and cilantro.

Spicy Cornbread Dressing with Chorizo

ACTIVE 15 MIN. - TOTAL 40 MIN.
SERVES 8

- 2 Tbsp. vegetable oil, divided, plus more for greasing pan
- 1 cup chopped yellow onion (from 1 small onion)
- 1 lb. fresh Mexican chorizo

SPICY CORNBREAD DRESSING WITH CHORIZO

- 1 cup chopped green bell pepper (from 1 small pepper)
- ¾ cup chopped celery (from 3 medium stalks)
- 1 Tbsp. chopped garlic (from 3 medium garlic cloves)
- 3 scallions, chopped, white and green parts separated
- 8 cups coarsely crumbled cornbread (from about 1½ lb.)
- ½ cup chopped fresh cilantro
- ⅓ cup chopped, seeded jalapeño chile (from 1 large or 2 small chiles)
- 1 tsp. kosher salt
- 1 tsp. black pepper
- 2 large eggs, well beaten
- 4 cups chicken stock

1. Generously grease a 13- x 9-inch baking dish with vegetable oil. Preheat oven to 375°F. Heat a large cast-iron or nonstick skillet over medium-high. Add 1 tablespoon of the oil to skillet, and heat until a piece of onion sizzles when added. Add chorizo, and cook, tossing often and breaking up meat with a spoon, until fragrant and nicely browned, 3 to 5 minutes. Transfer chorizo to a bowl, and set aside. Reserve drippings in skillet.
2. Add remaining 1 tablespoon vegetable oil to drippings in skillet. Once oil is hot, add chopped yellow onion, green bell pepper, and celery. Cook over medium-high, tossing often, until mixture is fragrant and softened, 3 to 4 minutes. Add chopped garlic and white parts of scallions, and cook, stirring constantly, until fragrant, about 1 minute. Remove pan from heat.
3. Transfer onion mixture to a large bowl, and add crumbled cornbread and cooked reserved chorizo. Stir mixture to combine well. Add chopped cilantro and jalapeño, salt, and black pepper, and stir to combine well. Add beaten eggs and chicken stock, and stir to combine well, making sure mixture is evenly moistened.
4. Transfer cornbread mixture to prepared baking dish. Bake in preheated oven until dressing is cooked through and browned, 25 to 35 minutes. Serve hot or warm. Sprinkle dressing with reserved green parts of scallions before serving.

FLUFFY CORN
PUDDING

SHRIMP-STUFFED
MIRLITONS

A Creole Classic

Unless you grew up in New Orleans, Baton Rouge, Lafayette, or their environs, the word "mirliton" (often pronounced "mel-ee-TAWN") in this recipe's title might not catch your eye. Whether pickled; glazed; or stuffed with crabmeat, sausage, and shrimp, mirlitons are beloved in Louisiana.

The pale green, pear-shape squash (also known as chayote) has roots in ancient Mayan and Aztec foodways. Mirlitons used their gourd-family DNA to spread swiftly on vines throughout the Caribbean. By the early 1800s, the plant could be found in New Orleans kitchens and backyard gardens. Then Hurricanes Katrina and Rita took their tolls, and the plump and curvaceous vegetable faced a crisis. But thanks to the dedication of home cooks, gardeners, and agricultural experts, it's making a comeback.

Case in point: About five years ago, New Orleans resident Renee Lapeyrolerie planted a mirliton sprout in her Tremé backyard. With lots of patience, as well as advice from family and friends, it is now flourishing. Mirliton.org, an organization committed to the survival and renaissance of this gourd, has named her plant the Lapeyrolerie mirliton in honor of her success with revitalizing this locally grown gem.

This is our version of a classic Creole dish, Shrimp-Stuffed Mirlitons, long a Thanksgiving standby in South Louisiana. Preparing the squash requires a little care, as you can easily cut through or tear the cooked halves, so take your time with this step. The rest of the recipe comes together effortlessly and makes a savory addition to your spread.

Shrimp-Stuffed Mirlitons

ACTIVE 30 MIN. - TOTAL 1 HOUR, 45 MIN.
SERVES 8

- 4 mirlitons (chayote squash), halved lengthwise
- 7 Tbsp. unsalted butter, divided
- 1 cup chopped yellow onion (from 1 small onion)
- ¾ cup chopped green bell pepper (from 1 medium pepper)
- ¾ cup chopped celery (from 4 medium stalks)
- 1 Tbsp. chopped garlic (from 3 garlic cloves)
- 3 scallions, chopped, white and green parts separated
- ¾ lb. peeled, deveined raw small- to medium-size shrimp, coarsely chopped (¾-inch pieces)
- ¾ cup chopped cooked ham
- 1 Tbsp. Creole seasoning or Cajun blackened seasoning
- 1 tsp. kosher salt
- ½ tsp. black pepper
- 2 large eggs, well beaten
- 1¾ cups fine fresh breadcrumbs, divided
- ¼ cup chopped fresh flat-leaf parsley, divided

1. Preheat oven to 400°F. Arrange squash halves, cut sides down, in a 13- x 9-inch baking dish. Add ¼ cup water, and cover with aluminum foil. Bake until squash is tender but still firm, 45 minutes to 1 hour. Set aside until cool enough to handle, about 20 minutes. Reduce oven temperature to 375°F.
2. While squash cools, melt 4 tablespoons of the butter in a large skillet over medium-high until a piece of chopped onion sizzles when added to butter. Add chopped onion, bell pepper, and celery. Cook, stirring occasionally, until mixture is fragrant, about 5 minutes. Add garlic and white parts of scallions. Cook, tossing often, until mixture is softened, about 2 minutes. Transfer mixture to a large bowl.
3. Add 2 tablespoons of the butter to skillet, and melt over medium-high. Once butter bubbles up, add shrimp. Cook, tossing often, until bright pink and firm, about 2 minutes. Add ham, Creole seasoning, salt, and black pepper. Remove from heat, and toss to combine. Add reserved onion mixture to shrimp mixture in skillet, and toss to combine. Transfer to a large bowl, and set aside.
4. Remove and discard seeds from cooled squash halves. Carefully scoop out flesh from each squash half using a spoon, leaving a ¼-inch shell. Set shells aside. Coarsely chop squash flesh, add to shrimp mixture in large bowl, and stir to combine. Add eggs, green parts of scallions, 1½ cups of the breadcrumbs, and 2 tablespoons of the parsley, and stir to combine. (Stuffing should be moist but not wet, with ingredients evenly mixed throughout.)
5. Arrange squash shells snugly in a 13- x 9-inch baking dish or a rimmed baking sheet, with larger, firmer shells around the edges and any torn or broken shells wedged in place among the sturdy ones. Fill shells evenly with prepared stuffing.
6. Melt remaining 1 tablespoon butter in a small microwavable bowl on HIGH for 30 seconds. Stir remaining ¼ cup breadcrumbs and 2 tablespoons parsley into butter. Sprinkle breadcrumb mixture evenly over stuffed squash.
7. Bake until stuffing is firm, fairly dry, and lightly browned, 30 to 40 minutes. Transfer squash to a serving platter, and serve hot or warm.

KENTUCKY

The Place for Corn Pudding

In the heart of the Bluegrass State, a beloved establishment prepares to welcome guests to its annual feast. The Beaumont Inn opened its doors 100 years ago, in Kentucky's oldest town of Harrodsburg, in what had been a college for women during the mid-1800s.

Family-owned and operated for five generations, it has grown from a small guesthouse for alumni of Beaumont College to an award-winning hotel. Its Thanksgiving menu draws return visitors along with new guests, not just for turkey with all the trimmings but also for corn pudding—which is one of the inn's signature dishes and most requested recipes.

Beaumont Inn's corn pudding was perfected in the 1960s and is served at lunch and dinner daily, earning generations of fans who've come to expect it on the menu. Its nontraditional recipe calls for white corn and involves three sessions of careful stirring with a fork during the baking process. The result is a dual-textured casserole with a delicate custard on top and the pleasing crunch of white corn beneath.

Our simplified recipe, which uses yellow corn for a pop of color (white corn will work just as well) and parsley and scallions for extra flavor, doesn't require nearly as much effort and has a light and fluffy texture that might just rival the original.

Fluffy Corn Pudding

ACTIVE 15 MIN. - TOTAL 1 HOUR, 5 MIN.
SERVES 8

- Baking spray with flour
- ¼ cup all-purpose flour
- 1 Tbsp. granulated sugar
- 1 tsp. kosher salt
- ½ tsp. black pepper
- 3 cups fresh or thawed frozen yellow or white corn kernels, divided
- 3 large eggs
- 2 cups whole milk
- ¼ cup unsalted butter, melted
- 1½ Tbsp. chopped fresh flat-leaf parsley
- 1½ Tbsp. finely chopped scallions, divided

1. Preheat oven to 350°F. Generously coat a 9-inch square glass or ceramic baking dish with baking spray with flour. Stir together flour, sugar, salt, and pepper in a small bowl, and set aside.
2. Pulse 1 cup of the corn kernels in a food processor until smooth, about 5 times, and set aside. Whisk eggs by hand in a large bowl until smooth and lightly beaten. Stir in flour mixture and milk until combined. Whisk in melted butter. Add corn puree, parsley, 1 tablespoon of the scallions, and remaining 2 cups corn kernels. Stir to combine well.
3. Transfer corn mixture to prepared baking dish. Bake in preheated oven until lightly browned, puffed up all over, and fairly firm, about 40 minutes. Sprinkle corn pudding with remaining ½ tablespoon scallions. Serve hot or warm.

Old-Fashioned Oysters

Bernie Herman, renowned folklorist and esteemed professor of Southern studies at The University of North Carolina at Chapel Hill, knows more than most people do about oysters. That's because he grew up in a community on Virginia's Eastern Shore, accessible to the waters of the Chesapeake Bay. In 2002, he bought land in the area, where he now tends his own small oyster-restoration project and supports efforts to rebuild and nourish the farming and seafood-harvesting communities, which have suffered great economic declines in recent decades.

For Herman, Thanksgiving means fresh oysters, roasted outdoors in the morning sunlight while the turkey (stuffed with the family's traditional dressing made with sausage, oysters, and hominy) cooks in the oven. He notes that today's scalloped oysters are likely descendants of oyster pie, a traditional Virginia dish that dates back to the 1700s. It's double crusted and features fresh oysters in an herbed cream sauce.

The modern culinary term "scalloped" denotes an ingredient—which could be anything from tomatoes to potatoes to oysters—layered in a casserole dish with breadcrumbs or cracker crumbs; enriched with cream and butter; and baked into a rich, satisfying side. Herman thinks the commercial production of saltines in the late 1800s may have led to the rise of scalloped oysters, the simpler—though no less delicious—dish we share here.

Scalloped Oysters

ACTIVE 20 MIN. - TOTAL 1 HOUR
SERVES 10

- 8 Tbsp. cold butter, divided, plus more for greasing dish
- 1½ tsp. kosher salt
- 1 tsp. black pepper
- 2 pt. fresh shucked oysters, undrained
- 1 cup heavy cream or whipping cream
- 5 cups finely crushed saltine crackers (from 2 cracker sleeves), divided
- 2 Tbsp. chopped fresh flat-leaf parsley

1. Generously butter a 13- x 9-inch baking dish. Preheat oven to 350°F. Cut 6 tablespoons of the butter into ½-inch pieces, and set aside. Stir together salt and pepper in a small bowl, and set aside.
2. Pour oysters in liquid over a fine-mesh strainer into a medium bowl. Measure ⅓ cup strained oyster liquid into a small bowl. (Discard remaining oyster liquid, or reserve for another use.) Stir cream into oyster liquid. Cut any large oysters into 2 or 3 pieces. Microwave remaining 2 tablespoons butter in a medium-size microwavable glass bowl on HIGH until melted, about 30 seconds. Add 1 cup of the crushed crackers. Stir to coat, and set aside.
3. Sprinkle bottom of prepared baking dish with 1 cup of the crushed crackers. Arrange one-fourth of the oysters, spaced a few inches apart, over crackers. Sprinkle with one-fourth of the salt-pepper mixture. Arrange one-fourth of the butter pieces around the oysters. Repeat layers 3 times using remaining crushed crackers, oysters, salt-pepper mixture, and butter pieces. Sprinkle evenly with reserved melted butter-cracker mixture.
4. Pour oyster liquid-cream mixture over layered mixture in baking dish. Bake in preheated oven until puffed up, firm, and heated through, 30 to 35 minutes. Sprinkle with parsley. Serve hot or warm.

Pass the Potatoes

Sweet potatoes grow well in many Southern states, but Mississippi takes particular pride in harvesting this crop. The North Mississippi town of Vardaman claims the title of Sweet Potato Capital of the World, and its regional agricultural tradition endures. The town will celebrate it at the 46th annual Vardaman Sweet Potato Festival this November.

We are saluting Mississippi's history with an old-school grated pudding, which is also known as a sweet potato pone. This near-forgotten classic calls for sweet potatoes, peeled and grated, sweetened with sugar (and sometimes molasses and spices), enriched with eggs, and baked into a rustic pudding.

The creamy dish is accented beautifully by a topping of crunchy chopped pecans, a reminder that wild pecan trees still thrive in the lower Mississippi Valley.

Grated Sweet Potato Pudding with Pecans

ACTIVE 20 MIN. - TOTAL 50 MIN.
SERVES 10

- ¼ cup unsalted butter
- 2 large eggs, well beaten
- ⅓ cup granulated sugar
- 2 Tbsp. all-purpose flour
- 2 tsp. kosher salt
- 1½ cups half-and-half
- 4 cups peeled, grated sweet potatoes (from 1½ lb. sweet potatoes)
- 1 cup chopped pecans

1. Preheat oven to 400°F. Melt butter in a deep 10-inch cast-iron skillet over medium-high. Remove from heat. Swirl to coat skillet with melted butter; then pour melted butter into a small bowl. Do not wipe skillet clean.
2. Stir together beaten eggs, sugar, flour, and salt in a large bowl. Gradually add half-and-half, stirring constantly. Stir in melted butter until mixture is combined and smooth. Add sweet potatoes; stir to combine.
3. Transfer sweet potato mixture to buttered skillet; spread in an even layer. Arrange chopped pecans in a ring around edge of skillet. Bake in preheated oven 10 minutes. Reduce oven temperature to 350°F; continue baking until pudding is puffed up, firm, and nicely browned, 25 to 35 minutes. Serve hot or warm.

GRATED SWEET
POTATO PUDDING
WITH PECANS

SCALLOPED
OYSTERS

251

The South's Soufflé

Spoon bread has been proudly present on our sideboards since the late 18th century. Composed of cornmeal, eggs, milk, and butter, it appears in early recipe books as "batter bread," "egg bread," and "cornmeal bread."

Spoon bread's appeal lies in its marriage of qualities found in three other favorite dishes: It's satisfying like cornbread, it's comforting like custard, and it creates anticipation and delight like an airy soufflé. Long enjoyed at celebrations throughout the region, it has a special resonance in South Carolina because of its signature ingredient, corn.

More than 20 years ago, Anson Mills opened its doors in Columbia under the direction of Glenn Roberts. Determined to recover and restore traditional cooking staples, Roberts and his team got to work bringing back heirloom grains and other ingredients that once flourished in the South—like Carolina Gold rice. They also tracked down nearly extinct types of corn, generating exceptional grits and cornmeal for today's kitchens.

Our spoon bread recipe calls for beating the egg whites and yolks separately and gently folding the puffy whites into the batter just before baking. This traditional method adds height and a little glamour to the dish.

Buttermilk Spoon Bread

ACTIVE 25 MIN. - TOTAL 1 HOUR
SERVES 6

- 3 Tbsp. unsalted butter, cut into small pieces, plus more for greasing dish
- 2 cups whole milk
- 1 cup whole buttermilk
- 1 cup finely ground white cornmeal
- 2 tsp. chopped fresh thyme
- 2 tsp. kosher salt
- ½ tsp. black pepper
- 3 large eggs, separated

1. Preheat oven to 350°F. Generously grease a 2-quart casserole dish with butter. Heat milk and buttermilk in a medium-size heavy saucepan over medium until steaming but not boiling. (Look for small bubbles forming around edges of saucepan.) Gradually pour cornmeal into milk mixture in a slow, steady stream, whisking or stirring with a large spoon. (Scrape sides of saucepan as you whisk to prevent lumps from forming.) Reduce heat to medium-low. Cook, stirring often, until cornmeal dissolves completely and mixture thickens, 10 to 12 minutes.
2. Remove cornmeal mixture from heat. Add butter, chopped thyme, salt, and pepper, stirring until butter melts and mixture is combined. Let stand 10 minutes.
3. Place egg yolks in a medium bowl. Stir in 2 cups of the cornmeal mixture until combined. Transfer cornmeal-egg yolk mixture to remaining cornmeal mixture in saucepan, stirring quickly until combined. (Mixture may still look a little grainy or lumpy.)
4. Beat egg whites in a medium bowl with an electric mixer fitted with a whisk attachment on medium-high speed until stiff peaks form, about 1½ minutes. Gently fold egg whites into cornmeal mixture using a spatula or large spoon until mixture becomes a smooth batter with no streaks remaining.
5. Spoon batter into prepared casserole dish. Bake in preheated oven until spoon bread is puffed up, firm, and lightly browned, 35 to 40 minutes. (Note that spoon bread will initially puff up to great heights but then deflate within minutes of leaving the oven.) Serve hot or warm.

Roll Call

Warm, light, and fluffy, these extra-special buns will be the talk of the buffet line

BAKING TIP
Use a light hand when flouring the work surface. You should be able to see the surface through the flour.

Sweet Potato Rolls with Cane Syrup Glaze

ACTIVE 30 MIN. - TOTAL 3 HOURS, 10 MIN.
MAKES 15

- 1 large sweet potato (about 12 oz.), peeled and cut into ½-inch pieces (about 2½ cups)
- ⅔ cup whole milk
- ¼ cup warm water (100°F to 110°F)
- 1 (¼-oz.) pkg. active dry yeast
- 3 Tbsp. plus 1 tsp. granulated sugar, divided
- 2 large eggs
- 6 Tbsp. butter, melted, divided
- 4½ cups bread flour, plus more for kneading
- 1½ Tbsp. kosher salt
- 2 Tbsp. cane syrup
- ¾ tsp. flaky sea salt

1. Bring sweet potato and milk to a boil in a small saucepan over medium-high. Reduce heat to medium-low. Cook, covered, stirring occasionally, until potatoes are very soft, about 20 minutes. Remove from heat. Using a potato masher or fork, mash potatoes with milk until very smooth. Transfer to a medium bowl to cool completely, about 30 minutes.
2. Stir together warm water, yeast, and 1 teaspoon of the sugar in a small bowl. Let stand until foamy, about 5 minutes.
3. Beat together sweet potato mixture, yeast mixture, eggs, 4 tablespoons of the melted butter, and remaining 3 tablespoons sugar in the bowl of a stand mixer fitted with a dough hook on low to combine. With mixer running, gradually add bread flour and kosher salt, beating on low until dough is soft and smooth, about 4 minutes. Transfer dough to a lightly floured surface. Knead until smooth and elastic, about 5 minutes,

adding up to ⅓ cup flour, as needed, if dough is very sticky. Transfer dough to a lightly greased large bowl, and cover with plastic wrap. Let stand at room temperature until doubled in size, 1 to 1½ hours.
4. Preheat oven to 375°F. Turn dough out onto a lightly floured surface, and divide into 15 balls. Place balls in a lightly greased 13- x 9-inch baking pan. Cover with plastic wrap, and let stand at room temperature until almost doubled in size, 45 minutes to 1 hour. Meanwhile, stir together cane syrup and remaining 2 tablespoons melted butter; set aside.
5. Uncover rolls, and bake in preheated oven until light golden brown, 18 to 22 minutes. Brush hot rolls with cane syrup butter; sprinkle with flaky sea salt. Serve immediately, or transfer rolls to a wire rack to cool completely, about 30 minutes.

The Giving Tree

If you're lucky enough to live near pecan trees, they will bestow upon you a mighty precious—and delicious—bounty

My family and I were in Big Level, Mississippi, to spend the holidays with my husband Patrick's relatives, and that always meant one thing: pecan time! Shortly after we arrived, my brother-in-law Jamie pointed to a table completely covered in shelled nuts. "Well, do you think we have enough?" he joked.

With help from his wife, Bethany, and their three kids, he had scooped up 90 pounds of pecans from beneath the huge tree at Uncle Kendell and Aunt Betty's place next door. Then they'd taken them to get "cracked and blown," which meant most of the shell had been removed, but the nuts still needed a final cleaning to take out any lingering pieces and those bitter, corky parts.

Over the course of our visit, we made memories around that table—gathering to tell stories, laugh, and sip bourbon, all while painstakingly picking through (and nibbling on) pecans. The little kids would sit in our laps and join in every now and then, filling their cheeks like chipmunks.

I've always loved local pecans. When I was growing up in small Mississippi towns, a wooden bowl of mixed shell-on nuts usually topped our coffee table in the winter. Sometimes there would just be pecans—I knew they were a gift from a kind friend or neighbor with a prolific tree.

Later, when Patrick and I lived near downtown Birmingham about 12 years ago, we had a pecan tree in our yard that proved fruitful around every other year. We'd sometimes notice people stopping on the sidewalk to gather nuts, and it made us happy to see others appreciate their worth too. These pecans might be longer and skinnier than the grocery store ones, but those idiosyncrasies speak to terroir, to being a natural, untouched product of your locale. And cracking them is part of what makes them special—like opening a present someone gives you, as opposed to buying one for yourself.
—Ann Taylor Pittman

SORGHUM-PECAN
MONKEY BREAD MUFFINS
(PAGE 257)

BAKED BRIE WITH
HONEYED FIVE SPICE
PECANS

Baked Brie with Honeyed Five Spice Pecans

ACTIVE 10 MIN. - TOTAL 30 MIN.
SERVES 8

- 1 (8-oz.) Brie round
- ¼ cup honey
- ¼ tsp. kosher salt
- ¼ tsp. Chinese five spice powder
- ½ cup chopped toasted pecans
- 2 Tbsp. chopped sweetened dried cherries
  Apple slices, crackers, and/or toasted baguette slices for serving

1. Preheat oven to 350°F. Line a small baking sheet with parchment paper or aluminum foil. Unwrap cheese, and place on prepared baking sheet. (Do not trim rind from cheese.) Bake until cheese is soft to the touch, 12 to 15 minutes. Remove from oven; cool on baking sheet 5 minutes.
2. Place honey, salt, and five spice powder in a small saucepan. Heat over medium-low until honey "melts," about 2 minutes. Stir in pecans and cherries; cook until warmed, about 2 minutes.
3. Carefully transfer cheese round to a platter; top with pecan mixture. Serve warm with apples, crackers, and/or toasted baguette slices.

Sorghum-Pecan Monkey Bread Muffins

(Photo, page 255)

ACTIVE 30 MIN. - TOTAL 50 MIN., PLUS 8 HOURS CHILLING
MAKES 1 DOZEN

- 1 cup chopped toasted pecans, divided
- 10 Tbsp. unsalted butter, melted and divided
- 1¼ lb. frozen white bread dough, thawed (such as Bridgford Frozen White Ready-Dough)
- ¾ cup granulated sugar
- 1 Tbsp. ground cinnamon
- ⅓ cup packed light brown sugar
- ⅓ cup sorghum syrup
- ¼ tsp. kosher salt

1. Coat a 12-cup muffin pan well with cooking spray. Sprinkle ½ cup of the pecans evenly into muffin cups.

2. Place 4 tablespoons of the melted butter in a medium bowl. Cut dough into ½- to ¾-inch pieces. Place pieces in bowl with butter; toss well to coat.
3. Stir together granulated sugar and cinnamon in a separate medium bowl. Add dough pieces; toss well to coat. Arrange half of pieces evenly in muffin pan; sprinkle remaining pecans evenly on top. Arrange remaining pieces evenly over pecans in muffin pan.
4. Combine brown sugar, sorghum, salt, and remaining 6 tablespoons butter in a small saucepan over medium-low. Cook, stirring occasionally, until mixture starts to bubble, about 5 minutes. Remove from heat; cool 10 minutes. Pour evenly over dough in muffin pan (about 1 tablespoon each). Cover loosely with plastic wrap. Chill 8 hours or up to overnight.
5. Remove pan from refrigerator, and uncover. Let stand at room temperature 20 minutes. Preheat oven to 350°F.
6. Place pan on a rimmed baking sheet to catch any drips. Bake in preheated oven until dough is puffed and cooked through, about 20 minutes. Remove pan from oven; let stand 5 minutes. Line a baking sheet with aluminum foil or parchment paper. Carefully invert muffins onto prepared baking sheet; transfer to a platter. Spoon any remaining syrup mixture from muffin pan over muffins. Serve warm.

Herby Pecan-Cornbread Dressing

(Photo, page 319)

ACTIVE 30 MIN. - TOTAL 1 HOUR, 45 MIN.
SERVES 12

CORNBREAD
- 2 cups medium-grind whole-grain cornmeal
- ⅔ cup white whole-wheat flour
- 1 tsp. baking powder
- 1 tsp. baking soda
- 1¼ tsp. kosher salt
- 1½ cups whole buttermilk
- ¼ cup canola oil or vegetable oil
- 2 large eggs, lightly beaten
- ¼ cup unsalted butter

DRESSING
- ½ cup unsalted butter
- 1 large yellow onion, chopped (about 2 cups)
- 8 stalks celery, chopped (about 2 cups)
- 2 Tbsp. fresh thyme leaves
- 2 Tbsp. finely chopped fresh sage
- 1¾ tsp. kosher salt
- 1 tsp. black pepper
- 3 cups unsalted chicken stock
- ⅓ cup chopped fresh flat-leaf parsley
- 2 large eggs, lightly beaten
- 1 cup toasted pecan halves

1. Prepare the Cornbread: Place a 10-inch cast-iron skillet in oven. Preheat oven to 450°F. (Leave skillet in oven as it heats.)
2. Stir together cornmeal, flour, baking powder, baking soda, and salt in a large bowl. Whisk together buttermilk, oil, and eggs in a medium bowl. Add buttermilk mixture to cornmeal mixture; stir until combined. Carefully add butter to hot skillet. Return skillet to oven; bake until butter melts and lightly browns, about 1 minute. Carefully add melted butter to batter, and stir to combine. Immediately pour batter into hot skillet. Bake until lightly browned and a wooden pick inserted in center comes out clean, about 20 minutes. Invert onto a wire rack; cool completely, about 30 minutes.
3. Prepare the Dressing: Reduce oven temperature to 375°F. Melt butter in a large skillet over medium. Add onion and celery. Cook, stirring occasionally, until tender, 12 to 14 minutes. Stir in thyme, sage, salt, and pepper. Cook until fragrant, about 2 minutes. Remove skillet from heat; cool 15 minutes.
4. Crumble Cornbread into a large bowl. Stir in onion mixture, stock, parsley, and eggs. Fold in pecans. Spoon mixture into a greased (with cooking spray) 13- x 9-inch baking dish. Bake until top is lightly browned and Dressing is set, 30 to 35 minutes. Cool 10 minutes before serving.

Roasted Root Vegetables with Spicy Pecan Topping

(Photo, page 317)

ACTIVE 25 MIN. - TOTAL 1 HOUR, 15 MIN.
SERVES 8

SPICY PECAN TOPPING

- 2 Tbsp. pure maple syrup
- 1 Tbsp. unsalted butter
- 1 cup pecan halves
- ½ tsp. chili powder
- ¼ tsp. smoked paprika
- ¼ tsp. cayenne pepper
- ½ tsp. kosher salt

ROASTED ROOT VEGETABLES

- 1 lb. sweet potatoes, peeled and cut into 1-inch cubes (3¼ cups)
- ¾ lb. golden beets (about 2 medium), peeled and cut into 1-inch wedges (2½ cups)
- ¾ lb. carrots (about 3 large), peeled and cut diagonally into 1½-inch pieces (2 cups)
- 5 Tbsp. olive oil, divided
- 1¾ tsp. kosher salt, divided
- 1 tsp. black pepper, divided
- ¾ lb. red beets (about 2 medium), peeled and cut into 1-inch wedges (2½ cups)
- 1 medium-size red onion, cut into 8 wedges with root intact
- 6 thyme sprigs, plus leaves for garnish

1. Prepare Spicy Pecan Topping: Preheat oven to 350°F. Combine syrup and butter in a medium microwavable bowl; microwave on HIGH until butter melts, about 45 seconds. Stir in pecans, chili powder, smoked paprika, cayenne, and salt. Spread in a single layer on a baking sheet lined with parchment paper. Bake 8 minutes. Stir mixture; bake until toasted, 4 to 6 more minutes. Remove from oven, and increase oven temperature to 450°F. Cool completely on baking sheet, about 30 minutes.
2. Prepare Roasted Root Vegetables: Line 2 baking sheets with parchment paper. Combine sweet potatoes, golden beets, and carrots in a large bowl. Drizzle with 3 tablespoons of the oil, and sprinkle with 1 teaspoon of the salt and ½ teaspoon of the black pepper. Toss well to combine. Spread mixture in a single layer on 1 baking sheet.
3. Combine red beets and red onion in same large bowl. Drizzle with remaining 2 tablespoons oil, and sprinkle with remaining ¾ teaspoon salt and ½ teaspoon black pepper. Toss well to combine. Spread mixture in a single layer on second baking sheet.
4. Bake vegetables for 20 minutes. Remove baking sheets from oven; stir vegetables. Tuck 4 thyme sprigs into orange vegetables and 2 thyme sprigs into red vegetables. Rotate baking sheets between top and bottom racks. Bake until vegetables are tender, 15 to 20 minutes.
5. Transfer vegetables to a serving bowl; gently toss together. Coarsely chop pecan topping. Sprinkle topping and thyme leaves over vegetables before serving warm or at room temperature.

Chocolate-Pecan Phyllo Turnovers

ACTIVE 40 MIN. - TOTAL 1 HOUR, 50 MIN.
MAKES 1½ DOZEN

- ¼ cup packed light brown sugar
- 1 Tbsp. honey
- 1 tsp. ground cinnamon
- ¼ tsp. ground cardamom
- ¼ tsp. kosher salt
- ½ cup, plus 2 Tbsp. unsalted butter, softened, divided
- ¾ cup chopped toasted pecans
- ⅔ cup semisweet chocolate chips, divided
- ½ (16-oz.) pkg. frozen phyllo dough (14- x 9-inch sheets, such as Athens), thawed overnight

1. Preheat oven to 375°F. Beat sugar, honey, cinnamon, cardamom, salt, and 2 tablespoons of the butter with a stand mixer fitted with paddle attachment on medium-high speed until well combined and creamy, about 3 minutes. Stir in pecans and ⅓ cup of the chocolate chips. Set aside.
2. Place remaining ½ cup butter in a small microwavable bowl. Microwave on HIGH until melted, about 30 seconds.
3. Place 1 phyllo sheet on a work surface.
(Cover remaining sheets with a damp paper towel to prevent drying.) Brush phyllo lightly with a small amount of melted butter. Top with another sheet; brush lightly with butter. Top with a third sheet; brush lightly with butter. Cut stack lengthwise into thirds. Spoon about 1 tablespoon of pecan mixture onto 1 end of each phyllo strip. Fold 1 corner of phyllo over filling to form a triangle; keep folding along length of strip. Place triangle, seam side down, on a baking sheet lined with parchment paper. Brush lightly with butter. Repeat with remaining phyllo, butter, and filling to make 18 turnovers. Reserve any remaining sheets for another use.
4. Bake turnovers in preheated oven until golden brown, 18 to 20 minutes. Cool turnovers on baking sheet 2 minutes. Transfer to a wire rack, and cool completely, about 30 minutes.
5. Place remaining ⅓ cup chocolate chips in a microwavable bowl. Microwave on HIGH until melted and smooth, about 1 minute, stirring every 30 seconds. Spoon melted chocolate into a small ziplock plastic bag. Seal bag, and snip a tiny hole in 1 corner. Squeeze to drizzle chocolate over turnovers. Let stand until set, about 20 minutes.

THE BEST WAY TO TOAST PECANS

If you toast a large batch, you can stash them in your freezer and consider yourself a step ahead for recipes or out-of-hand snacking. To get great results, use the oven instead of the stove top; the moderate heat ensures they're thoroughly toasted throughout, not just on the surface. Whether using 1 cup or 10, spread pecan halves in a single layer on a heavy rimmed baking sheet. Bake at 300°F for 23 to 25 minutes, stirring once halfway through. Cool completely before packing into ziplock plastic freezer bags and storing in the freezer for up to two years. They will maintain their rich flavor and crisp texture beautifully.

CHOCOLATE-
PECAN PHYLLO
TURNOVERS

Thanksgiving Classics

Enjoy all the traditional crowd-pleasers, from green bean casserole to pumpkin chess pie

Apple Brown Betty

The breadcrumb mixture on top of this dessert adds a delightful crunch!

ACTIVE 15 MIN. - TOTAL 1 HOUR, 10 MIN.
SERVES 6

- 4 cups soft white breadcrumbs
- ⅓ cup butter, melted
- 1 cup firmly packed brown sugar
- 1 Tbsp. ground cinnamon
- 4 large apples, peeled and cut into ¼-inch-thick slices
- 1 cup apple cider

1. Preheat oven to 350°F. Stir together breadcrumbs and butter.
2. Stir together brown sugar and cinnamon. Place half of the apple slices in a lightly greased 8-inch square baking dish; sprinkle apples with half of brown sugar mixture and half of breadcrumb mixture. Repeat procedure with remaining apples, brown sugar mixture, and breadcrumb mixture. Pour apple cider over top. Bake 45 to 55 minutes or until browned.

Butternut Squash Soup

All the comforts of the season in one delicious bow.

ACTIVE 25 MIN. - TOTAL 1 HOUR, 15 MIN.
SERVES 8

- 6 bacon slices
- 1 large onion, chopped
- 2 carrots, chopped
- 2 celery ribs, chopped
- 1 Granny Smith apple, peeled and finely chopped
- 2 garlic cloves, chopped
- 4 (12-oz.) pkg. frozen butternut squash, thawed
- 1 (32-oz.) container low-sodium, fat-free chicken broth
- 2 to 3 Tbsp. fresh lime juice
- 1½ Tbsp. honey
- 2 tsp. salt
- 1 tsp. black pepper
- ⅛ tsp. ground allspice
- ⅛ tsp. ground nutmeg
- ⅛ tsp. ground red pepper
- ¼ cup whipping cream
  Garnishes: sour cream, fresh thyme sprigs (optional)

1. Cook bacon slices in a Dutch oven until crisp. Remove bacon, and drain on paper towels, reserving 2 tablespoons drippings in Dutch oven. Coarsely crumble bacon, and set aside.
2. Saute onion and carrots in hot bacon drippings in Dutch oven over medium-high heat 5 minutes or until onion is tender. Add celery and apple, and saute 5 minutes. Add garlic, and saute 30 seconds. Add butternut squash and chicken broth. Bring to a boil; reduce heat, and simmer 20 minutes or until carrots are tender.
3. Process squash mixture, in batches, in a blender or food processor until smooth. Return to Dutch oven. Add lime juice and next 7 ingredients. Simmer 10 to 15 minutes or until thickened. Garnish, if desired. Top each serving with bacon.

Broccoli Dressing

Add a new twist to homemade pan dressing with this delicious mix of broccoli, cheese, onion, and celery.

ACTIVE 30 MIN. - TOTAL 1 HOUR, 5 MIN.
SERVES 8

- ½ cup chopped onion
- 1½ cups chopped celery
- ½ cup butter or margarine, melted
- 1 large egg, lightly beaten
- 1 tsp. salt
- ½ tsp. poultry seasoning
- ⅛ tsp. black pepper
- 4 cups soft bread cubes, lightly toasted
- 1 (8-oz.) pkg. Swiss cheese, cubed
- 1 (10-oz.) pkg. frozen chopped broccoli, thawed

1. Saute onion and celery in butter in a large skillet over medium-high until crisp-tender.
2. Combine egg and next 3 ingredients in a large bowl; gently stir in bread cubes, cheese, and broccoli. Spoon mixture into a greased 11- x 7-inch baking dish. Bake, uncovered, 35 minutes or until golden.

Cornbread Dressing

This Southern classic is a Thanksgiving dinner favorite. This version is quite moist; if you prefer a firmer dressing, use only four cans of broth.

ACTIVE 15 MIN. - TOTAL 1 HOUR, 25 MIN.
SERVES 16 TO 18

- 1 cup butter, divided
- 3 cups white cornmeal
- 1 cup all-purpose flour
- 2 Tbsp. sugar
- 2 tsp. baking powder
- 1½ tsp. salt
- 1 tsp. baking soda
- 7 large eggs, divided
- 3 cups buttermilk
- 3 cups soft breadcrumbs
- 3 cups finely chopped celery
- 2 cups finely chopped onion
- ½ cup finely chopped fresh sage or 1 Tbsp. dried rubbed sage
- 5 (10½-oz.) cans condensed chicken broth, undiluted
- 1 Tbsp. freshly ground black pepper

1. Preheat oven to 425°F. Place ½ cup butter in a 13- x 9-inch pan; heat in oven 4 minutes.
2. Combine cornmeal and next 5 ingredients; whisk in 3 eggs and buttermilk. Pour hot butter from pan into batter, stirring until blended. Pour batter into pan. Bake 30 minutes or until golden brown. Cool.
3. Crumble cornbread into a large bowl; stir in breadcrumbs, and set aside.

4. Melt remaining ½ cup butter in a large skillet over medium; add celery and onion, and saute until tender. Stir in sage, and saute 1 more minute.

5. Stir vegetables, remaining 4 eggs, chicken broth, and pepper into cornbread mixture; spoon into 1 lightly greased 13- x 9-inch baking dish and 1 lightly greased 8-inch square baking dish. Cover and chill 8 hours, if desired.

6. Preheat oven to 375°F. Bake dressing, uncovered, 35 to 40 minutes or until golden brown.

Crunch-Top Apple Pie

This pie showcases the best of both worlds—double piecrust and streusel topping. Braeburn apples work well in this pie because they hold their shape when cooked and provide contrast to the soft applesauce.

ACTIVE 20 MIN. - TOTAL 4 HOURS, 20 MIN., INCLUDING PASTRY AND CRUNCH TOPPING
SERVES 8 TO 10

	Pastry, divided (recipe follows)
¾	cup sugar
1	Tbsp. all-purpose flour
½	tsp. ground cinnamon
⅛	tsp. salt
4½	cups peeled and chopped cooking apples (about 4)
1	(16-oz.) jar applesauce
1	Tbsp. fresh lemon juice
1	Tbsp. butter, cut up
	Crunch Topping (recipe follows)

1. Preheat oven to 425°F. Roll half of Pastry to ⅛-inch thickness on a lightly floured surface; fit piecrust into a 9-inch pie plate, and trim off excess piecrust along edges. Combine sugar and next 3 ingredients; stir in apples and next 2 ingredients. Spoon apple mixture into prepared pie plate, and dot with butter.

2. Roll out remaining Pastry to ⅛-inch thickness on a lightly floured surface. Using the width of a ruler as a guide, cut piecrust into 9 (1-inch-wide) strips. Arrange strips in a lattice design over filling; gently press ends of strips, sealing to bottom piecrust. Prepare Crunch Topping, and sprinkle over lattice crust.

3. Bake 10 minutes (place foil on rack beneath pie to catch drips, if necessary); reduce oven temperature to 350°F, and bake 1 hour and 5 minutes or until crust is golden brown. Cool 2 hours.

Pastry

ACTIVE 10 MIN. - TOTAL 40 MIN.
MAKES ENOUGH FOR 1 DOUBLE-CRUST 9-INCH PIE

2½	cups all-purpose flour
1	tsp. salt
⅔	cup plus 2 Tbsp. shortening
½	cup ice water

Combine flour and salt; cut in shortening with a pastry blender until mixture is crumbly. Sprinkle ice water, 1 tablespoon at a time, evenly over surface; stir with a fork until dry ingredients are moistened. Shape into 2 balls; wrap in plastic wrap, and chill 30 minutes.

Crunch Topping

ACTIVE 5 MIN. - TOTAL 5 MIN.
MAKES ABOUT ¼ CUP

3	Tbsp. all-purpose flour
1	Tbsp. sugar
⅛	tsp. salt
1	Tbsp. butter, cut up

Combine first 3 ingredients; cut in butter with a fork until mixture is crumbly.

Favorite Southern Cornbread

"Perhaps no bread in the world is quite as good as Southern cornbread."—Mark Twain

ACTIVE 10 MIN. - TOTAL 42 MIN.
SERVES 8

¼	cup bacon drippings
2	cups self-rising cornmeal mix
½	tsp. baking soda
2	large eggs, lightly beaten
1½	cups buttermilk
	Butter

1. Preheat oven to 425°F. Place bacon drippings in a 9-inch cast-iron skillet; heat in oven 5 minutes.

2. Combine cornmeal mix and baking soda; make a well in center of mixture. Stir together eggs and buttermilk; add to dry mixture, stirring just until moistened. Remove skillet from oven; tilt skillet in all directions to coat bottom. Pour hot drippings into batter, whisking to blend. Pour batter into hot skillet.

3. Bake 27 minutes or until golden brown. Invert cornbread onto a serving plate; cut into wedges. Serve hot with butter.

FAVORITE SOUTHERN CORNBREAD

Field Greens, Crumbled Blue Cheese, and Spicy Pecans

All the tastes of fall mix together beautifully in this simple salad.

ACTIVE 15 MIN. - TOTAL 15 MIN.
SERVES 8

- ⅓ cup sugar
- ⅔ cup white vinegar
- 3 Tbsp. apple cider vinegar
- 2 Tbsp. Worcestershire sauce
- 1½ Tbsp. onion juice
- 1 tsp. salt
- 1 tsp. dry mustard
- 1 cup vegetable oil
- 4 cups loosely packed mixed greens
- 1 Granny Smith apple, unpeeled, cored and chopped
- 4 oz. blue cheese, crumbled
- ¼ cup coarsely chopped Spicy Pecans (recipe follows)
- 2 green onions, chopped

1. Combine first 7 ingredients, stirring until sugar dissolves. Slowly add oil, stirring constantly with a wire whisk until blended.
2. Combine greens and remaining 4 ingredients in a large bowl. Add desired amount of dressing, and toss gently. Serve immediately. Store any remaining dressing in refrigerator.

Spicy Pecans

ACTIVE 5 MIN. - TOTAL 35 MIN.
MAKES 5½ CUPS

- 2 egg whites
- 1½ tsp salt
- ¾ cup sugar
- 2 Tbsp. Hungarian paprika
- 1½ tsp. ground red pepper
- 2 tsp. Worcestershire sauce
- 4½ cups pecan halves
- ¼ cup plus 2 Tbsp. unsalted butter, melted

1. Preheat oven to 325°F. Beat egg whites and salt with a wire whisk until foamy. Add sugar and next 3 ingredients, beating well. Stir in pecans and butter. Spread coated pecans on a heavily greased large baking sheet.
2. Bake 30 minutes or until pecans are crisp and browned, stirring every 10 minutes. Remove from pan; cool completely. Store pecans in an airtight container.

Green Bean Casserole with Fried Leeks

Remember the old green bean casserole made with convenience products: frozen or canned green beans, cream of mushroom soup, and french-fried onions? Here it is again, better than ever with some scrumptious flavor twists.

ACTIVE 10 MIN. - TOTAL 36 MIN.
SERVES 6

- 2 Tbsp. butter
- 2 (8-oz.) pkg. sliced fresh mushrooms
- 1 tsp. dried thyme
- 2 shallots, finely chopped
- ½ cup Madeira
- 1 cup whipping cream
- 1¼ lb. fresh green beans, trimmed
   Vegetable or peanut oil
- 2 large leeks, cleaned and thinly sliced crosswise
   Salt to taste

1. Melt butter in large heavy skillet over medium-high. Add mushrooms and thyme; saute 5 minutes. Add shallots; saute 3 minutes or until tender. Add Madeira, and cook over medium-high 3 minutes or until liquid evaporates. Add whipping cream, and cook 2 to 5 minutes or until slightly thickened. Remove from heat.
2. Meanwhile, cook beans in a small amount of boiling water 5 minutes or just until crisp-tender; drain. Add beans to mushroom mixture, and toss gently. Spoon into a greased 2-quart gratin dish or shallow baking dish. Cover and keep warm. Preheat oven to 400°F. Pour oil to a depth of 2 inches into a 3-quart saucepan; heat to 350°F. Fry leeks, in 3 batches, 1 to 1½ minutes per batch or until golden. Remove leeks with a small metal strainer; drain on paper towels. Immediately sprinkle with salt. Sprinkle fried leeks over warm bean mixture.
3. Bake, uncovered, 5 minutes or until casserole is thoroughly heated.

Fresh Cranberry Congealed Salad

For a special presentation, chill the cranberry salad in individual teacups. This works particularly well for holiday luncheons.

ACTIVE 30 MIN. - TOTAL 9 HOURS, INCLUDING 8 HOURS CHILLING
SERVES 12

- 1 (12-oz.) pkg. fresh cranberries
- ½ cup sugar
- 3 (3-oz.) pkg. raspberry-flavored gelatin
- 2 cups boiling water
- 2 cups cranberry juice, chilled
- 1 (8-oz.) can crushed pineapple, undrained
- 2 celery ribs, diced (1 cup)
- ⅔ cup chopped pecans, toasted
   Lettuce leaves
   Garnishes: fresh cranberries, fresh mint sprigs (optional)

1. Process cranberries in a food processor 30 seconds or until coarsely chopped, stopping once to scrape down sides. Stir together cranberries and sugar in a bowl; set aside.
2. Stir together gelatin and boiling water in a large bowl 2 minutes or until gelatin dissolves. Add juice, and chill 30 minutes or until consistency of unbeaten egg whites. Stir in cranberry mixture, pineapple, celery, and pecans. Spoon mixture into a lightly greased 10-cup Bundt pan; cover and chill 8 hours or until firm.
3. Unmold salad onto a lettuce-lined platter. Garnish, if desired.

GREEN BEAN CASSEROLE WITH FRIED LEEKS

Herbed Turkey

Cook this tasty turkey over a hickory-smoke fire for a modern spin on a classic recipe.

SERVES 12

- 1 (12-lb.) turkey
- 2 Tbsp. salt
- 1 Tbsp. grated gingerroot
- 1 tsp. cumin seeds
- ½ cup butter, melted
- 1 bay leaf
- 1½ tsp. chopped fresh tarragon
- 1½ tsp. chopped fresh rosemary
- 1½ tsp. chopped fresh dill
- ½ cup dry sherry
- 1 Tbsp. steak sauce
- 1 Tbsp. honey

1. Remove giblets and neck; reserve for another use. Rinse turkey with cold water; pat dry.

2. Combine salt, gingerroot, and cumin seeds; crush until pulverized, using a mortar and pestle. Rub cavity and skin of turkey with salt mixture. Wrap turkey with plastic wrap, and chill 8 hours.

3. Combine butter and next 4 ingredients; cover and chill 8 hours. Let butter mixture stand at room temperature until softened.

4. Loosen skin from turkey breast and thighs without totally detaching skin. Spread butter mixture under skin on breast and thighs.

5. Combine sherry, steak sauce, and honey; set aside.

6. Soak hickory chunks in water at least 1 hour; drain. Wrap chips in heavy-duty aluminum foil, and make several holes in foil. Prepare a hot fire by piling charcoal on 1 side of grill, leaving other side empty. (For gas grills, light only 1 side.) Place foil-wrapped chips directly on hot coals. Coat grill rack on opposite side with cooking spray. Place food rack on grill. Arrange food over unlit side. Grill, covered with grill lid, basting occasionally with sherry mixture, 3 hours or until meat thermometer registers 180°F when inserted into meaty portion of thigh, making sure it does not touch bone. Let stand 15 minutes before carving.

FRESH CRANBERRY CONGEALED SALAD

Holiday Cranberry Salad

Remember the first time you tasted a gelatin salad? The squiggly mixture was magic in your mouth! Continue the fun and make this colorful, festive salad a part of your holiday menu.

ACTIVE 5 MIN. - TOTAL 1 HOUR, 38 MIN., PLUS 8 HOURS FOR CHILLING

SERVES 6 TO 8

- 1 cup chopped walnuts
- 2 cups fresh or frozen cranberries, thawed
- 1 cup sugar
- 1 (3-oz.) pkg. lemon-flavored gelatin
- 1 cup boiling water
- 1 cup chopped celery
   Lettuce leaves

1. Preheat oven to 350°F. Bake walnuts in a single layer in a shallow pan 8 to 10 minutes or until toasted, stirring halfway through.

2. Process cranberries in a food processor 30 seconds or until chopped, stopping to scrape down sides as needed.

3. Combine cranberries and sugar in a large bowl; let stand 1 hour or until sugar dissolves.

4. Combine gelatin and 1 cup boiling water in a large bowl; stir 2 minutes or until gelatin dissolves. Chill until the consistency of unbeaten egg white.

5. Stir cranberry mixture, celery, and walnuts into gelatin mixture. Pour into a lightly greased 4-cup mold. Cover and chill 8 hours or until firm.

6. Unmold salad onto a lettuce-lined plate.

Hot-Water Cornbread

So quick and easy to prepare, this recipe is one you'll turn to again and again.

ACTIVE 5 MIN. - TOTAL 11 MIN.

MAKES 1 DOZEN

- 2 cups white cornmeal
- ¼ tsp. baking powder
- 1¼ tsp. salt
- 1 tsp. sugar
- ¼ cup half-and-half
- 1 Tbsp. vegetable oil
- 1 to 2 cups boiling water
   Vegetable oil
   Softened butter

1. Combine first 4 ingredients in a bowl; stir in half-and-half and 1 tablespoon oil. Gradually add boiling water, stirring until batter is the consistency of grits (see note below).

2. Pour oil to a depth of ½ inch into a large heavy skillet; place over medium-high. Scoop batter into a ¼-cup measure; drop into hot oil, and fry, in batches, 3 minutes on each side or until golden. Drain on paper towels. Serve with softened butter.

Note: The amount of boiling water needed varies depending on the type of cornmeal used. Stone-ground (coarsely ground) cornmeal requires more liquid.

Pumpkin Chess Pie

Pumpkin pie is traditionally served around the holidays, but this version with its luscious sauce is so good you'll want to serve it year-round.

ACTIVE 15 MIN. - TOTAL 1 HOUR, 25 MIN., PLUS 8 HOURS CHILLING
SERVES 8

- ½ (15-oz.) pkg. refrigerated piecrusts
- 1 (15-oz.) can unsweetened pumpkin
- 2 cups sugar
- ½ cup butter, softened
- 3 large eggs
- ½ cup half-and-half
- 1½ tsp. vanilla extract
- ¾ tsp. salt
- ½ tsp. ground cinnamon
- ¼ tsp. ground ginger
- ¼ tsp. ground cloves
  Praline Sauce (recipe follows)

1. Preheat oven to 350°F. Fit piecrust in a 9-inch pie plate according to package directions; fold edges under, and crimp. Beat pumpkin, sugar, and butter in a large bowl at medium speed with an electric mixer until smooth. Add eggs and next 6 ingredients, beating until blended. Pour filling into prepared crust.
2. Bake 1 hour and 10 minutes or until almost set. Cool pie completely on a wire rack. Chill 8 hours. Serve with Praline Sauce.

Praline Sauce

This rich sauce is also good spooned over ice cream and makes a perfect holiday gift.

ACTIVE 5 MIN. - TOTAL 6 MIN.
MAKES ABOUT 2 CUPS

- 1 cup firmly packed brown sugar
- ½ cup half-and-half
- ½ cup butter
- ½ cup chopped pecans, toasted
- ½ tsp. vanilla extract

Combine first 3 ingredients in a small saucepan over medium. Bring to a boil; cook, stirring constantly, 1 minute. Remove from heat; stir in pecans and vanilla. Cool completely.

Roast Leg of Lamb

Surprise your guests with a new star of the show! This lamb is sure to please any crowd.

ACTIVE 15 MIN. - TOTAL 4 HOURS, 15 MIN.
SERVES 8

- 1 (5- to 6-lb.) leg of lamb
- ¼ cup butter, melted
- 2 tsp. salt
- 1 tsp. freshly ground black pepper
- 1 tsp. dried rosemary
  Mint Sauce or mint jelly (recipe follows)

1. Pat lamb dry, and place, fat side up, on a rack in a shallow roasting pan. Combine butter and next 3 ingredients; rub butter mixture over lamb. Cover loosely with aluminum foil, and let stand at room temperature 30 minutes.
2. Meanwhile, preheat oven to 400°F. Uncover lamb, and bake 2 hours and 30 minutes or until a meat thermometer inserted into thickest portion registers 145°F (medium-rare). Let stand 30 minutes before slicing. Serve with Mint Sauce.

Mint Sauce

ACTIVE 15 MIN. - TOTAL 15 MIN.
MAKES ½ CUP

- ¼ cup chopped fresh mint leaves
- ¼ cup light corn syrup
- 1½ Tbsp. white vinegar
- 1½ tsp. cornstarch

Combine mint leaves, corn syrup, and vinegar in a small saucepan. Whisk together cornstarch and ¼ cup water, whisking until blended. Add to mint mixture. Cook over medium, whisking constantly, 3 minutes or until thickened and bubbly. If desired, pour sauce through a fine wire-mesh strainer into a serving bowl, discarding solids.

Peppered Turkey Breast

If you are cooking for a small group and don't want to cook an entire bird, this is a perfect option!
SERVES 10

- 1 (5½ -lb.) bone-in turkey breast
- ½ cup black pepper
- ¼ cup salt

PUMPKIN CHESS PIE

¾ cup cider vinegar
¼ cup vegetable oil
3 garlic cloves, minced
1 medium onion, chopped
3 Tbsp. chopped fresh parsley
1 (10-oz.) bottle steak sauce
1 Tbsp. all-purpose flour
1 large oven cooking bag

1. Place turkey breast in a large heavy-duty zip-top plastic bag or large shallow dish; set aside.
2. Combine pepper and next 7 ingredients, stirring well; pour over turkey breast, coating thoroughly. Seal or cover, and marinate in refrigerator 8 hours, turning occasionally.
3. Preheat oven to 325°F. Remove turkey breast from marinade, discarding marinade. Add flour to oven bag, shaking to coat; place in a 13- x 9-inch baking pan. Add turkey breast to oven bag. Close bag with nylon tie; cut 6 (½-inch) slits in top of bag. Bake 1 hour and 35 minutes or until meat thermometer registers 170°F. Let stand 15 minutes before carving.
4. Cut top of oven bag, and remove turkey breast to a serving platter, reserving drippings. Strain drippings, and serve with turkey.

Refrigerator Yeast Rolls

You may know these as Parker House rolls, but whatever the name, they are classic buttery, soft, folded dinner rolls for any night of the week.

ACTIVE 18 MIN. · TOTAL 1 HOUR, 17 MIN., PLUS 8 HOURS CHILLING
MAKES ABOUT 3 DOZEN

1 (¼-oz.) envelope active dry yeast
2 cups warm water (100°F to 110°F)
6 cups bread flour
½ cup sugar
2 tsp. salt
½ cup shortening
2 large eggs, lightly beaten
½ cup butter, melted

1. Stir together yeast and warm water in a medium bowl; let stand 5 minutes. Stir together flour, sugar, and salt in a large bowl.
2. Cut shortening into flour mixture with a pastry blender until crumbly; stir in yeast mixture and eggs just until blended. (Do not overmix.) Cover and chill 8 hours.
3. Roll dough to ¼-inch thickness on a well-floured surface (dough will be soft); cut with a 2½-inch round cutter.

4. Brush rounds with melted butter. Make a crease across each round with the dull edge of a knife, and fold in half; gently press edges to seal. Place rolls in a greased 15- x 10-inch jelly-roll pan with sides touching or in 2 (9-inch) square pans. Cover and let rise in a warm place (85°F), free from drafts, 45 minutes or until doubled in bulk.
5. Preheat oven to 400°F. Bake 14 minutes or until golden.

Roast Turkey and Gravy

ACTIVE 14 MIN. · TOTAL 3 HOURS, 11 MIN.
SERVES 12 TO 14

1 (12- to 14-lb.) turkey
1 Tbsp. salt, divided
2 tsp. black pepper, divided
½ cup butter, softened
1 Golden Delicious apple, quartered
1 large yellow onion, quartered
2 large carrots, cut into 3-inch pieces
3 celery ribs with leaves, cut into 3-inch pieces
4 cups hot water
⅓ cup all-purpose flour
Cornbread Dressing (page 260)

1. Preheat oven to 425°F. Remove giblets and neck from turkey; rinse and reserve for another use. Rinse turkey with cold water, and pat dry. Sprinkle cavity with ½ tablespoon salt and 1 teaspoon pepper. Rub skin of turkey with butter, and sprinkle with remaining ½ tablespoon salt and 1 teaspoon pepper.
2. Place apple, onion, carrot, and celery in turkey cavity. Lift wingtips up and over back, and tuck under bird. Place turkey, breast side up, on a lightly greased rack in a roasting pan.
3. Bake on lower oven rack 20 minutes. Reduce oven temperature to 325°F. Add hot water to pan, and bake 2 to 2½ hours or until a meat thermometer inserted in turkey thigh registers 170°F, shielding turkey with foil after 1 hour and basting with pan juices every 20 minutes. Let stand 15 minutes. Transfer to a serving platter; reserve 2½ cups drippings.
4. Whisk together drippings and flour in a medium saucepan. Cook over medium, whisking constantly, 5 to 7 minutes or until thick and bubbly. Season gravy to taste. Serve gravy with Cornbread Dressing and turkey.

Roast Turkey with Chestnut Stuffing

For a festive and colorful presentation, decorate the serving platter with fresh herbs that echo the ones in the stuffing along with seasonal fruit such as kumquats and Concord grapes.

ACTIVE 40 MIN. · TOTAL 5 HOURS, 5 MIN.
SERVES 10 TO 12

1 (14-lb.) whole turkey
Chestnut Stuffing (recipe follows)
Kitchen string
½ cup butter, melted
1 tsp. kosher salt
1 tsp. black pepper
1 cup chicken broth
Giblet Gravy (recipe follows)
Garnishes: fresh oregano, fresh thyme, red grapes, kumquats

1. Preheat oven to 325°F. Remove giblets and neck from turkey; reserve for Giblet Gravy. Rinse turkey thoroughly with cold water. Drain cavity well; pat dry.
2. Place turkey on a work surface, and spoon Chestnut Stuffing into turkey. Tie ends of legs together with string. Tuck wingtips securely under bird.
3. Brush turkey with melted butter, and sprinkle with salt and pepper; place, breast side up, on a roasting rack in a roasting pan. Add broth to pan.
4. Bake 3 hours and 30 minutes, basting every 45 minutes with drippings. Bake an additional 30 minutes to 1 hour or until a meat thermometer inserted into thickest portion of thigh registers 180°F and center of stuffing registers 165°F. (Cover with aluminum foil during last hour of cooking to prevent excessive browning, if necessary.)
5. Transfer turkey to a serving platter, reserving drippings in roasting pan for Giblet Gravy. Skim fat from pan drippings, being careful not to loosen browned particles in pan; discard fat. Let turkey stand 15 minutes before carving. Serve with warm Giblet Gravy.

Chestnut Stuffing

ACTIVE 20 MIN. - TOTAL 20 MIN.
MAKES ABOUT 9 CUPS

1	cup butter
1½	cups chopped celery
1	medium onion, chopped
2	tsp. salt
1	Tbsp. chopped fresh thyme
1	Tbsp. chopped fresh oregano
½	tsp. black pepper
8	cups soft, fresh breadcrumbs
1	(14.8-oz.) jar whole chestnuts
1	cup chicken broth

Melt butter in a large Dutch oven over low. Add celery and next 5 ingredients, stirring well. Saute over medium heat 12 minutes or until celery and onion are tender. Remove from heat; gradually add breadcrumbs and chestnuts, stirring until combined. Add chicken broth, and stir to moisten.

Giblet Gravy

ACTIVE 25 MIN. - TOTAL 1 HOUR, 45 MIN.
MAKES ABOUT 2 CUPS

	Reserved giblets and neck from turkey
1	small onion, quartered
2	celery ribs, halved
½	tsp. salt
	Reserved pan drippings from turkey
3	Tbsp. all-purpose flour

1. Reserve turkey liver. Bring remaining giblets, neck, onion, celery, salt, and water to cover to a boil in a medium saucepan over medium. Cover, reduce heat to low, and simmer 45 minutes or until giblets are tender. Add liver, and simmer 10 minutes. Drain, reserving broth; discard onion and celery. When cool enough to handle, remove meat from neck; coarsely chop neck meat and giblets.
2. Add reserved broth to roasting pan; bring to a boil over medium-high, stirring to loosen browned particles from bottom of pan. Combine broth mixture and enough water to equal 1½ cups, if necessary. Pour mixture into a medium saucepan.
3. Whisk in flour, and cook, whisking constantly, over medium-high, 5 minutes or until thickened. Stir in neck meat and giblets. Season with salt and black pepper to taste.

Sausage-Cornbread Dressing

You can make your own cornbread muffins, but to save time, pick up some from the supermarket deli or from the freezer section.

ACTIVE 30 MIN. - TOTAL 1 HOUR, 40 MIN.
SERVES 8

10	(2-inch) cornbread muffins, crumbled (about 5⅓ cups)
6	white sandwich bread slices, torn into small pieces
2	(14-oz.) cans chicken broth
3	Tbsp. butter
2	medium onions, chopped
4	celery ribs, chopped
½	(1-lb.) pkg. mild ground pork sausage
2	large eggs, lightly beaten
¼	tsp. black pepper

1. Preheat oven to 350°F. Lightly grease a 13- x 9-inch baking dish. Soak cornbread and sandwich bread in chicken broth in a large bowl 10 minutes; stir until liquid is absorbed.
2. Melt butter in a large skillet over medium; add onions and celery, and saute 10 to 12 minutes or until tender. Add sausage, and cook, stirring often, over low 8 minutes or until sausage crumbles and is no longer pink; drain. Add sausage mixture, eggs, and pepper to bread mixture; stir well. Spoon dressing into prepared dish.
3. Bake 1 hour or until lightly browned.

Squash Casserole

Slightly sweet yellow squash is paired with tangy Cheddar and buttery crackers—what's not to love? This casserole is at its best in the summer when yellow squash is in season.

ACTIVE 15 MIN. - TOTAL 1 HOUR, 7 MIN.
SERVES 6 TO 8

8	large yellow squash, cut into ½-inch-thick slices
1	tsp. salt
¼	tsp. black pepper
1½	cups round buttery cracker crumbs
2	cups (8 oz.) shredded sharp Cheddar cheese, divided
¼	cup milk
¼	cup butter, cut into pieces

1. Preheat oven to 350°F. Lightly grease a 2-quart baking dish.
2. Combine squash and water to cover in a medium saucepan; bring to a boil. Cover, reduce heat, and simmer 12 minutes or until tender; drain. Mash squash.
3. Combine squash, salt, and pepper; stir well. Spoon half of mixture into prepared dish. Sprinkle ¾ cup cracker crumbs and 1½ cups cheese over squash. Repeat layers with remaining squash and cracker crumbs. Pour milk over top, and dot with butter.
4. Bake, uncovered, 30 minutes.
5. Sprinkle remaining ½ cup cheese over top; bake 5 minutes or until cheese melts.

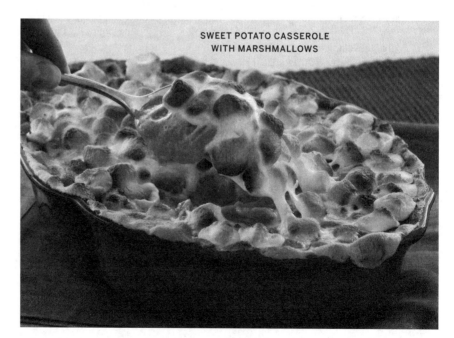

SWEET POTATO CASSEROLE
WITH MARSHMALLOWS

Walter's Favorite Pecan Pie

Chef Walter Royal of The Angus Barn in Raleigh, North Carolina, treats his customers to this fine holiday comfort fare. His pie received our staff's highest rating.

ACTIVE 5 MIN. · TOTAL 45 MIN.
SERVES 6

- ½ (15-oz.) pkg, refrigerated piecrusts
- 3 large eggs
- ½ cup sugar
- ¼ tsp. salt
- 3 Tbsp. butter, melted
- 1 cup dark corn syrup
- 1 tsp. vanilla extract
- 2 cups pecan halves

1. Preheat oven to 350°F. Fit piecrust into a 9-inch pie plate according to package directions. Fold edges under, and crimp.
2. Whisk together eggs and next 5 ingredients until thoroughly blended. Stir in pecans. Pour filling into piecrust.
3. Bake on lower rack 40 minutes or until pie is set, shielding edges with aluminum foil after 15 minutes. Cool completely on a wire rack. Serve with vanilla ice cream, if desired.

Sweet Potato Casserole

Sweet potato casserole is a favorite Thanksgiving side dish, but you don't have to wait until then for it. It teams well with turkey, but it's also perfect with pork or chicken.

ACTIVE 15 MIN. · TOTAL TIME: 1 HOUR, 20 MIN.
SERVES 8

- 6 medium-size sweet potatoes
- ½ cup butter, melted
- ½ cup sugar
- ⅓ cup milk
- 2 large eggs
- 1 tsp. vanilla extract
- ½ cup firmly packed light brown sugar
- ½ cup finely chopped pecans
- 2 Tbsp. all-purpose flour
- 2 Tbsp. butter, softened

1. Preheat oven to 350°F. Lightly grease an 11- x 7-inch baking dish.
2. Bring sweet potatoes and water to cover to a boil, and cook 30 to 35 minutes or until tender. When cool enough to handle, peel potatoes, place in a bowl, and mash.

WALTER'S FAVORITE
PECAN PIE

3. Combine mashed sweet potatoes, melted butter, and next 4 ingredients; beat at medium speed with an electric mixer until smooth. Spoon into prepared baking dish.
4. Combine brown sugar and remaining ingredients; sprinkle over sweet potato mixture.
5. Bake at 350° for 30 minutes.

Sweet Potato Casserole with Marshmallows

The iconic Thanksgiving side dish! It turns out perfectly every time.

ACTIVE 10 MIN. · TOTAL 40 MIN.
SERVES 8

- 3½ cups mashed cooked sweet potatoes
- ½ cup butter, melted
- ¼ cup milk or half-and-half
- 2 large eggs
- ¾ cup sugar
- 1 tsp. vanilla extract
- 3½ cups miniature marshmallows

1. Preheat oven to 375°F. Process first 3 ingredients in a food processor until very smooth, about 2 minutes. Add eggs, sugar, and vanilla; process until blended. Pour into a greased 11- x 7-inch baking dish or other 2-quart baking dish.
2. Cover and bake 10 minutes; uncover and sprinkle with marshmallows. Bake, uncovered, 15 to 20 minutes or until marshmallows are toasted. Serve hot.
Note: For best results, we recommend buying and cooking 3 large, deep orange sweet potatoes. Cut them in half crosswise; boil them in their skins 35 minutes or until very tender. Cool and slip potatoes out of their skins. Mash with a potato masher to equal 3½ cups. In a pinch, use 2 (29-oz.) cans candied yams as a substitute.

Mayo and sour cream make the dressing extra rich.

Dressing adheres better to shredded (not chopped) turkey.

Apple cider vinegar adds a tangy note.

Let's Talk Turkey Salad

The annual day-after sandwich gets a tasty twist

Stir together ½ cup **mayonnaise**; 2 Tbsp. each **sour cream** and chopped fresh flat-leaf **parsley**; 1 tsp. each **apple cider vinegar, Dijon mustard,** and kosher **salt**; and ¼ tsp. black **pepper** in a large bowl. Fold in ¾ cup finely chopped **celery** and ¼ cup finely chopped **shallot**. Fold mixture together with 4 cups shredded cooked **turkey** breast until fully coated. Store in an airtight container in refrigerator up to 4 days. SERVES 10 · ACTIVE 10 MIN. · TOTAL 10 MIN.

MIX IT UP *Use our classic turkey salad (above) as a starting point, and add these creative stir-ins.*

FRUIT-AND-NUT TURKEY SALAD
Prepare recipe as directed, stirring 1 cup **grapes,** 1 cup chopped **candied pecans,** and 1 Tbsp. chopped **fresh tarragon** into mayonnaise mixture.

GOLDEN CURRY TURKEY SALAD
Prepare recipe as directed, stirring ⅔ cup **golden raisins,** ½ cup chopped **roasted salted cashews,** 2 tsp. **curry powder,** and 1 tsp. **granulated sugar** into mayonnaise mixture.

PICKLE-AND-DILL TURKEY SALAD
Prepare recipe as directed, stirring ⅔ cup chopped **bread-and-butter pickles,** 2 Tbsp. chopped **fresh dill,** and 1 tsp. **celery seeds** into mayonnaise mixture.

Easiest-Ever Stock

Let turkey bones simmer in the slow cooker overnight

TURKEY STOCK
Place 1 **turkey carcass** (from a 5-lb. turkey) in a 4- to 6-qt. slow cooker. Add 8 cups **water,** 3 **large carrots** and **celery stalks** (cut into 3-inch pieces), and 1 **medium onion** (cut into 8 wedges). Cover and cook until stock develops a rich flavor and reduces slightly on HIGH 5 hours or on LOW 8 hours. Strain stock, discarding solids. Transfer to storage containers; cool completely, about 1 hour. Seal and store in refrigerator up to 1 week or in freezer up to 2 months.
MAKES 7 TO 7½ CUPS · ACTIVE 10 MIN. · TOTAL 6 HOURS, 10 MIN.

Time To Toss?

Here's how long to keep the remains of the feast

GRAVY
1 TO 2 DAYS

APPLE PIE
2 TO 3 DAYS

TURKEY
3 TO 4 DAYS

DRESSING AND CASSEROLES
3 TO 4 DAYS

CRANBERRY SAUCE
10 TO 14 DAYS

December

270 Spectacular Party Starters Whether you're swapping gifts with girlfriends, hosting a family get-together, or having the whole neighborhood over after the tree lighting, these delicious appetizers will suit any size or type of gathering

276 Bring a Side When the hostess requests your go-to dish, these make-and-take recipes deliver

280 The Art of the Roast Make the centerpiece of your feast look as incredible as it tastes

283 Spirited Desserts Three showstopping treats inspired by winter cocktails—featuring bourbon, whiskey, and rum

286 The Gift of Cookies Fourteen spectacular recipes for baking, sharing, and packaging with care

294 Christmas in Bloom The natural beauty of two iconic Southern flowers inspired this year's cover cake, a three-layer chocolate stunner with the best buttercream we've ever tasted

299 Pralines' Rich History These sweet, pecan-studded puddles are more than a treat for author Toni Tipton-Martin

300 Renaissance Woman New Orleans' most beloved hostess shares the tradition that binds her to the city

302 Bake Another Batch Ivy Odom, Test Kitchen professional and star of our IGTV series *Hey Y'all*, shares her best-ever brownie recipe and two sweet ways to serve them

303 Good to the Last Crumb Flavored with cranberries and a hint of cinnamon, this coffee cake makes a delicious breakfast treat

304 SL Cooking School Our Test Kitchen professionals share ideas for puff pastry and dressing up your dips

Spectacular Party Starters

Whether you're swapping gifts with girlfriends, hosting a family get-together, or having the whole neighborhood over after the tree lighting, these delicious appetizers will suit any size or type of gathering

Chipotle Cheese Straws

ACTIVE 20 MIN. - TOTAL 50 MIN.
MAKES 32

- ½ (17.3-oz.) pkg. frozen puff pastry sheets, thawed
  All-purpose flour, for work surface
- 1 large egg, lightly beaten
- 3 oz. sharp Cheddar cheese, finely shredded (about 1⅓ cups)
- ½ tsp. chipotle chile powder
- ½ tsp. kosher salt
- ¼ tsp. black pepper
- ⅛ tsp. onion powder
- ⅛ tsp. garlic powder

1. Preheat oven to 400°F. Line 2 baking sheets with parchment paper. Transfer puff pastry sheet to a lightly floured work surface; roll into a 16- x 10-inch rectangle (about ⅛ inch thick). Brush dough lightly with egg; reserve remaining egg. Sprinkle Cheddar, chile powder, salt, pepper, onion powder, and garlic powder over 1 long half of dough rectangle. Fold empty dough half over cheese mixture; press gently. Cut dough crosswise into 32 (5- x ½-inch) strips. Transfer to prepared baking sheets.
2. Working with 1 strip at a time, brush both sides lightly with reserved egg. Twist and gently stretch each strip to about 7 inches long. Bake in preheated oven until golden, 14 to 16 minutes, rotating baking sheets halfway through bake time. Transfer to a wire rack to cool completely, 15 minutes.

Baked Goat Cheese Spread with Pepper Jelly

ACTIVE 15 MIN. - TOTAL 30 MIN.
SERVES 14

- 2 (8-oz.) pkg. cream cheese, softened
- 10 oz. goat cheese, softened
- 1½ tsp. kosher salt
- 1 tsp. black pepper
- 2 garlic cloves, grated (about 1 tsp.)
- ¼ cup chopped fresh chives, plus more for garnish

- ¾ cup red pepper jelly
  Crudités and crackers, for serving

1. Preheat oven to 350°F. Combine cream cheese, goat cheese, salt, pepper, and garlic in a food processor. Process until smooth, about 1 minute, stopping to scrape down sides as needed. Transfer mixture to a medium bowl, and stir in ¼ cup chives.
2. Spoon mixture evenly into a shallow 1½-quart baking dish. Bake in preheated oven until heated through, 15 to 18 minutes. Place pepper jelly in a medium bowl, and whisk vigorously to loosen. Spread pepper jelly over hot dip, and garnish with additional chives. Serve immediately with crudités and crackers.

Mini Crab Cakes with Cajun Sauce

ACTIVE 35 MIN. - TOTAL 1 HR., 5 MIN.
MAKES 24

- ½ cup unsalted butter, divided
- 1 lb. fresh lump crabmeat, drained and picked over
- 1 large egg, lightly beaten
- 3 Tbsp. chopped fresh chives, plus more for garnish
- ½ tsp. lemon zest, plus 1½ Tbsp. fresh juice (from 1 lemon), divided
- 1½ cups panko breadcrumbs, divided
- 2 tsp. kosher salt, divided
- ¾ tsp. black pepper, divided
- ½ cup mayonnaise
- 2 tsp. Mexican-style hot sauce
- ½ tsp. Cajun seasoning
- ¼ cup olive oil, divided
- 24 large Gem lettuce leaves (from 4 heads)
  Lemon wedges

1. Place 4 tablespoons of the butter in a small microwavable bowl. Microwave on HIGH until melted, about 30 seconds. Gently stir together melted butter, crabmeat, egg, chives, lemon zest, 1 tablespoon of the lemon juice, ¾ cup of the panko, 1½ teaspoons of the salt, and

½ teaspoon of the pepper in a medium bowl. Shape into 24 (1½-inch) cakes. Sprinkle remaining ¾ cup panko on a large plate. Transfer cakes, in batches, to plate; dredge both sides in panko, pressing to adhere. Place cakes on a baking sheet lined with parchment paper. Cover; chill 15 minutes or up to 8 hours.
2. Stir together mayonnaise, hot sauce, Cajun seasoning, and remaining ½ tablespoon lemon juice, ½ teaspoon salt, and ¼ teaspoon pepper in a bowl; set aside.
3. Heat 2 tablespoons each of the butter and oil in a large nonstick skillet over medium. Add 12 cakes; cook until golden brown and heated through, 3 to 4 minutes per side. Transfer cakes to a plate; tent with foil to keep warm. Wipe skillet clean. Repeat with remaining 2 tablespoons butter, 2 tablespoons oil, and 12 cakes.
4. Place each crab cake on a lettuce leaf. Top each with about 1 teaspoon of the sauce. Garnish with chives and lemon wedges. Serve immediately.

Marinated Olives and Peppadews

ACTIVE 10 MIN. - TOTAL 10 MIN., PLUS 24 HOURS CHILLING, AND 1 HOUR STANDING
SERVES 14

Combine 2 cups (12 oz.) **Castelvetrano olives** (with pits), 2 cups (8 oz.) **Peppadew peppers**, 1 cup (6½ oz.) **Kalamata olives** (with pits), 2 Tbsp. **red wine vinegar**, and 3 (2-inch) **lemon peel strips** (from 1 lemon) in a bowl. Heat 1 cup **extra-virgin olive oil** and 3 finely chopped **anchovy fillets** in a saucepan over medium-low. Cook, stirring often, until anchovies dissolve, 5 minutes. Add 6 smashed **garlic** cloves, 4 **rosemary** sprigs, and 2 tsp. **fennel seeds**. Cook, stirring constantly, until fragrant, about 30 seconds. Pour hot oil mixture over olive mixture; stir to combine. Cover; chill at least 24 hours or up to 1 week. Let stand at room temperature 1 hour before serving.

CLOCKWISE FROM TOP LEFT:

- CHIPOTLE CHEESE STRAWS
  (PAGE 270)

- BAKED GOAT CHEESE SPREAD WITH
  PEPPER JELLY (PAGE 270)

- MARINATED OLIVES AND PEPPADEWS
  (PAGE 270)

- CHEESY MUSHROOM TARTLETS
  (PAGE 272)

- CREAMY FETA PHYLLO BITES (PAGE 273)

- BEEF TENDERLOIN CROSTINI (PAGE 272)

- SWEET-AND-SPICY MEATBALLS
  (PAGE 272)

- MINI CRAB CAKES WITH CAJUN SAUCE
  (PAGE 270)

Cheesy Mushroom Tartlets

(Photo, page 271)

ACTIVE 25 MIN. - TOTAL 1 HR., 10 MIN.
MAKES 18

- 1 (17.3-oz.) pkg. frozen puff pastry sheets, thawed
- 2½ oz. Parmesan cheese, finely shredded (about 1 cup)
- 6 Tbsp. chive-and-onion cream cheese
- 2 Tbsp. olive oil
- 1 lb. sliced wild mushrooms (from 2 [8-oz.] pkg.)
- 2 Tbsp. dry Marsala
- 1 tsp. kosher salt
- 1 tsp. chopped fresh thyme
- ½ tsp. black pepper
- 4 oz. fontina cheese, shredded (about 1 cup)
  Fresh thyme leaves

1. Preheat oven to 400°F. Sprinkle each puff pastry sheet with about ½ cup Parmesan, and gently press with a rolling pin to adhere. Cut each sheet into 9 (3-inch) squares. Gently press squares, cheese sides down, into 2 lightly greased (with cooking spray) 12-cup muffin pans. Place 1 teaspoon cream cheese into each tartlet. Chill, uncovered, while preparing mushrooms.
2. Heat oil in a large skillet over medium-high. Add mushrooms; cook, stirring occasionally, until browned and tender, 8 to 10 minutes. Add Marsala, salt, thyme, and pepper. Cook, stirring often, until liquid has evaporated, about 1 minute. Remove from heat; cool slightly, about 15 minutes.
3. Divide mushrooms among tartlets. Sprinkle evenly with fontina. Bake in preheated oven until pastry is golden brown and cheese is melted, 18 to 22 minutes. Run a small offset spatula around each tartlet to loosen. Transfer to a wire rack. Garnish with thyme leaves; serve warm.

Sweet-and-Spicy Meatballs

(Photo, page 271)

ACTIVE 20 MIN. - TOTAL 2 HOURS, 20 MIN.
MAKES 32

- 1 lb. ground pork
- ½ cup panko breadcrumbs
- 1 large egg, lightly beaten
- ¼ cup finely chopped scallions
- 1 tsp. kosher salt
- 2 Tbsp. toasted sesame oil, divided
- 2 tsp. finely chopped fresh ginger, divided
- 1 cup hoisin sauce
- 3 Tbsp. Asian chile-garlic sauce
- 2 Tbsp. rice vinegar
- 2 Tbsp. soy sauce
- 1 tsp. sesame seeds
  Sliced scallions

1. Combine pork, panko, egg, chopped scallions, salt, 1 tablespoon of the oil, and 1 teaspoon of the ginger. Gently mix with hands to combine. Form mixture into 32 (1-inch) meatballs; place in a lightly greased (with cooking spray) 6-quart slow cooker.
2. Whisk together hoisin sauce, chile-garlic sauce, vinegar, soy sauce, and remaining 1 tablespoon sesame oil and 1 teaspoon ginger. Pour over meatballs. Cover; cook on HIGH until meatballs are cooked through, about 2 hours. Using a slotted spoon, transfer meatballs to a serving platter. Garnish with sesame seeds and sliced scallions. Skim fat from sauce in cooker. Serve meatballs with sauce.

Beef Tenderloin Crostini

(Photo, page 271)

ACTIVE 30 MIN. - TOTAL 55 MIN.
MAKES 16

- 1 (1-lb.) center-cut beef tenderloin, tied at 2-inch intervals with kitchen twine
- 1 Tbsp. plus ¼ tsp. black pepper, divided
- 1 Tbsp. kosher salt, divided
- 5 Tbsp. olive oil, divided
- 16 (⅓-inch-thick) baguette slices (from 1 baguette), sliced at an angle
- ¾ cup very thinly sliced celery (from 2 stalks)
- 1½ Tbsp. red wine vinegar, divided
- ½ cup sour cream
- 1 garlic clove, grated
- 3 oz. blue cheese, crumbled (about ¾ cup), divided

1. Preheat oven to 400°F. Rub beef all over with 1 tablespoon of the pepper and 2 teaspoons of the salt. Heat 1 tablespoon of the oil in a large cast-iron skillet over medium-high until shimmering. Add beef; cook, turning occasionally, until browned all over, 6 to 8 minutes. Transfer skillet to oven. Roast until a thermometer in thickest portion of beef registers 115°F, 12 to 15 minutes. (Do not turn oven off.) Transfer beef to a cutting board; rest 20 minutes.
2. Meanwhile, brush both sides of baguette slices with 3 tablespoons of the oil. Arrange slices in a single layer on a baking sheet; sprinkle with ¼ teaspoon of the salt. Bake until lightly browned, 8 to 12 minutes. Cool 10 minutes.
3. Stir together celery, 1 tablespoon of the vinegar, ¼ teaspoon of the salt, and remaining 1 tablespoon oil in a small bowl. Let stand 10 minutes. Stir together sour cream, garlic, 2 ounces of the blue cheese, and remaining ½ tablespoon vinegar, ½ teaspoon salt, and ¼ teaspoon pepper in a medium bowl.
4. Thinly slice beef into ¼-inch-thick slices. Spread about 1½ teaspoons blue cheese mixture on each baguette slice. Top evenly with beef slices and celery mixture. Sprinkle with remaining 1 ounce blue cheese.

Rosemary-Bacon Nut Mix

(Photo, page 274)

ACTIVE 15 MIN. - TOTAL 1 HOUR
SERVES 12

Stir together 2 Tbsp. finely chopped fresh **rosemary**, 1 Tbsp. granulated **sugar**, 1 tsp. kosher **salt**, and ½ tsp. **cayenne pepper**. Set aside. Cook 6 oz. thick-cut **bacon** (about 5 slices) in a large skillet over medium, turning occasionally, until crisp, 14 to 18 minutes. Transfer bacon to a plate lined with paper towels; reserve for another use. Pour drippings through a fine-mesh strainer into a bowl; discard solids. Wipe skillet clean. Heat 3 tablespoons of the drippings in the skillet over medium. Add 1½ cups (7 oz.) **raw cashews**, 1½ cups (6 oz.) **raw pecan halves**, 1 cup (5 oz.) **raw almonds**, ½ cup (3 oz.) blanched **hazelnuts**, 1 Tbsp. **soy sauce**, and rosemary mixture. Cook, stirring often, until nuts are coated and sugar has melted, 2 to 4 minutes. Transfer nuts to a baking sheet lined with parchment paper; spread in one layer. Bake at 350°F until toasted, stirring occasionally, 10 to 14 minutes. Cool completely, 30 minutes. Store in an airtight container up to 1 week.

Beer-Cheese Fondue

(Photo, page 274)

ACTIVE 15 MIN. - TOTAL 15 MIN.
SERVES 8

- ¼ cup unsalted butter
- ⅓ cup all-purpose flour
- 1 (12-oz.) bottle lager beer
- ¼ cup heavy cream
- 6 oz. Gruyère cheese, shredded (about 1½ cups)
- 6 oz. mild Cheddar cheese, shredded (about 1½ cups)
- ½ tsp. Worcestershire sauce
- ½ tsp. dry mustard
   Serving suggestions: cubed bread, sliced cooked bratwurst, steamed broccoli florets, roasted Brussels sprouts, roasted fingerling potatoes

Melt butter in a medium saucepan over medium-low. Gradually whisk in flour. Cook, whisking constantly, until lightly browned, about 1 minute. Gradually whisk in beer and heavy cream. Cook, whisking constantly, until sauce has thickened and begins to bubble, 3 to 4 minutes. Gradually add Gruyère and Cheddar, whisking constantly, allowing each addition to melt and become incorporated before adding more. Whisk in Worcestershire sauce and dry mustard until smooth. Transfer mixture to a fondue pot; cover and keep warm. Serve immediately.

Smoked Sausage Pretzel Bites

(Photo, page 274)

ACTIVE 30 MIN. - TOTAL 40 MIN.
MAKES 32

- 2 lb. spicy smoked sausage
- 1 lb. fresh prepared pizza dough, at room temperature
   All-purpose flour, for surface
- ½ cup baking soda
- 1 large egg, lightly beaten
   Coarse sea salt or pretzel salt
- ½ cup Creole mustard
- 1 Tbsp. chopped fresh flat-leaf parsley
- 3 Tbsp. mayonnaise
- 1 Tbsp. honey

1. Preheat oven to 450°F. Cut sausage into 32 (1½-inch) straight pieces, reserving curved pieces for another use. Roll dough out on a lightly floured surface into a 16- x 12-inch rectangle (about ⅛ inch thick). Cut dough crosswise into 16 (1- x 12-inch) strips. Cut strips in half crosswise to yield 32 (1- x 6-inch) strips. Working with 1 dough strip at a time, stretch strip to about 12 inches. Wrap 1 stretched dough strip around 1 sausage piece, starting on one side and slightly overlapping in a spiral motion, pressing to seal and leaving ends exposed. Repeat with remaining dough and sausage.
2. Bring 10 cups of water and baking soda to a boil over high. Boil wrapped sausage bites, in batches, until slightly puffed, about 30 seconds. Using a slotted spoon, remove bites; place 1 inch apart and seam sides down on a lightly greased (with cooking spray) baking sheet lined with parchment paper. Brush lightly with egg; sprinkle with coarse sea salt. Bake in preheated oven until deep golden brown, 8 to 12 minutes.
3. Stir together Creole mustard, parsley, mayonnaise, and honey. Serve pretzel bites warm with mustard sauce for dipping.

Creamy Feta Phyllo Bites

(Photo, page 271)

ACTIVE 25 MIN. - TOTAL 25 MIN.
MAKES 30

- 2 (1.9-oz.) pkg. frozen mini phyllo pastry shells
- 6 oz. cream cheese, at room temperature
- 1 small garlic clove, grated
- 5 oz. feta cheese, crumbled (about 1¼ cups), divided
- 3 Tbsp. extra-virgin olive oil, divided
- 1 Tbsp. red wine vinegar, divided
- ¾ tsp. kosher salt, divided
- ½ tsp. black pepper, divided
- 1 cup finely chopped English cucumber (from 1 [12-oz.] cucumber)
- ½ cup finely chopped roasted red bell pepper
- 3 Tbsp. chopped fresh flat-leaf parsley
- 1 tsp. chopped fresh oregano

1. Preheat oven to 350°F. Place phyllo shells on a rimmed baking sheet. Bake until crisp, 5 minutes. Cool completely, 15 minutes.
2. Combine cream cheese, garlic, 4 ounces of the feta, 2 tablespoons of the oil, 1½ teaspoons of the vinegar, ¼ teaspoon of the salt, and ¼ teaspoon of the black pepper in a food processor. Process until smooth, about 1 minute, stopping to scrape down sides as needed. Transfer feta mixture to a ziplock plastic bag. Cut a ½-inch hole in 1 corner of the bag. Pipe about 1 tablespoon feta filling into each phyllo cup.
3. Stir together cucumber, bell pepper, parsley, oregano, and remaining 1 ounce feta, 1 tablespoon oil, 1½ teaspoons vinegar, ½ teaspoon salt, and ¼ teaspoon black pepper. Spoon about ½ tablespoon relish into each phyllo cup.

Pickled Shrimp and Citrus Endive Cups

(Photo, page 274)

ACTIVE 40 MIN. - TOTAL 1 HOUR, PLUS 24 HOURS CHILLING
MAKES 32

- ¼ cup plus ½ tsp. kosher salt, divided
- 1 lb. large peeled, deveined raw shrimp
- 1½ cups extra-virgin olive oil
- ½ cup fresh lemon juice (from 2 lemons)
- 4 garlic cloves, smashed
- 1 Tbsp. mustard seeds
- ½ tsp. crushed red pepper
- ½ cup shaved and finely chopped fennel (from 1 [6-oz.] fennel bulb), fronds reserved for garnish
- 2 fresh bay leaves
- 2 medium-size navel oranges
- 1 medium-size red grapefruit
- 32 Belgian endive leaves (from 4 heads)

1. Bring 4 quarts water and ¼ cup of the salt to a boil in a large saucepan over high. Add shrimp; cook until pink, about 45 seconds. Drain shrimp; transfer to a bowl of ice water. Let stand 5 minutes. Cut into ½-inch pieces. Set aside.
2. Whisk together oil, lemon juice, garlic, mustard seeds, crushed red pepper, and remaining ½ teaspoon salt in a large nonreactive bowl. Stir in chopped fennel, bay leaves, and shrimp. Cover; chill at least 24 hours or up to 2 days.
3. To serve, let shrimp mixture stand at room temperature 30 minutes. Cut around sides of citrus to remove peels. Cut citrus into segments; cut segments into ½-inch pieces. Strain shrimp mixture; discard oil mixture. Stir citrus pieces into shrimp mixture. Divide shrimp mixture evenly among endive leaves. Garnish with fennel fronds.

CLOCKWISE FROM TOP LEFT:

- ROSEMARY-BACON NUT MIX
(PAGE 272)

- BEER-CHEESE FONDUE (PAGE 273)

- PICKLED SHRIMP AND CITRUS ENDIVE
CUPS (PAGE 273)

- CREAMED SPINACH-STUFFED
MUSHROOMS (PAGE 275)

- PARMESAN GRITS TRIANGLES
WITH PESTO (PAGE 275)

- SMOKED SAUSAGE PRETZEL BITES
(PAGE 273)

- ROASTED OYSTERS WITH BACON-
SALTINE TOPPING (PAGE 275)

Creamed Spinach–Stuffed Mushrooms

ACTIVE 30 MIN. - TOTAL 1 HR.
MAKES 48

- 2 (10-oz.) pkg. frozen chopped spinach, thawed
- 6 Tbsp. unsalted butter, melted, divided
- 1 large shallot, finely chopped (about ¼ cup)
- 3 garlic cloves, chopped (about 1 Tbsp.)
- 2 Tbsp. all-purpose flour
- 1 cup heavy cream
- 1 oz. Parmesan cheese, finely shredded (about ⅓ cup)
- 2 tsp. kosher salt, divided
- 1 tsp. black pepper, divided
- 2 cups fresh breadcrumbs (from 1 [1-lb.] French bread loaf)
- 2 Tbsp. chopped fresh flat-leaf parsley
- 1 Tbsp. chopped fresh thyme
- 2½ lb. button mushrooms, stems removed and reserved for another use (about 48 mushrooms)

1. Preheat oven to 400°F. Drain spinach well, and press between paper towels to remove excess moisture.
2. Heat 2 tablespoons of the butter in a medium skillet over medium. Add shallot and garlic, and cook, stirring often, until softened, about 2 minutes. Add flour, and cook, whisking constantly, until lightly browned, about 1 minute. Whisk in cream until smooth. Add spinach, and cook, stirring occasionally, until mixture is very thick, 2 minutes. Stir in Parmesan, 1 teaspoon of the salt, and ½ teaspoon of the pepper. Remove skillet from heat, and cool 10 minutes.
3. Toss together breadcrumbs, parsley, thyme, ½ teaspoon of the salt, ¼ teaspoon of the pepper, and remaining 4 tablespoons butter in a medium bowl.
4. Sprinkle mushroom cavities evenly with remaining ½ teaspoon salt and ¼ teaspoon pepper. Spoon spinach filling into cavities. Top evenly with breadcrumb mixture, pressing gently to adhere. Arrange stuffed mushrooms on an aluminum foil-lined baking sheet. Bake in preheated oven until topping is golden brown and mushrooms are tender, 22 to 25 minutes. Serve stuffed mushrooms immediately.

Parmesan Grits Triangles with Pesto

ACTIVE 40 MIN. - TOTAL 55 MIN., PLUS 6 HOURS CHILLING
MAKES 48

- 4 cups whole milk
- 1 cup uncooked quick-cooking grits
- 3 oz. Parmigiano-Reggiano cheese, grated (about ¾ cup), divided, plus more (shaved) for garnish
- 2¾ tsp. kosher salt, divided
- 1 cup packed fresh basil leaves, plus small leaves for garnish
- 1 cup packed fresh flat-leaf parsley leaves
- ½ cup extra-virgin olive oil
- ⅓ cup pine nuts, toasted
- 1 cup finely ground yellow cornmeal Canola oil

1. Bring milk to a low simmer in a saucepan over medium. Gradually whisk in grits. Let come to a boil. Cover; reduce heat to medium-low. Cook, whisking occasionally, until very thick, about 12 minutes. Whisk in 2 ounces of the grated Parmigiano-Reggiano and 2 teaspoons of the salt. Pour grits onto a 13- x 9-inch rimmed baking sheet or quarter sheet pan, and spread evenly. Press plastic wrap directly on surface; chill until set, at least 6 hours or up to 3 days.
2. Combine basil, parsley, olive oil, and pine nuts in a food processor. Process until a paste forms, 15 seconds. Add remaining 1 ounce grated Parmigiano-Reggiano and ¾ teaspoon salt. Process until smooth, 15 seconds. Transfer to a bowl. Press plastic wrap directly on surface of pesto, and chill.
3. Cut chilled grits into 24 (2¼- x 2-inch) rectangles. Cut each rectangle in half diagonally to yield 48 triangles. Working in batches, dredge triangles in cornmeal; shaking off any excess. Arrange on a baking sheet lined with parchment paper. Chill at least 15 minutes or up to 4 hours.
4. Pour oil to a depth of 2 inches into a Dutch oven; heat over high to 360°F. Fry triangles, in batches, in hot oil until golden brown, 1½ to 2 minutes. Transfer to a baking sheet lined with paper towels to drain. Serve warm topped with pesto (reserving remaining pesto for another use). Garnish with shaved Parmigiano-Reggiano and small basil leaves.

Roasted Oysters with Bacon–Saltine Topping

ACTIVE 40 MIN. - TOTAL 45 MIN.
MAKES 48

- 3 thick-cut bacon slices, finely chopped (about ¾ cup)
- ½ cup finely chopped leek (from the white part of 1 [1-lb.] leek)
- ¼ cup unsalted butter
- 2 garlic cloves, finely chopped (about 2 tsp.)
- 1¼ cups crushed saltine or oyster crackers
- 2 Tbsp. finely chopped fresh flat-leaf parsley
- ½ tsp. kosher salt
- ½ tsp. black pepper
- ¼ tsp. lemon zest (from 1 lemon)
- ¼ tsp. paprika
- 7 cups coarse sea salt
- 48 large Gulf oysters on the half shell Lemon wedges

1. Cook bacon in a medium skillet over medium, stirring occasionally, until almost crisp, about 6 minutes. Add leek, butter, and garlic. Cook, stirring often, until leek is tender and bacon is crisp, 2 to 3 minutes. Remove from heat; stir in crackers, parsley, kosher salt, pepper, lemon zest, and paprika.
2. Preheat broiler to high with oven rack in center of oven. Spread coarse sea salt in an even layer on 2 rimmed baking sheets. Nestle oyster shells into salt. Top oysters evenly with cracker mixture (about 2 teaspoons each). Broil, 1 baking sheet at a time, until topping is golden brown, 1 to 2 minutes. Serve oysters with lemon wedges.

BRUSSELS SPROUTS SLAW WITH PECANS AND POMEGRANATE SEEDS

CREAMED GREENS WITH GARLIC BREADCRUMBS

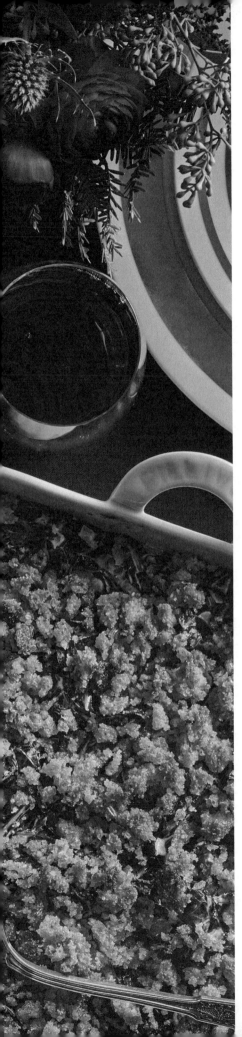

Bring a Side

When the hostess requests your go-to dish,
these make-and-take recipes deliver

Creamed Greens with Garlic Breadcrumbs

ACTIVE 30 MIN. · TOTAL 45 MIN.
SERVES 6

- 2 cups fresh breadcrumbs
- ¼ cup olive oil, divided
- 1½ tsp. finely chopped garlic (from 3 garlic cloves), divided
- 1¼ tsp. kosher salt, divided
- ½ cup chopped yellow onion (from 1 small onion)
- 3 (8-oz.) bunches fresh Lacinato kale, stemmed and thinly sliced (about 10 cups)
- 1 (1-lb.) bunch fresh collard greens, stemmed and thinly sliced (about 8 cups)
- 6 oz. cream cheese
- 4 oz. fontina cheese, shredded (about 1 cup)
- 1 cup half-and-half
- ¼ tsp. black pepper
- ¼ tsp. crushed red pepper (optional)

1. Preheat oven to 450°F. Stir together breadcrumbs, 2 tablespoons of the oil, ½ teaspoon of the garlic, and ¼ teaspoon of the salt in a medium bowl; set aside.
2. Heat remaining 2 tablespoons oil in a Dutch oven over medium-high. Add onion, and cook, stirring often, until softened, about 5 minutes. Add remaining 1 teaspoon garlic, and cook 30 seconds. Add kale, collards, and 3 tablespoons water. Cook, stirring often, until greens are wilted and tender, 10 to 12 minutes. Add cream cheese, fontina, half-and-half, black pepper, remaining 1 teaspoon salt, and (if desired) crushed red pepper. Cook, stirring constantly, until just heated through, about 8 minutes.
3. Transfer to a lightly greased (with cooking spray) 2-quart baking dish, and sprinkle with breadcrumb mixture.
4. Bake in preheated oven until golden and bubbly, about 15 minutes.

Brussels Sprouts Slaw with Pecans and Pomegranate Seeds

This tangy slaw comes together even faster with two preprepared ingredients from your supermarket's produce section: bagged shredded Brussels sprouts and refrigerated ready-to-eat pomegranate arils.

ACTIVE 15 MIN. · TOTAL 45 MIN.
SERVES 8

- ½ cup olive oil
- ¼ cup Champagne vinegar
- 2 tsp. Dijon mustard
- 2 tsp. kosher salt
- ½ tsp. black pepper
- 1½ lb. Brussels sprouts, thinly shaved
- 1 cup toasted pecans, chopped
- 1 Anjou pear, thinly sliced (about 1 cup)
- ¼ cup pomegranate arils (seeds)

1. Whisk together oil, vinegar, mustard, salt, and pepper in a small bowl. Place Brussels sprouts in a large bowl. Add ½ cup of the dressing, and toss to combine. Let stand at room temperature until softened, 30 minutes to 1 hour.
2. Add pecans, pear slices, and pomegranate arils to Brussels sprouts; toss to combine. Drizzle with remaining dressing just before serving.

CREAMY WHIPPED-POTATO CASSEROLE

Creamy Whipped-Potato Casserole

ACTIVE 35 MIN. - TOTAL 35 MIN.
SERVES 8

- 2 lb. russet potatoes, peeled and cut into 2-inch pieces
- 2 lb. Yukon Gold potatoes, cut into 2-inch pieces
- 1 Tbsp. plus 2½ tsp. kosher salt, divided
- 1 cup unsalted butter
- 1 cup heavy cream, divided
- 4 large egg yolks
- 2½ oz. Parmesan cheese, finely shredded (about 1 cup)
- ½ tsp. black pepper, plus more for garnish
- 1 Tbsp. chopped fresh chives

1. Place potatoes and 1 tablespoon of the salt in a large pot with water to cover by 1 inch. Bring to a boil; cook until potatoes pierce easily with a knife, 15 to 20 minutes.

2. Meanwhile, melt butter in a medium-size heavy saucepan over medium-high. Cook, stirring constantly, until butter browns and is fragrant, about 4 minutes. Remove from heat, and immediately pour into a medium-size heatproof bowl. Set aside at room temperature to cool slightly without stirring.

3. Preheat broiler to high with oven rack 8 inches from heat. Drain potatoes well, and return to pot. Add ½ cup of the cream, and blend with a hand mixer until potatoes are very smooth. Beat egg yolks, 1 at a time, into potatoes. Slowly pour in browned butter, discarding any browned bits that have settled at the bottom of the pan. Add Parmesan, ½ teaspoon pepper, and remaining ½ cup cream and 2½ teaspoons salt, and beat until smooth. Transfer to a lightly greased (with cooking spray) 3-quart baking dish.

4. Broil until top is golden, 5 to 8 minutes. Top with chives and sprinkle with pepper.

Melting Sweet Potatoes with Walnuts

Choose a rimmed baking sheet that has enough surface area so the potatoes don't overlap but is small enough so the butter and stock can cover the potatoes evenly. If using a 13- by 9-inch pan, fill it with just enough potatoes to make a single snug layer.

ACTIVE 10 MIN. - TOTAL 45 MIN.
SERVES 6

- ¾ cup unsalted butter, divided
- 2½ lb. medium-size sweet potatoes (about 4 potatoes), peeled and cut into ½-inch-thick rounds
- 1½ tsp. kosher salt, divided
- ½ tsp. black pepper, divided
- ¼ cup unsalted chicken stock
- ½ cup walnut pieces (black or English), toasted
- 2 Tbsp. pure maple syrup

1. Preheat oven to 450°F. Microwave ½ cup of the butter in a microwavable bowl on HIGH until melted, about

MELTING SWEET POTATOES
WITH WALNUTS

ROOT VEGETABLE-AND-
BUTTERNUT SQUASH GRATIN

30 seconds. Toss together potatoes and melted butter in a large bowl. Transfer to a large, rimmed baking sheet, spreading potatoes in a single layer; pour any remaining butter in the bowl over potatoes. Sprinkle with ½ teaspoon of the salt and ¼ teaspoon of the pepper. Roast potatoes in preheated oven until bottoms are lightly golden, about 15 minutes. Flip potatoes; sprinkle with ½ teaspoon of the salt and remaining ¼ teaspoon pepper. Return to oven, and bake until potatoes are very brown, about 10 minutes. Add stock to baking sheet, and bake at 450°F until most of the liquid has evaporated, about 10 minutes.

2. Meanwhile, combine walnuts, syrup, and remaining ¼ cup butter and ½ teaspoon salt in a saucepan over medium. Bring to a simmer, stirring to emulsify butter and syrup. Remove from heat.

3. Transfer potatoes to a platter. Drizzle with syrup mixture just before serving.

Root Vegetable–and–Butternut Squash Gratin

ACTIVE 30 MIN. - TOTAL 2 HOURS
SERVES 10

  2 **cups heavy cream**
2½ **Tbsp. all-purpose flour**
  2 **tsp. kosher salt**
 ½ **tsp. black pepper**
  1 **garlic clove, smashed**
  1 **bay leaf**
  1 **small butternut squash (about 2 lb.), peeled, halved, and seeded**
  2 **medium turnips (1 lb.), peeled and halved**
  1 **medium rutabaga (8 oz.), peeled and halved**
  8 **oz. Gruyère cheese, shredded (about 2 cups)**
 ¼ **cup vegetable oil**
 ¼ **cup fresh sage leaves**

1. Preheat oven to 350°F. Combine cream, flour, salt, pepper, garlic, and bay leaf in a medium saucepan over medium. Cook, stirring often, until hot and slightly thickened, about 5 minutes; do not boil. Reduce heat to low while assembling gratin.

2. Thinly slice squash, turnips, and rutabaga into ¼- to ⅛-inch-thick slices using a mandoline. Layer one-third of the vegetables in a lightly greased (with cooking spray) 13- x 9-inch baking dish. Top with one-third of the Gruyère. Repeat layers twice. Pour cream mixture over vegetables.

3. Cover with foil; bake in preheated oven until bubbly, about 1 hour and 20 minutes. Uncover, increase oven temperature to broil, and broil until top begins to brown, about 4 minutes. Remove from oven; let stand at room temperature 10 minutes.

4. Meanwhile, heat oil in a small skillet over medium. Working in small batches, fry sage leaves until edges begin to curl and leaves just begin to brown. Transfer to a plate lined with paper towels to drain, and cool slightly. Arrange sage leaves over gratin before serving.

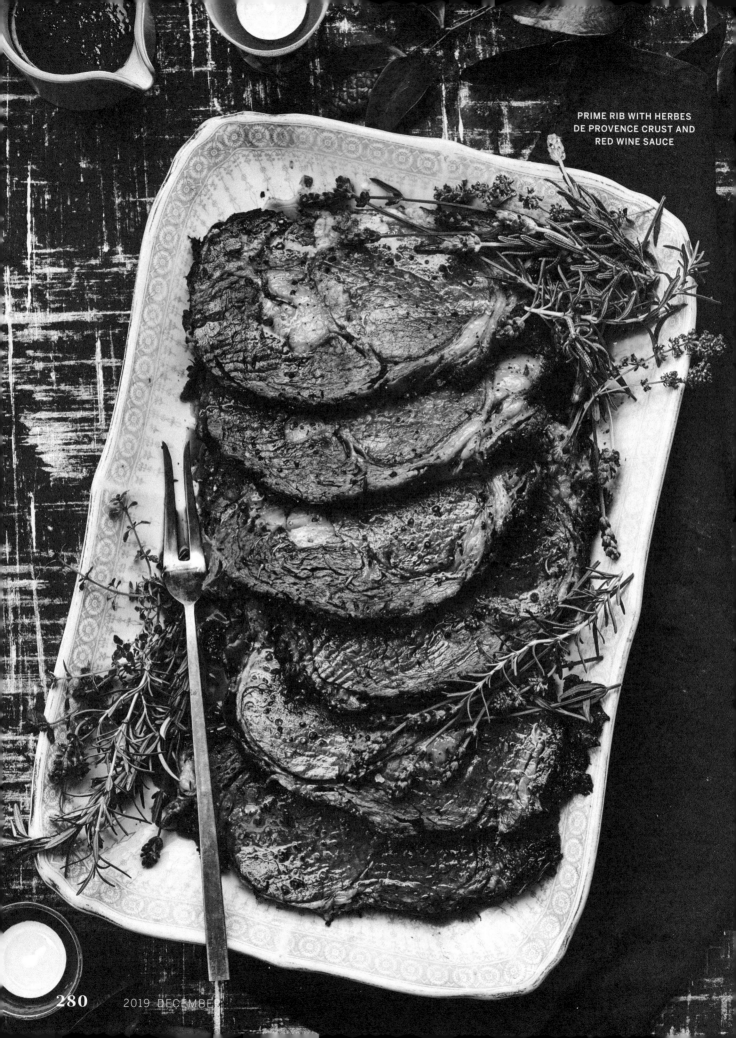

PRIME RIB WITH HERBES DE PROVENCE CRUST AND RED WINE SAUCE

The Art of the Roast

Make the centerpiece of your feast look as incredible as it tastes

Prime Rib with Herbes de Provence Crust and Red Wine Sauce

Instead of arranging a garland of herbs around the platter, garnish the sliced roast with a few loose "bouquets" of herbs (rosemary, lavender, thyme) inspired by the herbes de Provence used in the aromatic rub.

ACTIVE 30 MIN. - TOTAL 4 HOURS, 15 MIN., PLUS 12 HOURS CHILLING
SERVES 10

- 1 (8-lb.) 5-rib standing rib roast, chine bone removed
- 2 Tbsp. extra-virgin olive oil
- 3 Tbsp. herbes de Provence
- 4½ tsp. kosher salt, divided
- 2¼ tsp. black pepper, divided
- 2 Tbsp. butter
- ½ cup minced shallots (from 2 medium shallots)
- 1 cup (8 oz.) dry red wine
- 2 cups lower-sodium beef broth
- 2 Tbsp. Dijon mustard
  Fresh herb sprigs (such as rosemary, thyme, and lavender), for garnish

1. Rub rib roast evenly with oil. Stir together herbes de Provence, 4 teaspoons of the salt, and 2 teaspoons of the pepper in a small bowl. Spread mixture evenly over roast. Chill, uncovered, at least 12 hours or up to 24 hours.
2. Let roast stand at room temperature 1 hour. Meanwhile, preheat oven to 450°F with rack in lowest position.
3. Lightly coat a wire rack with cooking spray; set inside a roasting pan. Place roast, bone side down, on prepared rack. Bake in preheated oven on lowest oven rack 45 minutes. Reduce oven temperature to 350°F (do not remove roast from oven). Continue baking until a thermometer inserted in thickest portion of roast registers 120°F to 130°F for medium-rare (about 1 hour, 30 minutes) or 130°F to 135°F for medium (about 1 hour, 45 minutes). Remove from oven; let rest 30 minutes. Transfer roast to a serving platter, and cover with aluminum foil to keep warm. Discard drippings from pan, reserving any browned bits in pan.
4. Place roasting pan on stove top over 1 burner. Add butter to pan; and melt over medium-high, stirring occasionally and moving pan as needed to prevent hot spots. Add shallots; cook, stirring occasionally, until tender, 2 to 3 minutes. Stir in wine; cook, stirring occasionally, until liquid is mostly reduced, about 3 minutes. Stir in broth; cook, stirring constantly, until thickened, 3 to 4 minutes. Stir in mustard; cook, stirring constantly, until sauce thickens and reduces to 1½ cups, about 5 minutes. Stir in remaining ½ teaspoon salt and ¼ teaspoon pepper. Pour sauce into a serving bowl or gravy boat. Garnish roast with herb sprigs and serve with sauce.

Baked Ham with Brown Sugar-Citrus Glaze

Fresh orange juice and marmalade give this ham its sweet flavor. Pick a few types of citrus for garnishing, such as tangerines, kumquats, and blood oranges, and look for attached leaves. Slice larger fruit into halves or quarters, which will look and smell great and are easier to tuck in around the ham

ACTIVE 30 MIN. - TOTAL 2 HOURS, 45 MIN.
SERVES 12

- 1½ cups packed dark brown sugar
- ¾ cup orange marmalade
- ½ tsp. kosher salt
- ½ tsp. black pepper
- 1 cup fresh orange juice (from 2 large oranges), divided
- 1 (8- to 9-lb.) fully cooked bone-in spiral-cut ham half
  Assorted citrus (such as tangerines, blood oranges, and kumquats), for garnish

1. Preheat oven to 350°F. Line a baking pan with heavy-duty aluminum foil. Stir together brown sugar, marmalade, salt, pepper, and ½ cup of the orange juice in a small bowl.

2. Place ham sideways in prepared pan. Brush with ¼ cup of the brown sugar glaze, gently pushing glaze in between slices using your hands or a brush. Turn ham over, and repeat process with an additional ¼ cup of the glaze.
3. Turn ham cut side down in pan. Pour remaining ½ cup orange juice into bottom of pan. Cover tightly with aluminum foil.
4. Bake in preheated oven 1½ hours. Uncover ham, and brush evenly with ⅓ cup of the glaze. Bake an additional 15 minutes. Brush with an additional ⅓ cup of the glaze. Bake until a thermometer inserted in thickest portion of ham registers 140°F, about 15 minutes. Remove from oven. Brush ham with remaining glaze and pan drippings. Let stand 15 minutes. Garnish ham with whole and sliced citrus.

BAKED HAM WITH BROWN SUGAR-CITRUS GLAZE

ROASTED CHICKEN
WITH APPLES
AND HERBS

Roasted Chicken with Apples and Herbs

This golden-skinned bird is roasted with apples and shallots, which make a beautiful, no-effort garnish for the serving platter. Choose a few small apples and roast them whole for the prettiest presentation.

ACTIVE 30 MIN. - TOTAL 2 HOURS, 15 MIN.
SERVES 6

4 to 6 (about 2½ lb. total) apples (such as Gala, Fuji, or Granny Smith), cored and quartered lengthwise if large

12 small (about 12 oz. total) shallots, trimmed and peeled, divided

2 Tbsp. olive oil, divided

2½ tsp. kosher salt, divided

2½ tsp. black pepper, divided

1 (5- to 6-lb.) whole chicken, patted dry with paper towels

6 thyme sprigs, plus 1 tsp. chopped fresh thyme, divided

6 rosemary sprigs, plus 1 tsp. chopped fresh rosemary, divided

6 sage sprigs, plus 1 tsp. chopped fresh sage, divided

1. Preheat oven to 400°F. Place apples and 10 of the shallots in bottom of a roasting pan. Drizzle with 1 tablespoon of the oil, and sprinkle with ½ teaspoon each of the salt and pepper. Push apples and shallots to edges of roasting pan.

2. If present, remove giblets from chicken, and reserve for another use. Sprinkle ½ teaspoon each of the salt and pepper inside cavity of chicken. Place 3 of the thyme sprigs, 3 of the rosemary sprigs, 3 of the sage sprigs, and remaining 2 shallots inside cavity. Place chicken in center of roasting pan; tuck wings under. Brush chicken all over with remaining 1 tablespoon oil; sprinkle with remaining 1½ teaspoons each salt and pepper. Tie legs together with kitchen twine.

3. Roast chicken in preheated oven until a thermometer inserted in thickest portion of meat registers 160°F, about 1 hour, 30 minutes. Remove from oven, and let rest 15 minutes.

4. Transfer chicken to a serving platter. Remove and discard kitchen twine, if desired. Sprinkle apples and shallots with chopped thyme, chopped rosemary, and chopped sage. Arrange apples and shallots on the platter around the chicken. Spoon any pan drippings around chicken on platter. Garnish with remaining thyme, rosemary, and sage sprigs.

Spirited Desserts

Three showstopping treats inspired by winter cocktails—featuring bourbon, whiskey, and rum

Old-Fashioned Trifle

If whiskey-soaked cake cubes aren't enough reason to make this incredible trifle, the homemade orange-scented custard and tipsy cherries will send you running to the kitchen. For best results, use a fresh pound cake from the bakery, not the frozen kind.

ACTIVE 45 MIN. - TOTAL 1 HOUR, 20 MIN., PLUS 4 HOURS CHILLING

SERVES 12

CUSTARD
- 1 cup granulated sugar
- ½ cup all-purpose flour
- ½ tsp. kosher salt
- 4 cups whole milk
- 4 large egg yolks
- ¼ cup unsalted butter, cut into ½-inch pieces
- ¼ cup fresh orange juice (from 1 orange)
- 1 tsp. vanilla extract
- 1 tsp. Angostura bitters

CHERRIES
- 1 (12-oz.) pkg. frozen pitted dark cherries, thawed and drained
- ¼ cup cherry preserves
- 2 Tbsp. (1 oz.) whiskey

TRIFLE
- ¾ cup (6 oz.) whiskey
- ½ cup granulated sugar
- 2 (12-oz.) bakery pound cake loaves or 1 (24-oz.) round pound cake, cut into 1-inch-thick slices
- 2 cups sweetened whipped cream
  Orange peel twists

1. Prepare the Custard: Whisk together sugar, flour, and salt in a medium saucepan. Whisk in milk and egg yolks. Cook over medium-high, whisking constantly, until mixture begins to bubble, about 10 minutes. Continue to cook until thickened, about 4 more minutes. Remove from heat; whisk in butter, orange juice, vanilla, and bitters until smooth. Transfer to a heatproof glass bowl. Let stand at room temperature until slightly cool, about 30 minutes, stirring occasionally. Cover with plastic wrap, placing wrap directly on surface of custard; chill until cold, at least 4 hours.

2. Prepare the Cherries: Stir together cherries, preserves, and whiskey in a bowl. Set aside at room temperature.

3. Prepare the Trifle: Combine whiskey and sugar in a small saucepan. Bring to a boil over medium-high, whisking occasionally, until sugar dissolves. Remove from heat; cool to room temperature, 20 minutes. Place cake slices in a single layer on a work surface. Brush with cooled whiskey syrup; let stand 5 minutes. Cut cake into cubes.

4. Layer one-third of the cake cubes, one-third of the Custard, and one-third of the Cherries in a 4-quart trifle dish. Repeat layers twice. Top with whipped cream and orange peel twists. Serve immediately, or chill up to 12 hours.

Spiked Eggnog Bundt

Fans of the creamy cold weather drink will swoon for this ultrarich cake flavored with a little bourbon and finished with a sweet glaze. For the most tender crumb, don't overmix the wet and dry ingredients; stop stirring just after they are blended.

ACTIVE 30 MIN. - TOTAL 4 HOURS
SERVES 12

- 1½ cups unsalted butter, softened
- 3 cups granulated sugar
- 6 large eggs
- 3¾ cups all-purpose flour, plus more for pan
- 1½ tsp. kosher salt
- ¼ tsp. grated fresh nutmeg, plus more for garnish
- ¾ cup heavy cream
- ¼ cup, plus 1 Tbsp. (2½ oz.) bourbon, divided
- 2 Tbsp. vanilla extract, divided
- Vegetable shortening, for pan
- 2 cups powdered sugar
- 2–3 Tbsp. refrigerated eggnog

1. Preheat oven to 350°F. Beat butter with an electric mixer on medium speed until smooth, about 1 minute. Slowly add granulated sugar, beating until combined, about 2 minutes. Add eggs, 1 at a time, reducing speed to low to add each egg and increasing to medium speed for 30 seconds after each addition. Beat on medium for 1 minute after adding the last egg.

2. Whisk together flour, salt, and nutmeg in a medium bowl. Stir together cream, ¼ cup of the bourbon, and 1 tablespoon of the vanilla in small measuring cup. With mixer running on lowest speed, add flour mixture and cream mixture to butter mixture in batches, beginning and ending with flour mixture, beating until just blended after each addition and stopping to scrape bowl as needed. Transfer batter to a greased (with shortening) and floured 12- to 15-cup Bundt pan. (If using a 12-cup pan, cake may bake above rim; trim as needed to level.)

3. Bake in preheated oven until a toothpick inserted in middle of cake comes out clean, 1 hour to 1 hour, 10 minutes. Let cake cool in pan on a wire rack until pan is just cool enough to handle, 20 minutes. Turn cake out onto rack to cool, 1 hour.

4. Stir together powdered sugar, 2 tablespoons of the eggnog, and remaining 1 tablespoon each bourbon and vanilla in a large bowl until smooth, adding remaining 1 tablespoon eggnog, 1 teaspoon at a time, if needed for desired consistency. Transfer cooled cake to a platter; pour eggnog mixture over cake. Sprinkle with nutmeg; let stand 5 minutes before slicing.

Hot-Buttered-Rum Bread Pudding

Rum, brown sugar, and warming spices (don't skip the black pepper!) combine in this aromatic dessert. Brioche is often used in bread pudding, but a sturdy loaf of white bread from the bakery is best here because it won't break down as much.

ACTIVE 35 MIN. - TOTAL 50 MIN.
SERVES 10

2   cups half-and-half
2   cups whole milk
1½ cups granulated sugar
6   large eggs
¼   cup unsalted butter, melted
½   tsp. ground cinnamon
⅛   tsp. black pepper
4   tsp. vanilla extract, divided
1½ tsp. kosher salt, divided
15 cups bread cubes (from 1 [30-oz.]
      white bakery loaf)
1   cup golden raisins
1   cup (8 oz.) gold rum
½   cup packed light brown sugar
½   cup unsalted butter
¼   cup heavy cream

1. Preheat oven to 350°F. Whisk together half-and-half, milk, granulated sugar, eggs, melted butter, cinnamon, pepper, 2 teaspoons of the vanilla, and 1 teaspoon of the salt in a large bowl. Add bread and raisins; stir to combine. Let stand 15 minutes, stirring occasionally. Transfer to a lightly greased (with cooking spray) 13- x 9-inch baking dish. Bake until golden and set, 45 to 50 minutes. Cool on a wire rack.

2. Meanwhile, combine rum, brown sugar, ½ cup butter, and remaining ½ teaspoon salt in a saucepan over medium. Bring to a simmer; cook, stirring occasionally, until slightly thickened, 15 minutes. Remove from heat; stir in cream and remaining 2 teaspoons vanilla. Drizzle ½ cup sauce over bread pudding. Serve with remaining sauce.

The Gift of Cookies

Fourteen spectacular recipes for baking, sharing, and packaging with care

DIPPED PISTACHIO SHORTBREAD

AMBROSIA MACAROONS

When I was a child, December brought the mystery and magic of holiday tins, harbingers of the bounty of gifts to come. We never knew when the first one would arrive, but the pile peaked around a week before the big day, covering our largest kitchen counter. My mother stashed away at least one coffee cake topped with crumbled brown sugar and butter for Christmas morning, but everything else was there for the taking. Off-season limits on sweets didn't apply. My siblings and I closely monitored the growing heap, careful not to miss our favorites.

While we usually had ice cream in the freezer, or one of last year's repurposed tins full of my mother's oatmeal-raisin cookies, December's mountain of treats was unprecedented. In a home with four children, checking daily, hourly even, was essential, since the holiday tin buffet was first come, first served. Hiding a treat in the bread box was a solid strategy, at least until the rest of the family caught on.

We all had favorites, often cookies we knew our siblings weren't refined enough to appreciate. I loved butterscotch haystacks made with crispy chow mein noodles. Swedish wedding cookies were another sought-after treat. We called them "snowballs" because what did we know about snow in South Carolina? When my sisters pried the tops from tins decorated with smiling snowmen, sparkling trees, or delightfully garish poinsettias, they hoped for chocolate, especially peanut butter cookies topped with Hershey's Kisses. Christmas bark, eggnog snickerdoodles, and festive fudge were liberated by sticky fingers and popped into happy little mouths.

My brother, the baby, was at a disadvantage because his older sisters were quicker to pounce on the loot. But even he got his share of cookies. (Thank you, Mrs. Umbach, also a mother to four, who gave us a double gift every year because she knew we loved her baking.

She also knew how to keep the peace.) Missed out on crispy molasses cookies? Take a handful of divinity, eat a whole tin of jelly thumbprints, or dive into a dozen sugar cookies decorated with silver dragées (these are deemed inedible by the FDA, but the eighties were a time of innocence).

Cookie tins were the first sign of Christmas and everything we loved about the season: the brightly colored packaging, visits from the friends who brought them, and the containers' contents—enough for everyone. —Anne Wolfe Postic

Dipped Pistachio Shortbread

ACTIVE 40 MIN. - TOTAL 1 HOUR, 50 MIN.
MAKES 2 DOZEN

- 1 cup unsalted butter, softened
- ⅓ cup granulated sugar
- 2½ cups all-purpose flour
- ¼ tsp. salt
- ¾ cup finely chopped roasted unsalted pistachios, divided
- 2 (4-oz.) bittersweet baking chocolate bars, chopped
   Flaky sea salt (such as Maldon)

1. Preheat oven to 325°F. Beat butter with a stand mixer fitted with a paddle attachment on medium speed until creamy, about 2 minutes. Gradually add sugar, beating well. Stir together flour, salt, and ¼ cup of the pistachios in a bowl; gradually add to butter mixture, beating until just combined, 30 seconds. Divide dough into 3 equal portions.
2. Place 1 dough portion on a baking sheet lined with parchment paper. Roll or pat into a 6-inch circle. Score dough evenly into 8 triangles. Repeat procedure with remaining 2 portions on same baking sheet.
3. Bake shortbread in preheated oven until barely golden, 23 to 25 minutes. Cool on baking sheet 5 minutes. Using a very sharp knife, cut shortbread into triangles, following the scored lines in dough. Transfer shortbread to wire racks; cool completely, about 15 minutes.
4. Melt chocolate in a small microwavable bowl on MEDIUM (50%) power until melted and smooth, 2½ to 3 minutes, stopping to stir every 30 seconds.
5. Carefully dip the wide edge of 1 shortbread piece into melted chocolate. Transfer to a sheet of wax paper;

immediately sprinkle shortbread with some of the remaining ½ cup chopped pistachios and a small sprinkle of sea salt. Repeat procedure with remaining shortbread pieces, chocolate, pistachios, and salt. Let stand until chocolate is firm, about 30 minutes. Store in an airtight container up to 1 week.

Ambrosia Macaroons

ACTIVE 20 MIN. - TOTAL 1 HOUR, 15 MIN., PLUS 1 HOUR CHILLING
MAKES 4 DOZEN

- ⅓ cup unsalted butter, softened
- 1 (3-oz.) pkg. cream cheese, softened
- ¾ cup granulated sugar
- 1 large egg yolk
- 1 tsp. orange zest plus 1 Tbsp. fresh juice (from 1 orange)
- 1¼ cups all-purpose flour
- 2 tsp. baking powder
- ½ tsp. salt
- 1 (8-oz.) can crushed pineapple in juice, drained and patted very dry with paper towels
- 5 cups sweetened flaked coconut (from 1 [14-oz.] pkg.), divided
- 24 stemless red maraschino cherries, halved

1. Beat butter, cream cheese, and sugar with a stand mixer fitted with a paddle attachment on medium speed until blended, about 3 minutes. Add egg yolk, orange zest, and juice; beat on low speed until blended, about 1 minute.
2. Whisk together flour, baking powder, and salt in a bowl until combined; gradually add to butter mixture, beating on low speed until blended, about 1 minute. Stir in pineapple and 3 cups of the coconut. Cover; chill 1 hour.
3. Preheat oven to 350°F. Shape dough into 1-inch balls. Place remaining 2 cups coconut in a bowl; roll balls in coconut, and arrange on 2 baking sheets lined with parchment paper.
4. Working in 2 batches, bake macaroons in preheated oven until lightly browned, 12 to 14 minutes. Remove from oven; immediately press 1 cherry half into center of each warm macaroon. Cool on baking sheets 1 minute. Transfer macaroons to wire racks; cool completely, about 30 minutes. Store in an airtight container up to 3 days.

Cream Cheese Cookie Wreaths

ACTIVE 25 MIN. - TOTAL 1 HOUR, 20 MIN., PLUS 1 HOUR CHILLING
MAKES ABOUT 4 DOZEN

- 1 cup unsalted butter, softened
- 1 (8-oz.) pkg. cream cheese, softened
- 1½ cups granulated sugar
- 1 large egg
- 2 tsp. vanilla extract
- ¼ tsp. almond extract
- 3½ cups all-purpose flour, plus more for work surface
- 1 tsp. baking powder
- ½ tsp. salt
- 1 large egg white, beaten
   Green and red sanding sugar, small red sugar pearls, and red cinnamon candies, for decorating

1. Beat butter and cream cheese with a stand mixer fitted with a paddle attachment on medium speed until creamy, about 1 minute. Gradually add granulated sugar, beating until light and fluffy, about 1 minute. Add egg, vanilla, and almond extract, beating until just combined, about 30 seconds.
2. Stir together flour, baking powder, and salt in a bowl. Gradually add flour mixture to butter mixture, beating on low speed until just combined, about 1 minute. Shape dough evenly into 2 disks. Wrap each disk in plastic wrap; chill 1 hour.
3. Preheat oven to 375°F. Roll out 1 disk to ¼-inch thickness on a lightly floured work surface. Cut dough into wreath shapes using a 2½-inch fluted round cookie cutter; cut out centers of wreaths using a 1-inch fluted round cookie cutter (reserve center cutouts). Arrange center cutout pieces into circular wreath shapes, if desired, overlapping pieces slightly. Repeat procedure with remaining dough disk, rerolling scraps once. Arrange wreaths evenly on 2 baking sheets lined with parchment paper.
4. Brush wreaths evenly with egg white. Sprinkle with sanding sugar. Gently press red sugar pearls into cookies.
5. Working in 2 batches, bake in preheated oven until cookie edges turn light golden, 10 to 12 minutes. Remove from oven. Immediately gently press red cinnamon candies into hot cookies to make "berries." Cool on baking sheets 5 minutes. Transfer cookies to wire racks, and cool completely, about 30 minutes.

PEPPERMINT COOKIE TRUFFLES

CANDY CANE CAKE BARS

CHOCOLATE-PRALINE THUMBPRINTS

Peppermint Cookie Truffles

ACTIVE 25 MIN. - TOTAL 35 MIN., PLUS 2 HOURS CHILLING
MAKES ABOUT 30 TRUFFLES

- 3 cups crumbled chocolate-covered mint cookies (about 10 oz.; such as Thin Mints or Grasshopper)
- 4 oz. cream cheese, softened
- 1 (10-oz.) pkg. vanilla candy coating disks (such as Ghirardelli Chocolate White Melting Wafers)
- 10 round hard peppermint candies, crushed

1. Process crumbled cookies in a food processor until finely chopped and the consistency of sand, about 1 minute. Add cream cheese; pulse until mixture is well combined and cookies are finely crushed, about 10 times.
2. Shape mixture into 30 (1-inch) balls; arrange on a baking sheet lined with parchment paper. Cover; chill at least 2 hours or up to 24 hours.
3. Melt wafers in a microwavable bowl according to package directions.
4. Working with 1 at a time, dip truffles into melted wafers, using a fork to scoop up truffle and let excess drip off between fork tines; scrape down edges of bowl as needed. Place dipped truffle on a baking sheet lined with parchment paper; immediately sprinkle with some of the crushed peppermints.
5. Chill truffles until firm, about 10 minutes. Serve immediately, or refrigerate in an airtight container up to 1 week.

Candy Cane Cake Bars

ACTIVE 25 MIN. - TOTAL 1 HOUR, 15 MIN.
MAKES 4 DOZEN

- 1 (15¼-oz.) pkg. white cake mix
- 1 cup whole buttermilk
- ⅓ cup butter, melted
- 3 large egg whites
- 1 tsp. vanilla extract
- ¼ tsp. kosher salt
- ½ tsp. super red food coloring gel
- ½ cup seedless raspberry jam

1. Preheat oven to 350°F. Beat cake mix, buttermilk, melted butter, egg whites, vanilla, and salt with a stand mixer fitted with a paddle attachment on low speed until ingredients are incorporated, about 1 minute. Increase speed to medium; beat until completely smooth, about 2 minutes.
2. Coat 3 (9-inch) square baking pans with cooking spray. Spoon one-third of the cake batter into 1 of the prepared pans. Add 4 or 5 red food coloring gel drops to remaining batter; stir with a rubber spatula until fully incorporated. Divide red batter evenly between remaining 2 pans.
3. Bake cakes in preheated oven until a wooden pick inserted in middles comes out clean, 11 to 13 minutes. Cool in pans 5 minutes. Transfer cakes to a wire rack; cool completely, about 30 minutes.
4. Place 1 red cake layer on a serving plate; spread with ¼ cup jam. Top with white cake layer; spread with remaining ¼ cup jam. Top with remaining red cake layer. Cut cake into 4 equal-size rectangles. Cut each rectangle into 12 (about ½-inch) pieces.

Chocolate–Praline Thumbprints

ACTIVE 35 MIN. - TOTAL 1 HOUR, 35 MIN.
MAKES ABOUT 3½ DOZEN

COOKIES
- 1 cup butter, softened
- ¾ cup granulated sugar
- 2 large egg yolks
- 1 tsp. vanilla extract
- 2 cups all-purpose flour
- ¼ cup Dutch-process cocoa
- ½ tsp. salt

PRALINE FILLING
- 1 cup packed light brown sugar
- ¼ cup half-and-half
- 1 Tbsp. butter
- ¼ tsp. salt
- 1 cup unsifted powdered sugar
- ½ cup chopped toasted pecans

1. Prepare the Cookies: Beat butter in a stand mixer fitted with a paddle attachment on medium speed until creamy, about 30 minutes. Gradually add sugar, beating until light and fluffy, about 1 minute. Add egg yolks, 1 at a time, beating until incorporated after each addition. Beat in vanilla.
2. Stir together flour, cocoa, and salt in a bowl. Add flour mixture to butter mixture, beating on low speed until just combined, about 30 seconds.
3. Preheat oven to 300°F. Shape dough into 1-inch balls. Arrange balls 2 inches apart on 2 baking sheets lined with parchment paper. Press thumb into center of each ball to create an indentation.

4. Working in 2 batches, bake in preheated oven until Cookies are set, 15 to 18 minutes. Remove from oven; gently re-press thumb into indentions. Cool on baking sheets 5 minutes. Transfer Cookies to wire racks; cool completely, about 15 minutes.

5. Meanwhile, prepare the Praline Filling: Stir together brown sugar and half-and-half in a small saucepan. Cook over medium-high, stirring constantly, until mixture comes to a boil. Continue boiling, stirring constantly, 4 minutes. Remove from heat; stir in butter and salt. Whisk in powdered sugar until smooth, about 1 minute. Use immediately (filling hardens quickly).

6. Working with 1 Cookie at a time, fill each indentation with Praline Filling, and immediately sprinkle with some of the pecans. Let Cookies stand until set, about 20 minutes. Store in an airtight container between layers of wax paper or parchment paper up to 1 week.

Dark Chocolate–Ginger–Molasses Cookies

ACTIVE 15 MIN. · TOTAL 1 HOUR, 10 MIN.
MAKES ABOUT 2½ DOZEN

- ½ cup unsalted butter, softened
- ½ cup lightly packed light brown sugar
- 1 large egg
- 2 Tbsp. unsulphured molasses
- 1 tsp. vanilla extract
- 1½ cups all-purpose flour
- 3 Tbsp. unsweetened cocoa
- 3 Tbsp. finely chopped crystallized ginger
- 1 tsp. baking soda
- ½ tsp. ground cinnamon
- ½ tsp. salt
- ¼ tsp. ground ginger
- 3 oz. semisweet chocolate, chopped into small chunks
- ¼ cup granulated sugar

1. Preheat oven to 350°F. Beat butter and brown sugar in a stand mixer fitted with a paddle attachment on medium speed until smooth, about 1 minute. Add egg, and beat until just combined. Beat in molasses and vanilla.

2. Stir together flour, cocoa, crystallized ginger, baking soda, cinnamon, salt, and ground ginger in a bowl. Gradually add flour mixture to butter mixture, beating on low speed until just combined, about 1 minute. Fold in chocolate.

3. Shape dough into 30 (1½-inch) balls (dough will be sticky). Place granulated sugar in a bowl; roll balls twice in granulated sugar. Arrange balls 2 inches apart on 2 baking sheets lined with parchment paper.

4. Working in 2 batches, bake in preheated oven until tops are crackly but cookies are still soft to the touch, 10 to 12 minutes. Cool on baking sheets 5 minutes. Transfer cookies to wire racks; cool completely, about 30 minutes.

Sugar-and-Spice Rugelach

ACTIVE 40 MIN. · TOTAL 3 HOURS, 20 MIN., PLUS 2 HOURS CHILLING
MAKES 4 DOZEN

- 1 cup unsalted butter, softened
- 1 (8-oz.) pkg. cream cheese, softened
- ¼ cup granulated sugar
- 2 tsp. vanilla extract
- 2 cups all-purpose flour, plus more for work surface
- ¾ tsp. kosher salt, divided
- ¾ cup packed light brown sugar
- ½ tsp. ground cinnamon
- ½ tsp. ground cardamom
- ¼ tsp. ground ginger
- ¼ tsp. ground allspice
- 4 Tbsp. unsalted butter, very soft
- 1 cup toasted slivered almonds, chopped
- 1 large egg
- 1 Tbsp. water
  Sanding sugar, for decorating

1. Beat softened butter, cream cheese, granulated sugar, and vanilla with a stand mixer fitted with a paddle attachment on medium speed until creamy, about 1 minute. Stir together flour and ½ teaspoon of the salt in a small bowl. Gradually add flour mixture to butter mixture, beating on low speed until smooth, about 1 minute. Divide dough into 4 equal portions; flatten each into a disk. Wrap each disk in plastic wrap; chill 2 hours.

2. Stir together brown sugar, cinnamon, cardamom, ginger, allspice, and remaining ¼ teaspoon salt in a small bowl.

3. Working with 1 disk at a time, remove dough from refrigerator; roll into a 10-inch circle (about ¼ inch thick) on a lightly floured work surface. Spread disk with 1 tablespoon of the very soft butter, leaving a ½-inch border. Sprinkle butter evenly with one-fourth of the brown sugar mixture (about 3 packed tablespoons). Sprinkle evenly with one-fourth of the chopped almonds. Cut into 12 wedges; roll up each wedge starting at wide end. Arrange wedges, pointed sides down, on a baking sheet lined with parchment paper. Place in refrigerator. Chill rugelach 20 minutes. Repeat process with remaining dough, butter, brown sugar mixture, and almonds.

4. Preheat oven to 350°F. Whisk together egg and water in a small bowl; brush evenly over rugelach. Sprinkle evenly with sanding sugar. Working in 4 batches, bake until golden brown, 18 to 22 minutes. Cool on baking sheets 10 minutes. Transfer to wire racks; cool completely, about 15 minutes.

DARK CHOCOLATE-GINGER-MOLASSES COOKIES

SUGAR-AND-SPICE RUGELACH

SPRINKLE
SANDWICH COOKIES
(PAGE 292)

BROWN SUGAR
COOKIE STARS
(PAGE 292)

Sprinkle Sandwich Cookies

(Photo, page 290

ACTIVE 25 MIN. - TOTAL 1 HOUR, 5 MIN., PLUS
1 HOUR CHILLING

MAKES ABOUT 2 DOZEN SANDWICH COOKIES

- ¾ cup unsalted butter, softened
- 1 cup granulated sugar
- 2 large eggs
- 1 tsp. vanilla extract
- 2¼ cups all-purpose flour
- 1 tsp. baking powder
- ½ tsp. baking soda
- ¼ tsp. salt
- ¼ cup red and green candy sprinkles, or ¼ cup blue and white candy sprinkles, plus more for decorating
  Vanilla Buttercream (recipe follows)

1. Beat butter and sugar in a stand mixer fitted with a paddle attachment on medium speed until light and fluffy, about 1 minute. Add eggs, and beat until just incorporated; beat in vanilla.
2. Stir together flour, baking powder, baking soda, and salt in a small bowl. Gradually add flour mixture to butter mixture, beating on low speed until just incorporated, about 1 minute. Fold in either assorted red and green sprinkles or assorted blue and white sprinkles until evenly distributed throughout batter. Cover and chill at least 1 hour or up to overnight.
3. Preheat oven to 325°F. Shape chilled dough into 48 (1-inch) balls; arrange 2 inches apart on 2 baking sheets lined with parchment paper. Working in 2 batches, bake until cookies are lightly browned around edges, 8 to 10 minutes. Transfer cookies to wire racks; cool completely, about 20 minutes.
4. Spread about 1 tablespoon Vanilla Buttercream onto the flat sides of 24 of the cookies. Top with flat sides of remaining 24 cookies. Roll sides of cookie sandwiches in either assorted red and green sprinkles or assorted blue and white sprinkles (to match the colors used inside cookies). Store in an airtight container up to 1 week.

Vanilla Buttercream

ACTIVE 5 MIN. - TOTAL 5 MIN.

MAKES ABOUT 2 CUPS

- 1 cup unsalted butter, softened
- 4 cups unsifted powdered sugar
- 2 tsp. vanilla extract
- ¼ tsp. salt
- 1 to 2 tsp. whole milk, as needed

Beat butter with an electric mixer fitted with a paddle attachment on medium speed until creamy, about 30 seconds. Add powdered sugar, vanilla, salt, and 1 teaspoon milk, beating on low speed until smooth and creamy. If needed, beat in up to 1 teaspoon remaining milk to reach desired consistency. Store Vanilla Buttercream in an airtight container in the refrigerator up to 2 weeks.

Brown Sugar Cookie Stars

(Photo, page 291)

ACTIVE 35 MIN. - TOTAL 1 HOUR, 15 MIN.,
PLUS 1 HOUR CHILLING

MAKES ABOUT 4 DOZEN

- 1¼ cups unsalted butter, softened
- 1 cup granulated sugar
- 1 cup packed light brown sugar
- 2 large eggs
- 1 Tbsp. vanilla extract
- 4 cups all-purpose flour, plus more for work surface
- 1 tsp. baking powder
- ½ tsp. salt
  Royal Icing (recipe follows)
  Assorted gold candy sprinkles

1. Beat butter, granulated sugar, and brown sugar with a stand mixer fitted with a paddle attachment on medium speed until creamy, about 2 minutes. Add eggs, 1 at a time, beating until just incorporated; beat in vanilla on low speed.
2. Stir together flour, baking powder, and salt in a large bowl. Gradually add to butter mixture, beating on low speed until just blended, about 1 minute.
3. Divide dough into 4 equal portions; flatten each into a ½-inch-thick disk. Wrap each in plastic wrap; chill 30 minutes.
4. Working with 1 disk at a time, place on a lightly floured work surface; roll to ¼-inch thickness. Cut with assorted sizes of star-shaped cookie cutters. Arrange 1 inch apart on 2 baking sheets lined with parchment paper. Chill 30 minutes. Meanwhile, preheat oven to 350°F.
5. Working in 2 batches, bake in preheated oven until cookie edges begin to brown, 8 to 10 minutes. Cool on baking sheets 10 minutes. Transfer cookies to wire racks; cool completely, 20 to 30 minutes. Decorate with Royal Icing and sprinkles.

Royal Icing

ACTIVE 10 MIN. - TOTAL 10 MIN.

MAKES 2 CUPS

- 3 cups unsifted powdered sugar
- ¼ cup water, plus more as needed
- 2 Tbsp. meringue powder
- 1 tsp. vanilla extract

Beat all ingredients with a stand mixer fitted with a paddle attachment on medium speed until blended, smooth, and stiff, 1 minute (mixture should hold stiff peaks), stopping to scrape down sides as needed. Gradually add additional water, ½ teaspoon at a time, until desired consistency is reached. Spoon mixture into a piping bag fitted with desired tip; pipe onto cookies. Store in an airtight container up to 1 week.

Chocolate-Pecan Biscotti Thins

ACTIVE 25 MIN. - TOTAL 2 HOURS, 5 MIN.

MAKES ABOUT 4 DOZEN

- ½ cup unsalted butter, softened
- 1¼ cups granulated sugar
- 2 large eggs
- 1 tsp. vanilla extract
- 2½ cups all-purpose flour
- ½ cup unsweetened cocoa
- 1½ tsp. baking powder
- ½ tsp. salt
- ½ tsp. ground cinnamon
- 1 cup chopped toasted pecans
  Powdered sugar, for dusting

1. Preheat oven to 350°F. Beat butter and granulated sugar with a stand mixer fitted with a paddle attachment on medium speed until creamy, about 2 minutes. Add eggs, 1 at a time, beating until just combined after each addition. Beat in vanilla.
2. Stir together flour, cocoa, baking powder, salt, and cinnamon in a medium bowl. Gradually add flour mixture to butter mixture, beating on low speed until just combined. Beat in chopped pecans until just combined.
3. Lightly dust hands with powdered sugar. Divide dough in half. Shape each dough portion into a 12- x 3-inch log. Arrange logs 2 inches apart on a baking sheet lined with parchment paper.
4. Bake in preheated oven 25 minutes. Cool on baking sheet 30 minutes. Cut each log diagonally into ¼-inch-thick

slices using a serrated knife (use a gentle sawing motion). Arrange slices side by side on a baking sheet lined with parchment paper.

5. Return to oven, and bake at 350°F 7 to 8 minutes. Turn slices over, and bake until dry and crisp, an additional 7 to 8 minutes. Transfer to wire racks, and cool completely, about 20 minutes. Store cookies in an airtight container up to 1 week.

Cranberry-Orange Butter Cookies

ACTIVE 25 MIN. · TOTAL 1 HOUR, 10 MIN., PLUS 2 HOURS CHILLING

MAKES ABOUT 5 DOZEN

- 1½ cups unsalted butter, softened
- 1¼ cups unsifted powdered sugar
- 2 tsp. vanilla extract
- 3 cups all-purpose flour
- ¼ tsp. plus ⅛ tsp. baking powder
- ¼ tsp. salt
- ¾ cup chopped dried cranberries
- 1½ Tbsp. orange zest (from 3 oranges)
- 1 cup demerara sugar or sparkling sugar, as needed for decorating

1. Beat butter with a stand mixer fitted with a paddle attachment on medium speed until creamy, about 2 minutes. Gradually add powdered sugar, beating until smooth. Beat in vanilla.

2. Stir together flour, baking powder, and salt in a bowl. Gradually add flour mixture to butter mixture, beating on low speed until combined, about 1 minute. Beat in cranberries and orange zest until just combined, about 30 seconds.

3. Divide dough in half. Shape each half into a rectangular log about 9 inches long x 2 inches wide x 2 inches tall. Wrap in plastic wrap, and chill at least 2 hours or up to overnight.

4. Preheat oven to 350°F. Place demerara sugar in a shallow dish. Unwrap dough logs. Gently press demerara sugar into long sides of both logs.

5. Slice dough into ¼-inch-thick slices. Arrange slices 1 inch apart on 2 baking sheets lined with parchment paper.

6. Working in 2 batches, bake in preheated oven until cookie edges are lightly browned, 10 to 12 minutes. Cool on baking sheets 5 minutes. Transfer cookies to wire racks; cool completely, about 20 minutes. Store in airtight containers up to 1 week.

CHOCOLATE-PECAN
BISCOTTI THINS

CRANBERRY-ORANGE
BUTTER COOKIES

Christmas in Bloom

The natural beauty of two iconic Southern flowers inspired this year's cover cake, a three-layer chocolate stunner with the best buttercream we've ever tasted

Chocolate–Buttermilk Cake with Swiss Meringue Buttercream

ACTIVE 20 MIN. · TOTAL 2 HOURS
SERVES 12

- 1½ cups (9 oz.) semisweet chocolate chips
- 2 cups granulated sugar
- ½ cup unsalted butter, softened
- 3 large eggs
- 2¼ cups bleached cake flour (such as Swans Down), plus more for pans
- 1 tsp. baking soda
- ½ tsp. salt
- 1 cup whole buttermilk
- 1 cup hot water
- 2 tsp. vanilla extract
  Vegetable shortening, for greasing pans
  Swiss Meringue Buttercream (recipe follows)
  Magnolia or Camellia Cake Toppers (recipe follows)

1. Preheat oven to 350°F. Microwave chocolate chips in a microwavable bowl on MEDIUM (50%) power until melted, about 2½ minutes, stirring every 30 seconds. Stir until mixture is smooth. Cool 5 minutes.
2. Beat sugar and butter with a heavy-duty stand mixer fitted with a paddle attachment on medium speed until well blended, 3 to 5 minutes. Add eggs, 1 at a time, beating just until blended after each addition. Add melted chocolate, beating just until blended.
3. Sift together flour, baking soda, and salt in a bowl. Add to chocolate mixture in 3 additions alternately with buttermilk, beginning and ending with flour mixture. Beat on low speed just until blended after each addition. With mixer running on low speed, gradually add hot water in a slow, steady stream, beating just until blended. Add vanilla; beat on low until incorporated.

4. Grease (with shortening) and flour 3 (8-inch) round baking pans. Line bottoms with parchment paper; lightly grease. Pour batter into prepared pans. Bake in preheated oven until a wooden pick inserted in center comes out clean, 22 to 26 minutes. Cool in pans on wire racks 10 minutes. Remove from pans to wire racks, gently remove parchment paper, and cool completely, about 1 hour.
5. Place 1 cake layer on a cake stand. Top with 1 cup of the Swiss Meringue Buttercream. Spread to edges. Repeat with second cake layer and 1 cup of buttercream. Top with third cake layer. Frost top and sides of cake with remaining buttercream, using a small offset spatula to achieve textured look. Garnish with Magnolia or Camellia Cake Toppers.

Swiss Meringue Buttercream

ACTIVE 25 MIN. · TOTAL 35 MIN.
MAKES ABOUT 6 CUPS

- 6 large egg whites
- 1½ cups granulated sugar
- ½ tsp. kosher salt
- 2½ cups unsalted butter, cut into tablespoons and softened to room temperature
- 2 tsp. vanilla extract
- ¼ tsp. almond extract

1. Pour water to a depth of 1½ inches in a large saucepan; bring water to a boil over high. Reduce heat to low, maintaining a gentle simmer. Whisk together egg whites, sugar, and salt in bowl of a heavy-duty stand mixer. Crumple a large piece of aluminum foil; shape into a ring about 2 inches high. Place in simmering water in saucepan. (The foil ring will prevent the mixer bowl from touching the water.) Place mixer bowl on foil ring.
2. Cook egg white mixture, whisking constantly, until mixture registers 160°F on an instant-read thermometer, 10 to 12 minutes. Transfer bowl to heavy-duty stand mixer fitted with whisk attachment. Beat mixture on low speed for 1 minute; gradually increase speed to medium-high, beating until mixture is fluffy, glossy, and completely cool, 8 to 10 minutes total.
3. Reduce speed to medium-low, and add softened butter a few pieces at a time, beating well after each addition. Beat in vanilla and almond extracts. Remove whisk attachment; attach paddle attachment. Scrape down sides of bowl with a rubber spatula. Beat frosting on low until very smooth, 1 to 2 minutes. Use immediately, chill in an airtight container up to 3 days, or freeze up to 1 month. (Before using, let chilled or frozen buttercream come to room temperature and beat on low speed.)

THE FLOWERS

If you've played with modeling clay, you can make lifelike blooms from gum paste. All you need are a few things from the crafts store and two days for the flowers to dry.

Magnolia or Camellia Cake Toppers

ACTIVE 4 HOURS · TOTAL 4 HOURS,
PLUS 2 DAYS DRYING TIME

MAKES 4 FLOWERS AND ABOUT 15 MAGNOLIA LEAVES OR 24 CAMELLIA LEAVES

INGREDIENTS

- 1 (16-oz.) container ready-to-use gum paste (about 2 cups)
- ¼ cup vegetable shortening
- Red food coloring gel, for camellia flowers
- Green food coloring gel
- Brown food coloring gel, for magnolia leaves
- Edible glue (such as Wilton Dab-N-Hold Edible Adhesive)
- Green edible luster dust
- Yellow edible luster dust

TOOLS YOU WILL NEED

- Rolling pin
- 1-inch round cutter
- 2-inch round cutter
- Small pair of scissors
- Foam mat or linen towel
- Measuring teaspoon with rounded bottom
- Small (1-cup capacity) bowls
- 2-inch leaf-shaped cutter (optional)
- Leaf-shaped mold (optional)
- 4 wooden spoons with cylindrical handles
- Small food-safe paintbrush
- Vinyl disposable gloves

1. Make the Gum-Paste Mixture If making magnolias, knead together gum paste and shortening on a clean work surface until shortening is fully incorporated and gum paste is soft and malleable. (It may be easier to work with half of the gum paste and shortening at a time.) Wrap half of gum-paste mixture tightly in plastic wrap; set aside. If making camellias, follow method above, wearing gloves to knead 10 drops of red food coloring into half of gum-paste mixture until thoroughly blended, kneading in 1 more drop at a time until desired color is reached. Wrap remaining (white) half of gum-paste mixture tightly in plastic wrap; set aside.

2. Cut the Petals Use a rolling pin to roll remaining half of white or red gum-paste mixture to ⅛-inch thickness. Cut 12 circles out of gum-paste mixture using a 1-inch round cutter **[A]**. Cut 24 circles, using a 2-inch round cutter, rerolling scraps as needed. (To prevent gum-paste mixture from drying or cracking, work

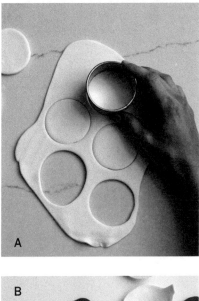

A

B

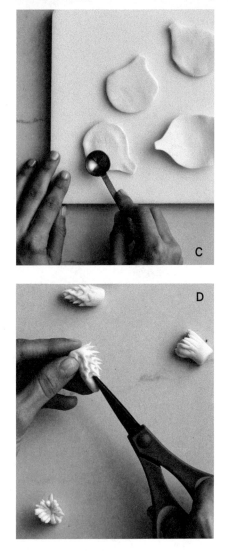

C

D

E

F

quickly and keep it covered with plastic wrap or a damp paper towel as you go.)

3. Shape the Petals For magnolia petals, use small scissors to cut each circle to create a light bulb or hot-air balloon shape **[B]**. Place each petal on a foam mat, and, using rounded bottom of a measuring teaspoon, gently and gradually smooth edges of petal until they are slightly thinner **[C]**. Place 3 or 4 petals in bottom and against side of a small bowl, shaping each petal to curvature of bowl. (Do not overlap petals.) Let stand, uncovered, overnight. For camellia petals, use small scissors to cut each circle into a teardrop shape with a pointed end. Place each petal on foam mat, and smooth the edges as directed above. Place in a small bowl, and let stand as directed above.

4. Make the Stamens For magnolia stamens, unwrap remaining half of gum-paste mixture. Pinch off 4 pea-size balls, and rewrap remaining gum-paste mixture. Roll each ball into a cone shape. Flatten bottom of wide end of

each cone, and stand upright on a work surface. Using small scissors, cut little incisions at a downward angle all over sides of cone **[D]**. Let stand, uncovered, overnight. For camellia stamens, pinch off 4 pea-size balls of gum-paste mixture as directed at left. Roll each ball into a 1-inch-long cylinder. Using small scissors, cut cylinders in half lengthwise, stopping about halfway. Cut each half in half again to create quarters. Cut each quarter into thirds. Stand cylinders upright on a work surface; let stand, uncovered, overnight.

5. Make the Leaves For magnolia leaves, divide reserved gum-paste mixture from Step 4 into 2 equal portions. Wearing gloves, knead 8 drops of green food coloring into 1 portion until thoroughly blended, kneading in 1 more drop at a time until color resembles green side of a magnolia leaf. Cover with plastic wrap. Knead 8 drops of brown food coloring into remaining portion of gum-paste mixture until thoroughly blended, kneading in 1 more drop at a time until color

resembles brown side of a magnolia leaf. Roll each green and brown portion into 1 (⅛-inch-thick) sheet. Place green sheet on top of brown sheet, and roll together to ⅛-inch thickness **[E]**. Cut out about 15 leaves using a leaf-shape cutter. (Or, using a 2-inch round cutter, cut into about 15 circles **[F]**, and, using small scissors, trim into a leaf shape **[G]**.) Place each leaf on foam mat, and, using rounded bottom of a measuring teaspoon, gently and gradually smooth edges of leaf until they are slightly thinner. Using dull side of a paring knife, create a vein pattern on the leaves. (If using a leaf-shape mold, press each leaf into mold, and gently remove.) For camellia leaves, wearing gloves, knead 10 drops of green food coloring into reserved portion of gum-paste mixture from Step 4 until thoroughly blended, kneading in 1 more drop at a time until color resembles the deep green shade of a camellia leaf. Roll mixture into a ⅛-inch-thick sheet. Cut out about 24 leaves using a leaf-shaped cutter. (Or,

G

I

H

J

K

using a 2-inch round cutter, cut into about 24 circles, and, using small scissors, trim into a leaf shape.) Place leaves on foam mat. Smooth the edges of the leaves, and create a vein pattern as directed on page 297. Place 2 of the wooden spoons side by side, with handles as close as possible. Drape leaves over handles, with center vein of leaf between and parallel to handles [H]. (Do not let leaves touch each other.) Repeat with remaining leaves and spoons. Let stand, uncovered, overnight. (This will give the leaves a natural curve.)

6. Assemble the Flowers To make magnolias or camellias (the following day), place a 1-inch square piece of paper towel in center of a small bowl. Arrange 3 large petals in bowl, allowing the narrow ends to overlap in the bottom center of the bowl. Dab a generous amount of edible glue in

between each petal end, and gently press to adhere. Place 3 large petals on top, arranging them in gaps of petals already in bowl. Dab a generous amount of edible glue in and around the center of the petals, and press to adhere [I]. Place a small ball of aluminum foil behind each petal to keep layers of petals from touching. Place 3 small petals on top, arranging them in gaps of petals already in bowl. Dab a generous amount of edible glue in and around the center of the petals, and press to adhere. Place a small ball of aluminum foil behind each petal to keep layers of petals from touching. Repeat with remaining large and small petals in 3 separate bowls, to form 3 more flowers.

7. Attach the Stamens Using a food-safe paintbrush, brush 1 stamen (for magnolia or camellia flowers) with a mixture of

green and yellow luster dust [J]; blow off excess. Dab a small amount of edible glue on flat end of stamen, and press into center of 1 flower [K]. Place small aluminum foil balls around the stamen to hold upright. Repeat with remaining stamens and flowers. Let stand, uncovered, at least 24 hours or up to 48 hours.

8. Arrange the Flowers Once glue has dried, remove and discard aluminum foil balls from between petals and from around stamens; remove and discard paper towel squares. Place magnolia or camellia flowers on top of frosted cake, pressing lightly to secure. Arrange leaves around each flower or along bottom of cake, forming a garland. (Flowers will keep in an airtight container in a cool, dry place up to 4 months.)

Pralines' Rich History

These sweet, pecan-studded puddles are more than a treat for author Toni Tipton-Martin

Whether they are packaged in pretty gift boxes or served at the end of a festive evening with tea or coffee, pralines are a Christmas tradition in many homes throughout the South. These beloved sweets, associated with both the city Creoles of New Orleans and Cajuns in the country, vividly illustrate how black cooks turned leftovers into financial advantage.

Most people know about the ways yesterday's black cooks perfected survival cooking, teaching children to pull thick molasses syrup until it turned into taffy at Christmastime. We hear less, though, about black culinary professionals like the "pralinieres" who refined their skills on the job, revealing the art of imaginative cooking that is spurred when resources are plentiful. In my new book, *Jubilee: Recipes from Two Centuries of African American Cooking,* I restore dignity to the entrepreneurial and hospitable spirits of Creole pralinieres and so many more of this country's well-trained cooks while memorializing their recipes.

Mirroring a treat once called "hard times candy" or "groundnut cakes," pralines originally were made with molasses and then evolved to a boiled sugar-syrup base when this commodity was no longer a luxury. The process for making pralines was detailed this way in *Soul and Spice: African Cooking in the Americas*: "The sugar syrup was heated until dark and caramelized and mixed with peanuts, pecans, benne (sesame) seeds, or sometimes cornflakes. A little butter might be added to make a creamy praline. The nutty confections were poured out onto corn husks to set up."

For me, making these treats to share with friends and family during the holidays is a hospitality tradition that preserves the timeless wisdom of my ancestors, a forgotten culinary class.

Pralines

This is my adaptation of the pecan candy in Cleora's Kitchens: The Memoir of a Cook & Eight Decades of Great American Food. *I swapped in molasses for her dark corn syrup and heavy cream for the milk, resulting in pralines that are thick and chewy.*

ACTIVE 20 MIN. - TOTAL 30 MIN.
MAKES ABOUT 2 DOZEN

- 1½ cups packed dark brown sugar
- 1½ cups granulated sugar
- 1 cup heavy cream or whole milk
- 3 Tbsp. molasses or dark corn syrup
- 2 Tbsp. unsalted butter
- 1 cup pecans, toasted and coarsely chopped
- 1 tsp. vanilla extract
  Pinch of kosher salt

1. Line a baking sheet with parchment or wax paper.

2. Stir together brown sugar, granulated sugar, cream, and molasses in a saucepan. Cook over medium-high, stirring constantly with a wooden spoon, until sugars dissolve and mixture begins to boil, about 5 minutes.

3. Boil, stirring constantly, until a candy thermometer registers 240°F or mixture begins to thicken and form a soft ball when a small amount is dropped from a spoon into a bowl of cold water, about 4 to 5 minutes.

4. Remove pan from heat. Using a wooden spoon, stir in butter, pecans, vanilla, and salt. Continue to stir vigorously until mixture is thick and just begins to lose its gloss, 9 to 11 minutes. Working quickly, drop heaping tablespoons of mixture 2 inches apart onto prepared baking sheet. Cool completely, 10 minutes. Store in an airtight container at room temperature up to 3 days.

Renaissance Woman

New Orleans' most beloved hostess shares the tradition that binds her to the city

JoAnn Clevenger walks between the two dining rooms of her restaurant, Upperline, broom in hand like a spear. She spots a painting of the pianist James Booker that's tilting askew and nudges it straight. Walking back to her podium near the front door, she stops at a table to move a few pieces of silverware a couple of millimeters this way or that until the setting feels just right.

At 5:30 p.m., she adjusts her oversize cockatiel brooch and turns the open sign around. The first guests arrive, Clevenger leads them to their tables, where she hands them the Upperline réveillon menu: "12 Hour" Roast Duck, Crispy Oysters St. Claude, Sautéed Baby Drum Fish Meunière, and the dish she's famous for creating, Fried Green Tomato with Shrimp Rémoulade. They're the kind of dishes the city is known for, but so hard to find now.

Originally, Catholics in 1800s New Orleans celebrated réveillon (which comes from the French word for "awakening") as a breakfast-for-dinner spread after midnight mass on Christmas Eve. By the 1940s, presents had taken precedence, and hardly anyone observed réveillon anymore.

Now a celebration of place instead of piety, it has been reinvented as a month-long affair with restaurants serving festive, prix fixe menus—a campaign started by the nonprofit French Quarter Festivals to drum up business in the slower months.

Clevenger joined in from the start in 1993, and now réveillon has become her most anticipated time of year. "It has always appealed to me greatly because it gives people a reason to arrange time with those they value," she says. "Sometimes, guests come in with friends they haven't seen since last year or people they went to high school with. Connections are what we human beings are. Réveillon does that for people."

Upperline, originally a house built in 1877, was supposed to be a second location for Clevenger's vintage-clothing business. But when she found out the building was for sale instead of for rent, she knew she had to open a restaurant. Her husband took a second mortgage on their house; her son took the helm as the first chef.

Eventually, Upperline went from having 40 chairs to 74 with the purchase of an adjoining hair salon. Connected by a sunporch, the dining rooms feel closer to their original purpose, like a home rather than a restaurant, and Clevenger intentionally sustains that dynamic.

"To me, the most important thing about New Orleans is that people who are different from each other rub shoulders," Clevenger says. "The neighborhoods are mixed up with a big house here and a little house next to it there. On the streetcar, you see a banker next to a carpenter. Traditions like réveillon unify us; they bind us together. And that's something that can nourish us just like a good meal."

When she was a senior in high school, her family was living in Superior, Arizona, when her mother contracted a rare fungal disease. Doctors sent her back home to Louisiana—Charity Hospital in New Orleans, specifically—and Clevenger accompanied her.

The hospital's food was miserable, so she would walk across the street to the A&G Cafeteria to get her mom lunch.

It was behind the glass display case at the cafeteria that she saw shrimp rémoulade for the first time. "I didn't know people ate shrimp cold," she says.

When she was 53, she paired this city dish with the fried green tomatoes of her country childhood in Louisiana, inadvertently creating a classic in a city with a 300-year-old culinary canon.

"When you go into a CVS or a Walmart, no one looks at you. You're alone," Clevenger says. "But here, the server looks at you. The people at your table look at you. You see the expressions on their faces if you tell a joke. And if someone at the table next to you is looking at your plate to see what you had, you might smile and say, 'It was a rack of lamb.' It's a very intimate thing. You're not anonymous."

After her last guest departs, Clevenger snuffs out the candles and prepares to drive home, down the cratered streets of the Garden District. She'll return tomorrow and do it all over again—her own ritual that binds her to New Orleans.

Spicy Shrimp with Jalapeño Cornbread and Aïoli

ACTIVE 40 MIN.-TOTAL 1 HOUR
SERVES 4

JALAPEÑO CORNBREAD
- ⅓ cup whole milk
- ¼ cup heavy cream
- ¼ cup canned cream-style corn
- 1 Tbsp. unsalted butter, melted, plus more for greasing pan
- 1 Tbsp. drained and finely chopped pickled jalapeño chile
- ½ tsp. black pepper
- ½ tsp. ground cumin
- ½ tsp. crushed red pepper
- 1 large egg
- 1 (8½-oz.) pkg. corn muffin mix (such as Jiffy)

SHRIMP
- 2 Tbsp. canola oil
- 1 cup thinly sliced red onion (from 1 medium [10 oz.] onion)
- 24 large peeled, deveined raw shrimp (about 1 lb.)
- ½ cup shrimp stock
- ¼ cup (2 oz.) white wine
- ¼ cup Spicy Butter (recipe follows)
- 1 Tbsp. fresh lemon juice (from 1 lemon)
- 1 tsp. kosher salt
  Aïoli (recipe follows)
- 2 Tbsp. chopped fresh flat-leaf parsley

1. To prepare Jalapeño Cornbread, preheat oven to 350°F. Grease an 8-inch square baking pan with butter. Whisk together milk and next 8 ingredients in a large bowl until well combined. Stir in corn muffin mix until blended; pour batter into prepared pan. Bake in preheated oven 15 to 17 minutes. Cool in pan 10 minutes. Remove from pan; let cool completely, about 15 minutes. Cut into 4 (4-inch) squares. Set aside.
2. To prepare Shrimp: Heat oil in a large skillet over high. Add onion; cook, stirring often, until lightly browned, about 3 minutes. Add raw shrimp; cook, stirring often, until they turn opaque, about 2 minutes. Add shrimp stock and wine, and let come to a boil. Cook until liquid reduces by three-fourths, about 5 minutes. Remove from heat; stir in Spicy Butter, lemon juice, and salt until melted.
3. To serve, spread each piece of cornbread with a thin layer of Aïoli. Top evenly with Shrimp, and sprinkle with parsley.

SPICY SHRIMP WITH
JALAPEÑO CORNBREAD
AND AÏOLI

Spicy Butter

ACTIVE 5 MIN.-TOTAL 5 MIN.
MAKES 1¼ CUPS

Process 1 cup softened **unsalted butter**, 3 Tbsp. **paprika**, 1 Tbsp. **chili powder**, 1 Tbsp. **ground cumin**, 1½ tsp. minced **garlic** (from 2 cloves), 1½ tsp. **smoked paprika**, 1½ tsp. **cayenne pepper**, 1½ tsp. **Worcestershire sauce**, 1½ tsp. **granulated sugar**, and 2 dashes of **hot sauce (such as Crystal)** in a food processor until smooth, about 10 seconds. Refrigerate Spicy Butter, covered, up to 1 month.

Aïoli

ACTIVE 5 MIN.-TOTAL 5 MIN.
MAKES 1 CUP

Process 1 cup mayonnaise; 2 Tbsp. **fresh lemon juice** (from 1 lemon); 3 **medium garlic cloves**, grated (1 Tbsp.); ½ tsp. **Worcestershire sauce**; ⅛ tsp. **cayenne pepper**; and 2 dashes of **hot sauce (such as Crystal)** in a food processor until smooth. Chill, covered, up to 5 days.

Bake Another Batch

Ivy Odom, Test Kitchen professional and star of our IGTV series *Hey Y'all*, shares her best-ever brownies and two sweet ways to serve them

I am a huge fan of brownies, but to be honest, I've never met a homemade version that could stand up to the boxed mix. Most from-scratch recipes tend to be dry and cakey, so I set out to develop the ultimate chewy, extra-chocolatey treat. After testing many versions, I finally found the one. And unlike boxed mixes, this recipe yields two pans of gooey, fudgy perfection, which is especially handy during the holidays. I think handmade gifts make recipients feel special. Prepare one batch in a gift-worthy dish, and save the other to serve at a party. For an easy and impressive presentation, I cut brownies into diamond shapes instead of the traditional squares.

Ivy's Best-Ever Brownies

ACTIVE 15 MIN. - TOTAL 1 HOUR, 40 MIN.
MAKES 2 (8-INCH-SQUARE) PANS

1	cup butter
1½	(4-oz.) semisweet chocolate baking bars, chopped (6 oz.)
2½	tsp. vanilla extract
1¼	cups all-purpose flour
1	cup Dutch-process cocoa
1¼	tsp. kosher salt
1⅔	cups granulated sugar
1	cup packed light brown sugar
3	large eggs
1	large egg yolk

1. Preheat oven to 350°F. Line 2 (8-inch-square) baking pans with parchment paper, leaving a 2-inch overhang on all sides to easily lift brownies out of pans.
2. Place butter in a microwavable bowl, and heat on HIGH in 30-second intervals, stirring after each, until melted (about 1 minute total). Stir in chocolate until melted; stir in vanilla, and set aside.
3. Stir together flour, cocoa, and salt in a large bowl; set aside.
4. Place granulated sugar, brown sugar, eggs, and yolk in a large bowl. Beat with an electric mixer on high speed until pale and thick, about 1½ to 2 minutes. Stir in melted chocolate mixture. Using a rubber spatula, gently fold in flour mixture. (Batter will be very thick.) Fold in stir-ins

(below), if desired. Divide batter evenly between prepared pans.
5. Bake in preheated oven until a wooden pick inserted in center of each pan comes out with a few moist crumbs and tops are set and shiny, 25 to 28 minutes. Remove from oven; cool completely in pans on wire racks, 1 hour. Use parchment handles to lift cooled brownies from pans; cut and serve.

STIR-IN SURPRISES
Chocolate Chunk-Sea Salt (photo above): 1¼ cups semisweet chocolate chunks; garnish with 1½ tsp. flaky sea salt
Go Nuts: 1 cup chopped toasted walnuts or pecans
Chocolate-Mint: ½ cup chopped thin crème de menthe chocolate mints (such as Andes) + ½ cup semisweet chocolate chip

Good to the Last Crumb

Flavored with cranberries and a hint of cinnamon, this coffee cake makes a delicious breakfast treat

Cranberry-Pecan Coffee Cake

ACTIVE 25 MIN. - TOTAL 1 HOUR, 10 MIN.,
PLUS 1 HOUR, 15 MIN. COOLING
SERVES 12

- ¾ cup toasted chopped pecans
- ½ tsp. ground cinnamon
- 3¼ cups all-purpose flour, divided, plus more for pan
- 1¼ cups packed light brown sugar, divided
- 1 tsp. kosher salt, divided
- ⅓ cup unsalted butter, melted
  Vegetable shortening, for greasing pan
- 1 cup frozen cranberries
- 1 cup granulated sugar, divided
- ¾ cup unsalted butter, softened
- 2 large eggs
- 1 large egg yolk
- 2 tsp. vanilla extract
- 2 tsp. baking powder
- ¼ tsp. baking soda
- 1 (8-oz.) container sour cream

1. Stir together pecans, cinnamon, ¾ cup of the flour, ¾ cup of the brown sugar, and ½ teaspoon of the salt in a bowl. Stir in melted butter. Freeze until hardened, about 20 minutes.

2. Meanwhile, preheat oven to 350°F. Grease a 10-inch tube pan with shortening; dust pan with flour. Pulse cranberries and ¼ cup of the granulated sugar in a food processor until finely chopped, 6 to 8 times. Transfer to a bowl; chill until ready to use.

3. Beat softened butter, remaining ½ cup brown sugar, and remaining ¾ cup granulated sugar with a stand mixer fitted with a paddle attachment on medium-high speed until light and fluffy, 2 minutes. Add eggs and yolk 1 at a time, beating well on low speed after each addition. Stir in vanilla.

4. Stir together baking powder, baking soda, remaining 2½ cups flour, and remaining ½ teaspoon salt in a bowl. Add flour mixture to softened butter mixture alternately with sour cream in 3 additions (beginning and ending with flour mixture), beating on low speed until just combined after each addition.

5. Stir ¾ cup of the batter into chilled cranberry mixture. Spoon half of the remaining plain batter into prepared pan. Spoon cranberry-batter mixture over, smoothing into an even layer. Top with remaining plain batter. Crumble frozen pecan-cinnamon mixture into chunks. Sprinkle evenly over cake.

6. Bake in preheated oven until a wooden pick inserted in center comes out clean, 45 to 55 minutes, tenting with aluminum foil after 35 minutes, if needed, to prevent excessive browning. Cool in pan on a wire rack 15 minutes. Remove from pan. Cool completely on rack, 1 hour.

COOKING ⓈⓁ SCHOOL

TIPS AND TRICKS FROM THE SOUTH'S MOST TRUSTED KITCHEN

Puff Pastry in a Pinch

From puffs to triangles, three fast and flavorful ways to show its versatility

Cacio e Pepe Puffs

Cut 2 thawed **puff pastry sheets** into 20 (2-inch) fluted rounds. Brush rounds with **extra-virgin olive oil.** Sprinkle with grated **Parmesan cheese, black pepper,** and **flaky sea salt.** Bake at 400°F for 15 minutes. Sprinkle with chopped **fresh chives** and additional grated **Parmesan.**

Cheesy Garlic-Herb-and-Ham Bites

Cut 2 thawed **puff pastry sheets** into 20 (2-inch) rounds. Brush rounds with melted **butter.** Spread with **garlic-and-herb spreadable cheese (such as Boursin).** Bake at 400°F for 20 minutes. Top with thin strips of **prosciutto** and chopped **fresh flat-leaf parsley.**

Butternut Squash Triangles

Brush 2 thawed **puff pastry sheets** with melted **butter.** Top evenly with shaved **butternut squash,** leaving a ½-inch border. Brush squash with **olive oil;** sprinkle with **kosher salt** and **black pepper.** Bake at 400°F for 20 minutes. Cut into triangles. Sprinkle with shaved **ricotta salata,** and drizzle with **balsamic glaze.**

> "The best place to thaw frozen puff pastry is in the refrigerator. Once soft-ened, use it right away because it doesn't hold up well after multiple days in the fridge."

—Robby Melvin
Test Kitchen Director

Dress Up Your Dip

Simple styling tweaks to upgrade a party-worthy platter

FILL 'ER UP Cover the serving dish completely. Nestle the vegetables close together, and tuck in more to fill any empty spaces.

SWOOP AND SWIRL Scoop the dip, such as hummus, into a serving bowl. Make a few indentations over the top using the back of a spoon. Drizzle a topping (such as harissa, pesto, or tapenade) into the indentations. Using a toothpick or skewer, drag the topping across the indentations to create a swirled effect. Top with olive oil, and sprinkle with chopped fresh herbs.

GO LONG Raw vegetables look their best when cut lengthwise with a little bit of the stem still intact (if possible).

PERSIMMON
PUDDING
(PAGE 227)

CLOCKWISE FROM TOP LEFT:

- ORANGE-BUTTERMILK TRIFLE
  (PAGE 220)

- OYSTER STEW (PAGE 219)

- CLEMENTINE WHISKEY SOUR
  (PAGE 218)

- WOOD-FIRED ROOT
  VEGETABLES WITH CHARRED
  SCALLION AÏOLI (PAGE 219)

JOHNNYCAKES WITH
LEEKS AND COLLARD
GREENS (PAGE 219)

SALTED CARAMEL-
APPLE HAND PIES
(PAGE 223)

CLOCKWISE FROM TOP LEFT:

• SWEET-AND-SALTY AUTUMN SNACK MIX (PAGE 222)

• SPARKLING CARAMEL-APPLE SANGRÍA (PAGE 222)

• DINER-STYLE PATTY MELTS (PAGE 226)

• QUICK MISSISSIPPI POT ROAST (PAGE 229)

SPICED COCONUT-
PUMPKIN PIE
(PAGE 237)

DULCE DE LECHE-
CHEESECAKE PECAN PIE
(PAGE 238)

311

POMEGRANATE-
CHESS TART
(PAGE 238)

CLOCKWISE FROM TOP LEFT:

- PEAR-CRANBERRY PIE WITH
  GINGER-ALMOND STREUSEL
  (PAGE 239)

- CREAMY BAKED MACARONI
  AND CHEESE WITH BACON
  (PAGE 244)

- COLLARD GREENS WITH
  GARLIC AND SIPPETS
  (PAGE 242)

- SHRIMP-STUFFED MIRLITONS
  (PAGE 249)

SEA ISLAND CRAB FRIED
RICE (PAGE 246)

SIMPLE MASHED RUTABAGAS
AND POTATOES (PAGE 245)

FRIED ARKANSAS
BLACK APPLES
(PAGE 245)

SPICY CORNBREAD
DRESSING
WITH CHORIZO
(PAGE 247)

CLOCKWISE FROM TOP LEFT:

• SCALLOPED OYSTERS
(PAGE 250)

• GRATED SWEET POTATO
PUDDING WITH PECANS
(PAGE 250)

• BUTTERMILK SPOON BREAD
(PAGE 252)

• SWEET POTATO ROLLS
WITH CANE SYRUP GLAZE
(PAGE 254)

ROASTED ROOT
VEGETABLES WITH
SPICY PECAN TOPPING
(PAGE 258)

CHOCOLATE-PECAN
PHYLLO TURNOVERS
(PAGE 258)

HERBY PECAN-
CORNBREAD DRESSING
(PAGE 257)

SORGHUM-PECAN
MONKEY BREAD MUFFINS
(PAGE 257)

Our Favorite Holiday Recipes

When the winter holidays arrive, you may reach for your tried-and-true standards—the special recipes you know never fail to please. After all, making and eating good food is one of the most wonderful ways to celebrate the season and make holiday guests in your home feel welcome and loved. The recipes on these pages are our proven winners, and we think you'll find them more than worthy of adding to your repertoire. There's something for every occasion and mood. From tasty appetizers, brunch dishes and breads to celebratory main dishes, sides, soups, salads and desserts. It's all here in one convenient place. Homey Chicken and Cornbread Casserole is just the thing for a casual gathering. Or treat guests at a fancy sit-down dinner to Fennel-Crusted Rib Roast topped off by Brandy Alexander Cheesecake or Fudge Truffle Pecan Tart. Get into the spirit of giving with a gift from your kitchen, whether that's something as simple as Lime Sea Salt or whimsical Reindeer Gingersnaps. Celebrate with something new this year!

Appetizers

Buttery Toasted Pecans

Patiently roasting pecans (the entire 25 minutes!) at 325°F to coax out their flavor and essential oils takes them from good to great.

ACTIVE 10 MIN. - TOTAL 35 MIN.
MAKES 4 CUPS

- ¼ cup butter, melted
- 4 cups pecan halves
- 1 Tbsp. kosher salt
- ½ tsp. ground red pepper

Preheat oven to 325°F. Toss together butter and pecans. Spread pecans in a single layer in a jelly-roll pan; bake 25 minutes or until toasted and fragrant, stirring halfway through. Remove from oven, and sprinkle with salt and red pepper, tossing to coat. Cool completely. Store up to 1 week.

Spinach-Sausage Turnovers

ACTIVE 50 MIN. - TOTAL 1 HOUR, 15 MIN.
SERVES 40

- 1 (12-oz.) pkg. frozen spinach soufflé
- ½ lb. hot Italian sausage, casings removed
- 4 scallions, minced
- ⅓ cup (1½ oz.) shredded Parmesan cheese
- 1 (17.3-oz.) package frozen puff pastry sheets, thawed
- 2 Tbsp. olive oil

1. Preheat oven to 400°F. Microwave spinach soufflé at MEDIUM 6 to 7 minutes or until thawed.
2. Cook sausage and scallions in a medium skillet over medium-high, stirring often, 12 to 15 minutes or until sausage is finely crumbled and is no longer pink. Stir in spinach soufflé and cheese. Remove from heat.
3. Roll each pastry sheet into a 15- x 12-inch rectangle on a lightly floured surface. Cut into 3-inch squares. Cover and chill 10 to 15 minutes.
4. Spoon about 1 tablespoon spinach mixture onto center of each square. Moisten edges of pastry with water, and fold 2 opposite corners together over spinach mixture, forming a triangle. Press edges with a fork to seal, and place on lightly greased baking sheets. Brush lightly with olive oil.
5. Bake 12 to 15 minutes or until lightly browned. Serve immediately.
Note: For testing purposes only, we used Stouffer's Spinach Soufflé.
Note: To make ahead, prepare recipe as directed through Step 4, omitting olive oil. Arrange turnovers in a single layer on a parchment paper-lined baking sheet; cover with plastic wrap. Freeze 1 hour. Transfer turnovers to a heavy-duty zip-top plastic freezer bag. Freeze up to 3 months. Arrange frozen turnovers on parchment paper-lined baking sheets. Brush lightly with olive oil. Bake at 400° for 20 to 25 minutes or until golden brown.

Black-Eyed Pea Cakes

ACTIVE 40 MIN. - TOTAL 1 HOUR, 40 MIN.
SERVES 30

- 1 small onion, chopped
- 4 Tbsp. olive oil, divided
- 2 (15.5-oz.) cans black-eyed peas, rinsed and drained, divided
- 1 (8-oz.) container chive-and-onion cream cheese, softened
- 1 large egg
- 1 tsp. hot sauce
- ½ tsp. salt
- 1 (8-oz.) pkg. hush puppy mix with onion
  Toppings: sour cream, green tomato relish, chopped fresh chives

1. Saute onion in 1 tablespoon hot oil in a large skillet over medium-high 5 minutes or until tender.
2. Process onion, 1 can of peas, and next 4 ingredients in a food processor 30 seconds or until smooth, stopping to scrape down sides. Stir in hush puppy mix; gently fold in remaining can of peas.
3. Shape mixture into 30 (3-inch) patties (about 2 tablespoons each); place on a wax paper-lined baking sheet. Cover and chill 1 hour.
4. Cook patties, in batches, in remaining 3 tablespoons hot oil in skillet over medium 1½ minutes on each side or until golden brown, adding additional oil as needed. Drain on paper towels; keep warm. Serve with desired toppings.

Lump Crab Mornay

This creamy dip is adapted from a recipe in Bayou Cuisine *by St. Stephen's Episcopal Church in Indianola, Mississippi.*

ACTIVE 20 MIN. - TOTAL 20 MIN.
SERVES 10 TO 12

- ½ cup butter, softened
- 1 bunch scallions, chopped
- 2 Tbsp. all-purpose flour
- 2 cups heavy cream
- 1 cup freshly grated Gruyère or Swiss cheese
- 2 Tbsp. dry sherry
- ¼ tsp. kosher salt
- ¼ tsp. ground red pepper
- 1 lb. fresh jumbo lump crabmeat
- ½ cup chopped fresh flat-leaf parsley
  Store-bought or homemade toast points

Melt butter in a heavy saucepan over medium-high; add onions, and saute 3 minutes or until tender. Whisk in 2 tablespoons all-purpose flour, and cook, whisking constantly, 2 minutes. Add cream, and cook, whisking constantly, until smooth and sauce begins to bubble. Remove from heat, and stir in cheese until smooth. Stir in dry sherry, kosher salt, and ground red pepper. Gently fold in crabmeat and parsley. Keep warm in a chafing dish or slow cooker set on WARM or LOW. Serve with toast points.

Cherry-Pecan Brie

ACTIVE 10 MIN. - TOTAL 10 MIN.
SERVES 6 TO 8

- 1 (8-oz.) Brie round
- ⅓ cup cherry preserves
- 1 Tbsp. balsamic vinegar
- ⅛ tsp. freshly ground black pepper
- ⅛ tsp. salt
  Chopped toasted pecans
  Assorted crackers

1. Preheat oven to 400°F. Trim and discard rind from top of Brie. Place Brie on a lightly greased baking sheet. Bake 7 to 9 minutes or until cheese is just melted.
2. Meanwhile, stir together preserves and next 3 ingredients in a bowl.
3. Transfer Brie to serving dish; drizzle preserves mixture over warm Brie, and top with pecans. Serve with crackers.

Parmesan Cheese Bites

Baked cheese bites may be frozen up to two months.

ACTIVE 15 MIN. - TOTAL 1 HOUR, 30 MIN.
SERVES 32

- 1 cup all-purpose flour
- ⅔ cup grated Parmesan cheese
- ¼ tsp. ground red pepper
- ½ cup butter, cut up
- 2 Tbsp. milk

1. Preheat oven to 350°F. Combine first 3 ingredients in a medium bowl; cut in butter with a pastry blender or 2 forks until crumbly. (Mixture will look very dry.) Gently press mixture together with hands, pressing until blended and smooth (about 2 to 3 minutes).
2. Shape dough into 2 (4-inch-long) logs. Wrap in plastic wrap, and chill 1 hour. Cut each log into ¼-inch-thick slices, and place on lightly greased baking sheets. Brush with milk.
3. Bake 12 to 15 minutes or until lightly browned.
Parmesan Cheese Squares: Roll dough into a 10- x 8-inch rectangle on a lightly floured surface. Cut into 32 squares using a pastry wheel or knife. Place squares on lightly greased baking sheets; brush with milk, and bake as directed. Makes 32 squares.

Garlic Butter–Roasted Shrimp Cocktail

ACTIVE 20 MIN. - TOTAL 25 MIN.
SERVES 8 TO 10

- ⅔ cup ketchup
- ⅓ cup chili sauce
- 3 Tbsp. grated fresh horseradish
- 1 tsp. lemon zest plus 1 Tbsp. fresh juice (from 1 lemon)
- ½ tsp. Old Bay seasoning
- ½ tsp. hot sauce (such as Tabasco)
- ½ cup (4 oz.) salted butter
- 4 garlic cloves, minced
- 1 lemon, cut into ¼-inch-thick slices
- ¼ tsp. crushed red pepper
- 2 lb. large peeled, deveined raw shrimp, tails on
- 2 Tbsp. chopped fresh flat-leaf parsley
- ½ tsp. kosher salt
- ¼ tsp. black pepper

1. Stir together ketchup, chili sauce, horseradish, lemon zest, lemon juice, Old Bay seasoning, and hot sauce in a medium bowl; chill until ready to use.
2. Preheat oven to 450°F. Place butter, garlic, lemon slices, and crushed red pepper in the center of a rimmed baking sheet. Place baking sheet in oven, and heat until butter melts and garlic is fragrant, about 5 minutes. Add shrimp, and toss in butter mixture; spread in a single layer. Roast in preheated oven until shrimp turn pink and are just cooked through, 4 to 5 minutes.
3. Transfer shrimp and pan juices to a large platter. Squeeze juice from roasted lemon slices over shrimp; sprinkle with parsley, salt, and black pepper. Serve with chilled cocktail sauce.

Millionaire's Candied Bacon

ACTIVE 10 MIN. - TOTAL 1 HOUR, 25 MIN.
SERVES 10 TO 12

Preheat oven to 350°F. Arrange 1 (16-oz.) package thick **bacon** slices in a single layer on 2 lightly greased wire racks in 2 aluminum foil-lined broiler pans. Let stand 10 minutes. Top bacon with 1 cup firmly packed **dark brown sugar**, pressing lightly to adhere. Bake 45 to 50 minutes or until done. Cool completely (about 20 minutes). Cut into bite-size pieces.

Tortellini Caprese Bites

ACTIVE 30 MIN. - TOTAL 2 HOURS, 47 MIN., INCLUDING VINAIGRETTE
SERVES 12

- 1 (9-oz.) pkg. refrigerated cheese-filled tortellini
- 3 cups halved grape tomatoes
- 3 (8-oz.) containers fresh small mozzarella cheese balls
- 60 (6-inch) wooden skewers
  Basil Vinaigrette (recipe follows)

1. Prepare tortellini according to package directions. Rinse under cold running water.
2. Thread 1 tomato half, 1 cheese ball, another tomato half, and 1 tortellini onto each skewer. Place skewers in a 13- x 9-inch baking dish. Pour Basil Vinaigrette over skewers, turning to coat. Cover and chill 2 hours. Transfer skewers to a serving platter; sprinkle with salt and black pepper to taste. Discard any remaining vinaigrette.

Basil Vinaigrette

ACTIVE 10 MIN. - TOTAL 10 MIN.
MAKES 1½ CUPS

- ½ cup white balsamic vinegar
- 1 tsp. kosher salt
- ⅔ cup extra-virgin olive oil
- 6 Tbsp. chopped fresh basil

Whisk together vinegar and salt until blended. Gradually add oil in a slow, steady stream, whisking constantly until smooth. Stir in basil and freshly ground black pepper to taste.

Colby–Pepper Jack Cheese Dip

Prepare up to a day ahead; cover and chill in an airtight container, and bake just before serving.

ACTIVE 15 MIN. - TOTAL 45 MIN.
SERVES 10

- 1 (8-oz.) pkg. cream cheese, softened
- ⅔ cup sour cream
- ⅓ cup mayonnaise
- 1 Tbsp. finely chopped canned chipotle peppers in adobo sauce
- 2 tsp. chili powder
- 2 cups chopped cooked chicken
- 2 cups (8 oz.) shredded colby-Jack cheese
- 1 (4-oz.) can chopped green chiles
- 4 scallions, finely chopped
- 2 jalapeño peppers, seeded and minced
- ¼ cup chopped fresh cilantro
  Garnish: fresh cilantro sprig (optional)
  Tortilla and sweet potato chips

Preheat oven to 350°F. Stir together first 5 ingredients in a large bowl until smooth. Stir in chicken and next 5 ingredients until blended. Spoon cheese mixture into a lightly greased 8-inch square baking dish. Bake 30 minutes or until bubbly. Spoon into a serving bowl. Garnish, if desired. Serve dip with tortilla and sweet potato chips.

Beverages

Apple–Ale Wassail

ACTIVE 5 MIN. - TOTAL 3 HOURS, 5 MIN.
SERVES 8

Stir together 2 (12-oz.) bottles **ale**; 2 cups **apple cider**; 1 cup **port**; 1 cup **lemonade**; ¾ cup firmly packed **light brown sugar**; 1 **apple**, diced; 2 **whole allspice**; 2 (3-inch) **cinnamon sticks**; 6 **whole cloves**; and ⅛ teaspoon **ground cardamom** in a 5-quart slow cooker. Cover and cook on LOW 3 hours or until hot. Remove diced apple, if desired. Ladle into mugs. Garnish with lemon wedges and cinnamon sticks, if desired.

Cherry Frost

ACTIVE 5 MIN. - TOTAL 5 MIN.
SERVES 1

Combine 3 tablespoons **black cherry liqueur**, 1 tablespoon **brandy**, and 1 cup crushed **ice** in a cocktail shaker. Cover with lid, and shake vigorously until thoroughly chilled (about 30 seconds). Strain into a Champagne flute, and top with 4 tablespoons **sparkling white wine**. Garnish with **maraschino cherries**, if desired.

Classic Eggnog

ACTIVE 35 MIN. - TOTAL 4 HOURS, 5 MIN.
SERVES 12

  6 cups **milk**
  2 cups **heavy cream**
  ⅛ tsp. **ground nutmeg**
  12 **pasteurized egg yolks**
  2 cups **sugar**
     Praline or bourbon liqueur
     (optional)
     Freshly ground nutmeg

1. Cook first 3 ingredients in a large saucepan over medium, stirring occasionally, 5 to 7 minutes or until steaming or a candy thermometer registers about 150°F. Reduce heat to low.
2. Whisk together yolks and sugar in a large saucepan until smooth. Cook over low, whisking constantly, until a candy thermometer registers at least 160°F (about 25 minutes). Whisk milk mixture into egg mixture. Cool 30 minutes; transfer to a pitcher.
3. Cover and chill 3 to 24 hours. Pour desired amount of praline or bourbon liqueur into each glass, if desired. Top with eggnog. Sprinkle with freshly ground nutmeg.

Perky Cranberry Punch

ACTIVE 10 MIN. - TOTAL 20 MIN.
SERVES 14

  10 whole **allspice**
  10 whole **cloves**
  4   (3-inch) **cinnamon sticks**
      Cheesecloth
      Kitchen string
  1   (64-oz.) bottle **cranberry juice**
  1   (46-oz.) can **pineapple juice**
  1   cup firmly packed **brown sugar**
      Garnish: assorted fruit-flavored candy sticks (optional)

1. Place first 3 ingredients on a 3-inch square of cheesecloth; tie with kitchen string. Place in a Dutch oven.
2. Stir juices and brown sugar into Dutch oven, and bring to a boil. Reduce heat, and simmer 5 minutes. Discard spices. Garnish, if desired.

Cranberry Sangría Punch

This wintry, ruby-red spin on sangría is a staff favorite but comes with a warning: It goes down easy. Make it a day ahead, and add the Champagne right before serving.

ACTIVE 20 MIN. - TOTAL 40 MIN.
SERVES 10

  2   cups frozen or fresh **cranberries**
  1   cup **granulated sugar**
  1   cup **water**
  1   (750-ml) bottle **sangría**, chilled
  ¼   cup (2 oz.) **Campari**
  1   large navel **orange**, thinly sliced
  1   large **Granny Smith apple**, thinly sliced
  1   (750-ml) bottle **brut Champagne**, chilled

1. Combine cranberries, sugar, and water in a medium saucepan over medium-high; bring to a boil, stirring often until sugar dissolves and berries just begin to pop, about 3 to 4 minutes. Remove from heat; cool 30 minutes.
2. Stir together sangría, Campari, and cooled cranberries with liquid in a large pitcher or a small punch bowl. Add orange and apple slices. Just before serving, add Champagne.
3. Serve over ice with a few pieces of fruit in each glass.

Hot Spiced Wine

To serve, use a tempered glass heatproof pitcher, a thermal carafe, or simply return mixture to Dutch oven and ladle into mugs.

ACTIVE 5 MIN. - TOTAL 25 MIN.
SERVES 10

  2 (750-ml) bottles **red wine**
  2 cups **apple juice**
  1 cup **sugar**
  6 Tbsp. **mulling spices**

1. Bring all ingredients to a boil in a Dutch oven; reduce heat, and simmer 15 minutes. Pour mixture through a wire-mesh strainer into a pitcher, discarding mulling spices. Serve wine hot.
Note: For best results, use a fruity red wine, such as a Beaujolais or Pinot Noir.

CRANBERRY
SANGRÍA PUNCH

White Sangria Fizz

ACTIVE 5 MIN. - TOTAL 8 HOURS, 5 MIN.,
INCLUDING 8 HOURS CHILLING
SERVES 8

- 1 cup fresh orange juice
- ½ cup sugar
- 1 (750-ml) bottle dry white wine
- 1½ cups sparkling water, chilled
  Garnishes: lime, orange, and
  lemon wedges (optional)

1. Stir together orange juice and sugar in a large pitcher until sugar dissolves. Stir in wine; cover and chill 8 hours.
2. Stir sparkling water into wine mixture just before serving. Garnish, if desired.

Breads

Hurry-Up Homemade Cornbread Yeast Rolls

ACTIVE 45 MIN. - TOTAL 4 HOURS, 15 MIN.,
INCLUDING 3 HOURS RISING
MAKES 18 ROLLS

- 1 (¼-oz.) envelope active dry yeast
- 1 cup warm water (105°F to 115°F)
- 1 Tbsp. sugar
- 4 cups bread flour, divided
- ¼ cup honey
- 4 Tbsp. butter, melted
- 2 large eggs
- 1¼ tsp. salt
- ¾ cup plain yellow cornmeal
  Vegetable cooking spray
- 2 Tbsp. plain yellow cornmeal
- 1 large egg, lightly beaten
- 1 Tbsp. sesame seeds
- ½ tsp. freshly ground black pepper

1. Stir together yeast, 1 cup warm water, and sugar in a 2-cup glass measuring cup; let stand 5 minutes.
2. Beat yeast mixture and 2 cups flour at low speed with a heavy-duty electric stand mixer, using dough hook attachment, until combined. Add honey, butter, 2 eggs, salt, and ¾ cup cornmeal; beat at medium-low speed until well blended, scraping bowl as needed. Gradually beat in remaining 2 cups flour. Continue beating until a dough forms and begins to pull away from sides of bowl. (Dough will be sticky.) Beat dough 1 minute.

3. Coat a large bowl with cooking spray; place dough in bowl, turning to grease top. Cover with plastic wrap, and let rise in a warm place (85°F), free from drafts, 2 hours or until doubled in bulk.
4. Line 2 baking sheets with parchment paper; dust each with 1 tablespoon cornmeal.
5. Punch dough down; turn out onto a lightly floured surface. Knead 1 minute. Shape dough into 18 balls; place on prepared baking sheets. Cover with a clean kitchen towel, and let rise 1 to 1½ hours or until almost doubled in bulk.
6. Preheat oven to 375°F. Gently brush rolls with lightly beaten egg, and sprinkle with sesame seeds and pepper. Bake 18 to 22 minutes or until golden on top, browned on bottom, and sound hollow when tapped on base. Let cool on baking sheets 5 minutes. Serve immediately.
Note: To make ahead, prepare recipe as directed through Step 5; cover loosely with plastic wrap or aluminum foil. Chill 24 hours. Uncover and bake as directed in Step 6.

Crescent Rolls

ACTIVE 25 MIN. - TOTAL 1 HOUR, 40 MIN.
MAKES 12 ROLLS

- 1 (¼-oz.) envelope active dry yeast
- ¾ cup warm water (105°F to 115°F)
- 3 to 3½ cups all-purpose baking mix
- 2 Tbsp. sugar
  All-purpose flour

1. Combine yeast and warm water in a 1-cup measuring cup; let stand 5 minutes. Combine 3 cups baking mix and sugar in a large bowl; gradually stir in yeast mixture.
2. Turn dough out onto a floured surface, and knead, adding additional baking mix (up to ½ cup) as needed, until dough is smooth and elastic (about 10 minutes).
3. Roll dough into a 12-inch circle; cut circle into 12 wedges. Roll up each wedge, starting at wide end, to form a crescent shape; place, point sides down, on a lightly greased baking sheet. Cover and let rise in a warm place (85°), free from drafts, 1 hour or until doubled in bulk.
4. Preheat oven to 425°F. Bake 10 to 12 minutes or until golden.
Note: To make rolls in a heavy-duty electric stand mixer, prepare as directed in Step 1. Beat dough at medium speed, using dough hook attachment, about 5 minutes, beating in ½ cup additional

baking mix, if needed, until dough leaves the sides of the bowl and pulls together, becoming soft and smooth. Proceed with recipe as directed in Step 3.
Note: We tested with Bisquick All-Purpose Baking Mix.
To Make Ahead: Rolls may be frozen up to 2 months. Bake at 425°F for 5 minutes; cool completely (about 30 minutes). Wrap in aluminum foil, and freeze in an airtight container. Thaw at room temperature on a lightly greased baking sheet; bake at 425°F for 7 to 8 minutes or until golden.

Sour Cream Pocketbook Rolls

ACTIVE 30 MIN. - TOTAL 9 HOURS, 32 MIN.,
INCLUDING 8 HOURS CHILLING
MAKES 54 ROLLS

- 1 (8-oz.) container sour cream
- ½ cup butter
- ½ cup sugar
- 1¼ tsp. salt
- 2 (¼-oz.) envelopes active dry yeast
- ½ cup warm water (105°F to 110°F)
- 2 large eggs, lightly beaten
- 4 cups all-purpose flour
- ¼ cup butter, melted, divided

1. Cook first 4 ingredients in a saucepan over medium-low, stirring occasionally, 3 to 4 minutes or until butter melts. Let cool to 115°F.
2. Combine yeast and warm water in a liquid measuring cup; let stand 5 minutes. Stir together eggs, flour, yeast mixture, and sour cream mixture in a large bowl until well blended. Cover and chill 8 to 24 hours.
3. Divide dough into fourths, and shape each portion into a ball. Roll each ball to ¼-inch thickness on a floured surface; cut dough into rounds with a 2½-inch round cutter.
4. Brush rounds with 2 tablespoons melted butter. Make a crease across each round with a knife, and fold in half; gently press edges to seal. Place rolls, with sides touching, in a lightly greased 15- x 10-inch jelly-roll pan. Place any remaining rolls on a lightly greased baking sheet. Cover and let rise in a warm place (85°F), free from drafts, 45 minutes or until doubled in bulk.
5. Preheat oven to 375°F. Bake rolls 12 to 15 minutes or until golden brown. Brush rolls with remaining 2 tablespoons melted butter.

SEA SALT–POPPY SEED CLOVERLEAF ROLLS

Sea Salt–Poppy Seed Cloverleaf Rolls

There is nothing quite like freshly baked rolls, but if pushed for time, make these a day in advance and reheat just before serving. Wrap tightly in aluminum foil and store at room temperature.

ACTIVE 25 MIN. - TOTAL 2 HOURS, 15 MIN.
MAKES 12 ROLLS

- 1 cup warm milk (100°F to 110°F)
- 1 (¼-oz.) envelope active dry yeast
- 2 Tbsp. sugar, divided
- 3 cups all-purpose flour
- 1¼ tsp. table salt
- 6 Tbsp. butter, melted, divided
- 1 large egg, lightly beaten
- 1½ tsp. poppy seeds
- 1½ tsp. flaky sea salt

1. Stir together milk, yeast, and 1 tablespoon of the sugar in a 2-cup glass measuring cup; let stand 5 minutes.
2. Combine flour, table salt, and remaining 1 tablespoon sugar in bowl of a heavy-duty electric stand mixer; let stand 5 minutes. Add 4 tablespoons of the melted butter, egg, and yeast mixture; beat at low speed, using paddle attachment, 3 minutes or until blended and a soft, sticky dough forms. Increase speed to medium, attach dough hook, and beat 6 minutes or until dough is smooth and elastic but still slightly sticky. Cover bowl with plastic wrap, and let rise in a warm place (85°F), free from drafts, 1 hour or until doubled in bulk.

3. Punch dough down. Turn out onto a lightly floured surface. Divide dough into 12 equal portions (about 2 ounces each). Gently shape each portion into 3 (1¼-inch) balls; place in 12 buttered muffin cups. Brush tops of dough with remaining 2 tablespoons melted butter. Cover and let rise in a warm (85°F) place, free from drafts, 30 to 45 minutes or until doubled in bulk.
4. Preheat oven to 375°F. Sprinkle rolls with poppy seeds and sea salt.
5. Bake 15 to 17 minutes or until golden brown. Transfer to a wire rack. Serve warm, or cool completely (about 30 minutes).

Butter Muffins

For pretty, rounded muffin tops, use a small ice-cream scoop to fill the muffin cups.

ACTIVE 15 MIN. - TOTAL 40 MIN.
MAKES 24 MUFFINS

- 2 cups self-rising flour
- 1 (8-oz.) container sour cream
- ½ cup butter, melted

Preheat oven to 350°F. Stir together all ingredients in a large bowl just until blended. Spoon batter into 2 lightly greased 12-cup miniature muffin pans, filling completely full. Bake 25 to 28 minutes or until muffins are golden brown.

Breakfast and Brunch

Best-Ever Sticky Buns

These ooey-gooey, pecan-topped cinnamon rolls live up to their name. Prepare the dough on Christmas Eve, and bake the sticky buns first thing in the morning.

ACTIVE 40 MIN. - TOTAL 9 HOURS, 50 MIN., INCLUDING 8 HOURS CHILLING
MAKES 12 BUNS

DOUGH
- 1 (8-oz.) container sour cream
- 6 Tbsp. salted butter, plus more for greasing pan
- 1 tsp. salt
- ⅓ cup, plus 1 tsp. granulated sugar, divided
- ⅓ cup warm water (100°F to 110°F)
- 1 (¼-oz.) pkg. active dry yeast
- 2 large eggs, beaten
- 3¾ to 4½ cups bread flour, divided, plus more for dusting

FILLING
- 1 cup packed dark brown sugar
- 2 tsp. ground cinnamon

TOPPING
- ½ cup packed dark brown sugar
- 6 Tbsp. salted butter, melted
- ¼ cup granulated sugar
- ¼ cup light corn syrup
- 2 Tbsp. heavy cream
- ¼ tsp. salt
- 1 cup toasted pecans, coarsely chopped

1. Prepare the Dough: Combine sour cream, butter, salt, and ⅓ cup of the granulated sugar in a small saucepan. Cook over medium-low, stirring occasionally, just until butter melts, about 4 minutes. Remove from heat, and cool to 100°F to 110°F.
2. Stir together warm water, yeast, and remaining 1 teaspoon granulated sugar in a small bowl. Let stand until foamy, about 5 minutes.
3. Combine sour cream mixture, yeast mixture, and eggs in the bowl of a heavy-duty electric stand mixer fitted with a dough hook attachment. With mixer running on medium-low speed, gradually add 3¾ cups of the flour, beating until

a soft dough forms and pulls away from sides but still adheres to bottom of bowl.

4. Turn it out onto a lightly floured surface. Knead until smooth and elastic, about 10 minutes, adding up to ¾ cup flour, in very small amounts, if necessary to keep it workable. (Dough should be tacky but not sticky.) Place in a lightly greased bowl, turning to coat all sides. Cover and chill 8 hours or overnight.

5. Turn dough out onto a lightly floured work surface. Roll into a 16- x 20-inch rectangle.

6. Prepare the Filling: Stir together brown sugar and cinnamon in a small bowl.

7. Sprinkle filling evenly over dough rectangle, pressing gently to adhere, leaving a 1-inch border on both long sides. Starting at 1 long side, roll up dough, jelly-roll style. Using a piece of unflavored dental floss, cut off and discard 1 inch from each end of roll. Cut roll crosswise into 12 (1½-inch-wide) pieces.

8. Prepare the Topping: Stir together all ingredients except pecans in a small bowl.

9. Assemble the sticky buns: Pour Topping into a lightly greased 13- x 9-inch metal baking pan. Spread to coat bottom of pan evenly. Sprinkle evenly with pecans. Place rolls, cut sides down, in baking pan with sides touching. Cover with plastic wrap, and let stand in a warm place until rolls double in size, 45 minutes to 1 hour.

10. Preheat oven to 375°F. Remove and discard plastic wrap from buns. Bake until golden brown, 20 to 22 minutes. Cool in pan 5 minutes. Carefully invert buns onto a serving platter. Serve warm.

Homemade Waffles

ACTIVE 20 MIN. - TOTAL 25 MIN.
MAKES 12 (4-INCH) BELGIAN WAFFLES

- 1½ cups water
- ½ cup vegetable oil or melted butter
- 2 large egg yolks
- 2 large egg whites
- 2¾ cups Homemade All-Purpose Biscuit, Pancake, and Waffle Mix (recipe follows)
  Cooking spray
  Maple syrup

1. Whisk water and oil with egg yolks. Beat egg whites at high speed with an electric mixer until stiff, about 2 minutes. Gently whisk Homemade All-purpose Biscuit, Pancake, and Waffle Mix into oil mixture and fold in beaten egg whites.

2. Coat a preheated waffle iron with cooking spray, and add ½ cup batter to waffle iron. Cook 2 to 3 minutes or until golden. Serve with maple syrup.

Homemade All-Purpose Biscuit, Pancake, and Waffle Mix

ACTIVE 5 MIN. - TOTAL 5 MIN.
MAKES ABOUT 8 CUPS

- 6 cups all-purpose flour
- 1½ cups powdered buttermilk
- ¼ cup granulated sugar
- 2 Tbsp. baking powder
- 1 Tbsp. baking soda
- 1½ tsp. salt

Whisk together all ingredients in a large bowl. Store in an airtight container up to 6 months.
Note: We tested with Saco Cultured Buttermilk Powder.

Creamy Egg Strata

ACTIVE 35 MIN. - TOTAL 10 HOURS, 10 MIN., INCLUDING 8 HOURS CHILLING
SERVES 8 TO 10

- ½ (16-oz.) French bread loaf, cubed (about 5 cups)
- 6 Tbsp. butter, divided
- 2 cups (8 oz.) shredded Swiss cheese
- ½ cup freshly grated Parmesan cheese
- ⅓ cup chopped onion
- 1 tsp. minced garlic
- 3 Tbsp. all-purpose flour
- 1½ cups chicken broth
- ¾ cup dry white wine
- ½ tsp. salt
- ½ tsp. freshly ground black pepper
- ¼ tsp. ground nutmeg
- ½ cup sour cream
- 8 large eggs, lightly beaten
  Garnish: chopped fresh chives (optional)

1. Place bread cubes in a well-buttered 13- x 9-inch baking dish. Melt 3 tablespoons butter, and drizzle over bread cubes. Sprinkle with cheeses.

2. Melt remaining 3 tablespoons butter in a medium saucepan over medium; add onion and garlic. Saute 2 to 3 minutes or until tender. Whisk in flour until

smooth; cook, whisking constantly, 2 to 3 minutes or until lightly browned. Whisk in broth and next 4 ingredients until blended. Bring mixture to a boil; reduce heat to medium-low, and simmer, stirring occasionally, 15 minutes or until thickened. Remove from heat. Stir in sour cream. Add salt and black pepper to taste.

3. Gradually whisk about one-fourth of hot sour cream mixture into eggs; add egg mixture to remaining sour cream mixture, whisking constantly. Pour mixture over cheese in baking dish. Cover with plastic wrap; chill 8 to 24 hours.

4. Let strata stand at room temperature 1 hour. Preheat oven to 350°F. Remove plastic wrap, and bake 30 minutes or until set. Garnish, if desired. Serve immediately.

One-Dish Blackberry French Toast

ACTIVE 21 MIN. - TOTAL 8 HOURS, 51 MIN., INCLUDING 8 HOURS CHILLING
SERVES 8 TO 10

- 1 cup blackberry jam
- 1 (12-oz.) French bread loaf, cut into 1½-inch cubes
- 1 (8-oz.) pkg. ⅓-less-fat cream cheese, cut into 1-inch cubes
- 4 large eggs
- 2 cups half-and-half
- 1 tsp. ground cinnamon
- 1 tsp. vanilla extract
- ½ cup firmly packed brown sugar
  Maple syrup

1. Cook jam in a small saucepan over medium 1 to 2 minutes or until melted and smooth, stirring once.

2. Place half of bread cubes in bottom of a lightly greased 13- x 9-inch baking dish. Top with cream cheese cubes, and drizzle with melted jam. Top with remaining bread cubes.

3. Whisk together eggs and next 3 ingredients. Pour over bread mixture. Sprinkle with brown sugar. Cover tightly, and chill 8 to 24 hours.

4. Preheat oven to 325°F. Bake, covered, 20 minutes. Uncover and bake 10 to 15 minutes or until bread is golden brown and mixture is set. Serve with maple syrup.

Dessert

Buttered Rum Pound Cake with Bananas Foster Sauce

ACTIVE 30 MIN. - TOTAL 6 HOURS, 15 MIN., INCLUDING 4 HOURS STANDING
SERVES 10 TO 12

- 1 cup butter, softened
- 3 cups sugar, divided
- 6 large eggs, separated
- 3 cups all-purpose flour
- ¼ tsp. baking soda
- 1 (8-oz.) container sour cream
- 1 tsp. vanilla extract
- 1 tsp. lemon extract
  Buttered Rum Glaze
  (recipe follows)
  Bananas Foster Sauce
  (recipe follows)

1. Preheat oven to 325°F. Beat butter at medium speed with a heavy-duty electric stand mixer until creamy. Add 2½ cups sugar, beating 4 to 5 minutes or until fluffy. Add egg yolks, 1 at a time, beating just until yellow disappears.
2. Combine flour and baking soda; add to butter mixture alternately with sour cream, beginning and ending with flour mixture. Beat at medium speed just until blended after each addition. Stir in extracts.
3. Beat egg whites until foamy; gradually add remaining ½ cup sugar, 1 tablespoon at a time, beating until stiff peaks form. Fold into batter. Pour batter into a greased and floured 10-inch (16-cup) tube pan.
4. Bake 1 hour and 30 minutes or until a long wooden pick inserted in center comes out clean. Cool in pan 10 to 15 minutes; remove from pan, and place on a serving plate. Prick warm cake surface at 1-inch intervals with a long wooden pick; spoon warm Buttered Rum Glaze over cake. Let stand, covered, at least 4 hours or overnight. Serve with Bananas Foster Sauce.
Lemon Pound Cake: Prepare recipe as directed through Step 3, adding 2 tablespoons grated lemon zest to batter. Proceed with recipe as directed. Omit Buttered Rum Glaze; do not serve with sauce.

Buttered Rum Glaze

ACTIVE 10 MIN. - TOTAL 15 MIN.
MAKES 1¼ CUPS

- ½ cup chopped pecans
- 6 Tbsp. butter
- 3 Tbsp. light rum
- ¾ cup sugar

1. Preheat oven to 350°F. Arrange pecans in a single layer in a shallow pan, and bake 5 minutes or until toasted and fragrant.
2. Combine butter, rum, sugar, and 3 tablespoons water in a small saucepan; bring to a boil. Boil, stirring constantly, 3 minutes. Remove from heat, and stir in pecans.

Bananas Foster Sauce

ACTIVE 5 MIN. - TOTAL 13 MIN.
SERVES 8

- ¼ cup butter
- ½ cup firmly packed brown sugar
- ⅓ cup banana liqueur
- ¼ tsp. ground cinnamon
- 4 bananas, peeled and sliced
- ⅓ cup light rum

1. Melt butter in a large skillet over medium; add next 3 ingredients. Cook, stirring constantly, 3 minutes or until bubbly. Add bananas, and cook 2 to 3 minutes or until thoroughly heated. Remove from heat.
2. Heat rum in a small saucepan over medium (do not boil). Remove saucepan from heat; quickly pour rum over banana mixture, and carefully ignite the fumes just above the mixture with a long match or long multipurpose lighter. Let flames die down; serve immediately with Buttered Rum Pound Cake.

Apple-Gingerbread Cobbler

ACTIVE 20 MIN. - TOTAL 55 MIN.
SERVES 8

- 1 (14.5-oz.) pkg. gingerbread mix, divided
- ¼ cup firmly packed light brown sugar
- ½ cup butter, divided
- ½ cup chopped pecans
- 2 (21-oz.) cans apple pie filling
  Vanilla ice cream

1. Preheat oven to 375°F. Stir together 2 cups gingerbread mix and ¾ cup water until smooth.
2. Stir together remaining gingerbread mix and brown sugar; cut in ¼ cup butter with a pastry blender or fork until mixture is crumbly. Stir in pecans.
3. Combine apple pie filling and remaining ¼ cup butter in a large saucepan, and cook over medium, stirring often, 5 minutes or until thoroughly heated.
4. Spoon hot apple mixture into a lightly greased 11- x 7-inch baking dish. Spoon gingerbread-water mixture over hot apple mixture; sprinkle with gingerbread-pecan mixture.
5. Bake 30 to 35 minutes or until set. Serve cobbler with vanilla ice cream.

Cranberry-Apple Pie

Sparkling sugar can be found in specialty supermarkets and stores that carry cake-decorating products.

ACTIVE 15 MIN. - TOTAL 2 HOURS, 15 MIN.
SERVES 8

- 1 (15-oz.) pkg. refrigerated piecrusts, divided
- 1 large egg, lightly beaten
  Cranberry-Apple Pie Filling
  (recipe follows)
- 4 Tbsp. sparkling sugar*, divided

1. Preheat oven to 400°F. Fit 1 piecrust into a 9-inch pieplate according to package directions. Brush edges of piecrust with egg. Spoon Cranberry-Apple Pie Filling into piecrust, mounding filling in center of pie.
2. Unroll remaining piecrust on a lightly floured surface. Brush piecrust lightly with egg; sprinkle with 2 tablespoons sparkling sugar. Using the width of a ruler as a guide, cut the piecrust into 9 (1-inch-wide) strips. Arrange strips in a lattice design over filling; fold excess bottom piecrust under and along edges of top piecrust. Gently press ends of strips, sealing to bottom piecrust. Brush lattice with egg; sprinkle with remaining 2 tablespoons sparkling sugar. Place pie on a baking sheet.
3. Bake on lower oven rack 45 minutes, shielding with aluminum foil after 30 minutes to prevent excessive browning. Remove from oven, and let cool on a wire rack 1 hour.
*Note: Regular or turbinado sugar may be substituted.

Cranberry-Apple Pie Filling

ACTIVE 30 MIN. - TOTAL 1 HOUR 15 MIN.
MAKES ENOUGH FOR 1 (9-INCH) PIE

  12 large apples, peeled (about 6 lb.)
1½ cups sugar
⅓ cup all-purpose flour
½ cup butter
  1 cup sweetened dried cranberries

Cut apples into wedges; toss with 1½ cups sugar and ⅓ cup flour.

Melt butter in a large skillet over medium; add apple mixture to skillet, and saute 10 to 15 minutes or until apples are tender. Stir in sweetened dried cranberries; remove from heat, and let cool 45 minutes or until completely cool.

Mrs. Billett's White Cake

Think of this instant classic as the little black dress of white cakes. Cake Contest Winner Sue Winter says, "My mother always made this cake for my birthday. I have no idea where she got the recipe, but it is always requested by my children and grandchildren for their birthdays. I don't know who Mrs. Billett is, but she has become our family's best friend!"

ACTIVE 40 MIN. - TOTAL TIME 2 HOURS, INCLUDING FROSTING
SERVES 10 TO 12

  1 cup milk
1½ tsp. vanilla extract
  1 cup butter, softened
  2 cups sugar
  3 cups cake flour
  1 Tbsp. baking powder
  5 egg whites
     Vanilla Buttercream Frosting
       (recipe follows)
     Garnish: Fondant Snowflakes
       (directions follow)

1. Preheat oven to 350°F. Grease 3 (8-inch) round cake pans; line bottoms with parchment paper, and grease and flour paper.
2. Stir together milk and vanilla.
3. Beat butter at medium speed with a heavy-duty electric stand mixer until creamy; gradually add sugar, beating until light and fluffy. Sift together flour and baking powder; add to butter mixture alternately with milk mixture, beginning and ending with flour mixture. Beat at low speed just until blended after each addition.

4. Beat egg whites at medium speed until stiff peaks form; gently fold into batter. Pour batter into prepared pans.
5. Bake 20 to 23 minutes or until a wooden pick inserted in centers comes out clean. Cool in pans on wire racks 10 minutes. Remove from pans to wire racks; discard parchment paper. Cool completely (about 40 minutes).
6. Spread Vanilla Buttercream Frosting between layers (about 1 cup per layer) and on top and sides of cake. Apply Fondant Snowflakes.

Vanilla Buttercream Frosting

ACTIVE 10 MIN. - TOTAL 10 MIN.
MAKES 4½ CUPS

  1 cup butter, softened
¼ tsp. salt
  1 (32-oz.) pkg. powdered sugar
  6 to 7 Tbsp. milk
  1 Tbsp. vanilla extract

Beat butter and salt at medium speed with an electric mixer 1 to 2 minutes or until creamy; gradually add powdered sugar alternately with 6 tablespoons milk, beating at low speed until blended and smooth after each addition. Stir in vanilla. If desired, beat in remaining 1 tablespoon milk, 1 teaspoon at a time, until frosting reaches desired consistency.

Fondant Snowflakes

Don't let the cake bakers extraordinaire fool you. Smooth, pliable, decorative fondant is easy to use, particularly one straight from the box. Follow our directions, applying a little edible glitter and pearl sparkling dust, such as Wilton Shimmer Dust. Don't forget the pearls!

Dust work surface with **powdered sugar**. Roll out half of 1 (24-oz.) package **white fondant** to ¼ inch. Cut fondant with snowflake or holly leaf cutters. Transfer to baking sheets; let dry 12 hours. Add glimmer: Brush garnishes lightly with **vodka**. Sprinkle with **edible glitter** and **sparkling dust**.

MRS. BILLETT'S WHITE CAKE

Triple-Decker Strawberry Cake

This showstopping dessert will be the hit of any gathering!

ACTIVE 25 MIN. - TOTAL 1 HOUR, 58 MIN.
SERVES 12

- 1 (18.25-oz.) pkg. white cake mix
- 1 (3-oz.) pkg. strawberry gelatin
- 4 large eggs
- ½ cup sugar
- ½ cup finely chopped fresh strawberries
- ½ cup milk
- ½ cup vegetable oil
- ⅓ cup all-purpose flour
- Strawberry Buttercream Frosting (recipe follows)
- Garnish: halved strawberries

1. Preheat oven to 350°F. Beat cake mix and next 7 ingredients at low speed with an electric mixer 1 minute. Scrape down sides of bowl, and beat at medium speed 2 more minutes, stopping to scrape down sides as needed. (Strawberries should be well blended.)
2. Pour batter into 3 greased and floured 9-inch round cake pans.
3. Bake 23 minutes or until cakes spring back when pressed lightly with a finger. Cool in pans on wire racks, and let cool 1 hour or until cool completely.
4. Spread Strawberry Buttercream Frosting between layers and on top and sides of cake. Garnish, if desired. Serve immediately, or chill up to 1 week.

To make ahead: Prepare recipe as directed. Chill, uncovered, 20 minutes or until frosting is set. Cover with wax paper; store in refrigerator up to 1 week. To freeze, wrap chilled frosted cake with aluminum foil, and freeze up to 6 months. Thaw in refrigerator 24 hours.

Strawberry Buttercream Frosting

ACTIVE 10 MIN. - TOTAL 10 MIN.
MAKES 2½ CUPS

- 1 cup butter, softened
- 1 (32-oz.) pkg. powdered sugar
- 1 cup finely chopped fresh strawberries

Beat butter at medium speed with an electric mixer until fluffy (about 20 seconds). Add sugar and strawberries; beat at low speed until creamy. Add more sugar if frosting is too thin, or add more strawberries if too thick.

Four-Layer Coconut Cake

ACTIVE 45 MIN. - TOTAL 2 HOURS, 25 MIN.
SERVES 14 TO 16

- 3 cups all-purpose flour
- 2⅔ cups granulated sugar
- 1½ cups butter, softened
- 1 cup milk
- 1 tsp. baking powder
- ½ tsp. salt
- 2 tsp. coconut extract
- 1 tsp. vanilla extract
- 5 large eggs
- 1 (6-oz.) pkg. frozen flaked coconut, thawed
- 1 cup coconut shavings
- Coconut Filling (recipe follows)
- 2 cups whipping cream
- ¼ cup powdered sugar

1. Preheat oven to 400°F. Beat first 6 ingredients at medium speed with an electric mixer until well blended. Add extracts, beating well. Add eggs, 1 at a time, beating until blended after each addition. Stir in flaked coconut. Pour batter into 4 greased and floured 9-inch round cake pans.
2. Bake 20 minutes or until a wooden pick inserted in centers comes out clean. Cool in pans on wire racks 10 minutes. Remove from pans to wire racks, and let cool 1 hour or until completely cool.
3. Meanwhile, reduce oven temperature to 350°F. Arrange coconut shavings in a single layer in a shallow pan. Bake 8 to 10 minutes or until toasted, stirring occasionally.
4. Spread Coconut Filling between layers, leaving a 1-inch border. Beat whipping cream at high speed until foamy. Gradually add powdered sugar, beating until soft peaks form. Spread on top and sides of cake. Sprinkle toasted coconut on top and sides of cake, pressing gently to adhere.

Coconut Filling

ACTIVE 25 MIN. - TOTAL 55 MIN.
MAKES 5½ CUPS

- 2 cups sugar
- 2 cups milk
- 4 large eggs, lightly beaten
- ¼ cup all-purpose flour
- 2 (6-oz.) pkg. frozen flaked coconut, thawed
- 2 tsp. vanilla extract

Cook first 4 ingredients in a large saucepan over medium, whisking constantly, 12 to 15 minutes or until thickened and bubbly. Remove from heat, and stir in coconut and vanilla. Let cool 30 minutes or until completely cool.

Chocolate-Covered Cherry Pie

ACTIVE 35 MIN. - TOTAL 9 HOURS, 30 MIN., INCLUDING 8 HOURS CHILLING
SERVES 8

- 2 cups semisweet chocolate morsels
- ½ cup butter or margarine, cut into pieces
- 1 (6-oz.) ready-made chocolate crumb piecrust
- 1 (21-oz.) can cherry pie filling
- 1 (8-oz.) pkg. cream cheese, softened
- ⅓ cup powdered sugar
- 1 large egg
- ¼ tsp. almond extract
- 16 maraschino cherries with stems
- 2 cups thawed whipped topping or sweetened whipped cream

1. Microwave chocolate morsels and cream in a glass bowl at MEDIUM 1 to 2 minutes or until chocolate begins to melt. Whisk in butter until smooth. Let cool, whisking occasionally, 5 to 10 minutes or to desired consistency.
2. Spoon half of chocolate mixture into piecrust. Cover and chill remaining chocolate mixture.
3. Spoon cherry pie filling evenly over chocolate mixture in piecrust. Place piecrust on a baking sheet, and set aside.
4. Beat cream cheese and next 3 ingredients at medium speed with an electric mixer until smooth. Pour cream cheese mixture evenly over cherry pie filling mixture. (Piecrust will be full, but contents will not overflow when baking.)
5. Bake 30 minutes or until center is set. Remove from oven, and cool on a wire rack. Cover and chill 8 hours.
6. Drain cherries on paper towels; pat dry. Microwave reserved chocolate mixture at MEDIUM 1 minute. Remove from microwave, and stir until spreading consistency, reheating as necessary. Dip cherries in chocolate mixture, and place on a baking sheet lined with wax paper; chill for 15 minutes.

BRANDY ALEXANDER CHEESECAKE

Chocolate Tart Shell. Bake 20 minutes. Let cool on a wire rack 1 hour. Garnish, if desired.

Chocolate Tart Shell: Preheat oven to 350°F. Combine 1¼ cups chocolate graham cracker crumbs* and ⅓ cup melted butter; press onto bottom of an 11-inch tart pan with removable bottom. Bake 6 minutes. Let cool on a wire rack 30 minutes or until completely cool.
*Note: Chocolate-flavored teddy bear-shape graham crackers, crushed, may be substituted.

7. Spread remaining chocolate mixture evenly over pie. Spoon 8 dollops of whipped cream around outer edge of pie; place 2 chocolate covered-cherries in center of each dollop. Serve immediately.

Brandy Alexander Cheesecake

ACTIVE 20 MIN. - TOTAL 11 HOURS, 8 MIN., INCLUDING 8 HOURS CHILLING
SERVES 10 TO 12

- 1 (10-oz.) box chocolate-flavored bear-shape graham crackers, crushed (about 2¼ cups)
- 6 Tbsp. butter, melted
- 2 Tbsp. sugar, divided
- 4 (8-oz.) pkg. cream cheese, softened
- 1¼ cups sugar
- 3 Tbsp. cornstarch
- 4 large eggs, at room temperature
- 4 Tbsp. brandy, divided
- 4 Tbsp. crème de cacao, divided*
- 1 (16-oz.) container sour cream
  Garnishes: Blackberries, currants, raspberries, strawberries, cocoa (optional)

1. Preheat oven to 325°F. Stir together crushed graham crackers, butter, and 1 tablespoon sugar. Press mixture on bottom and halfway up sides of a 9-inch springform pan. Freeze 10 minutes.
2. Beat cream cheese, 1¼ cups sugar, and cornstarch at medium speed with an electric mixer 2 to 3 minutes or until smooth. Add eggs, 1 at a time, beating at low speed just until yellow disappears after each addition. Add 3 tablespoons brandy and 3 tablespoons crème de cacao, and beat just until blended. Pour into prepared crust.
3. Bake 1 hour or just until center is almost set.

4. During last 2 minutes of baking, stir together sour cream and remaining 1 tablespoon sugar, 1 tablespoon brandy, and 1 tablespoon crème de cacao.
5. Spread sour cream mixture over cheesecake. Bake 8 more minutes. Remove from oven; gently run a knife along outer edge of cheesecake, and cool completely in pan on a wire rack (about 1½ hours). Cover and chill 8 to 24 hours.
6. Remove sides of springform pan, and place cheesecake on a serving plate. Garnish, if desired.
*Note: Coffee liqueur may be substituted. We tested with Kahlúa.

Fudge Truffle–Pecan Tart

ACTIVE 20 MIN. - TOTAL 1 HOUR, 40 MIN.
SERVES 10 TO 12

- 1 (12-oz.) pkg. semisweet chocolate morsels
- ¾ cup firmly packed light brown sugar
- ½ cup butter, softened
- 3 large eggs
- 1 tsp. vanilla extract
- 1 cup finely chopped pecans
- ½ cup all-purpose flour
- 2 tsp. instant coffee granules
  Chocolate Tart Shell
  Garnish: Shaved chocolate curls (optional)

1. Preheat oven to 375°F. Microwave chocolate in a microwave-safe bowl at HIGH 1½ minutes or until melted and smooth, stirring at 30-second intervals.
2. Beat brown sugar and butter at medium speed with an electric mixer until blended; add eggs, beating well. Stir in melted chocolate, vanilla, and next 3 ingredients. Pour batter into prepared

Tiramisú Toffee Trifle Pie

ACTIVE 25 MIN. - TOTAL 8 HOURS, 25 MIN., INCLUDING 8 HOURS CHILLING
SERVES 8 TO 10

- 1½ Tbsp. instant coffee granules
- ¾ cup warm water
- 1 (10.75-oz.) frozen pound cake, thawed
- 1 (8.8-oz.) pkg. mascarpone or cream cheese, softened
- ½ cup powdered sugar
- ½ cup chocolate syrup
- 1 (12-oz.) container frozen whipped topping, thawed, divided
- 2 (1.4-oz.) English toffee candy bars, coarsely chopped*

1. Stir together coffee and ¾ cup warm water until coffee is dissolved. Let cool.
2. Meanwhile, cut cake into 14 slices. Cut each slice in half crosswise. Place cake slices in bottom and overlapping up sides of a 9-inch deep-dish pieplate. Drizzle coffee mixture over cake slices.
3. Beat mascarpone cheese, sugar, and chocolate syrup at medium speed with an electric mixer until smooth. Add 2½ cups whipped topping, and beat until light and fluffy.
4. Spread cheese mixture over cake. Dollop remaining whipped topping in center of pie. Sprinkle with chopped candy bars. Cover and chill 8 hours.
*Note: 10 miniature English toffee candy bars (from 1 [12-oz.] pkg.), coarsely chopped, may be substituted.

Red Velvet Layer Cake

ACTIVE 15 MIN. - TOTAL 1 HOUR, 45 MIN.
SERVES 12

- 1 cup butter, softened
- 2½ cups sugar
- 6 large eggs
- 3 cups all-purpose flour
- 3 Tbsp. unsweetened cocoa
- ¼ tsp. baking soda
- 1 (8-oz.) container sour cream
- 2 tsp. vanilla extract
- 2 (1-oz.) bottles red food coloring
- 1½ recipes 5-Cup Cream Cheese Frosting (recipe follows)

1. Preheat oven to 350°F. Beat butter at medium speed with an electric mixer until creamy. Gradually add sugar, beating until light and fluffy. Add eggs, 1 at a time, beating just until blended after each addition.
2. Combine flour, cocoa, and baking soda. Add to butter mixture alternately with sour cream, beginning and ending with flour mixture. Beat at low speed just until blended after each addition. Stir in vanilla; stir in red food coloring. Spoon cake batter into 3 greased and floured 8-inch round cake pans.
3. Bake 18 to 20 minutes or until a wooden pick inserted in centers comes out clean. Cool in pans on wire racks 10 minutes. Remove from pans to wire racks, and let cool 1 hour or until completely cool.

4. Spread 5-Cup Cream Cheese Frosting between layers and on top and sides of cake.

5-Cup Cream Cheese Frosting

ACTIVE 10 MIN. - TOTAL 10 MIN.
MAKES ABOUT 5 CUPS

- 2 (8-oz.) pkg. cream cheese, softened
- ½ cup butter, softened
- 1 (32-oz.) pkg. powdered sugar
- 2 tsp. vanilla extract

Beat cream cheese and butter at medium speed with an electric mixer until creamy. Gradually add powdered sugar, beating until fluffy. Stir in vanilla.

Chocolate-Peppermint Candy Cupcakes

ACTIVE 25 MIN. - TOTAL 1 HOUR, 58 MIN.
MAKES 3 DOZEN

- Chocolate Velvet Cake Batter (recipe follows)
- 1 (12-oz.) package white chocolate morsels
- ½ cup crushed peppermint candy canes
- Vanilla Buttercream Frosting (recipe follows)

1. Preheat oven to 350°F. Place 36 paper baking cups in muffin pans; spoon Chocolate Velvet Cake Batter evenly into baking cups, filling two-thirds full.
2. Bake 18 minutes or until a wooden pick inserted in centers comes out clean. Remove from pans to wire racks, and let cool 45 minutes or until completely cool.
3. Melt white chocolate morsels in a microwave-safe bowl at HIGH 1½ minutes or until melted and smooth, stirring at 30-second intervals. Spread melted chocolate in a ¼-inch-thick layer on an aluminum foil-lined baking sheet. Sprinkle with peppermint candy. Chill 30 minutes or until firm. Remove from baking sheet, and chop.
4. Spread cupcakes with Vanilla Buttercream Frosting; sprinkle with chopped candy mixture.

CHOCOLATE-
PEPPERMINT
CANDY CUPCAKES

Chocolate Velvet Cake Batter

ACTIVE 20 MIN. - TOTAL 20 MIN.
MAKES ENOUGH BATTER FOR 3 DOZEN CUPCAKES

- 1½ cups semisweet chocolate morsels
- ½ cup butter, softened
- 1 (16-oz.) pkg. light brown sugar
- 3 large eggs
- 2 cups all-purpose flour
- 1 tsp. baking soda
- ½ tsp. salt
- 1 (8-oz.) container sour cream
- 1 cup hot water
- 2 tsp. vanilla extract

1. Melt chocolate in a microwave-safe bowl at HIGH 1½ minutes or until melted and smooth, stirring at 30-second intervals. Beat butter and brown sugar at medium speed with an electric mixer until well blended (about 5 minutes). Add eggs, 1 at a time, beating just until blended after each addition. Add melted chocolate, beating just until blended.
2. Sift together flour, baking soda, and salt. Gradually add to chocolate mixture alternately with sour cream, beginning and ending with flour mixture. Beat at low speed just until blended after each addition. Gradually add 1 cup hot water in a slow, steady stream, beating at low speed just until blended. Stir in vanilla.

Vanilla Buttercream Frosting

ACTIVE 10 MIN. - TOTAL 10 MIN.
MAKES 6 CUPS

- 1 cup butter, softened
- 1 (32-oz.) pkg. powdered sugar
- ⅔ cup milk
- 1 Tbsp. vanilla extract

Beat butter at medium speed with an electric mixer until creamy; gradually add powdered sugar alternately with milk, beating at low speed until blended after each addition. Stir in vanilla.

White Chocolate–Raspberry Cheesecake Bars

Raspberry preserves and syrup combine to make a luscious, spreadable layer in this cheesecake. Raspberry syrup can be found near the pancake syrup at your local grocery store.

ACTIVE 34 MIN. - TOTAL 10 HOURS, 19 MIN., INCLUDING 8 HOURS CHILLING
MAKES ABOUT 4 DOZEN

- 2 cups graham cracker crumbs
- ½ cup butter, melted
- 3 Tbsp. sugar
- 1 (12-oz.) pkg. white chocolate morsels
- 5 (8-oz.) packages cream cheese, softened
- 1 cup sugar
- 2 large eggs
- 1 Tbsp. vanilla extract
- 1½ cups seedless raspberry preserves
- 2 Tbsp. raspberry syrup (optional)
  Garnish: fresh mint sprigs (optional)

1. Preheat oven to 350°F. Combine first 3 ingredients; press onto bottom of lightly greased aluminum foil-lined 13- x 9-inch pan. Bake 8 to 10 minutes.
2. Place white chocolate morsels in top of a double boiler; bring water to a boil. Reduce heat to low; cook, stirring constantly, 3 to 4 minutes or until chocolate is melted.
3. Beat cream cheese at medium speed with an electric mixer until creamy; gradually add 1 cup sugar, beating well. Add eggs, 1 at a time, beating until blended after each addition. Stir in vanilla. Add melted chocolate, beating well.
4. Microwave raspberry preserves in a microwave-safe glass bowl at HIGH 1½ minutes or until smooth, stirring at 30-second intervals. Stir in raspberry syrup, if desired.
5. Spoon half of cream cheese batter into prepared crust; drizzle half of raspberry mixture over batter, leaving a ¾-inch border. Spoon remaining cream cheese batter around edges of pan, spreading towards the center. Cover and chill remaining raspberry mixture.
6. Bake cheesecake 30 to 35 minutes or until almost set. Turn oven off; let cheesecake stand in oven, with door partially open, 1 hour. Remove from oven; gently run a knife around edge of cheesecake to loosen. Cover and chill at least 8 hours or up to 24 hours.
7. Cut cheesecake into 1½-inch squares; drizzle with remaining raspberry mixture. Garnish, if desired. Store in an airtight container in refrigerator up to 1 week.

Lemon-Poppy Seed Cakes

Mini Bundt pans (not to be confused with small Bundt pans) look like regular muffin pans; however, they have Bundt-shape cups. The cups in mini Bundt pans can vary in size and shape, so your yield can also vary. For this recipe, we used 2 (12-cup) pans to make 18 miniature Bundt cakes.

ACTIVE 25 MIN. - TOTAL 1 HOUR
MAKES 18 MINI BUNDT CAKES

- ½ cup butter, softened
- 2 oz. cream cheese, softened
- 1¼ cups granulated sugar
- 2 large eggs
- ¾ cup milk
- ¾ tsp. poppy seeds
- ¾ tsp. almond extract
- 2 tsp. lemon zest, divided
- 1¾ cups all-purpose flour
- ¾ tsp. baking powder
- ⅛ tsp. salt
- 1¼ cups powdered sugar
- ¼ cup fresh lemon juice

1. Preheat oven to 350°F. Beat butter and cream cheese at medium speed with an electric mixer until well blended. Gradually add granulated sugar, beating until creamy and fluffy. Add eggs, 1 at a time, beating just until yellow disappears after each addition. Beat in milk, poppy seeds, almond extract, and 1½ teaspoons lemon zest. (Mixture will be slightly lumpy.)
2. Whisk together flour and next 2 ingredients in a large bowl. Gradually add to butter mixture, beating until blended. Spoon batter into 1 greased and floured (12-cup) miniature Bundt pan, filling all cups three-fourths full. Spoon remaining batter into a second pan, filling only 6 cups. Bake miniature cakes 24 to 26 minutes or until a wooden pick inserted in centers comes out clean. Remove from pans to wire racks, and let cakes cool 10 minutes.
3. Whisk together powdered sugar, fresh lemon juice, and remaining ½ teaspoon lemon zest until smooth. Drizzle glaze evenly over warm cakes. Let cakes stand 4 to 5 minutes or until glaze is set.

Brown Sugar Bread Pudding with Rich Bourbon Sauce

ACTIVE 25 MIN. - TOTAL 1 HOUR, 50 MIN.
SERVES 10

- 3 large eggs
- 3 cups milk
- 1 cup firmly packed dark brown sugar
- ¼ cup melted butter
- 1 Tbsp. vanilla extract
- ¾ tsp. ground cinnamon
- ¼ tsp. ground nutmeg
- ¼ tsp. salt
- 1 (8-oz.) French bread loaf, cut into 1-inch cubes (about 8 cups)
  Garnish: cinnamon sticks (optional)
  Rich Bourbon Sauce (recipe follows)

1. Preheat oven to 325°F. Whisk together first 8 ingredients in a large bowl; add bread cubes; cover and chill 10 minutes. Spoon soaked bread cubes into 10 lightly greased (6-oz.) ramekins, and place on a jelly-roll pan.
2. Bake 40 to 45 minutes or until set. Remove from oven, and let stand 30 minutes before serving. Garnish, if desired. Serve with Rich Bourbon Sauce.

Rich Bourbon Sauce

ACTIVE 10 MIN. - TOTAL 20 MIN.
MAKES 1 CUP

- ½ cup butter
- ⅓ cup firmly packed dark brown sugar
- ⅓ cup heavy whipping cream
- 2 Tbsp. bourbon

Melt butter and sugar in a heavy 2-quart saucepan over low, stirring until smooth. Stir in cream. Cook, stirring constantly, 5 minutes or until thickened. Remove from heat, and stir in bourbon.

Orange–Sweet Potato Pie with Rosemary–Cornmeal Crust

ACTIVE 35 MIN. - TOTAL 4 HOURS, 35 MIN., INCLUDING 3 HOURS CHILLING AND COOLING
SERVES 8

ROSEMARY-CORNMEAL CRUST*
- ¾ cup all-purpose flour
- ½ cup plain white cornmeal
- ¼ cup powdered sugar
- 2 tsp. chopped fresh rosemary
- ¼ tsp. salt
- ½ cup cold butter, cut into pieces
- ¼ cup very cold water

ORANGE-SWEET POTATO FILLING
- 1½ lb. sweet potatoes
- 3 large eggs
- ¾ cup granulated sugar
- 1 cup evaporated milk
- 3 Tbsp. butter, melted
- 2 tsp. orange zest
- 1 Tbsp. fresh orange juice
- ½ tsp. ground cinnamon
- ¼ tsp. ground nutmeg
- 1½ tsp. vanilla extract

1. Prepare crust: Whisk together first 5 ingredients in a medium bowl until well blended. Cut butter into flour mixture with a pastry blender or fork until mixture resembles small peas and is crumbly.
2. Sprinkle cold water, 1 tablespoon at a time, over surface of mixture in bowl; stir with a fork until dry ingredients are moistened. Place dough on a plastic wrap-lined flat surface, and shape into a disc. Wrap in plastic wrap, and chill 30 minutes.
3. Unwrap dough, and roll between 2 new sheets of lightly floured plastic wrap into a 12-inch circle. Fit into a 9-inch pie plate. Fold edges under, and crimp. Chill 30 minutes.
4. Preheat oven to 400°F. Bake crust 20 minutes, shielding edges with aluminum foil to prevent excessive browning. Cool completely on a wire rack (about 1 hour). Meanwhile, prepare filling: Bake sweet potatoes on a baking sheet 50 to 55 minutes or until tender. Let stand 5 minutes. Cut potatoes in half lengthwise; scoop out pulp into a bowl. Mash pulp. Discard skins.
5. Whisk together eggs and granulated sugar until well blended. Add milk, next 6 ingredients, and sweet potato pulp, stirring until blended. Pour mixture into prepared crust.
6. Bake 20 minutes. Reduce heat to 325°F, and bake 20 to 25 minutes or until center is set. Let cool completely on a wire rack (about 1 hour).

*Note: Substitute ½ (15-oz.) package refrigerated piecrusts for cornmeal crust ingredients. Unroll on a lightly floured surface. Sprinkle with 1 tablespoon plain white cornmeal and 2 teaspoons chopped fresh rosemary. Lightly roll cornmeal and rosemary into crust. Fit into a 9-inch pie plate according to package directions. Fold edges under; crimp. Proceed as directed, beginning with Step 5.

Gifts from the Kitchen

Italian Parmesan Herb Mix

ACTIVE 5 MIN. - TOTAL 5 MIN.
MAKES ABOUT 2 CUPS

- 1 (8-oz.) container grated Parmesan cheese
- 3 Tbsp. dried Italian seasoning
- 3 Tbsp. dried parsley flakes
- 1 Tbsp. granulated garlic
- ½ tsp. ground red pepper

Stir together all ingredients. Store mixture in airtight containers in refrigerator up to 6 weeks.

Holiday Herb Butter

ACTIVE 5 MIN. - TOTAL 5 MIN.
MAKES 1 CUP

Stir together 1 cup **softened butter** and ¼ cup **Italian Parmesan Herb Mix.**
Note: Pack this flavorful butter into colorful pottery crocks, or mold into festive shapes using holiday cookie cutters. Inexpensive sheets of plastic candy molds, sold at crafts stores, are perfect for shaping individual portions of butter. To make the Christmas tree-shape butter, place a tree-shape cookie cutter on a plate lined with wax paper; fill with butter, and garnish with pink peppercorns. Freeze 4 hours or until firm enough to remove from mold. Place in a zip-top plastic freezer bag, and freeze up to 1 month.

Sweet Hot Honey Mustard

Sweet Hot Honey Mustard is a delicious complement to holiday ham and turkey. Spread it on a grilled chicken sandwich or over the crust of a quiche before adding the filling. Straight from the jar, it makes a bold and spicy dip for egg rolls. Or mix with equal parts mayo, and then serve with fried chicken tenders.

ACTIVE 15 MIN. - TOTAL 15 MIN.
MAKES 4 CUPS

- 2 cups sugar
- 1½ cups dry mustard
- 2 cups white vinegar
- 3 large eggs, lightly beaten
- ½ cup honey

1. Whisk together sugar and mustard in a heavy 3-quart saucepan; gradually whisk in vinegar and eggs until blended.
2. Cook mustard mixture over medium, whisking constantly, 10 to 12 minutes or until smooth and thickened. Remove from heat, and whisk in honey. Let cool, and store in airtight containers in the refrigerator up to 1 month.

Butter–Pecan Granola

The pecan lover in your life will be more than thrilled with this tasty and impressive gift.

ACTIVE 15 MIN. - TOTAL 1 HR., 10 MIN.
MAKES ABOUT 8 CUPS

- ½ cup melted butter
- ¼ cup honey
- 2 Tbsp. light brown sugar
- 1 tsp. vanilla extract
- ⅛ tsp. salt
- 3 cups uncooked regular oats
- 1½ cups coarsely chopped pecans
- ½ cup toasted wheat germ
- ½ cup toasted sesame seeds
- 1 (8-oz.) pkg. chopped dates
  Wax paper

Preheat oven to 325°F. Stir together butter and next 4 ingredients in a large bowl. Add oats, pecans, wheat germ, and sesame seeds; stir until mixture is evenly coated. Spread oat mixture on a lightly greased 15- x 10-inch jelly-roll pan. Bake 25 to 30 minutes or until toasted, stirring every 10 minutes. Spread granola onto wax paper; cool completely (about 30 minutes). Stir in dates. Store in an airtight container at room temperature up to 3 days, or freeze up to 6 months.

Cranberry-Pecan Chicken Salad

ACTIVE 20 MIN. - TOTAL 20 MIN.
SERVES 6 TO 8

Stir together 8 cups chopped cooked **chicken**; 3 **celery ribs**, diced; 5 **scallions**, thinly sliced; 1½ cups chopped toasted **pecans**; 1 (6-oz.) package sweetened **dried cranberries**; 1 cup **mayonnaise**; and ½ cup **Sweet Hot Honey Mustard**. Season with **salt** and **black pepper** to taste. Cover and chill up to 3 days.
Note: For holiday gift-giving, pack into pretty jars and deliver to family and friends along with a fresh loaf of bakery bread.

Peanut Butter Bonbons

ACTIVE 15 MIN. - TOTAL 1 HOUR, 15 MIN.
MAKES ABOUT 7 DOZEN

- 1 (18-oz.) jar creamy or chunky peanut butter
- 1 cup butter, softened
- 1½ cups finely crushed graham cracker crumbs
- 4 cups powdered sugar
- 1½ cups finely chopped roasted peanuts
  Powdered sugar

Beat peanut butter and butter at medium speed with an electric mixer until creamy; add graham cracker crumbs, beating until blended. Gradually add powdered sugar, beating at low speed until blended. Shape into 1-inch balls, and roll in peanuts. Cover and chill 1 hour. Store in refrigerator. Dust with powdered sugar just before serving.

Salty Chocolate-Pecan Candy

Once it's removed from the refrigerator, this candy will soften slightly at room temperature.

ACTIVE 10 MIN. - TOTAL 1 HOUR, 25 MIN., INCLUDING 1 HOUR CHILLING
MAKES 1¾ POUNDS

- 1 cup pecans, coarsely chopped
- 3 (4-oz.) bittersweet chocolate baking bars
- 3 (4-oz.) white chocolate baking bars
- 1 tsp. coarse sea salt*

1. Preheat oven to 350°F. Place pecans in a single layer on a baking sheet. Bake 8 to 10 minutes or until toasted.

2. Line a 17- x 12-inch jelly-roll pan with parchment paper. Break each chocolate bar into 8 equal pieces. (You will have 48 pieces total.) Arrange in a checkerboard pattern in jelly-roll pan, alternating dark and white chocolate. (Pieces will touch.)
3. Bake at 225°F for 5 minutes or just until chocolate is melted. Remove pan to a wire rack. Swirl chocolates into a marble pattern, using a wooden pick. Sprinkle evenly with pecans and salt.
4. Chill 1 hour or until firm. Break into pieces. Store in an airtight container in refrigerator up to 1 month.
***Note:** ¾ teaspoon kosher salt may be substituted.

Reindeer Gingersnaps

ACTIVE 45 MIN. - TOTAL 1 HOUR, 25 MIN.
MAKES 16 COOKIES

- 1 (14.5-oz.) pkg. gingerbread mix
- 1 tsp. meringue powder
- ½ tsp. hot water
- 1 (12-oz.) container ready-to-spread fluffy white frosting
  Decorations: 32 miniature candy canes, 32 licorice candies, and 16 sour cherry candies

1. Preheat oven to 375°. Prepare gingerbread dough according to package instructions for gingersnap cookies.
2. Roll dough out on a lightly floured surface, and cut into 3½-inch ovals, using an egg-shape or oval cookie cutter. Place 2 inches apart on parchment paper-lined baking sheets.
3. Bake 8 to 10 minutes or until edges are lightly browned. Remove to wire racks, and let cool 30 minutes.
4. Stir together meringue powder and water until combined; stir in frosting. Spoon frosting mixture into a zip-top plastic freezer bag; snip 1 corner of bag to make a small hole. Pipe 1 dot of frosting mixture at top of 1 cookie; press straight ends of 2 candy canes into piped dot to form antlers (prop up candy canes as needed). Pipe 2 large ovals in center of cookie; press 1 licorice candy in each oval to form eyes. Pipe 1 dot at bottom of cookie; press 1 cherry candy in dot to form a nose. Repeat procedure with remaining cookies, frosting mixture, and candies. Let stand 24 hours to dry, if desired.

Merry Margarita Mix Pineapple Craft Cocktail

When poured into a glass bottle, this tangy mixer makes a fantastic hostess gift, especially when it's packaged with a batch of Lime Sea Salt and a bottle of tequila.

ACTIVE 10 MIN. - TOTAL 10 MIN.
MAKES 2½ CUPS

Add 1 cup **pineapple juice** and 2 tablespoons granulated **sugar** to a 16-oz. glass bottle with a tight-fitting lid. Cover with lid; shake vigorously until sugar dissolves, 1 minute. Add ¾ cup **orange liqueur** (such as Cointreau or Grand Marnier) and ¾ cup fresh **lime juice**. Cover with lid; shake until well combined. Give as a gift with a bottle of tequila and Lime Sea Salt. This mix can be refrigerated up to 3 days; shake before serving.

Lime Sea Salt

ACTIVE 20 MIN. - TOTAL 20 MIN.
MAKES 1 CUP

Line a rimmed baking sheet with parchment paper. Spread 1½ tablespoons **fresh lime zest** across prepared baking sheet. Bake at 150°F (or lowest temperature) until zest is fragrant and dry but not browned, 10 minutes. Remove from oven; cool on baking sheet set on a wire rack. Combine 1 cup **coarse sea salt** and cooled zest. Store in an airtight container up to 6 months.

Main Dishes

Shepherd's Pie

ACTIVE 40 MIN. · TOTAL 1 HOUR, 20 MIN.
SERVES 8

1½ lb. ground round
1 cup chopped onion
½ (8-oz.) pkg. fresh mushrooms, sliced
1 garlic clove, minced
1 cup frozen peas, thawed
4 tsp. beef bouillon granules
½ tsp. salt
½ tsp. dried thyme
¼ tsp. freshly ground black pepper
1 Tbsp. all-purpose flour
1 (14½-oz.) can stewed tomatoes
1 bay leaf
2 Tbsp. red wine vinegar
Cheese-and-Carrot Mashed Potatoes (recipe follows)

1. Preheat oven to 400°F. Brown beef in a large nonstick skillet over medium-high, stirring often, 10 minutes or until meat crumbles and is no longer pink. Remove ground beef from skillet using a slotted spoon; reserve 2 tablespoons drippings in skillet. Reduce heat to medium.
2. Saute onion, mushrooms, and garlic in hot drippings over medium 10 to 11 minutes or until tender. Stir in ground beef, peas, and next 4 ingredients. Sprinkle flour over meat mixture. Increase heat to medium-high, and cook, stirring constantly, 1 minute. Stir in tomatoes, bay leaf, and vinegar, breaking up large tomato pieces with a spoon. Reduce heat to medium; cook, stirring often, 3 minutes or until slightly thickened. Remove bay leaf. Transfer mixture to a lightly greased 3-quart baking dish or pan. Spoon Cheese-and-Carrot Mashed Potatoes evenly over meat mixture, smoothing with back of spoon.
3. Bake 15 minutes or until thoroughly heated. Let stand 5 minutes before serving.

Cheese-and-Carrot Mashed Potatoes

ACTIVE 20 MIN. · TOTAL 20 MIN.
SERVES 8

1 (1-lb.) pkg. baby carrots
1 Tbsp. butter
3 cups mashed potatoes
1 cup (4 oz.) shredded Cheddar cheese
1 Tbsp. fresh thyme leaves
1 tsp. salt
¼ tsp. black pepper

1. Place carrots and ¼ cup water in a large microwave-safe bowl. Cover tightly with plastic wrap; fold back a small edge to allow steam to escape. Microwave at HIGH 8 to 10 minutes or until carrots are tender. Drain.
2. Stir in butter. Coarsely mash carrots with a potato masher. Stir in mashed potatoes and next 4 ingredients until well blended.

Dinner Mac and Cheese

ACTIVE 30 MIN. · TOTAL 1 HOUR
SERVES 8

1 (16-oz.) pkg. uncooked cellentani (corkscrew) pasta
3 Tbsp. butter
¼ cup all-purpose flour
4 cups milk
1 cup (4 oz.) shredded sharp Cheddar cheese
1 (10-oz.) block sharp white Cheddar cheese, shredded
1 (3-oz.) pkg. cream cheese, softened
½ tsp. salt
2 cups chopped cooked ham
2 cups coarsely chopped assorted roasted vegetables
1¼ cups crushed round buttery crackers
2 Tbsp. butter, melted

1. Preheat oven to 400°F. Prepare cellentani according to package directions.
2. Meanwhile, melt 3 tablespoons butter in a Dutch oven over medium. Gradually whisk in flour; cook, whisking constantly, 1 minute. Gradually whisk in milk until smooth; cook, whisking constantly, 8 to 10 minutes or until slightly thickened. Whisk in 1 cup sharp Cheddar cheese and next 3 ingredients until smooth. Remove from heat, and stir in ham, vegetables, and hot cooked pasta.
3. Spoon pasta mixture into a lightly greased 13- x 9-inch baking dish. Stir together crushed cracker crumbs and the melted butter; sprinkle over pasta mixture.
4. Bake 25 to 30 minutes or until golden and bubbly. Let stand 5 minutes before serving.

Chicken-and-Cornbread Casserole

ACTIVE 20 MIN. · TOTAL 1 HOUR, 7 MIN.
SERVES 6

2 celery ribs, chopped
½ medium onion, chopped
1 Tbsp. vegetable oil
3 cups packed crumbled cornbread
1 Tbsp. poultry seasoning
3½ cups chopped cooked chicken
1¼ cups low-sodium chicken broth
1 cup sour cream
1 large egg, lightly beaten
1 (4.5-oz.) jar sliced mushrooms, drained
¼ tsp. crushed red pepper
¼ tsp. salt
2 Tbsp. butter, melted
1 cup (4 oz.) shredded sharp Cheddar cheese
Garnish: chopped fresh parsley (optional)

1. Preheat oven to 350°F. Saute celery and onion in hot oil in a medium skillet over medium-high 7 minutes or until vegetables are tender; set aside.
2. Combine cornbread and poultry seasoning in a large bowl. Layer half of cornbread mixture on bottom of a lightly greased 11- x 7-inch baking dish.
3. Combine onion mixture, chicken, and next 6 ingredients in a bowl. Spoon mixture in dish. Top evenly with remaining half of cornbread mixture, and drizzle with butter.
4. Bake, covered, 30 minutes or until bubbly. Remove from oven; top with cheese. Bake, uncovered, 10 more minutes or until cheese is melted and golden brown. Garnish, if desired.

Ham-and-Vegetable Cobbler

Leftover holiday ham plays the starring role in this comforting cobbler.

ACTIVE 30 MIN. - TOTAL 50 MIN.
SERVES 6

- ¼ cup butter
- ¼ cup all-purpose flour
- 3½ cups milk
- ½ tsp. dried thyme
- 1 tsp. chicken bouillon granules
- 2 cups diced cooked ham
- 1 (10-oz.) pkg. frozen sweet peas and mushrooms
- 1 cup frozen crinkle-cut carrots
- 1 (14.1-oz.) pkg. refrigerated piecrusts

1. Preheat oven to 450°F. Melt butter in a large saucepan over medium. Gradually whisk in flour, and cook, whisking constantly, 1 minute. Add milk and next 2 ingredients; cook, stirring constantly, 6 to 8 minutes or until thickened and bubbly. Stir in ham and next 2 ingredients; cook 4 to 5 minutes or until mixture is thoroughly heated. Spoon into a lightly greased 11- x 7-inch baking dish.
2. Unroll each piecrust on a lightly floured surface. Cut piecrusts into 1¼-inch-wide strips. Arrange strips in a lattice design over ham mixture.
3. Bake 40 minutes or until crust is browned and filling is bubbly.

Fennel-Crusted Rib Roast

ACTIVE 20 MIN. - TOTAL 3 HOURS, 5 MIN.
SERVES 8

- 1 (7- to 9-lb.) 4-rib prime rib roast, trimmed
- 2 tsp. black peppercorns
- 2 tsp. fennel seeds
- 1½ tsp. coriander seeds
- 1 Tbsp. olive oil
- 4 tsp. kosher salt
  Garnishes: fresh cranberries, oranges with stems, gray sea salt (optional)

1. Preheat oven to 400°F. Let prime rib roast stand at room temperature 30 minutes.

2. Pulse peppercorns, fennel, and coriander in a spice grinder 5 times or until coarsely ground. (Or place spices in a zip-top plastic freezer bag, and crush using a skillet or rolling pin.) Rub roast with oil, and sprinkle with kosher salt. Press spice mixture onto all sides of roast. Place on a rack in a roasting pan.
3. Bake 2 hours or until a meat thermometer inserted into thickest portion registers 120°F to 125°F (medium-rare) or to desired degree of doneness. Let stand 15 minutes to 1 hour before slicing. Garnish, if desired.

Citrus-Grilled Turkey Breast

ACTIVE 40 MIN. - TOTAL 3 HOURS, 40 MIN.
SERVES 6

- 1 (5- to 6-lb.) skin-on, bone-in turkey breast
- ¼ cup chopped fresh flat-leaf parsley
- 2 garlic cloves, minced
- 1 Tbsp. lemon zest
- 2 Tbsp. olive oil
- 1 tsp. freshly ground black pepper
- 2 tsp. salt, divided
  Garnishes: Grilled citrus slices, fresh cranberries, lemon leaves (optional)

1. Let turkey breast stand at room temperature 30 minutes; rinse with cold water, and pat turkey dry.
2. Stir together parsley, next 4 ingredients, and 1 teaspoon salt. Loosen and lift skin from turkey without totally detaching skin, and rub parsley mixture under skin. Replace skin. Sprinkle cavity with ½ teaspoon salt; rub into cavity. Sprinkle remaining ½ teaspoon salt on skin, and rub into skin.
3. Light 1 side of grill, heating to 350°F to 400°F (medium-high) heat; leave other side unlit. Place turkey over lit side, and grill, without grill lid, 4 minutes on each side or until golden brown. Transfer turkey to unlit side, and grill, covered with grill lid, 2 to 2½ hours or until a meat thermometer inserted into thickest portion registers 165°F. Remove from heat, and let stand 30 minutes before slicing. Garnish, if desired.

CREOLE DEEP-FRIED TURKEY

Creole Deep-Fried Turkey

ACTIVE 20 MIN. - TOTAL 2 HOURS, 10 MIN.
SERVES 8

- Peanut oil (about 3 gal.)
- 1 (12- to 14-lb.) whole fresh turkey*
- 4 Tbsp. Creole seasoning, divided
  Garnishes: figs, fig leaves, apples, fresh cranberries (optional)

1. Pour oil into a deep propane turkey fryer 10 to 12 inches from top; heat to 350° over a medium-low flame according to manufacturer's instructions (about 45 minutes).
2. Meanwhile, remove giblets and neck from turkey, and rinse turkey with cold water. Drain cavity well; pat dry. Loosen and lift skin from turkey with fingers, without totally detaching skin; spread 1 tablespoon Creole seasoning under skin. Carefully replace skin. Sprinkle 1 tablespoon Creole seasoning inside cavity; rub into cavity. Sprinkle outside of turkey with remaining 2 tablespoons Creole seasoning, and rub into skin. Let turkey stand at room temperature 30 minutes.
3. Place turkey on fryer rod. Carefully lower turkey into hot oil with rod attachment.
4. Fry 35 to 45 minutes or until a meat thermometer inserted in thickest portion of thigh registers 165°F (about 3 minutes per pound, plus an additional 5 minutes. Keep oil temperature between 300°F and 325°F). Remove turkey from oil; drain and let stand 30 minutes before slicing. Garnish, if desired.
*Note: Frozen whole turkey, thawed, may be substituted.

Cranberry-Turkey Panini

If you don't have a panini press, place the sandwiches in a hot skillet, and press with a smaller heavy pan. Cook until bread is golden brown; turn and continue to cook until the other side is golden brown and the cheese is melted.

ACTIVE 15 MIN. - TOTAL 23 MIN.
SERVES 6

- 4 Tbsp. mayonnaise
- 4 Tbsp. horseradish-Dijon mustard
- 4 soft sandwich rolls, cut in half
- 8 Swiss or provolone cheese slices
- 8 oz. roasted turkey slices
- 1 cup cranberry sauce
  Vegetable cooking spray

1. Preheat panini press. Spread mayonnaise and mustard on cut sides of rolls. Layer each bottom roll half with 1 cheese slice, and top evenly with turkey, cranberry, and remaining cheese slices. Cover with roll tops; spray tops with cooking spray.
2. Cook in a preheated panini press 2 to 3 minutes or until golden brown.

Next-Day Turkey Bake

If the mashed potatoes won't spread, warm them slightly in the microwave with a little milk.

ACTIVE 15 MIN. - TOTAL 1 HOUR, 35 MIN.
SERVES 6

- 2½ cups coarsely chopped cooked turkey
- 2½ cups prepared cornbread dressing
- 1½ cups chilled prepared turkey gravy
- 3 cups prepared mashed potatoes
- ½ Tbsp. butter

1. Preheat oven to 325°F. Layer a lightly greased 8-inch-square baking dish with turkey, dressing, and gravy. Spread mashed potatoes evenly over gravy, sealing to edges. Dot evenly with butter.
2. Bake 1 hour and 15 minutes. Let casserole stand 5 minutes before serving.

Turkey Pot Pie with Cranberry-Pecan Crusts

If you're in a hurry and don't have time for the Cranberry-Pecan Crusts, you can use refrigerated piecrusts as your topping; cut into shapes or strips and follow baking instructions on the piecrust package.

ACTIVE 20 MIN. - TOTAL 1 HR., 13 MIN. INCLUDING CRUSTS
SERVES 10 TO 12

- 3 Tbsp. butter, divided
- 2 large sweet onions, diced
- ¼ cup all-purpose flour
- 1 tsp. salt
- 1 tsp. black pepper
- 3 lb. turkey tenderloins, cut into 1½-inch cubes
- 2 Tbsp. vegetable oil
- 1½ cups chicken broth
- 1 cup milk
- 1 (9-oz.) pkg. fresh spinach, torn
  Cranberry-Pecan Crusts (recipe follows)

1. Preheat oven to 350°F. Melt 1 tablespoon butter in a large skillet over medium-high; add onions, and saute 15 minutes or until caramel colored. Place onions in a bowl.
2. Combine flour, salt, and pepper; dredge turkey tenderloin cubes in flour mixture.
3. Melt remaining 2 tablespoons butter with oil in skillet over medium-high; add turkey tenderloin cubes, and brown on all sides. Gradually stir in chicken broth and milk. Bring to a boil, and cook, stirring constantly, 1 minute or until thickened. Stir in onions. Add spinach, stirring just until wilted. Pour turkey mixture into a lightly greased 13- x 9-inch baking dish.
4. Bake, covered, 30 minutes. Remove from oven, and arrange desired amount of Cranberry-Pecan Crusts over pie before serving. Serve with any remaining Cranberry-Pecan Crusts on the side.

Cranberry-Pecan Crusts

ACTIVE 15 MIN. - TOTAL 23 MIN.
MAKES 3 TO 4 DOZEN

- 1 (14.1-oz.) pkg. refrigerated piecrusts
- ½ cup finely chopped pecans, toasted
- ½ cup finely chopped sweetened dried cranberries

1. Preheat oven to 425°F. Unroll 1 piecrust on a lightly floured surface; sprinkle with pecans and cranberries; top with remaining piecrust. Roll into a 14-inch circle, sealing together piecrusts. Cut into desired shapes with a 2- to 3-inch cutter. Place pastry shapes on a lightly greased baking sheet.
2. Bake 8 to 10 minutes or until golden.

Honey-Curry Glazed Lamb with Roasted Grapes and Cranberries

ACTIVE 15 MIN. - TOTAL 1 HOUR, 30 MIN., INCLUDING GRAPES AND CRANBERRIES
SERVES 6

- 3 (8-rib) lamb rib roasts (1½ lb. each), trimmed
- 1 Tbsp. red curry powder
- 1½ tsp. kosher salt
- 1½ tsp. freshly ground black pepper
  Roasted Grapes and Cranberries (recipe follows)
- 5 Tbsp. olive oil, divided
- 2 Tbsp. honey

1. Preheat oven to 425°F. Sprinkle lamb on all sides with curry powder, kosher salt, and ground black pepper. Let stand 30 minutes.
2. Meanwhile, prepare Roasted Grapes and Cranberries.
3. Cook lamb in 1 tablespoon hot oil in a 12-inch cast-iron skillet over medium 6 to 7 minutes, turning often to brown tops and sides. Place roasts, meat sides up, in skillet. Stir together honey and remaining 4 tablespoons olive oil; brush mixture on tops and sides of lamb.
4. Bake 15 to 18 minutes or until a meat thermometer inserted into thickest portion registers 135°F. Remove from oven; let stand 10 minutes. Cut into chops. Serve with Roasted Grapes and Cranberries.

Roasted Grapes and Cranberries

ACTIVE 5 MIN. - TOTAL 20 MIN.
SERVES 6

- 6 to 8 seedless green or red grape clusters (about 1 lb.)
- 1 cup fresh cranberries
- 1 Tbsp. olive oil
- 1 tsp. chopped fresh rosemary

1. Preheat oven to 400°F. Place grape clusters on a 15- x 10-inch jelly-roll pan. Stir together cranberries, olive oil, and rosemary in a small bowl. Spoon mixture over grape clusters.
2. Bake 15 to 18 minutes or until grapes begin to blister and cranberry skins begin to split, shaking pan occasionally. Serve immediately, or let stand up to 4 hours.

Cornish Game Hens with Butternut Croutons

ACTIVE 30 MIN. - TOTAL 2 HOURS, 25 MIN., INCLUDING CROUTONS
SERVES 6

- Wooden picks
- 6 (1- to 1½-lb.) Cornish game hens, rinsed and patted dry
- 4½ tsp. salt, divided
- 2 tsp. freshly ground black pepper, divided
- 2 clementines, unpeeled and quartered
- 6 fresh sage leaves
- Kitchen string
- 3 Tbsp. butter, softened
- Butternut Croutons (recipe follows)

1. Preheat oven to 450°F. Soak wooden picks in water to cover 30 minutes.
2. Meanwhile, season each hen cavity with ½ teaspoon salt and ¼ teaspoon pepper, and insert 1 clementine quarter.
3. Loosen and lift skin from hen breasts with fingers, without totally detaching skin. Place 1 sage leaf under skin of each hen. Carefully replace skin, and secure using wooden picks. Tie ends of legs together with string; tuck wingtips under.
4. Arrange hens, tail to tail in 2 rows, on a jelly-roll pan. Rub hens with butter, and sprinkle with remaining 1½ teaspoon salt and ½ teaspoon pepper.
5. Bake 45 to 50 minutes or until golden brown and a meat thermometer inserted into thickest portion of thighs registers 165°F. Transfer hens to a serving platter, and cover loosely with heavy-duty aluminum foil. Let stand 5 minutes before serving. Serve with warm Butternut Croutons.

Butternut Croutons

ACTIVE 35 MIN. - TOTAL 1 HOUR, 5 MIN.
SERVES 6

- 3 cups (¾-inch) cubed fresh peasant-style bread
- 1½ lb. butternut squash, peeled and cut into ½-inch pieces (about 4 cups)
- 10 shallots, quartered (about 9 to 10 oz.)
- 1½ Tbsp. dark brown sugar
- 3 Tbsp. olive oil
- 1½ tsp. salt
- ¾ tsp. freshly ground white pepper
- 2 Tbsp. chopped fresh sage

1. Preheat oven to 400°F. Bake bread cubes on a baking sheet 10 to 12 minutes or until lightly browned and toasted. Let cool. Increase oven temperature to 450°F.
2. Mound squash and shallots in center of a lightly greased jelly-roll pan. Whisk together sugar and next 3 ingredients in a small bowl. Pour over squash and shallots, and toss to coat. Spread vegetables in a single layer in jelly-roll pan, using 2 pans if necessary.
3. Bake 20 minutes or until tender, stirring halfway through. Toss warm squash mixture with croutons and sage in a bowl.

Spice-Rubbed Smoked Turkey Breast with Mushroom Gravy

ACTIVE 25 MIN. - TOTAL 6 HOURS, 51 MIN., INCLUDING GRAVY
SERVES 8

- Hickory wood chunks
- 2 Tbsp. mayonnaise
- 2 Tbsp. Creole mustard
- 1 tsp. Worcestershire sauce
- 1 (5- to 6-lb.) bone-in turkey breast
- 2 Tbsp. brown sugar
- 1½ tsp. paprika
- 1 tsp. kosher salt
- ¾ tsp. garlic powder
- ½ tsp. celery salt
- ½ tsp. ground cumin
- ½ tsp. freshly ground black pepper
- ¼ tsp. onion powder
- 3 Tbsp. butter, melted
- ¼ cup apple butter
- 1 Tbsp. honey
- Mushroom Gravy (recipe follows)

1. Soak hickory wood chunks in water 30 minutes. Prepare smoker according to manufacturer's directions, bringing internal temperature to 225°F to 250°F; maintain temperature for 15 to 20 minutes. Drain wood chunks, and place on coals. Add water to pan to depth of fill line.
2. Combine mayonnaise, Creole mustard, and Worcestershire sauce; rub evenly over turkey breast. Combine brown sugar and next 7 ingredients; sprinkle evenly over turkey, pressing to adhere.
3. Place turkey on upper cooking grate; cover with smoker lid. Smoke 3½ hours, maintaining smoker temperature between 225°F and 250°F.
4. Stir together butter, apple butter, and honey. Baste turkey with half of butter mixture.
5. Cover and cook 1½ more hours or until a meat thermometer inserted in thickest portion registers 165°F, basting with remaining butter mixture during last 30 minutes. Remove turkey from smoker, and let stand 15 minutes before slicing. Serve with Mushroom Gravy.

Mushroom Gravy

ACTIVE 26 MIN. - TOTAL 26 MIN.
SERVES 10 TO 12

- 2 Tbsp. butter
- 1 (8-oz.) pkg. sliced baby portobello mushrooms
- ¼ cup dry sherry
- 2 Tbsp. all-purpose flour
- 2 cups vegetable broth
- ½ cup whipping cream
- 2 tsp. chopped fresh thyme
- ½ tsp. salt
- ½ tsp. freshly ground black pepper

1. Melt butter in a large skillet over medium-high. Add mushrooms; saute 5 to 6 minutes or until tender. Stir in sherry, and cook 1 minute or until liquid almost evaporates. Stir in flour, and cook, stirring constantly, 1 minute. Gradually stir in broth. Bring to a boil; reduce heat, and simmer, stirring constantly, 5 minutes or until slightly thickened.
2. Stir in cream. Simmer 8 minutes, stirring constantly, or until thickened. Remove from heat, and stir in thyme, salt, and pepper.

Classic Lasagna

ACTIVE 31 MIN. · TOTAL 2 HOURS, 30 MIN.
SERVES 8 TO 10

    Italian Meat Sauce (recipe follows)
12 lasagna noodles
8 cups boiling water
1 Tbsp. olive oil
1 (16-oz.) container ricotta cheese
2 large eggs, lightly beaten
¼ cup grated Parmesan cheese
¼ tsp. salt
¼ tsp. black pepper
18 thin part-skim mozzarella cheese
    slices, divided

1. Prepare Italian Meat Sauce. Meanwhile, place noodles in a 13- x- 9-inch pan. Carefully pour 8 cups boiling water and olive oil over noodles. Let stand 15 minutes; drain and pat dry. Stir together ricotta cheese and next 4 ingredients.
2. Preheat oven to 350°F. Discard bay leaf from sauce. Spoon 2 cups sauce into a lightly greased 13- x 9-inch baking dish. Arrange one-third of noodles over sauce; top with about ¾ cup ricotta mixture and 6 mozzarella cheese slices. Repeat layers twice.
3. Bake, covered, 55 minutes. Uncover and bake 15 minutes or until bubbly. Let stand 10 minutes.

Italian Meat Sauce

ACTIVE 15 MIN. · TOTAL 1 HOUR
SERVES 10

2 medium onions, chopped
1 Tbsp. olive oil
4 garlic cloves, minced
1 lb. lean ground beef
1 (14.5-oz.) can basil, garlic, and
    oregano diced tomatoes
2 (6-oz.) cans tomato paste
1 (8-oz.) can basil, garlic, and
    oregano tomato sauce
1 bay leaf
1 tsp. dried Italian seasoning
1 tsp. salt
½ tsp. black pepper

Saute onions in hot oil in a 3-quart skillet over medium-high 5 minutes or until tender. Add garlic; saute 1 minute. Add beef; cook, stirring occasionally, 10 minutes or until beef crumbles and is no longer pink. Stir in remaining ingredients, and bring to a boil. Cover, reduce heat, and simmer, stirring occasionally, 30 minutes.

Pecan-and-Dill-Crusted Salmon

ACTIVE 10 MIN. · TOTAL 30 MIN.
SERVES 10 TO 12

1½ cups pecan halves
6 Tbsp. butter, melted
2 garlic cloves, minced
1½ tsp. dried dill weed
1 (3- to 3½-lb.) boneless, skinless
    side of salmon
1¼ tsp. kosher salt
½ tsp. freshly ground black pepper

Preheat oven to 400°F. Pulse first 4 ingredients in a food processor 5 or 6 times or until mixture resembles coarse crumbs. Sprinkle salmon with salt and pepper; place on a parchment paper-lined baking sheet. Spread pecan mixture over salmon. Bake 18 to 20 minutes or just until salmon flakes with a fork.

Spicy Fruit-Stuffed Pork Loin with Roasted Pears and Onions

ACTIVE 1 HOUR · TOTAL 2 HOURS, 20 MIN.
SERVES 8 TO 10

PORK LOIN
2 (7-oz.) pkg. mixed dried fruit bits
2 Tbsp. dark brown sugar
1 Tbsp. chopped fresh sage
¼ tsp. dried crushed red pepper
1 (4-lb.) boneless pork loin
1½ tsp. kosher salt, divided
1½ tsp. coarsely ground black pepper,
    divided
2 Tbsp. olive oil
ROASTED PEARS AND ONIONS
6 firm, ripe Seckel pears*
2 Tbsp. butter, melted
2 tsp. fresh lemon juice
2 tsp. honey**
¼ tsp. finely chopped fresh rosemary
¼ tsp. kosher salt
¼ tsp. freshly ground pepper
2 (10-oz.) packages cipollini onions,
    peeled
GLAZE
½ cup pear preserves

1. Prepare Pork Loin: Bring first 4 ingredients and 1 cup water to a boil in a small saucepan over medium-high. Cook 2 minutes, stirring once. Remove from heat; cool completely (about 40 minutes).

2. Meanwhile, butterfly pork by making a lengthwise cut down center of 1 flat side, cutting to within ½ inch of other side. (Do not cut all the way through pork.) Open pork, forming a rectangle; place between 2 sheets of heavy-duty plastic wrap. Flatten to ½-inch thickness using a meat mallet or rolling pin. Sprinkle with ½ teaspoon each salt and pepper.
3. Spoon fruit mixture over pork, leaving a ½-inch border around edges. Roll up pork, jelly-roll fashion, starting at 1 long side. Tie with string at 1½-inch intervals. Sprinkle with remaining 1 teaspoon salt and 1 teaspoon pepper.
4. Preheat oven to 375°. Brown pork in hot oil in a large roasting pan over medium-high until browned on all sides (about 2 to 3 minutes per side). Place, seam side down, in pan.
5. Prepare Roasted Pears and Onions: Cut pears in half lengthwise, and remove cores. Stir together butter and next 5 ingredients. Stir in onions; gently stir in pear halves. Spoon mixture around roast in pan.
6. Bake 1 hour to 1 hour and 5 minutes or until a meat thermometer inserted into thickest portion of stuffing registers 135°F, stirring pear mixture halfway through. Cover with aluminum foil, and let stand 15 minutes.
7. Prepare Glaze: Microwave preserves in a microwave-safe bowl at HIGH 1 minute or until thoroughly heated. Pour warm preserves over pork. Slice pork, and serve with Roasted Pears and Onions and pan juices. Garnish, if desired.
*****Note:** 3 firm, ripe Bartlett pears may be substituted. Core each pear, and cut into 4 wedges.
****** Note:** Sugar may be substituted.

Herb-and-Potato Chip-Crusted Beef Tenderloin

ACTIVE 40 MIN. · TOTAL 2 HOURS, 20 MIN.
SERVES 6 TO 8

1 (4- to 5-lb.) beef tenderloin,
    trimmed
3 tsp. kosher salt, divided
¾ cup panko (Japanese breadcrumbs)
3 garlic cloves, pressed
2 tsp. coarsely ground black pepper,
    divided
3 Tbsp. olive oil, divided
1¼ cups crushed, plain kettle-cooked
    potato chips
¼ cup finely chopped fresh parsley

1 Tbsp. finely chopped fresh thyme
1 bay leaf, crushed
1 egg white, lightly beaten
1 Tbsp. Dijon mustard
   Garnish: Fresh sage (optional)

1. Preheat oven to 400°F. Sprinkle tenderloin with 2 teaspoons salt. Let stand 30 to 45 minutes.
2. Meanwhile, saute panko, garlic, 1 teaspoon pepper, and remaining 1 teaspoon salt in 1 tablespoon hot oil in a skillet over medium 2 to 3 minutes or until deep golden brown. Let cool completely (about 10 minutes). Stir in potato chips and next 4 ingredients.
3. Pat tenderloin dry with paper towels, and sprinkle with remaining 1 teaspoon pepper. Brown beef in remaining 2 tablespoons hot oil in a roasting pan over medium-high heat until browned on all sides (about 2 to 3 minutes per side). Transfer tenderloin to a wire rack in an aluminum foil-lined jelly-roll pan. Let stand 10 minutes.
4. Spread mustard over tenderloin. Press panko mixture onto top and sides.
5. Bake 40 to 45 minutes or until coating is crisp and a meat thermometer inserted into thickest portion registers 130°F (rare). Let stand 10 minutes. Garnish, if desired.
Note: For medium-rare, cook tenderloin to 135°F; for medium, cook to 150°F.

Stuffed Beef Tenderloin

Stuffed beef tenderloin pairs well with a classic Béarnaise sauce for the perfect sumptuous holiday meal.

ACTIVE 30 MIN. - TOTAL 1 HOUR, 15 MIN.
SERVES 12

BEEF
1 lb. fresh Swiss chard, stemmed and chopped
2 Tbsp. olive oil
2 garlic cloves, minced
½ tsp. kosher salt, divided
¼ tsp. freshly ground black pepper, divided
1 Tbsp. butter
2 (4-oz.) pkg. exotic blend mushrooms, chopped
1 (5-lb.) beef tenderloin, trimmed
RUB
1 Tbsp. kosher salt
1 Tbsp. fennel seeds, toasted and crushed

STUFFED BEEF TENDERLOIN

1 Tbsp. chopped fresh rosemary
1 Tbsp. freshly ground black pepper
5 garlic cloves, pressed
1 Tbsp. olive oil

1. Prepare Beef: Preheat oven to 500°F. Cook Swiss chard in hot oil in a large nonstick skillet over medium-high, stirring constantly, until chard begins to wilt. Cook 1 minute or until wilted. Add minced garlic, ¼ teaspoon of the salt, and ⅛ teaspoon of the pepper; saute 1 minute. Transfer to a bowl; let stand until cool enough to handle.
2. Gently squeeze moisture from chard.
3. Melt butter in skillet over medium-high. Add mushrooms and remaining salt and pepper. Cook, stirring occasionally, 8 minutes or until browned. Stir into chard.
4. Butterfly beef by making a lengthwise cut in 1 side, but not through the opposite side (leave about ½ inch); unfold. Flatten to a uniform thickness (about ¾ inch), using a rolling pin or flat side of a meat mallet. Sprinkle with salt and pepper. Spoon chard mixture down center of beef, leaving a ¼-inch border. Fold beef over chard, and tie with kitchen string at 2-inch intervals. Place beef, seam side down, on a lightly greased rimmed baking pan.
5. Prepare Rub: Stir together kosher salt and next 4 ingredients in a small bowl. Stir in oil to form a paste. Rub mixture over beef.
6. Bake 10 minutes. Reduce oven temperature to 350°F. Bake 25 minutes or until a meat thermometer inserted into thickest portion of tenderloin registers 130°F (rare). Let stand 15 minutes before slicing.

Béarnaise Sauce

Classic Béarnaise Sauce is emulsified in the blender for an easy yet elegant sauce to accompany roasted beef tenderloin. If your Béarnaise is too thick, gradually whisk in very hot water, 1 teaspoon at a time, until desired consistency is reached.

ACTIVE 15 MIN. TOTAL 15 MIN.
MAKES 1¼ CUPS

¼ cup Champagne vinegar
¼ cup dry white wine
2 Tbsp. minced shallots
2 Tbsp. chopped fresh tarragon, divided
1 cup butter
3 large egg yolks
¼ tsp. salt
¼ tsp. freshly ground black pepper
1 tsp. fresh lemon juice (optional)

1. Combine first 3 ingredients and 1 tablespoon of the tarragon in a small saucepan. Bring to a simmer over medium-high, and cook 3 minutes or until reduced to 2 tablespoons. Pour through a fine-mesh strainer into a blender. Discard solids. Let cool slightly.
2. Meanwhile, microwave butter in a microwave-safe bowl at HIGH 1 minute or until melted.
3. Place egg yolks in blender, and process until smooth. With blender running, add hot butter in a slow, steady stream, processing until smooth. Add salt, pepper, 1 tablespoon hot water, and, if desired, lemon juice. Process until blended.
4. Transfer to a bowl, and stir in remaining 1 tablespoon tarragon. Store at room temperature until ready to use (up to 1 hour).

Perfect Beef Tenderloin

ACTIVE 10 MIN. - TOTAL 50 MIN.
SERVES 12 TO 14

- 1 (5- to 7-lb.) beef tenderloin, trimmed
- 3 Tbsp. butter, softened
- 5 to 7 tsp. kosher salt
- ¾ tsp. cracked black pepper

1. Preheat oven to 425°F. Place beef on a wire rack in a jelly-roll pan. Rub butter over beef, and sprinkle with salt and pepper.
2. Bake 25 to 35 minutes or until a meat thermometer inserted into thickest portion registers 135°F (medium-rare). Cover loosely with aluminum foil; let stand 15 minutes before slicing.

Smoked Pork Tenderloins with Sherry-Mushroom Sauce

ACTIVE 50 MIN. - TOTAL 11 HOURS, INCLUDING 8 HOURS CHILLING
SERVES 6

PORK
- 2 pork tenderloins (about 2 lbs.)

BRINE
- 2 Tbsp. kosher salt
- 3 garlic cloves, peeled and smashed
- 5 black peppercorns, cracked
- 2 thyme sprigs
- 3 cups apple cider, divided

RUB
- 2 Tbsp. dry mustard
- ½ Tbsp. onion powder
- ½ Tbsp. garlic powder
- ½ Tbsp. ground coriander
- 1 tsp. black pepper

- 3 large applewood chunks, soaked in water to cover 1 hour

SAUCE
- 2 Tbsp. olive oil
- 1 lb. sliced cremini mushrooms
- ⅔ cup dry sherry
- 1 Tbsp. chopped fresh thyme leaves
- ½ tsp. kosher salt
- ¼ tsp. black pepper
- 3 Tbsp. heavy cream
- 2 Tbsp. chopped fresh flat-leaf parsley

1. Prepare the Pork: Remove pork tenderloins from wrapper; rinse and pat dry. Place on work surface, and trim any silver skin. Trim small, thinner ends, leaving tenderloin pieces that are uniform in thickness from end to end.
2. Prepare the Brine: Stir together salt, garlic cloves, peppercorns, thyme sprigs, and 1½ cups apple cider in a medium saucepan over medium. Warm gently, stirring just until salt is dissolved, about 3 minutes. Remove from heat, and stir in remaining 1½ cups apple cider. Remove and reserve ¼ cup of the brine liquid.
3. Place tenderloins in a zip-top plastic bag, and pour remaining brine with solids into bag, making sure all pieces of pork are submerged. Seal bag, and chill 8 hours or overnight. Remove pork from brine; rinse with cold water, and pat dry. Discard brine. Tie tenderloins at intervals with kitchen twine so they are round and of even thickness from end to end.
4. Prepare the Rub: Stir together dry mustard, onion powder, garlic powder, ground coriander, and pepper in a small bowl. Rub mixture evenly over pork, and let stand at room temperature 30 minutes.
5. Prepare smoker according to manufacturer's instructions, bringing internal temperature to 225°F; maintain temperature 20 minutes. Smoke tenderloins on the top rack of the smoker 1 hour, maintaining smoker temperature at 225°F and basting pork twice with reserved ¼ cup brine. Add soaked applewood chunks to the wood reservoir. Continue to smoke pork until a thermometer registers 140°F to 142°F when inserted in thickest portion of pork, about 1 more hour, maintaining internal temperature at 225°F and basting pork twice with reserved brine. Remove pork from smoker, and let stand 10 minutes before removing twine and slicing.
6. While pork cooks, prepare the Sauce: Heat oil in a large skillet over medium-high; add mushrooms, and cook, stirring occasionally, until mushrooms are tender and liquid has completely evaporated, about 12 minutes. Stir in sherry, thyme, salt, and pepper; simmer until sherry has reduced by half, about 6 minutes. Stir in heavy cream, and cook until sauce has thickened slightly, 2 to 3 minutes. Remove from heat, and stir in parsley. Serve with pork.

Salads

Turkey Salad with Cranberry Dressing

ACTIVE 20 MIN. - TOTAL 35 MIN.
SERVES 8

- 2 Tbsp. butter, melted
- ½ tsp. dried Italian seasoning
- 4 medium-size dinner rolls, cut into 2-inch cubes (about 2 cups)
- 1 (5.5-oz.) pkg. spring greens mix
- 1 small head romaine lettuce, chopped
- 2 cups coarsely chopped turkey or ham
- ½ English cucumber, thinly sliced
- ½ cup balsamic vinegar
- ½ cup canola oil
- ¼ cup whole-berry cranberry sauce
- 2 Tbsp. Dijon mustard
- 2 garlic cloves, minced
- ¼ tsp. salt
- ¼ tsp. black pepper

1. Preheat oven to 425°F. Stir together first 2 ingredients in a bowl. Add bread cubes; toss to coat. Bake cubes in a single layer in a jelly-roll pan 3 to 5 minutes or until golden, stirring once. Cool completely on a wire rack (about 15 minutes).
2. Combine spring greens, next 3 ingredients, and toasted bread cubes in a serving bowl. Process vinegar and next 6 ingredients in a blender until smooth. Serve with salad.

Bing Cherry Salad

ACTIVE 12 MIN. - TOTAL 9 HOURS, 50 MIN., INCLUDING 9 HOURS, 30 MIN. CHILLING
SERVES 8

- 1 (15-oz.) can Bing cherries (dark, sweet pitted cherries)
- 2 (8-oz.) cans crushed pineapple in juice
- 1 (6-oz.) pkg. cherry-flavored gelatin
- 1 cup cold water
  Mayonnaise (optional)
  Garnishes: poppy seeds, arugula leaves (optional)

1. Drain cherries and pineapple, reserving 1½ cups juice in a saucepan. (If necessary, add water to equal 1½ cups.) Bring juice

mixture to a boil over medium heat; stir in gelatin, and cook, stirring constantly, 2 minutes or until gelatin dissolves. Remove from heat, and stir in 1 cup cold water. Chill until consistency of unbeaten egg whites (about 1½ hours).
2. Gently stir in drained cherries and pineapple. Pour mixture into an 8-inch square baking dish or 8 (²⁄₃-cup) molds. Cover and chill 8 hours or until firm. Dollop with mayonnaise, and garnish, if desired.

Basil-And-Blue Cheese Salad

It's ideal to slice pears and avocados at the last minute so they won't turn brown. But you can do this one hour ahead—just toss in a small amount of lemon juice. Too much will alter the flavor of the vinaigrette.

ACTIVE 20 MIN. - TOTAL 20 MIN.
SERVES 10 TO 12

- ⅓ cup olive oil
- ⅓ cup seasoned rice vinegar
- 1 tsp. country-style Dijon mustard
- ½ tsp. salt
- ¼ tsp. dried crushed red pepper
- 10 cups mixed salad greens
- ½ cup firmly packed fresh basil leaves, coarsely chopped
- 2 ripe pears, thinly sliced
- 2 fresh navel oranges, sectioned
- 2 avocados, sliced
- 1 (4-oz.) package blue cheese, crumbled

1. Whisk together first 5 ingredients. Cover and chill until ready to use (up to 24 hours).
2. Toss together greens and basil. Top with pears, oranges, avocados, and blue cheese; toss. Drizzle with vinaigrette. Serve immediately.

Bacon-Mandarin Salad

Wash the lettuces the night before. Wrap the leaves in a damp paper towel, and chill in zip-top plastic bags. Cook the bacon, and toast the almonds ahead too. Assemble and dress the salad right before serving.

ACTIVE 15 MIN. - TOTAL 33 MIN.
SERVES 12

- ½ cup olive oil
- ¼ cup red wine vinegar
- ¼ cup sugar
- 1 Tbsp. chopped fresh basil

- ⅛ tsp. hot sauce
- 2 (15-oz.) cans mandarin oranges, drained and chilled*
- 1 bunch red leaf lettuce, torn
- 1 head romaine lettuce, torn
- 1 (16-oz.) pkg. bacon, cooked and crumbled
- 1 (4-oz.) pkg. sliced almonds, toasted

Whisk together first 5 ingredients in a large bowl, blending well. Add oranges and lettuces, tossing gently to coat. Sprinkle with crumbled bacon and sliced almonds. Serve immediately.
*Note: Fresh orange segments can be substituted for canned mandarin oranges, if desired.

Spinach Salad with Apricot Vinaigrette

This light and colorful salad is sweet, sour, and full of veggies. To serve salad for dinner, top it with grilled chicken or tuna.

ACTIVE 10 MIN. - TOTAL 10 MIN.
SERVES 6

- 2 (6-oz.) pkg. fresh baby spinach
- 1 pink grape tomatoes, halved
- 1 small red onion, thinly sliced
- ½ cup chopped dried apricots
- 1 ripe avocado, peeled and diced
- ½ cup chopped pecans, toasted Apricot Vinaigrette (recipe follows)

Place first 6 ingredients in a large bowl, tossing gently. Drizzle with Apricot Vinaigrette, tossing gently to coat.

Apricot Vinaigrette

ACTIVE 3 MIN. - TOTAL 5 MIN.
MAKES ½ CUP

- ⅓ cup vegetable oil
- 2 Tbsp. white wine vinegar
- 2 Tbsp. orange juice
- 2 Tbsp. apricot jam
- ½ tsp. salt
- ½ tsp. ground coriander
- ½ tsp. freshly ground black pepper

Whisk together all ingredients in a small bowl.

Sides

Perfect Green Beans

As the name of this recipe states, these beans are PERFECT every time.

ACTIVE 3 MIN. - TOTAL 5 MIN.
SERVES 4 TO 6

- 1 lb. fresh green beans
- ⅛ tsp. salt
- ½ tsp. black pepper

Cook beans in boiling salted water to cover 3 to 5 minutes or until crisp-tender; drain and sprinkle with freshly-ground black pepper.

Sweet Onion Pudding

ACTIVE 1 HOUR - TOTAL 1 HOUR, 30 MIN.
SERVES 6 TO 8

- 6 large eggs
- 2 cups whipping cream
- 1 (3-oz.) pkg. shredded Parmesan cheese
- 3 Tbsp. all-purpose flour
- 2 Tbsp. sugar
- 2 tsp. baking powder
- 1 tsp. salt
- ½ cup butter
- 6 medium-size sweet onions, thinly sliced

1. Preheat oven to 350°F. Stir together first 3 ingredients in a large bowl, blending well. Combine flour and next 3 ingredients. Gradually stir into egg mixture.
2. Melt butter in a large skillet over medium. Add onions, and cook 30 to 40 minutes or until caramel colored, stirring often. Remove skillet from heat.
3. Stir onions into egg mixture; spoon onto a lightly greased 13- x 9-inch or 3-quart baking dish.
4. Bake 30 minutes or until set.

Baked Smokin' Macaroni and Cheese

ACTIVE 25 MIN. - TOTAL 1 HOUR
SERVES 8

- 1 lb. uncooked cellentani (corkscrew) pasta
- 2 Tbsp. butter
- ¼ cup all-purpose flour
- 3 cups fat-free milk
- 1 (12-oz.) can fat-free evaporated milk
- 1 cup (4 oz.) shredded smoked Gouda cheese
- ½ cup (2 oz.) shredded 1.5% reduced-fat sharp Cheddar cheese
- 3 oz. fat-free cream cheese, softened
- ½ tsp. salt
- ¼ tsp. ground red pepper, divided
- 1 (8-oz.) package chopped smoked ham
  Vegetable cooking spray
- 1¼ cups cornflakes cereal, crushed
- 1 Tbsp. butter, melted

1. Preheat oven to 350°F. Prepare cellentani pasta according to package directions.
2. Meanwhile, melt 2 tablespoons butter in a Dutch oven over medium. Gradually whisk in flour; cook, whisking constantly, 1 minute. Gradually whisk in milk and evaporated milk until smooth; cook, whisking constantly, 8 to 10 minutes or until slightly thickened. Whisk in Gouda cheese, next 3 ingredients, and ⅛ teaspoon ground red pepper until smooth. Remove from heat, and stir in ham and pasta.
3. Pour pasta mixture into a 13- x 9-inch baking dish coated with cooking spray. Stir together crushed cereal, 1 tablespoon melted butter, and remaining ⅛ teaspoon ground red pepper; sprinkle over pasta mixture.
4. Bake 30 minutes or until golden and bubbly. Let stand 5 minutes before serving.
Pepper Jack Macaroni and Cheese: Substitute 1½ cups 1.5% reduced-fat pepper Jack cheese for Gouda and Cheddar cheeses. Omit ground red pepper, if desired. Stir 1 (4.5-oz.) can chopped green chiles into pasta mixture.
Sweet Pea-and-Prosciutto Macaroni and Cheese: Omit ham. Saute 2 oz. thin prosciutto slices, cut into thin strips, in a small skillet over medium-high 2 minutes or until slightly browned. Stir prosciutto and 1 cup frozen sweet peas, thawed, into pasta mixture.

Pimiento Macaroni and Cheese: Substitute 1½ cups 2% reduced-fat sharp Cheddar cheese for Gouda and Cheddar cheeses. Stir 1 (4-oz.) jar diced pimiento, drained, into pasta mixture.

Butternut Squash Gratin

Slice the potatoes as you use them in each layer (rather than all at once) to help prevent oxidation.

ACTIVE 45 MIN. - TOTAL 3 HOURS, 30 MIN.
SERVES 8

- 1 (3-lb.) butternut squash
- 1 (3-lb.) spaghetti squash
- 2 Tbsp. butter, melted
- 1 cup firmly packed light brown sugar, divided
- ½ tsp. ground cinnamon
- ¼ tsp. ground nutmeg
- 3 cups whipping cream
- 5 large Yukon gold potatoes (about 2½ lb.), divided
- 1 tsp. salt, divided
- 1 tsp. freshly ground black pepper, divided
- 4 cups (16 oz.) freshly shredded Fontina cheese*, divided
  Garnish: fresh rosemary sprigs (optional

1. Preheat oven to 450°F. Cut butternut and spaghetti squash in half lengthwise; remove and discard seeds. Place squash, cut sides up, in a lightly greased 17- x 12-inch jelly-roll pan. Drizzle with butter, and sprinkle with ½ cup brown sugar. Bake 40 minutes or until tender. Cool 20 minutes.
2. Using a fork, scrape inside of spaghetti squash to remove strands, and place in a large bowl. Scoop pulp from butternut squash; coarsely chop pulp, and toss with spaghetti squash.
3. Stir together cinnamon, nutmeg, and remaining ½ cup brown sugar.
4. Cook cream in a heavy non-aluminum saucepan over medium, stirring often, 5 minutes or just until it begins to steam (do not boil); remove from heat.
5. Using a mandoline or sharp knife, cut potatoes into ⅛-inch-thick slices.
6. Arrange one-fourth of potato slices in a thin layer on bottom of a buttered 13- x 9-inch baking dish. Spoon one-third of squash mixture over potatoes (squash layer should be about ¼ inch thick); sprinkle with ¼ teaspoon salt,

¼ teaspoon pepper, 1 cup Fontina cheese, and ¾ cup hot cream. Repeat layers twice, sprinkling one-third of sugar mixture over each of second and third squash layers. (Do not sprinkle sugar mixture over first squash layer.) Top with remaining potato slices, ¼ teaspoon salt, and ¼ teaspoon pepper. Gently press layers down with back of a spoon. Sprinkle top with remaining 1 cup cheese and ¾ cup hot cream; sprinkle with remaining brown sugar mixture. Place baking dish on an aluminum foil-lined baking sheet.
7. Bake, covered with foil, 1 hour; uncover and bake 25 more minutes or until golden brown and potatoes are tender. Cool on a wire rack 20 minutes before serving. Garnish, if desired.
***Note:** Gouda cheese may be substituted.

Shrimp And Grits Dressing

ACTIVE 35 MIN. - TOTAL 1 HOUR, 50 MIN.
SERVES 6 TO 8

- 1 lb. peeled, medium-size raw shrimp
- 3 cups chicken broth
- ½ tsp. salt
- ¼ tsp. ground red pepper
- 1 cup uncooked regular grits
- ½ cup butter
- 3 large eggs, lightly beaten
- 1 red bell pepper, diced
- 1 cup fine dry breadcrumbs
- 1 cup chopped green onions
- ½ cup grated Parmesan cheese

1. Preheat oven to 325°F. Devein shrimp, if desired.
2. Bring broth and next 2 ingredients to a boil in a large saucepan over medium-high. Whisk in grits, and return to a boil; reduce heat to low, and stir in butter. Cover and simmer, stirring occasionally, 10 minutes or until liquid is absorbed. Remove from heat.
3. Stir together eggs and next 4 ingredients in a large bowl. Gradually stir about one-fourth of hot grits mixture into egg mixture; add egg mixture to remaining hot grits mixture, stirring constantly. Stir in shrimp until blended. Pour grits mixture into a lightly greased 11- x 7-inch baking dish.
4. Bake 55 minutes to 1 hour or until mixture is set. Let stand 10 minutes.

Classic Parmesan Scalloped Potatoes

This tasty dish will be the hit of any holiday gathering!

ACTIVE 20 MIN. - TOTAL 1 HOUR, 15 MIN.
SERVES 8 TO 10

- 2 lb. Yukon gold potatoes, peeled and thinly sliced
- 3 cups whipping cream
- ¼ cup chopped fresh flat-leaf parsley
- 2 garlic cloves, chopped
- 1½ tsp. salt
- ¼ tsp. freshly ground black pepper
- ⅓ cup grated Parmesan cheese

1. Preheat oven to 400°F. Layer potatoes in a 13- x 9-inch or 3-quart baking dish.
2. Stir together whipping cream and next 4 ingredients in a large bowl. Pour cream mixture over potatoes.
3. Bake 30 minutes, stirring gently every 10 minutes. Sprinkle with cheese; bake 15 to 20 minutes or until bubbly and golden brown. Let stand on a wire rack 10 minutes before serving.

Smoky Pimiento Cheese Deviled Eggs

ACTIVE 20 MIN. - TOTAL 35 MIN.
MAKES 2 DOZEN

- 12 large eggs
- ¼ cup mayonnaise
- ¾ cup freshly grated smoked or sharp Cheddar cheese
- ¼ cup finely chopped jarred roasted red bell pepper
- 1 Tbsp. Dijon mustard
  Pinch of ground red pepper
  Toppings: sliced green onions, diced country ham, sliced pickled okra, spiced pecans

1. Place eggs in a large stainless-steel saucepan (not nonstick). Add water to depth of 3 inches. Bring to a rolling boil; cook 1 minute. Cover, remove from heat, and let stand 10 minutes. Drain.
2. Place eggs under cold running water until cool enough to handle. Peel under cold running water. Cut eggs in half lengthwise; remove yolks. Reserve 6 yolks for another use.
3. Mash remaining 6 yolks with mayonnaise using a fork. Stir in cheese and next 3 ingredients. Season with salt and black pepper to taste. Spoon into egg whites. Serve with desired toppings.

Cornflake, Pecan, and Marshmallow-Topped Sweet Potato Casserole

For even better flavor, make this casserole the night before because the flavor gets better as the dish sits. Remember to put the topping on just before baking.

ACTIVE 20 MIN. - TOTAL 2 HOURS, 30 MIN.
SERVES 8

SWEET POTATO FILLING
- 2½ lb. sweet potatoes (about 5 medium)
- 2 Tbsp. butter, softened
- ½ cup firmly packed brown sugar
- ½ cup 2% reduced-fat milk
- 1 large egg
- ½ tsp. salt
- ½ tsp. vanilla extract
  Vegetable cooking spray
CORNFLAKE, PECAN, AND MARSHMALLOW TOPPING
- 1¼ cups cornflakes cereal, crushed
- ¼ chopped pecans
- 1 Tbsp. brown sugar
- 1 Tbsp. melted butter
- 1¼ cups miniature marshmallows

1. Prepare filling: Preheat oven to 400°F. Bake sweet potatoes on a baking sheet 1 hour or until tender. Reduce oven temperature to 350°F. Let potatoes stand until cool to touch (about 20 minutes); peel and mash with a potato masher.
2. Beat mashed sweet potatoes, 2 tablespoons softened butter, and next 5 ingredients at medium speed with an electric mixer until smooth. Spoon mixture into an 11- x 7-inch baking dish coated with cooking spray.
3. Prepare topping: Stir together crushed cornflakes cereal and next 3 ingredients. Sprinkle over sweet potato mixture in diagonal rows 2 inches apart.
4. Bake 30 minutes. Remove from oven; let stand 10 minutes. Sprinkle miniature marshmallows in alternate rows between cornflake mixture, and bake 10 more minutes.
To make ahead: Prepare recipe as directed through step 2. Cover and refrigerate up to 24 hours. Remove cover; let stand at room temperature 30 minutes. Proceed with recipe as directed in steps 3 and 4.

Crumb-Topped Spinach Casserole

ACTIVE 20 MIN. - TOTAL 50 MIN.
SERVES 8 TO 10

- 2 Tbsp. butter
- 1 medium onion, diced
- 2 garlic cloves, minced
- 4 (10-oz.) pkg. frozen chopped spinach, thawed
- ½ (8-oz.) pkg. cream cheese, softened
- 2 Tbsp. all-purpose flour
- 2 large eggs
- ½ tsp. table salt
- ¼ tsp. freshly ground black pepper
- 1 cup milk
- 1 (8-oz.) pkg. shredded Cheddar cheese
- 1 cup Italian-seasoned panko (Japanese breadcrumbs) or homemade breadcrumbs
- 3 Tbsp. butter, melted

1. Preheat oven to 350°F. Melt 2 tablespoons butter in a large nonstick skillet over medium. Add onion and garlic, and saute 8 minutes or until tender.
2. Meanwhile, drain spinach well, pressing between paper towels to remove excess moisture.
3. Combine cream cheese and flour in a large bowl until smooth. Whisk in eggs, salt, and pepper. Gradually whisk in milk until blended. Add sauteed onion mixture, spinach, and Cheddar, stirring to blend. Spoon into a lightly greased 11- x 7-inch baking dish.
4. Combine breadcrumbs and 3 tablespoons melted butter in a small bowl; toss well, and sprinkle over casserole.
5. Bake, uncovered, 30 to 35 minutes or until thoroughly heated and breadcrumbs are browned.

CORNBREAD
DRESSING CAKES

Cornbread Dressing Cakes

ACTIVE 40 MIN. - TOTAL 1 HOUR 40 MIN.,
INCLUDING CORNBREAD
MAKES 24 CAKES

  Cornbread, crumbled
    (recipe follows)
 1 cup soft, fresh breadcrumbs
 4 ears fresh corn
 2 Tbsp. butter
 2 medium-size sweet onions, diced
 2 celery ribs, diced
 3 large eggs, lightly beaten
 1 cup mayonnaise
 ½ cup chopped fresh parsley
 ¼ cup chopped fresh sage
 2 tsp. seasoned pepper
 1 tsp. garlic salt
 4½ Tbsp. vegetable oil, divided

1. Combine crumbled Cornbread and
breadcrumbs in a large bowl.
2. Cut corn kernels from cob.
3. Melt butter in a large nonstick skillet
over medium-high; add onions and celery,
and saute 5 minutes or until tender. Add
corn, and saute 5 minutes.
4. Stir together onion mixture, cornbread
mixture, eggs, and next 5 ingredients.
Shape mixture into 24 (3-inch) patties.
Cover and chill up to 8 hours, if desired.
5. Cook 8 patties in 1½ tablespoons hot
oil in a large nonstick skillet over medium
2 to 3 minutes on each side or until golden
brown. Repeat procedure with remaining
patties and oil.
6. Serve immediately, or remove to a wire
rack to cool. Garnish, if desired.
To make ahead: Prepare recipe as
directed through Step 5. Cover and chill
up to a day ahead, if desired. To reheat,
bake in a single layer on a baking sheet at
400°F 8 to 10 minutes or until thoroughly
heated. Garnish, if desired.

Cornbread

PREP: 10 MIN. - BAKE: 30 MIN.
MAKES 1 (13- X 9-INCH) PAN

 ½ cup butter
 2 cups white cornmeal mix
 2 cups buttermilk
 1 cup all-purpose flour
 2 Tbsp. sugar
 2 large eggs

1. Preheat oven to 425°F. Melt butter in a
13- x 9-inch pan in oven 5 minutes.
2. Stir together cornmeal mix and next
4 ingredients in a large bowl.
3. Tilt pan to coat with butter; pour butter
into cornmeal mixture, and stir until well
blended. Pour batter into hot pan.
4. Bake 30 minutes or until golden brown.

Roasted Garlic Mashed Potatoes

ACTIVE 15 MIN. - TOTAL 2 HOURS
SERVES 4 TO 6

 1 garlic bulb
 2½ lb. Yukon gold potatoes, peeled
    and cut into 2-inch pieces
    Cold water
 ½ cup whipping cream
 ⅓ cup sour cream
 ¼ cup butter, melted
 1¼ tsp. salt
 ½ tsp. black pepper

1. Preheat oven to 400°F. Cut off pointed
end of garlic; place garlic on a piece of
aluminum foil. Fold foil to seal.
2. Bake 1 hour. Let cool 10 minutes.
Squeeze pulp from garlic bulb.
3. Place potatoes in a large Dutch oven;
add water to cover. Bring to a boil; boil
25 minutes or until tender. Drain. Place

back in Dutch oven, and heat over low 3 to
5 minutes or until potatoes are dry.
4. Heat whipping cream in a small
saucepan over low 4 minutes or just
until warm; remove from heat, and stir in
sour cream.
5. Press potatoes through a ricer into
Dutch oven. Let stand 1 minute. Stir in
roasted garlic pulp, melted butter, salt,
and pepper until blended. Gradually stir
in warm whipping cream mixture, stirring
just until blended. Serve immediately.

Savory Bacon–and–Leek Bread Pudding

*We love how buttery Gouda and nutty
Parmesan lend richness and depth of flavor
to this dish.*

ACTIVE 40 MIN. - TOTAL 1 HOUR, 20 MIN.
SERVES 6 TO 8

 8 large eggs, lightly beaten
 1 cup half-and-half
 1 cup heavy cream
 2 tsp. kosher salt
 1 tsp. dried thyme
 1 tsp. dried marjoram
 1 tsp. freshly ground black pepper
 6 cups cubed challah bread (about
    1-inch cubes)
 1¼ cups grated Gouda cheese, divided
 1¼ cups freshly grated Parmesan
    cheese, divided
 2 leeks, thinly sliced
 2 Tbsp. butter
 2 garlic cloves, minced
 8 cooked bacon slices, crumbled

1. Preheat oven to 350°F. Whisk together
first 7 ingredients in a large bowl; stir in
bread cubes and 1 cup each Gouda and
Parmesan cheeses.
2. Remove and discard root ends and dark
green tops of leeks. Cut in half lengthwise,
and rinse thoroughly under cold running
water to remove grit and sand.
3. Melt butter in a medium skillet over
medium. Add leeks, and cook, stirring
occasionally, 7 to 8 minutes or until tender.
Add garlic, and cook, stirring constantly,
1 minute. Fold leek mixture and bacon
into egg mixture. Pour into a lightly
greased 11- × 7-inch baking dish. Sprinkle
with remaining ¼ cup each Gouda and
Parmesan cheeses.
4. Bake 35 to 40 minutes or until center is
set. Let stand 5 minutes.

Green Beans with Hollandaise Sauce

ACTIVE 15 MIN. - TOTAL 15 MIN.
SERVES 8

½ cup butter
4 large pasteurized egg yolks
2 Tbsp. fresh lemon juice
½ tsp. kosher salt
⅛ tsp. ground white pepper
Dash of hot sauce (optional)
1 lb. haricots verts (thin green beans), blanched or steamed

Melt butter in a small saucepan over medium; reduce heat to low, and keep warm. Process egg yolks, next 3 ingredients, 1 tablespoon water, and, if desired, hot sauce in a blender or food processor 2 to 3 minutes or until pale and fluffy. With blender running, add melted butter in a slow stream, processing until smooth. Serve warm with beans.

Perfect Mashed Potatoes

ACTIVE 22 MIN. - TOTAL 43 MIN.
MAKES ABOUT 6 CUPS

3 lb. Yukon gold potatoes
2 tsp. salt, divided
⅓ cup butter
⅓ cup half-and-half
4 oz. cream cheese, softened
¾ tsp. coarsely ground black pepper

1. Peel potatoes, and cut into 1-inch pieces. Bring potatoes, 1 teaspoon salt, and cold water to cover to a boil in a medium-size Dutch oven over medium-high. Reduce heat to medium-low, and cook 16 to 20 minutes or until fork-tender; drain.
2. Return potatoes to Dutch oven. Cook until water evaporates and potatoes look dry. Mound potatoes on 1 side; add butter, next 3 ingredients, and remaining 1 teaspoon salt to opposite side of Dutch oven. Cook 1 to 2 minutes or until butter is melted and mixture boils.
3. Beat until smooth. Remove from heat; beat at medium speed with a handheld electric mixer 30 seconds to 1 minute or to desired degree of smoothness. (Do not overbeat.) Serve immediately.

Make-Ahead Turkey Gravy

To make ahead: Cool gravy 45 minutes. Cover and chill up to 3 days. When ready to serve, add a few tablespoons of broth, and reheat over medium.

ACTIVE 37 MIN. - TOTAL 1 HOUR, 52 MIN.
MAKES 4 CUPS

2¼ lb. turkey drumsticks
3 carrots, cut into pieces
1 large onion, quartered
6 fresh parsley sprigs
⅓ cup vegetable oil
½ cup all-purpose flour
6 cups low-sodium chicken broth
½ tsp. black pepper
Salt to taste

1. Preheat oven to 400°F. Pat drumsticks dry. Cook drumsticks and next 3 ingredients in hot oil in a large roasting pan over medium-high. Cook drumsticks 3 minutes on each side; cook carrots, onion, and parsley at the same time, stirring often.
2. Bake drumsticks and carrot mixture in pan 30 minutes or until a meat thermometer inserted into thickest portion of drumsticks registers 160°F. Remove from oven. Remove and discard vegetables and parsley using a slotted spoon. Reserve drumsticks for another use.
3. Whisk flour into hot drippings in pan, and cook over medium, whisking constantly, 1 minute. Gradually whisk in chicken broth until mixture is smooth. Whisk in pepper.
4. Bring to a boil over medium-high, whisking occasionally. Reduce heat to medium, and gently boil, whisking occasionally, 45 minutes or until thick enough to coat the back of a spoon. Season with salt to taste.

Roasted Onions

ACTIVE 45 MIN. - TOTAL 1 HOUR, 15 MIN.
SERVES 8 TO 10

¼ cup firmly packed light brown sugar
¼ cup olive oil
¼ cup balsamic vinegar
½ tsp. salt
4 small red onions, quartered
1 lb. pearl onions
1 lb. cipollini onions
1 lb. shallots

1. Preheat oven to 450°F. Whisk together first 4 ingredients in a large bowl.
2. Toss red onions and next 3 ingredients with oil mixture. Arrange in a single layer on a lightly greased 17- x 12-inch jelly-roll pan. Bake 30 to 40 minutes or until tender and golden brown, stirring twice.

Wild Rice Salad

If you think the amount of rosemary in this recipe seems like overkill, just wait until you taste it.

ACTIVE 20 MIN. - TOTAL 1 HOUR, 10 MIN.
SERVES 6 TO 8

1½ cups long-grain brown rice
⅔ cup wild rice
½ cup pine nuts
3 (4-inch) rosemary sprigs
½ cup olive oil
Pinch of kosher salt
⅓ cup dried cranberries
2 Tbsp. sherry vinegar
1 tsp. kosher salt
¼ tsp. freshly ground black pepper
2 tsp. honey
3 scallions, finely sliced (about ½ cup)

1. Prepare brown rice and wild rice according to package directions.
2. Meanwhile, heat pine nuts in a small skillet over medium-low, stirring often, until toasted and fragrant. Remove from skillet.
3. Cook rosemary in hot oil in skillet over medium 1 minute, turning with tongs halfway through. Transfer to a paper towel-lined plate to drain, and sprinkle with a pinch of kosher salt. Let oil cool. Reserve ¼ cup oil.
4. Combine cranberries and next 3 ingredients in a small bowl. Let stand 15 minutes. Whisk in honey and reserved ¼ cup rosemary oil.
5. Combine brown rice, wild rice, pine nuts, and scallions in a large bowl. Crush fried rosemary, and sprinkle over rice mixture. Add cranberry mixture, and toss to combine.
6. Let salad cool 30 minutes before serving, or cover with plastic wrap and chill up to 1 day. Let chilled salad stand at room temperature 15 minutes before serving.
Tip: Test the readiness of the oil with 1 rosemary leaf (needle). It should start to sizzle. If not, wait a few seconds and test again.

Smoky Cranberry–Apple Sauce

ACTIVE 25 MIN. - TOTAL 25 HOURS, 3 MIN., INCLUDING 24 HOURS CHILLING

MAKES 3½ CUPS

- 1 (12-oz.) pkg. fresh cranberries
- 1 cup sugar
- ¾ cup apple juice
- ¼ cup minced red onion
- 2 Tbsp. butter
- 2 Granny Smith apples, peeled and coarsely chopped
- ½ cup smoky barbecue sauce
  Garnish: Fresh parsley sprigs (optional)

1. Stir together cranberries and next 4 ingredients in a medium saucepan. Bring to a boil over medium-high; reduce the heat to low, and simmer, stirring occasionally, 10 minutes or until cranberry skins begin to split and pop and mixture begins to thicken.

2. Stir apples and barbecue sauce into cranberry mixture, and simmer 5 minutes or just until apples are tender. Let cool 30 minutes. Cover and chill 24 hours before serving. Store in refrigerator up to 3 days. Let stand 30 minutes before serving. Garnish, if desired.

Fennel–Potato Gratin

ACTIVE 45 MIN. - TOTAL 1 HOUR, 45 MIN.

SERVES 12

- 2 Tbsp. butter
- 1 Tbsp. olive oil
- 2 fennel bulbs (about 2¼ lb.), halved and thinly sliced crosswise (about ⅛ inch thick)
- 1 tsp. kosher salt, divided
- ½ tsp. freshly ground black pepper, divided
- ⅓ cup dry white wine
- 2½ lbs. Yukon gold potatoes, peeled and cut into ⅛-inch-thick slices
- 3 garlic cloves, minced
- 3 cups heavy cream
- 2 cups (8 oz.) shredded Comté cheese

1. Preheat oven to 350°F. Melt butter with oil in a large skillet over medium. Add fennel, ½ teaspoon of the salt, and ¼ teaspoon of the pepper. Cook, stirring occasionally, 2 minutes. Add wine; cover, reduce heat to medium-low, and cook, stirring occasionally, 20 minutes or until fennel is tender.

2. Increase heat to medium-high, and cook, uncovered and stirring often, 7 to 8 minutes or until fennel is lightly browned.

3. Bring potatoes, garlic, cream, and remaining ½ teaspoon salt and ¼ teaspoon pepper to a low simmer in a Dutch oven over medium-high. Cover, reduce heat to medium-low, and simmer 10 minutes or until potatoes are almost tender.

4. Place one-third of potatoes in an even layer in a lightly greased 3-quart baking dish, using a slotted spoon. Sprinkle with ⅔ cup cheese. Top with half of fennel. Repeat layers once. Top with remaining potatoes and ⅔ cup cheese. Pour remaining cream mixture over top. Cover with aluminum foil.

5. Bake 20 minutes. Uncover and bake 30 to 35 minutes or until bubbly and golden brown. Let stand 10 minutes.

Roasted Heirloom Root Vegetables in Lemon–Horseradish Butter

Roasting brings out the natural sweetness and earthiness of these beautiful root vegetables and is one of the easiest methods of cooking.

ACTIVE 20 MIN. - TOTAL 5 HOURS, 35 MIN., INCLUDING 4 HOURS CHILLING

SERVES 12

- 1 cup butter, softened
- 1 Tbsp. chopped fresh thyme
- 1 Tbsp. chopped fresh flat-leaf parsley
- 2 to 3 Tbsp. freshly grated horseradish
- 1 tsp. lemon zest
- 2 Tbsp. fresh lemon juice
- 2 lbs. Chioggia beets, trimmed (about 6 medium)
- 2 lbs. golden beets, trimmed (about 5 medium)
- 3 (6-oz.) pkg. fresh baby rainbow carrots, cut into 1-inch pieces
- 1 lb. parsnips, cut into ¾-inch-thick slices
- 3 Tbsp. extra-virgin olive oil

1. Mash together first 6 ingredients in a medium bowl, using a fork.

2. Place butter mixture on a large piece of parchment or wax paper. Bring 1 side of paper over mixture. Hold down other end of paper. Place flat edge of a baking sheet or other sturdy flat object next to butter on paper. Using your other hand, hold end of baking sheet, and push bottom of baking sheet away from you into base of butter mixture, forming a 1½-inch-wide log. Chill 4 hours.

3. Meanwhile, preheat oven to 425°F. Cut all beets into ¾- to 1-inch wedges, if needed, for uniform pieces. Toss together beets, carrots, and next 2 ingredients in a large bowl. Season lightly with desired amount of kosher salt and freshly ground black pepper, and toss. Place in a single layer on 2 large baking sheets, leaving space between vegetables.

4. Bake 1 hour and 15 minutes to 1½ hours or until tender and golden brown, stirring every 20 minutes.

5. Transfer roasted vegetables to a large bowl. Add ¼ cup butter mixture. Toss until well coated. Serve immediately with remaining butter mixture.

Lemon Broccolini

ACTIVE 20 MIN. - TOTAL 20 MIN.

SERVES 6 TO 8

- 1 cup (½-inch) French bread baguette cubes
- 2 Tbsp. butter
- 1 garlic clove, pressed
- 2 Tbsp. chopped fresh flat-leaf parsley
- 2 tsp. lemon zest
- 1½ lb. fresh Broccolini
- 2 Tbsp. fresh lemon juice
- 1 Tbsp. olive oil
  Salt and freshly ground black pepper to taste

1. Process bread in a food processor 30 seconds to 1 minute or until coarsely crumbled.

2. Melt butter with garlic in a large skillet over medium; add breadcrumbs, and cook, stirring constantly, 2 to 3 minutes or until golden brown. Remove from heat, and stir in parsley and lemon zest.

3. Cook Broccolini in boiling salted water to cover 3 to 4 minutes or until crisp-tender; drain well. Toss Broccolini with lemon juice, olive oil, and salt and pepper. Transfer to a platter; sprinkle with breadcrumb mixture.

Soups

Pecan Soup

This velvety, rich appetizer is like chestnut soup with Southern flair.

ACTIVE 36 MIN. - TOTAL 1 HOUR, 6 MIN.
MAKES 13 CUPS

- ½ cup butter
- 3 celery ribs, coarsely chopped
- 2 sweet onions, chopped
- 1 large baking potato, peeled and coarsely chopped
- 4 cups chicken broth
- 3 cups heavy cream
- 1 tsp. salt
- ½ tsp. ground white pepper
- 1 lb. toasted pecan halves
  Garnishes: crème fraîche, chopped chives, additional toasted pecan halves (optional)

1. Melt butter in a Dutch oven over medium; add celery and onion. Sauté 20 minutes or until tender.
2. Add potato, chicken broth, and next 4 ingredients. Bring to a boil; reduce heat to medium-low, and simmer, uncovered, 30 minutes or until slightly thickened and potato is very tender. Remove from heat; cool slightly.
3. Process soup mixture, in batches, in a blender until smooth, stopping to scrape down sides as needed. Ladle into serving bowls. Serve hot with desired garnishes.

Tortilla Turkey Soup

ACTIVE 30 MIN. - TOTAL 40 MIN.
MAKES 8 CUPS

- 10 (6-inch) fajita-size corn tortillas, cut into ½-inch-wide strips
  Vegetable cooking spray
- 1 small onion, chopped
- 2 garlic cloves, chopped
- 1 small jalapeño pepper, seeded and minced
- 1 Tbsp. olive oil
- 1 (32-oz.) container chicken broth
- 1 (10-oz.) can enchilada sauce
- 2 cups chopped cooked turkey
- 1 tsp. ground cumin
  Toppings: chopped avocado, shredded sharp Cheddar cheese, chopped fresh cilantro, chopped tomatoes

1. Preheat oven to 450°F. Place half of tortilla strips in a single layer on a baking sheet. Coat strips with cooking spray, and bake 10 minutes or until strips are browned and crisp, stirring once.
2. Saute chopped onion and next 2 ingredients in hot olive oil in a Dutch oven over medium-high 5 to 6 minutes or until browned.
3. Add chicken broth and remaining unbaked tortilla strips to onion mixture. Cook broth mixture over medium 3 to 5 minutes or until tortilla strips soften and broth mixture thickens slightly.
4. Stir in enchilada sauce and next 2 ingredients, and cook 6 to 8 minutes or until mixture is thoroughly heated. (Do not boil.) Serve with baked tortilla strips and desired toppings.

Sausage-Tortellini Soup

ACTIVE 38 MIN. - TOTAL 1 HOUR
MAKES 4 QUARTS

- 1½ lb. hot Italian sausage, casings removed*
- 1 medium onion, diced
- 3 garlic cloves, minced
- 2 (15-oz.) cans Italian-style stewed tomatoes
- 1 (16-oz.) pkg. frozen cut green beans
- 1 (8-oz.) pkg. sliced fresh mushrooms
- 1 (8-oz.) can tomato sauce
- 4 beef bouillon cubes
- 3 carrots, sliced
- 3 medium zucchini, quartered and sliced
- 1 cup dry red wine
- 2 tsp. dried Italian seasoning
- 1 (20-oz.) pkg. refrigerated cheese-filled tortellini
  Freshly grated Parmesan cheese

1. Saute sausage, onion, and garlic in a Dutch oven over medium 8 minutes or until sausage crumbles and is no longer pink; drain. Stir in tomatoes, next 8 ingredients, and 10 cups water; bring to a boil. Cover, reduce heat to low, and cook 20 minutes or until carrots are crisp-tender.
2. Cook tortellini according to package directions; drain. Stir into soup just before serving. Serve with Parmesan cheese.
*Note: 1 lb. turkey Italian sausage may be substituted.

Tomato Bisque

ACTIVE 15 MIN. - TOTAL 45 MIN.
MAKES ABOUT 2 QUARTS

- 3 (14.5-oz.) cans good-quality diced tomatoes
- 2 large onions, diced (about 2 cups)
- 2 garlic cloves, minced
- 2 bay leaves
- 4 Tbsp. tomato paste
- 3 Tbsp. fresh brewed coffee
- 1 Tbsp. jarred beef soup base
- 1 tsp. jarred chicken soup base
- 2 fresh flat-leaf parsley sprigs
- 1½ tsp. dried thyme
- ½ cup heavy cream
- 2 tsp. fresh lemon juice
- 1½ tsp. kosher salt
- ½ tsp. black pepper
  Garnishes: whipped cream, golden caviar, fresh parsley or chive sprigs (optional)

1. Bring first 10 ingredients and 5 cups water to a boil in a large stockpot over high. Reduce heat to medium-high; simmer, stirring occasionally, 20 minutes or until reduced by one-fourth. Cool 15 minutes.
2. Process with a handheld blender until smooth. Stir in the heavy cream, fresh lemon juice, kosher salt, and black pepper. Garnish as desired. Serve immediately.
Note: Refrigerate in an airtight container up to 4 days, or freeze up to 8 weeks. Reheat over medium until soup simmers. (Do not boil.)

PECAN SOUP

Baking at High Altitudes

Liquids boil at lower temperatures (below 212°F), and moisture evaporates more quickly at high altitudes. Both of these factors significantly impact the quality of baked goods. Also, leavening gases (air, carbon dioxide, water vapor) expand faster. If you live at 3,000 feet or below, first try a recipe as is. Sometimes few, if any, changes are needed. But the higher you go, the more you'll have to adjust your ingredients and cooking times.

A Few Overall Tips

- Use shiny new baking pans. This seems to help mixtures rise, especially cake batters.
- Use butter, flour, and parchment paper to prep your baking pans for nonstick cooking. At high altitudes, baked goods tend to stick more to pans.
- Be exact in your measurements (once you've figured out what they should be). This is always important in baking, but especially so when you're up so high. Tiny variations in ingredients make a bigger difference at high altitudes than at sea level.
- Boost flavor. Seasonings and extracts tend to be more muted at higher altitudes, so increase them slightly.
- Have patience. You may have to bake your favorite sea-level recipe a few times, making slight adjustments each time, until it's worked out to suit your particular altitude.

Ingredient/Temperature Adjustments

CHANGE	AT 3,000 FEET	AT 5,000 FEET	AT 7,000 FEET
Baking powder or baking soda	Reduce each tsp. called for by up to ⅛ tsp.	Reduce each tsp. called for by ⅛ to ¼ tsp.	Reduce each tsp. called for by ¼ to ½ tsp.
Sugar	Reduce each cup called for by up to 1 Tbsp.	Reduce each cup called for by up to 2 Tbsp.	Reduce each cup called for by 2 to 3 Tbsp.
Liquid	Increase each cup called for by up to 2 Tbsp.	Increase each cup called for by 2 to 4 Tbsp.	Increase each cup called for by up to 3 to 4 Tbsp.
Oven temperature	Increase 3° to 5°	Increase 15°	Increase 21° to 25°

Metric Equivalents

The recipes that appear in this cookbook use the standard United States method for measuring liquid and dry or solid ingredients (teaspoons, tablespoons, and cups). The information on this chart is provided to help cooks outside the U.S. successfully use these recipes. All equivalents are approximate.

METRIC EQUIVALENTS FOR DIFFERENT TYPES OF INGREDIENTS

A standard cup measure of a dry or solid ingredient will vary in weight depending on the type of ingredient. A standard cup of liquid is the same volume for any type of liquid. Use the following chart when converting standard cup measures to grams (weight) or milliliters (volume).

Standard Cup	Fine Powder (ex. flour)	Grain (ex. rice)	Granular (ex. sugar)	Liquid Solids (ex. butter)	Liquid (ex. milk)
1	140 g	150 g	190 g	200 g	240 ml
¾	105 g	113 g	143 g	150 g	180 ml
⅔	93 g	100 g	125 g	133 g	160 ml
½	70 g	75 g	95 g	100 g	120 ml
⅓	47 g	50 g	63 g	67 g	80 ml
¼	35 g	38 g	48 g	50 g	60 ml
⅛	18 g	19 g	24 g	25 g	30 ml

USEFUL EQUIVALENTS FOR DRY INGREDIENTS BY WEIGHT
(To convert ounces to grams, multiply the number of ounces by 30.)

1 oz.	=	1/16 lb.	=	30 g
4 oz.	=	¼ lb.	=	120 g
8 oz.	=	½ lb.	=	240 g
12 oz.	=	¾ lb.	=	360 g
16 oz.	=	1 lb.	=	480 g

USEFUL EQUIVALENTS FOR LENGTH
(To convert inches to centimeters, multiply the number of inches by 2.5.)

1 in.				=	2.5 cm		
6 in.	=	½ ft.		=	15 cm		
12 in.	=	1 ft.		=	30 cm		
36 in.	=	3 ft.	= 1 yd.	=	90 cm		
40 in.				=	100 cm	=	1 m

USEFUL EQUIVALENTS FOR LIQUID INGREDIENTS BY VOLUME

¼ tsp.						=	1 ml		
½ tsp.						=	2 ml		
1 tsp.						=	5 ml		
3 tsp.	=	1 Tbsp.		=	½ fl oz.	=	15 ml		
		2 Tbsp.	= ⅛ cup	=	1 fl oz.	=	30 ml		
		4 Tbsp.	= ¼ cup	=	2 fl oz.	=	60 ml		
		5⅓ Tbsp.	= ⅓ cup	=	3 fl oz.	=	80 ml		
		8 Tbsp.	= ½ cup	=	4 fl oz.	=	120 ml		
		10⅔ Tbsp.	= ⅔ cup	=	5 fl oz.	=	160 ml		
		12 Tbsp.	= ¾ cup	=	6 fl oz.	=	180 ml		
		16 Tbsp.	= 1 cup	=	8 fl oz.	=	240 ml		
1 pt.	=	2 cups	=	16 fl oz.	=	480 ml		
1 qt.	=	4 cups	=	32 fl oz.	=	960 ml		
				33 fl oz.	=	1000 ml	=	1 l

USEFUL EQUIVALENTS FOR COOKING/OVEN TEMPERATURES

	Fahrenheit	Celsius	Gas Mark
Freeze Water	32° F	0° C	
Room Temperature	68° F	20° C	
Boil Water	212° F	100° C	
Bake	325° F	160° C	3
	350° F	180° C	4
	375° F	190° C	5
	400° F	200° C	6
	425° F	220° C	7
	450° F	230° C	8
Broil			Grill

Recipe Title Index

This index alphabetically lists every recipe by exact title

A

Aïoli, 301
All-Purpose Red Onions, 160
Ambrosia Macaroons, 287
"Any-Berry" Muffins with Cornmeal
        Streusel, 155
Apple-Ale Wassail, 324
Apple Brown Betty, 260
Apple-Gingerbread Cobbler, 328
Apricot Vinaigrette, 343
Asparagus-and-Goat Cheese
        Quiche, 72

B

Bacon-Cheddar Dutch Baby, 211
Bacon Deviled Eggs, 204
Bacon-Mandarin Salad, 343
Bacon with Ranch Drizzle, 139
Baked Apple-Cranberry-Pecan
        Oatmeal, 231
Baked Brie with Honeyed Five-Spice
        Pecans, 257
Baked Chicken Wings with Pepper
        Jelly Glaze, 204
Baked Goat Cheese Spread with
        Pepper Jelly, 270
Baked Ham with Brown Sugar-Citrus
        Glaze, 281
Baked Mini Pumpkin-Pecan
        Doughnuts, 223
Baked Smokin' Macaroni and
        Cheese, 344
Bananas Foster Sauce, 328
Basil-and-Blue Cheese Salad, 343
Basil Butter, 122
Basil Butter with Parmesan, 139
Basil Fried Rice with Butter Peas, 117
Basil Oil, 122
Basil Shrimp Scampi, 104
Basil Simple Syrup, 122
Basil Sugar, 122
Basil Vinaigrette, 323
Basmati Rice, 201
BBQ-Glazed Cedar-Plank Salmon, 135
Béarnaise Sauce, 341
Beef-and-Vegetable Soup with
        Gnocchi, 225
Beef Tenderloin Crostini, 272
Beefy Butternut Squash Pasta, 225
Beer-Cheese Fondue, 273
Best-Ever Sticky Buns, 326

Bing Cherry Salad, 342
Black-and-Blue Buttermilk Tart, 141
Black-Eyed Pea Cakes, 322
Brandy Alexander Cheesecake, 331
Broccoli Dressing, 260
Brown Butter-Caramel Blondies, 48
Brown Sugar Bread Pudding with Rich
        Bourbon Sauce, 333
Brown Sugar Cookie Stars, 292
Brussels Sprouts Slaw with Pecans
        and Pomegranate Seeds, 277
Buttered Rum Glaze, 328
Buttered Rum Pound Cake with
        Bananas Foster Sauce, 328
Buttermilk Spoon Bread, 252
Butter Muffins, 326
Butter-Pecan Granola, 334
Butternut Croutons, 339
Butternut Squash Gratin, 344
Butternut Squash Soup, 260
Butternut Squash Triangles, 304
Buttery Chive-and-Mustard Drop
        Biscuits, 37
Buttery Toasted Pecans, 322

C

Cacio e Pepe Puffs, 304
Candy Cane Cake Bars, 288
Candy Roaster Squash with
        Sorghum, Black Walnuts, and
        Cranberries, 242
Cappuccino Swirl Bars, 46
Carrot-and-Fennel Salad, 31
Cauliflower with Cheese Sauce, 31
Charred Onion Dip, 134
Charred Potato-Okra Salad, 135
Charred Tomatillo-Avocado Salsa, 142
Cheerwine Cherry Cupcakes with
        Cherry-Swirl Frosting, 149
Cheese-and-Carrot Mashed
        Potatoes, 336
Cheese Sauce, 31
Cheesy Beef-and-Spinach Ravioli, 69
Cheesy Garlic-Herb-and-Ham
        Bites, 304
Cheesy Mushroom Tartlets, 272
Cheesy Sheet Pan Pasta, 54
Cherry Frost, 324
Cherry-Pecan Brie, 322
Cherry-Swirl Frosting, 149
Chestnut Stuffing, 266

Chicken-and-Cornbread Casserole, 336
Chicken-Mushroom Skillet, 230
Chicken Salad-Stuffed Tomatoes, 154
Chicken-Tortellini Salad with Basil
        Vinaigrette, 140
Chipotle Cheese Straws, 270
Chocolate Bundt Cake, 64
Chocolate-Buttermilk Cake
        with Swiss Meringue
        Buttercream, 295
Chocolate-Coconut Pavlova Cake, 91
Chocolate-Covered Cherry Pie, 330
Chocolate-Pecan Biscotti Thins, 292
Chocolate-Pecan Phyllo Turnovers, 258
Chocolate-Peppermint Candy
        Cupcakes, 332
Chocolate-Praline Thumbprints, 288
Chocolate Velvet Cake Batter, 332
Chocolate-Zucchini Cake, 114
Chopped Salad with Buttermilk
        Dressing, 132
Cinnamon Whipped Cream, 227
Citrus-Grilled Turkey Breast, 337
Classic Boiled Peanuts, 215
Classic Eggnog, 324
Classic Grilled Corn, 139
Classic Lasagna, 340
Classic Parmesan Scalloped
        Potatoes, 345
Clementine-and-Collard Salad, 38
Clementine Whiskey Sour, 218
Coca-Cola Layer Cake with Fudgy
        Cola Frosting, 146
Coconut-Buttermilk Sauce, 199
Coconut Filling, 330
Colby-Pepper Jack Cheese Dip, 323
Collard Greens with Garlic and
        Sippets, 242
Company Quiche, 86
Corn Custards with Berry Compote, 114
Cornbread, 346
Cornbread Dressing, 260
Cornbread Dressing Cakes, 346
Cornflake, Pecan, and Marshmallow-
        Topped Sweet Potato
        Casserole, 345
Cornish Game Hens with Butternut
        Croutons, 339
Cranberry-Apple Pie, 328
Cranberry-Apple Pie Filling, 329
Cranberry-Orange Butter Cookies, 293

Cranberry-Pecan Chicken Salad, 335
Cranberry-Pecan Coffee Cake, 303
Cranberry-Pecan Crusts, 338
Cranberry Sangría Punch, 324
Cranberry-Turkey Panini, 338
Cream Cheese Cookie Wreaths, 287
Creamed Greens with Garlic
    Breadcrumbs, 277
Creamed Spinach-Stuffed
    Mushrooms, 275
Creamy Baked Macaroni and Cheese
    with Bacon, 244
Creamy Cheddar-Potato Soup with
    Bacon, 71
Creamy Chicken-and-Rice Soup with
    Collard Greens, 32
Creamy Chicken Spaghetti, 107
Creamy Egg Strata, 327
Creamy Feta Phyllo Bites, 273
Creamy Peach Icebox Cake, 158
Creamy Pesto-and-Shrimp Penne
    with Peas, 153
Creamy Southwest Black-Eyed Pea
    Dip, 57
Creamy Whipped-Potato
    Casserole, 278
Creole Deep-Fried Turkey, 337
Crescent Rolls, 325
Crispy Catfish Tacos with Slaw, 51
Crispy Chicken-and-Broccoli Salad, 157
Crispy Fried Turkey with Creole
    Spices, 235
Crumb-Topped Spinach Casserole, 345
Crunch-Top Apple Pie, 261
Crunch Topping, 261
Curried Chicken Pot Pie, 208

D

Dark Chocolate-Ginger-Molasses
    Cookies, 289
Diner-Style Patty Melts, 226
Dinner Mac and Cheese, 336
Dipped Pistachio Shortbread, 287
Dr Pepper Texas Sheet Cake, 147
Dry-Brined Beer-Can Chickens, 131
Dulce de Leche-Cheesecake Pecan
    Pie, 238

E

Easy Steak Fajitas, 151

F

Favorite Southern Cornbread, 261
Favorite Strawberry Shortcakes, 109
Fennel-Crusted Rib Roast, 337
Fennel-Potato Gratin, 348
Field Greens, Crumbled Blue Cheese,
    and Spicy Pecans, 262
Field Pea Cakes with Tomato-Ginger
    Jam, 99

Field Pea-Tomato Salad with Lemon
    Vinaigrette, 100
Field Peas, Corn, and Okra in
    Country-Ham Cream, 100
Field Peas in Herbed Broth, 99
5-Cup Cream Cheese Frosting, 332
Five-Spice Almonds, 80
Fluffy Corn Pudding, 249
Foil-Pack Clams with White Wine and
    Herbs, 133
Fondant Snowflakes, 329
Four-Layer Coconut Cake, 330
Fresh Cranberry Congealed Salad, 262
Fried Arkansas Black Apples , 245
Fried Red Quinoa, 80
Fruit-and-Nut Turkey Salad, 268
Fudge Truffle-Pecan Tart, 331
Fudgy Cola Frosting, 147

G

Garlic Butter-Roasted Shrimp
    Cocktail, 323
Garlic-Butter Shrimp, 203
Giblet Gravy, 266
Gingery Carrots with Pistachios and
    Coconut-Buttermilk Sauce, 199
Golden Curry Turkey Salad, 268
Grapefruit Cheesecake, 41
Grated Sweet Potato Pudding with
    Pecans, 250
Greek Stuffed Peppers, 208
Green Bean Casserole with Fried
    Leeks, 262
Green Beans with Hollandaise
    Sauce, 347
Green Chile-Chicken Soup, 207
Green Tomato Skillet Pie, 113
Grilled Chicken with Quick-Pickled
    Squash Salad, 118
Grilled Garlic Bread, 133
Grilled Oysters, 218
Grilled Salmon Panzanella Salad, 151
Grilled Steak Salad with Potatoes and
    Pickled Red Onion, 120
Grilled Sweet Potato Fries, 131

H

Ham-and-Vegetable Cobbler, 337
Hazelnut Financiers with Strawberry
    Jam and Lemon Puree, 79
Heirloom Tomato Pie with Parmesan-
    Buttermilk Crust, 136
Herb-and-Potato Chip-Crusted Beef
    Tenderloin, 340
Herbed Turkey, 263
Herby Pecan-Cornbread Dressing, 257
Holiday Cranberry Salad, 263
Holiday Herb Butter, 334
Homemade All-Purpose Biscuit,
    Pancake, and Waffle Mix, 327

Homemade Waffles, 327
Honey-Chipotle Glaze, 139
Honey-Curry Glazed Lamb with Roasted
    Grapes and Cranberries, 338
Honey-Mustard Salmon
    and Vegetables, 90
Hot-Buttered-Rum Bread Pudding, 285
Hot Pepper Vinegar, 218
Hot Spiced Tea, 222
Hot Spiced Wine, 324
Hot-Water Cornbread, 263
Huevos Rancheros Bake, 84
Hurry-Up Homemade Cornbread
    Yeast Rolls, 325

I

Instant Pot Beef-and-Barley Soup
    with Mushrooms, 34
Italian Meat Sauce, 340
Italian Parmesan Herb Mix, 334
Ivy's Best-Ever Brownies, 302

J

Jambalaya Skewers, 105
Johnnycakes with Leeks and Collard
    Greens, 219

L

Leek-and-Mushroom Grits Frittata, 69
Lemon Broccolini, 348
Lemon-Coconut Chess Bars, 48
Lemon-Garlic Butter Shrimp and
    Broccoli, 53
Lemon-Lime Cream Cheese
    Frosting, 146
Lemon-Lime Meringue Pie, 31
Lemon-Poppy Seed Cakes, 333
Lemon-Vanilla Buttercream, 64
Lemony Potato-and-Beet Salad with
    Dill, 81
Lentil Soup with Sweet Potatoes and
    Bacon, 36
Lime Sea Salt, 335
Lump Crab Mornay, 322

M

Magnolia or Camellia Cake
    Toppers, 296
Make-Ahead Turkey Gravy, 347
Mama's Rum Cake, 96
Marinated Olives and Peppadews, 270
Marinated Watermelon-and-Tomato
    Salad, 126
Master Pickling Brine, 160
Melting Sweet Potatoes with
    Walnuts, 278
Merry Margarita Mix Pineapple Craft
    Cocktail, 335
Meyer Lemon-Ginger Mignonette, 218
Millionaire's Candied Bacon, 323

Mini Bananas Foster Sticky Buns, 39
Mini Confetti Cakes, 61
Mini Crab Cakes with Cajun
          Sauce, 270
Mint Sauce, 264
Mixed Herb-and-Tomato Salad, 133
Mrs. Billett's White Cake, 329
Mushroom Gravy, 339

N

"Naked" Lemon Cake with a Flower
          Crown, 61
Nehi Orange Poke Cake, 148
Next-Day Turkey Bake, 338

O

Old-Fashioned Apple Pie, 195
Old-Fashioned Trifle, 283
One-Dish Blackberry French
          Toast, 327
One-Pan Hot Honey Chicken and
          Rice, 205
Orange-Buttermilk Trifle, 220
Orange-Sweet Potato Pie with
          Rosemary-Cornmeal
          Crust, 334
Orange-Vanilla French Toast
          Casserole with Bourbon-Maple
          Syrup, 85
Oven-Fried Pork Chops with Sweet
          Potatoes and Green Beans, 52
Oven-Fried Zucchini Sticks, 132
Oyster Stew, 219

P

Pan-Roasted Okra and Sweet Onions
          with Lemony Masala, 201
Parmesan-Buttermilk Crust, 136
Parmesan Cheese Bites, 323
Parmesan Cheese Squares, 323
Parmesan Grits Triangles with
          Pesto, 275
Pasta with Summer Beans and
          Bacon, 119
Pastry, 261
Peach-Ricotta-Prosciutto Toasts, 135
Peanut Butter Bonbons, 335
Peanut Butter-Fudge Bars, 45
Pear-Cranberry Pie with Ginger-
          Almond Streusel, 239
Pecan-and-Dill-Crusted Salmon, 340
Pecan Soup, 349
Pepper Jack Macaroni and Cheese, 344
Pepper Jelly-Glazed Baby Turnips, 83
Peppered Turkey Breast, 264
Peppermint Cookie Truffles, 288
Perfect Beef Tenderloin, 342
Perfect Green Beans, 343
Perfect Mashed Potatoes, 347
Perky Cranberry Punch, 324

Persimmon Pudding, 227
Pickled Onions, 201
Pickled Shrimp and Citrus Endive
          Cups, 273
Pickle-and-Dill Turkey Salad, 268
Pico de Gallo Pork Chops, 117
Pimiento Macaroni and Cheese, 344
Pomegranate-Chess Tart, 238
Pork Paillards with Lemony Squash
          Salad, 108
Pralines, 299
Praline Sauce, 264
Prime Rib with Herbes de Provence
          Crust and Red Wine Sauce, 281
Pumpkin Chess Pie, 264

Q

Quick Mississippi Pot Roast, 229
Quick Shrimp-and-Corn
          Chowder, 106

R

Rajma (Punjabi Red Beans), 198
Raspberry-Almond Crumble Bars, 48
Red Velvet Layer Cake, 332
Refrigerator Yeast Rolls, 265
Reindeer Gingersnaps, 335
Rich Bourbon Sauce, 333
Roast Leg of Lamb, 264
Roast Turkey and Gravy, 265
Roast Turkey with Chestnut
          Stuffing, 265
Roasted Baby Turnips with Turnip
          Green Pesto, 83
Roasted Beef Tenderloin, 28
Roasted Carrots with Spiced Pecans
          and Sorghum, 83
Roasted Chicken with Apples and
          Herbs, 282
Roasted Garlic Mashed Potatoes, 346
Roasted Granny Smith Apple Pie, 241
Roasted Grapes and Cranberries, 339
Roasted Heirloom Root Vegetables
          in Lemon-Horseradish
          Butter, 348
Roasted Onions, 347
Roasted Oysters with Bacon-Saltine
          Topping, 275
Roasted Root Vegetables with Spicy
          Pecan Topping, 258
Roasted Tomato-Cheddar Soup, 33
Root Vegetable-and-Butternut Squash
          Gratin, 279
Rosemary-Bacon Nut Mix, 272
Rosemary Chicken Thighs and
          Vegetables, 66
Rose Petal Cupcakes, 64
Rose-Vanilla Buttercream, 64
Royal Icing, 292

S

Salmon with Lemony Greens and
          Grains, 66
Salted Butter-Pecan Shortbread
          Cookies, 228
Salted Caramel-Apple Hand Pies, 223
Salty Chocolate-Pecan Candy, 335
Sausage-and-Shrimp Pizzas with
          Spinach-Basil Pesto, 132
Sausage-Cornbread Dressing, 266
Sausage, Egg, and Cheddar Biscuit
          Sandwiches, 121
Sausage-Hashbrown Casserole, 87
Sausage-Tortellini Soup, 349
Sautéed Radishes with Bacon and
          Cilantro, 83
Savory Bacon-and-Leek Bread
          Pudding, 346
Scalloped Oysters, 250
Sea Island Crab Fried Rice, 246
Sea Salt-Poppy Seed Cloverleaf
          Rolls, 326
7UP Bundt Cake, 146
Shaved Carrot, Asparagus, and Apple
          Salad, 83
Sheet Pan Chicken with Dressing, 50
Shepherd's Pie, 336
Shrimp-and-Bacon Stir-Fry, 103
Shrimp and Grits Casserole, 88
Shrimp and Grits Dressing, 344
Shrimp-and-Sausage Skillet Corn, 119
Shrimp Cakes with Smoky
          Horseradish Sauce, 103
Shrimp Fajita Bowls, 207
Shrimp-Stuffed Mirlitons, 249
Simple Mashed Rutabagas and
          Potatoes, 245
Simple Raita, 201
Skillet Chicken with Beans and
          Greens, 56
Skillet Pot Pie with Chicken and
          Spring Vegetables, 89
Skillet Turkey Meatballs, 210
Skillet Vegetable Pie with Goat
          Cheese, 40
Slow-Cooker Winter Vegetable Soup
          with Bacon, 55
Smashed Bacon Cheeseburgers, 134
Smoked-Pork-Stuffed Shells, 209
Smoked Pork Tenderloins with
          Sherry-Mushroom Sauce, 342
Smoked Sausage Pretzel Bites, 273
Smoked Turkey-and-Andouille
          Gumbo, 25
Smoky Barbecue Rub, 139
Smoky Cranberry-Apple Sauce, 348
Smoky Field Pea-and-Greens
          Dip, 101
Smoky Grilled BLTs, 152
Smoky Kimchi Pimiento Cheese, 202

Smoky Pimiento Cheese Deviled
    Eggs, 345
Smoky Split Pea-and-Sausage Soup, 35
Sorghum-Pecan Monkey Bread
    Muffins, 257
Sour Cream Pocketbook Rolls, 325
Sparkling Caramel-Apple Sangría, 222
Speedy Skillet Beef and Broccoli, 224
Spiced Coconut-Pumpkin Pie, 237
Spiced Pecan Pie Bars, 45
Spice-Rubbed Smoked Turkey Breast
    with Mushroom Gravy, 339
Spicy Butter, 301
Spicy Cornbread Dressing
    with Chorizo, 247
Spicy Fruit-Stuffed Pork Loin
    with Roasted Pears
    and Onions, 340
Spicy Green and Yellow Beans, 160
Spicy Pecans, 262
Spicy Pepper Jelly Coleslaw, 131
Spicy Shrimp with Jalapeño
    Cornbread and Aïoli, 301
Spicy-Sweet Refrigerator Pickles, 134
Spiked Eggnog Bundt, 284
Spinach Salad with Apricot
    Vinaigrette, 343
Spinach-Sausage Turnovers, 322
Spring Shrimp-and-Orzo Salad with
    Lemon Dressing, 70
Sprinkle Sandwich Cookies, 292
Squash Casserole, 266
Strawberry Buttercream Frosting, 330
Strawberry Gelato with Almond
    Shortbread and Elderflower
    Crème, 79
Strawberry-Rhubarb Crisps with
    Sweet-and-Savory Granola, 80
Stuffed Beef Tenderloin, 341
Sugar-and-Spice Rugelach, 289
Sugared Lemon-Lime Zest, 146
Sweet-and-Salty Autumn Snack
    Mix, 222
Sweet-and-Spicy Meatballs, 272
Sweetened Whipped Cream, 64
Sweet Hot Honey Mustard, 334
Sweet Onion Pudding, 343
Sweet Pea-and-Prosciutto Macaroni
    and Cheese, 344
Sweet Potato Casserole, 267
Sweet Potato Casserole with
    Marshmallows, 267
Sweet Potato Rolls with Cane Syrup
    Glaze, 254
Swiss Meringue Buttercream, 295

T
Tiramisú Toffee Trifle Pie, 331
Toasted Israeli Couscous and
    Shrimp, 65

Tomato-Basil Couscous with Chicken
    and Smoked Sausage, 156
Tomato Bisque, 349
Tomato-Ginger Jam, 99
Tortellini Caprese Bites, 323
Tortilla Turkey Soup, 349
Triple-Decker Strawberry Cake, 330
Turkey, Brie, and Fig
    Pressed Sandwiches, 223
Turkey Pot Pie with Cranberry-Pecan
    Crusts, 338
Turkey Salad, 268
Turkey Salad with Cranberry
    Dressing, 342
Turmeric-Dill Onions, 160
Tuscan Cherry Tomatoes, 160

U
Ultimate Dark Chocolate Brownies, 46

V
Vanilla Buttercream, 64
Vanilla Buttercream, 292
Vanilla Buttercream Frosting, 329
Vanilla Buttercream Frosting, 332
Vanilla Layer Cake with a Flower
    Cuff, 64
Vidalia Onion-and-Vinegar Sauce, 29

W
Walter's Favorite Pecan Pie, 267
Watermelon Chiffon Pie, 128
Watermelon-Ginger Mojitos, 127
White Chocolate-Buttermilk
    Cake, 220
White Chocolate-Raspberry
    Cheesecake Bars, 333
White Sangria Fizz, 325
Wild Rice Salad, 347
Wood-Fired Root Vegetables with
    Charred Scallion Aïoli, 219

Y
Yellow Squash Bundt Cake, 113

Z
Zesty Okra, 160

Month-by-Month Index

This index alphabetically lists every food article and accompanying recipes by month

January

A Matter of Taste, 26
Carrot-and-Fennel Salad, 31
Cauliflower with Cheese Sauce, 31
Cheese Sauce, 31
Lemon-Lime Meringue Pie, 31
Roasted Beef Tenderloin, 28
Vidalia Onion-and-Vinegar Sauce, 29
Award-Winning Gumbo, 24
Smoked Turkey-and-Andouille
Gumbo, 25
Bananas for Sticky Buns, 39
Mini Bananas Foster Sticky Buns, 39
Go for the Greens, 38
Clementine-and-Collard Salad, 38
Just Add Sunshine, 41
Grapefruit Cheesecake, 41
SL Cooking School, 42
Tastes Like Comfort, 32
Buttery Chive-and-Mustard Drop
Biscuits, 37
Creamy Chicken-and-Rice Soup
with Collard Greens, 32
Instant Pot Beef-and-Barley Soup
with Mushrooms, 34
Lentil Soup with Sweet Potatoes and
Bacon, 36
Roasted Tomato-Cheddar Soup, 33
Smoky Split Pea-and-Sausage
Soup, 35
Winter Layers, 40
Skillet Vegetable Pie with Goat
Cheese, 40

February

Chicken in a Snap, 56
Skillet Chicken with Beans and
Greens, 56
Make Your Famous Dip!, 57
Creamy Southwest Black-Eyed Pea
Dip, 57
Raising the Bar, 44
Brown Butter-Caramel Blondies, 48
Cappuccino Swirl Bars, 46
Lemon-Coconut Chess Bars, 48
Peanut Butter-Fudge Bars, 45
Raspberry-Almond Crumble Bars, 48
Spiced Pecan Pie Bars, 45
Ultimate Dark Chocolate Brownies, 46
SL Cooking School, 58

Soup's On, 55
Slow-Cooker Winter Vegetable Soup
with Bacon, 55
Weeknight Cheat Sheets, 50
Cheesy Sheet Pan Pasta, 54
Crispy Catfish Tacos with Slaw, 51
Lemon-Garlic Butter Shrimp
and Broccoli, 53
Oven-Fried Pork Chops with Sweet
Potatoes and Green Beans, 52
Sheet Pan Chicken with Dressing, 50

March

A Quick Shrimp Supper, 70
Spring Shrimp-and-Orzo Salad with
Lemon Dressing, 70
Garden Party, 60
Chocolate Bundt Cake, 64
Lemon-Vanilla Buttercream, 64
Mini Confetti Cakes, 61
"Naked" Lemon Cake with a Flower
Crown, 61
Rose Petal Cupcakes, 64
Rose-Vanilla Buttercream, 64
Sweetened Whipped Cream, 64
Vanilla Buttercream, 64
Vanilla Layer Cake with a Flower
Cuff, 64
Hot Potato, 71
Creamy Cheddar-Potato Soup with
Bacon, 71
Party Perfect, 72
Asparagus-and-Goat Cheese
Quiche, 72
Skillet Sensations, 65
Cheesy Beef-and-Spinach Ravioli, 69
Leek-and-Mushroom Grits
Frittata, 69
Rosemary Chicken Thighs and
Vegetables, 66
Salmon with Lemony Greens
and Grains, 66
Toasted Israeli Couscous
and Shrimp, 65
SL Cooking School, 74

April

Back to Your Roots, 81
Lemony Potato-and-Beet Salad with
Dill, 81
Pepper Jelly-Glazed Baby Turnips, 83

Roasted Baby Turnips with Turnip
Green Pesto, 83
Roasted Carrots with Spiced Pecans
and Sorghum, 83
Sautéed Radishes with Bacon and
Cilantro, 83
Shaved Carrot, Asparagus, and
Apple Salad, 83
Easter Brunch for a Bunch, 84
Company Quiche, 86
Huevos Rancheros Bake, 84
Orange-Vanilla French Toast
Casserole with Bourbon-
Maple Syrup, 85
Sausage-Hash Brown Casserole, 87
Shrimp and Grits Casserole, 88
Fabulous and Flourless, 91
Chocolate-Coconut Pavlova Cake, 91
Pretty Tasty Pot Pie, 89
Skillet Pot Pie with Chicken and
Spring Vegetables, 89
SL Cooking School, 92
Speedy Sheet Pan Salmon, 90
Honey-Mustard Salmon and
Vegetables, 90
Virginia's Sweet Spot, 76
Five-Spice Almonds, 80
Fried Red Quinoa, 80
Hazelnut Financiers with Strawberry
Jam and Lemon Puree, 79
Strawberry Gelato with Almond
Shortbread and Elderflower
Crème, 79
Strawberry-Rhubarb Crisps with
Sweet-and-Savory Granola, 80

May

A New Spin on Chicken Spaghetti, 107
Creamy Chicken Spaghetti, 107
Eat Your Peas, 98
Field Pea-Tomato Salad with Lemon
Vinaigrette, 100
Field Pea Cakes with Tomato-Ginger
Jam, 99
Field Peas, Corn, and Okra in
Country-Ham Cream, 100
Field Peas in Herbed Broth, 99
Smoky Field Pea-and-Greens Dip, 101
Tomato-Ginger Jam, 99
Hooked on Shrimp, 102
Basil Shrimp Scampi, 104

Jambalaya Skewers, 105
Quick Shrimp-and-Corn Chowder, 106
Shrimp-and-Bacon Stir-Fry, 103
Shrimp Cakes with Smoky
    Horseradish Sauce, 103
It's Shortcake Season, 109
Favorite Strawberry Shortcakes, 109
Pork Perfection, 108
Pork Paillards with Lemony Squash
    Salad, 108
SL Cooking School, 110
The House That Mama Built, 94
Mama's Rum Cake, 96

June
Fresh in a Flash, 116
Basil Fried Rice with Butter Peas, 117
Grilled Chicken with Quick-Pickled
    Squash Salad, 118
Pasta with Summer Beans and
    Bacon, 119
Pico de Gallo Pork Chops, 117
Shrimp-and-Sausage Skillet Corn, 119
SL Cooking School, 122
Basil Butter, 122
Basil Oil, 122
Basil Simple Syrup, 122
Basil Sugar, 122
Steak Salad with a Kick, 120
Grilled Steak Salad with Potatoes
    and Pickled Red Onion, 120
Sunrise Sliders, 121
Sausage, Egg, and Cheddar Biscuit
    Sandwiches, 121
Veggie Delights, 112
Chocolate-Zucchini Cake, 114
Corn Custards with Berry
    Compote, 114
Green Tomato Skillet Pie, 113
Yellow Squash Bundt Cake, 113

July
Berry Delicious, 141
Black-and-Blue Buttermilk Tart, 141
Heavenly Corn, 138
Bacon with Ranch Drizzle, 139
Basil Butter with Parmesan, 139
Classic Grilled Corn, 139
Honey-Chipotle Glaze, 139
Smoky Barbecue Rub, 139
Gather Round the Grill, 130
BBQ-Glazed Cedar-Plank Salmon, 135
Charred Onion Dip, 134
Charred Potato-Okra Salad, 135
Chopped Salad with Buttermilk
    Dressing, 132
Dry-Brined Beer-Can Chickens, 131
Foil-Pack Clams with White Wine
    and Herbs, 133
Grilled Garlic Bread, 133

Grilled Sweet Potato Fries, 131
Mixed Herb-and-Tomato Salad, 133
Oven-Fried Zucchini Sticks, 132
Peach-Ricotta-Prosciutto Toasts, 135
Sausage-and-Shrimp Pizzas with
    Spinach-Basil Pesto, 132
Smashed Bacon Cheeseburgers, 134
Spicy Pepper Jelly Coleslaw, 131
Spicy-Sweet Refrigerator Pickles, 134
SL Cooking School, 142
Charred Tomatillo-Avocado Salsa, 142
The Bradford Melon, 124
Marinated Watermelon-and-Tomato
    Salad, 126
Watermelon Chiffon Pie, 128
Watermelon-Ginger Mojitos, 127
Time for Tomato Pie!, 136
Heirloom Tomato Pie with Parmesan-
    Buttermilk Crust, 136
Parmesan-Buttermilk Crust, 136
Tortellini with a Twist, 140
Chicken-Tortellini Salad with Basil
    Vinaigrette, 140

August
5-Ingredient Suppers, 150
Chicken Salad-Stuffed Tomatoes, 154
Creamy Pesto-and-Shrimp Penne
    with Peas, 153
Easy Steak Fajitas, 151
Grilled Salmon Panzanella Salad, 151
Smoky Grilled BLTs, 152
Berry Good Breakfast, 155
"Any-Berry" Muffins with
    Cornmeal Streusel, 155
Break Out the Broccoli, 157
Crispy Chicken-and-Broccoli
    Salad, 157
Fresh from the Garden, 156
Tomato-Basil Couscous with Chicken
    and Smoked Sausage, 156
Just Add Fizz, 144
7UP Bundt Cake, 146
Cheerwine Cherry Cupcakes with
    Cherry-Swirl Frosting, 149
Cherry-Swirl Frosting, 149
Coca-Cola Layer Cake with Fudgy
    Cola Frosting, 146
Dr Pepper Texas Sheet Cake, 147
Fudgy Cola Frosting, 147
Lemon-Lime Cream Cheese
    Frosting, 146
Nehi Orange Poke Cake, 148
Sugared Lemon-Lime Zest, 146
Peaches and Cream, 158
Creamy Peach Icebox Cake, 158
SL Cooking School, 159
All-Purpose Red Onions, 160
Master Pickling Brine, 160
Spicy Green and Yellow Beans, 160

Turmeric-Dill Cucumbers, 160
Tuscan Cherry Tomatoes, 160
Zesty Okra, 160

September
Easy, Cheesy Meatballs, 210
Skillet Turkey Meatballs, 210
Fix & Freeze, 206
Curried Chicken Pot Pie, 208
Greek Stuffed Peppers, 208
Green Chile-Chicken Soup, 207
Shrimp Fajita Bowls, 207
Smoked-Pork-Stuffed Shells, 209
Finding Her Groove, 196
Basmati Rice, 201
Coconut-Buttermilk Sauce, 199
Gingery Carrots with Pistachios and
    Coconut-Buttermilk Sauce, 199
Pan-Roasted Okra and Sweet Onions
    with Lemony Masala, 201
Pickled Onions, 201
Rajma (Punjabi Red Beans), 198
Simple Raita, 201
For the Love of Apple Pie, 194
Old-Fashioned Apple Pie, 195
Game Day Snack Trays, 202
Bacon Deviled Eggs, 204
Baked Chicken Wings with Pepper
    Jelly Glaze, 204
Garlic-Butter Shrimp, 203
Smoky Kimchi Pimiento Cheese, 202
Going Dutch, 211
Bacon-Cheddar Dutch Baby, 211
Kickin' Chicken, 205
One-Pan Hot Honey Chicken and
    Rice, 205
SL Cooking School, 212

October
Boiled-Peanut Perfection, 214
Classic Boiled Peanuts, 215
Bring Out the Beef, 224
Beef-and-Vegetable Soup with
    Gnocchi, 225
Beefy Butternut Squash Pasta, 225
Diner-Style Patty Melts, 226
Speedy Skillet Beef and Broccoli, 224
Falling for Persimmons, 227
Cinnamon Whipped Cream, 227
Persimmon Pudding, 227
Pumpkin Picking Time!, 221
Baked Mini Pumpkin-Pecan
    Doughnuts, 223
Hot Spiced Tea, 222
Salted Caramel-Apple Hand Pies, 223
Sparkling Caramel-Apple Sangría, 222
Sweet-and-Salty Autumn Snack
    Mix, 222
Turkey, Brie, and Fig Pressed
    Sandwiches, 223

Mushrooms Make It Better, 230
Chicken-Mushroom Skillet, 230
Not Your Ordinary Oatmeal, 231
Baked Apple-Cranberry-Pecan
Oatmeal, 231
***SL* Cooking School, 232**
Sweet on Shortbread, 228
Salted Butter-Pecan Shortbread
Cookies, 228
The Instant Pot Roast, 229
Quick Mississippi Pot Roast, 229
The Oyster Feast, 216
Clementine Whiskey Sour, 218
Grilled Oysters, 218
Hot Pepper Vinegar, 218
Johnnycakes with Leeks and Collard
Greens, 219
Meyer Lemon-Ginger Mignonette, 218
Orange-Buttermilk Trifle, 220
Oyster Stew, 219
White Chocolate-Buttermilk Cake, 220
Wood-Fired Root Vegetables with
Charred Scallion Aïoli, 219

November
A Texas-Size Thank-You, 234
Crispy Fried Turkey with Creole
Spices, 235
Picture-Perfect Pies, 236
Dulce de Leche-Cheesecake
Pecan Pie, 238
Pear-Cranberry Pie with Ginger-
Almond Streusel, 239
Pomegranate-Chess Tart, 238
Roasted Granny Smith Apple Pie, 241
Spiced Coconut-Pumpkin Pie, 237
Roll Call, 254
Sweet Potato Rolls with Cane Syrup
Glaze, 254
***SL* Cooking School, 268**
Tastes Like Home, 242
Buttermilk Spoon Bread, 252
Candy Roaster Squash with
Sorghum, Black Walnuts,
and Cranberries, 242
Collard Greens with Garlic and
Sippets, 242
Creamy Baked Macaroni and
Cheese with Bacon, 244
Fluffy Corn Pudding, 249
Fried Arkansas Black Apples , 245
Grated Sweet Potato Pudding with
Pecans, 250
Scalloped Oysters, 250
Sea Island Crab Fried Rice, 246
Shrimp-Stuffed Mirlitons, 249
Simple Mashed Rutabagas
and Potatoes, 245
Spicy Cornbread Dressing
with Chorizo, 247

Thanksgiving Classics, 260
Apple Brown Betty, 260
Broccoli Dressing, 260
Butternut Squash Soup, 260
Chestnut Stuffing, 266
Cornbread Dressing, 260
Crunch-Top Apple Pie, 261
Crunch Topping, 261
Favorite Southern Cornbread, 261
Field Greens, Crumbled Blue
Cheese, and Spicy Pecans, 262
Fresh Cranberry Congealed Salad, 262
Giblet Gravy, 266
Green Bean Casserole with Fried
Leeks, 262
Herbed Turkey, 263
Holiday Cranberry Salad, 263
Hot-Water Cornbread, 263
Mint Sauce, 264
Pastry, 261
Peppered Turkey Breast, 264
Praline Sauce, 264
Pumpkin Chess Pie, 264
Refrigerator Yeast Rolls, 265
Roast Leg of Lamb, 264
Roast Turkey and Gravy, 265
Roast Turkey with Chestnut
Stuffing, 265
Sausage-Cornbread Dressing, 266
Spicy Pecans, 262
Squash Casserole, 266
Sweet Potato Casserole, 267
Sweet Potato Casserole with
Marshmallows, 267
Walter's Favorite Pecan Pie, 267
The Giving Tree, 255
Baked Brie with Honeyed Five-Spice
Pecans, 257
Chocolate-Pecan Phyllo
Turnovers, 258
Herby Pecan-Cornbread Dressing, 257
Roasted Root Vegetables with Spicy
Pecan Topping, 258
Sorghum-Pecan Monkey Bread
Muffins, 257

December
Bake Another Batch, 302
Ivy's Best-Ever Brownies, 302
Christmas in Bloom, 294
Chocolate-Buttermilk Cake with Swiss
Meringue Buttercream, 295
Magnolia or Camellia Cake
Toppers, 296
Swiss Meringue Buttercream, 295
Bring a Side, 276
Brussels Sprouts Slaw with Pecans
and Pomegranate Seeds, 277
Creamed Greens with Garlic
Breadcrumbs, 277

Creamy Whipped-Potato
Casserole, 278
Melting Sweet Potatoes with
Walnuts, 278
Root Vegetable-and-Butternut
Squash Gratin, 279
Good to the Last Crumb, 303
Cranberry-Pecan Coffee Cake, 303
Pralines' Rich History, 299
Pralines, 299
Renaissance Woman, 300
Aïoli, 301
Spicy Butter, 301
Spicy Shrimp with Jalapeño
Cornbread and Aïoli, 301
***SL* Cooking School, 304**
Butternut Squash Triangles, 304
Cacio e Pepe Puffs, 304
Cheesy Garlic-Herb-and-Ham
Bites, 304
Spectacular Party Starters, 270
Baked Goat Cheese Spread with
Pepper Jelly, 270
Beef Tenderloin Crostini, 272
Beer-Cheese Fondue, 273
Cheesy Mushroom Tartlets, 272
Chipotle Cheese Straws, 270
Creamed Spinach-Stuffed
Mushrooms, 275
Creamy Feta Phyllo Bites, 273
Marinated Olives and Peppadews, 270
Mini Crab Cakes with Cajun Sauce, 270
Parmesan Grits Triangles
with Pesto, 275
Pickled Shrimp and Citrus Endive
Cups, 273
Roasted Oysters with Bacon-Saltine
Topping, 275
Rosemary-Bacon Nut Mix, 272
Smoked Sausage Pretzel Bites, 273
Sweet-and-Spicy Meatballs, 272
Spirited Desserts, 283
Hot-Buttered-Rum Bread Pudding, 285
Old-Fashioned Trifle, 283
Spiked Eggnog Bundt, 284
The Art of the Roast, 280
Baked Ham with Brown Sugar-
Citrus Glaze, 281
Prime Rib with Herbes de Provence
Crust and Red Wine Sauce, 281
Roasted Chicken with Apples and
Herbs, 282
The Gift of Cookies, 286
Ambrosia Macaroons, 287
Brown Sugar Cookie Stars, 292
Candy Cane Cake Bars, 288
Chocolate-Pecan Biscotti Thins, 292
Chocolate-Praline Thumbprints, 288
Cranberry-Orange Butter Cookies, 293
Cream Cheese Cookie Wreaths, 287

Dark Chocolate-Ginger-Molasses Cookies, 289
Dipped Pistachio Shortbread, 287
Peppermint Cookie Truffles, 288
Royal Icing, 292
Sprinkle Sandwich Cookies, 292
Sugar-and-Spice Rugelach, 289
Vanilla Buttercream, 292

Our Favorite Holiday Recipes

Appetizers, 322
Buttery Toasted Pecans, 322
Spinach-Sausage Turnovers, 322
Black-Eyed Pea Cakes, 322
Lump Crab Mornay, 322
Cherry-Pecan Brie, 322
Parmesan Cheese Bites, 323
Parmesan Cheese Squares, 323
Garlic Butter-Roasted Shrimp Cocktail, 323
Millionaire's Candied Bacon, 323
Tortellini Caprese Bites, 323
Basil Vinaigrette, 323
Colby-Pepper Jack Cheese Dip, 323

Beverages, 324
Apple-Ale Wassail, 324
Cherry Frost, 324
Classic Eggnog, 324
Perky Cranberry Punch, 324
Cranberry Sangría Punch, 324
Hot Spiced Wine, 324
White Sangria Fizz, 325

Breads, 325
Hurry-Up Homemade Cornbread Yeast Rolls, 325
Crescent Rolls, 325
Sour Cream Pocketbook Rolls, 325
Sea Salt-Poppy Seed Cloverleaf Rolls, 326
Butter Muffins, 326

Breakfast and Brunch, 326
Best-Ever Sticky Buns, 326
Homemade Waffles, 327
Homemade All-Purpose Biscuit, Pancake, and Waffle Mix, 327
Creamy Egg Strata, 327
One-Dish Blackberry French Toast, 327

Dessert, 328
Buttered Rum Pound Cake with Bananas Foster Sauce, 328
Buttered Rum Glaze, 328
Bananas Foster Sauce, 328
Apple-Gingerbread Cobbler, 328
Cranberry-Apple Pie, 328
Cranberry-Apple Pie Filling, 329
Mrs. Billett's White Cake, 329
Vanilla Buttercream Frosting, 329
Fondant Snowflakes, 329
Triple-Decker Strawberry Cake, 330

Strawberry Buttercream Frosting, 330
Four-Layer Coconut Cake, 330
Coconut Filling, 330
Chocolate-Covered Cherry Pie, 330
Brandy Alexander Cheesecake, 331
Fudge Truffle-Pecan Tart, 331
Tiramisú Toffee Trifle Pie, 331
Red Velvet Layer Cake, 332
5-Cup Cream Cheese Frosting, 332
Chocolate-Peppermint Candy Cupcakes, 332
Chocolate Velvet Cake Batter, 332
Vanilla Buttercream Frosting, 332
White Chocolate-Raspberry Cheesecake Bars, 333
Lemon-Poppy Seed Cakes, 333
Brown Sugar Bread Pudding with Rich Bourbon Sauce, 333
Rich Bourbon Sauce, 333
Orange-Sweet Potato Pie with Rosemary-Cornmeal Crust, 334

Gifts from the Kitchen, 334
Italian Parmesan Herb Mix, 334
Holiday Herb Butter, 334
Sweet Hot Honey Mustard, 334
Butter-Pecan Granola, 334
Cranberry-Pecan Chicken Salad, 335
Peanut Butter Bonbons, 335
Salty Chocolate-Pecan Candy, 335
Reindeer Gingersnaps, 335
Merry Margarita Mix Pineapple Craft Cocktail, 335
Lime Sea Salt, 335

Main Dishes, 336
Shepherd's Pie, 336
Cheese-and-Carrot Mashed Potatoes, 336
Dinner Mac and Cheese, 336
Chicken-and-Cornbread Casserole, 336
Ham-and-Vegetable Cobbler, 337
Fennel-Crusted Rib Roast, 337
Citrus-Grilled Turkey Breast, 337
Creole Deep-Fried Turkey, 337
Cranberry-Turkey Panini, 338
Next-Day Turkey Bake, 338
Turkey Pot Pie with Cranberry-Pecan Crusts, 338
Cranberry-Pecan Crusts, 338
Honey-Curry Glazed Lamb with Roasted Grapes and Cranberries, 338
Roasted Grapes and Cranberries, 339
Cornish Game Hens with Butternut Croutons, 339
Butternut Croutons, 339
Spice-Rubbed Smoked Turkey Breast with Mushroom Gravy, 339
Mushroom Gravy, 339
Classic Lasagna, 340

Italian Meat Sauce, 340
Pecan-and-Dill-Crusted Salmon, 340
Spicy Fruit-Stuffed Pork Loin with Roasted Pears and Onions, 340
Herb-and-Potato Chip-Crusted Beef Tenderloin, 340
Stuffed Beef Tenderloin, 341
Béarnaise Sauce, 341
Perfect Beef Tenderloin, 342
Smoked Pork Tenderloins with Sherry-Mushroom Sauce, 342

Salads, 342
Turkey Salad with Cranberry Dressing, 342
Bing Cherry Salad, 342
Basil-and-Blue Cheese Salad, 343
Bacon-Mandarin Salad, 343
Spinach Salad with Apricot Vinaigrette, 343
Apricot Vinaigrette, 343

Sides, 343
Perfect Green Beans, 343
Sweet Onion Pudding, 343
Baked Smokin' Macaroni and Cheese, 344
Butternut Squash Gratin, 344
Shrimp and Grits Dressing, 344
Classic Parmesan Scalloped Potatoes, 345
Smoky Pimiento Cheese Deviled Eggs, 345
Cornflake, Pecan, and Marshmallow-Topped Sweet Potato Casserole, 345
Crumb-Topped Spinach Casserole, 345
Cornbread Dressing Cakes, 346
Cornbread, 346
Roasted Garlic Mashed Potatoes, 346
Savory Bacon-and-Leek Bread Pudding, 346
Green Beans with Hollandaise Sauce, 347
Perfect Mashed Potatoes, 347
Make-Ahead Turkey Gravy, 347
Roasted Onions, 347
Wild Rice Salad, 347
Smoky Cranberry-Apple Sauce, 348
Fennel-Potato Gratin, 348
Roasted Heirloom Root Vegetables in Lemon-Horseradish Butter, 348
Lemon Broccolini, 348

Soups, 349
Pecan Soup, 349
Tortilla Turkey Soup, 349
Sausage-Tortellini Soup, 349
Tomato Bisque, 349

General Recipe Index

This index lists every recipe by food category and/or major ingredient.

A

Appetizers and snacks. *See also*
Dips and spreads
Bacon Deviled Eggs, 204
Baked Chicken Wings with Pepper
    Jelly Glaze, 204
Beef Tenderloin Crostini, 272
Black-Eyed Pea Cakes, 322
Butternut Squash Triangles, 304
Buttery Toasted Pecans, 322
Cacio e Pepe Puffs, 304
Cheesy Garlic-Herb-and-Ham
    Bites, 304
Cheesy Mushroom Tartlets, 272
Cherry-Pecan Brie, 322
Chipotle Cheese Straws, 270
Classic Boiled Peanuts with
    variations, 215
Creamed Spinach-Stuffed
    Mushrooms, 275
Creamy Feta Phyllo Bites, 273
Garlic Butter-Roasted Shrimp
    Cocktail, 323
Garlic-Butter Shrimp, 203
Lump Crab Mornay, 322
Marinated Olives and
    Peppadews, 270
Millionaire's Candied Bacon, 323
Mini Crab Cakes with Cajun
    Sauce, 270
Parmesan Cheese Bites, 323
Parmesan Cheese Squares, 323
Parmesan Grits Triangles with
    Pesto, 175
Pickled Shrimp and Citrus Endive
    Cups, 273
Roasted Oysters with Bacon-
    Stuffing Topping, 275
Rosemary-Bacon Nut Mix, 172
Smoked Sausage Pretzel Bites, 273
Smoky Pimiento Cheese Deviled
    Eggs, 345
Spinach-Sausage Turnovers, 322
Sweet-and-Salty Autumn Snack
    Mix, 222
Sweet-and-Spicy Meatballs, 272
Tortellini Caprese Bites, 323
Apples
Apple-Ale Wassail, 324
Apple Brown Betty, 260
Apple-Gingerbread Cobbler, 328

Baked Apple-Cranberry-Pecan
    Oatmeal, 231
Cranberry-Apple Pie, 328
Cranberry-Apple Pie Filling, 329
Cranberry Sangria Punch, 324
Crunch-Top Apple Pie, 261
Fried Arkansas Black Apples, 245
Old-Fashioned Apple Pie, 195
Roasted Chicken with Apples and
    Herbs, 282
Roasted Granny Smith Apple Pie, 241
Salted Caramel-Apple Hand
    Pies, 223
Shaved Carrot, Asparagus, and
    Apple Salad, 83
Sheet Pan Chicken with Dressing, 50
Smoky Cranberry-Apple Sauce, 348
Sparkling Caramel-Apple
    Sangria, 222
Asparagus
Asparagus-and-Goat Cheese
    Quiche, 72
Company Quiche, 86
Shaved Carrot, Asparagus, and
    Apple Salad, 83
Spring Shrimp-and-Orzo Salad with
    Lemon Dressing, 70
Avocados
Basil-and-Blue Cheese Salad, 343
Charred Tomatillo-Avocado
    Salsa, 142
Chopped Salad with Buttermilk
    Dressing, 132
Crispy Catfish Tacos with Slaw, 51
Huevos Rancheros Bake, 84
Sausage, Egg, and Cheddar Biscuit
    Sandwiches, 121

B

Bacon
Bacon-Cheddar Dutch Baby, 211
Bacon Deviled Eggs, 204
Bacon-Mandarin Salad, 343
Bacon with Ranch Drizzle, 139
Creamy Baked Macaroni and
    Cheese with Bacon, 244
Creamy Cheddar-Potato Soup with
    Bacon, 71
Lentil Soup with Sweet Potatoes and
    Bacon, 36
Millionaire's Candied Bacon, 323

Pasta with Summer Beans and
    Bacon, 119
Roasted Oysters with Bacon-
    Stuffing Topping, 275
Rosemary-Bacon Nut Mix, 172
Sautéed Radishes with Bacon and
    Cilantro, 83
Savory Bacon-and-Leek Bread
    Pudding, 346
Shrimp-and-Bacon Stir-Fry, 103
Slow-Cooker Winter Vegetable Soup
    with Bacon, 55
Smashed Bacon Cheeseburgers, 134
Smoky Grilled BLTs, 152
Bananas
Banana Nut Shortcakes, 109–110
Bananas Foster Sauce, 328
Buttered Rum Pound Cake with
    Bananas Foster Sauce, 328
Mini Bananas Foster Sticky
    Buns, 39
Bar cookies and brownies
Brown Butter-Caramel Blondies, 48
Candy Cane Cake Bars, 288
Cappuccino Swirl Bars, 46
Ivy's Best-Ever Brownies, 302
Lemon-Coconut Chess Bars, 48
Peanut Butter Fudge Bars, 45
Raspberry-Almond Crumble Bars, 48
Spiced Pecan Pie Bars, 45
Ultimate Dark Chocolate
    Brownies, 46
White Chocolate-Raspberry
    Cheesecake Bars, 333
Beans. *See also* **Green beans**
Beans and lentils
Huevos Rancheros Bake, 84
Lentil Soup with Sweet Potatoes and
    Bacon, 36
Pasta with Summer Beans and
    Bacon, 119
Rajma (Punjabi Red Beans), 198
Skillet Chicken with Beans and
    Greens, 56
Slow-Cooker Winter Vegetable Soup
    with Bacon, 55
Beef
Beef-and-Vegetable Soup with
    Gnocchi, 225
Beef Tenderloin Crostini, 272
Beefy Butternut Squash Pasta, 225

Cheesy Beef and Spinach Ravioli, 69
Classic Lasagna, 340
Diner-Style Patty Melts, 226
Easy Steak Fajitas, 151
Fennel-Crusted Rib Roast, 337
Greek Stuffed Peppers, 208
Grilled Steak Salad with Potatoes
    and Pickled Red Onion, 120
Herb-and-Potato Chip-Crusted Beef
    Tenderloin, 340
Instant Pot Beef-and-Barley Soup
    with Mushrooms, 34
Italian Meat Sauce, 340
Perfect Beef Tenderloin, 342
Prime Rib with Herbes de Provence
    Crust and Red Wine Sauce, 281
Quick Mississippi Pot Roast, 229
Roasted Beef Tenderloin, 28
Shepherd's Pie, 336
Smashed Bacon Cheeseburgers, 134
Speedy Skillet Beef and
    Broccoli, 224
Stuffed Beef Tenderloin, 341

Beets
Lemony Potato-and-Beet Salad with
    Dill, 81
Roasted Heirloom Root Vegetables
    in Lemon-Horseradish
    Butter, 348
Roasted Root Vegetable with Spicy
    Pecan Topping, 258

Beverages
Apple-Ale Wassail, 324
Cherry Frost, 324
Classic Eggnog, 324
Clementine Whiskey Sour, 218
Cranberry Sangria Punch, 324
Hot Spiced Tea, 222
Hot Spiced Wine, 324
Merry Margarita Pineapple Craft
    Cocktail, 335
Perky Cranberry Punch, 324
Sparkling Caramel-Apple
    Sangria, 222
Watermelon-Ginger Mojitos, 127
White Sangria Fizz, 325

Blackberries
"Any-Berry" Muffins with Cornmeal
    Streusel, 155
Berry Compote, 114
Black-and-Blue Buttermilk Tart, 141
Corn Custards with Berry
    Compote, 114
One-Dish Blackberry French
    Toast, 327
Zesty Blackberry Shortcakes, 109–110

Black-eyed peas
Black-Eyed Pea Cakes, 322
Chicken-Tortellini Salad with Basil
    Vinaigrette, 140

Creamy Southwest Black-Eyed Pea
    Dip, 57
Salmon with Lemony Greens and
    Grains, 66

Blueberries
"Any-Berry" Muffins with Cornmeal
    Streusel, 155
Black-and-Blue Buttermilk Tart, 141

Breads. See also Rolls and buns
"Any-Berry" Muffins with Cornmeal
    Streusel, 155
Baked Mini Pumpkin-Pecan
    Doughnuts, 223
Buttermilk Spoon Bread, 252
Butter Muffins, 326
Buttery Chive-and-Mustard Drop
    Biscuits, 37
Cornbread, 346
Favorite Southern Cornbread, 261
Grilled Garlic Bread, 133
Homemade All-Purpose Biscuit,
    Pancake, and Waffle Mix, 327
Homemade Waffles, 327
Hot-Water Cornbread, 263
Johnnycakes with Leeks and Collard
    Greens, 219
Mini Bananas Foster Sticky Buns, 39
Sorghum-Pecan Monkey Bread
    Muffins, 257

Broccoli
Broccoli Dressing, 260
Crispy Chicken-and-Broccoli
    Salad, 157
Lemon-Garlic Butter Shrimp and
    Broccoli, 53
Speedy Skillet Beef and Broccoli, 224

Broccolini
Lemon Broccolini, 348
Skillet Vegetable Pie with Goat
    Cheese, 40

Brussels sprouts
Brussels Sprouts Slaw with Pecans
    and Pomegranate Seeds, 277
Rosemary Chicken Thighs and
    Vegetables, 66

C

Cabbage
Crispy Catfish Tacos with Slaw, 51
One-Pan Hot Honey Chicken and
    Rice, 205
Shaved Carrot, Asparagus, and
    Apple Salad, 83
Spicy Pepper Jelly Coleslaw, 131

Cakes
Buttered Rum Pound Cake with
    Bananas Foster Sauce, 328
Cheerwine Cherry Cupcakes with
    Cherry-Swirl Frosting, 149
Chocolate Bundt Cake, 64

Chocolate-Buttermilk Cake
    with Swiss Meringue
    Buttercream, 295
Chocolate-Coconut Pavlova Cake, 91
Chocolate-Peppermint Candy
    Cupcakes, 332
Chocolate Velvet Cake Batter, 332
Chocolate-Zucchini Cake, 114
Coca-Cola Layer Cake with Fudgy
    Cola Frosting, 146
Cranberry-Pecan Coffee Cake, 303
Creamy Peach Icebox Cake, 158
Dr Pepper Texas Sheet Cake, 147
Four-Layer Coconut Cake, 330
Hazelnut Financiers with Strawberry
    Jam and Lemon Puree, 79
Lemon-Poppy Seed Cakes, 333
Lemon Pound Cake, 328
Mama's Rum Cake, 96
Mini Confetti Cakes, 61
Mrs. Billett's White Cake, 329
"Naked" Lemon Cake with a Flower
    Crown, 61
Nehi Orange Poke Cake, 148
Red Velvet Layer Cake, 332
Rose Petal Cupcakes, 64
7UP Bundt Cake, 146
Spiked Eggnog Bundt, 284
Triple-Decker Strawberry Cake, 330
Vanilla Layer Cake with a Flower
    Cuff, 64
White Chocolate-Buttermilk
    Cake, 220
Yellow Squash Bundt Cake, 113

Candy
Peanut Butter Bonbons, 335
Pralines, 299
Salty Chocolate-Pecan Candy, 335

Carrots
Carrot-and-Fennel Salad, 31
Cheese-and-Carrot Mashed
    Potatoes, 336
Gingery Carrots with Pistachios and
    Coconut-Buttermilk Sauce, 199
Roasted Carrots with Spiced Pecans
    and Sorghum, 83
Roasted Heirloom Root Vegetables in
    Lemon-Horseradish Butter, 348
Shaved Carrot, Asparagus, and
    Apple Salad, 83
Wood-Fired Root Vegetables with
    Charred Scallion Aïoli, 219

Cauliflower
Cauliflower with Cheese Sauce, 31

Cherries
Ambrosia Macaroons, 287
Bing Cherry Salad, 342
Cheerwine Cherry Cupcakes with
    Cherry-Swirl Frosting, 149
Cherry Frost, 324

Cherry-Pecan Brie, 322
Cherry-Swirl Frosting, 149
Chocolate-Covered Cherry Pie, 330
Old-Fashioned Trifle, 283

Chicken
Baked Chicken Wings with Pepper
  Jelly Glaze, 204
Chicken-and-Cornbread
  Casserole, 336
Chicken-Mushroom Skillet, 230
Chicken Salad-Stuffed Tomatoes, 154
Chicken-Tortellini Salad with Basil
  Vinaigrette, 140
Clementine-and-Collard Salad, 38
Colby-Pepper Jack Cheese Dip, 323
Cornish Game Hens with Butternut
  Croutons, 339
Cranberry-Pecan Chicken Salad, 335
Creamy Chicken-and-Rice Soup
  with Collard Greens, 32
Creamy Chicken Spaghetti, 107
Crispy Chicken-and-Broccoli
  Salad, 157
Curried Chicken Pot Pie, 208
Dry-Brined Beer-Can Chicken, 131
Green Chile-Chicken Soup, 207
Grilled Chicken with Quick-Pickled
  Squash Salad, 118
One-Pan Hot Honey Chicken and
  Rice, 205
Roasted Chicken with Apples and
  Herbs, 282
Rosemary Chicken Thighs and
  Vegetables, 66
Sheet Pan Chicken with
  Dressing, 50
Skillet Chicken with Beans and
  Greens, 56
Skillet Pot Pie with Chicken and
  Spring Vegetables, 89
Tomato-Basil Couscous with
  Chicken Smoked Sausage, 156

Chocolate. *See also* White chocolate
Brown Butter-Caramel Blondies, 48
Cappuccino Swirl Bars, 46
Chocolate Bundt Cake, 64
Chocolate-Buttermilk Cake
  with Swiss Meringue
  Buttercream, 295
Chocolate-Coconut Pavlova Cake, 91
Chocolate-Covered Cherry Pie, 330
Chocolate-Pecan Biscotti Thins, 292
Chocolate-Pecan Phyllo
  Turnovers, 258
Chocolate-Peppermint Candy
  Cupcakes, 332
Chocolate-Praline Thumbprints, 288
Chocolate Tart Shell, 331
Chocolate Velvet Cake Batter, 332
Chocolate-Zucchini Cake, 114

Coca-Cola Layer Cake with Fudgy
  Cola Frosting, 146
Dark Chocolate-Ginger-Molasses
  Cookies, 289
Dipped Pistachio Shortbread, 287
Dr Pepper Texas Sheet Cake, 147
Fudge Truffle-Pecan Tart, 331
Fudgy Cola Frosting, 147
Ivy's Best-Ever Brownies, 302
Peanut Butter Fudge Bars, 45
Peppermint Cookie Truffles, 288
Raspberry Truffle Shortcakes, 110
Red Velvet Layer Cake, 332
Rich Fudge Icing, 147
Salty Chocolate-Pecan Candy, 335
Tiramisú Toffee Trifle Pie, 331
Ultimate Dark Chocolate
  Brownies, 46

Collard greens
Beefy Butternut Squash Pasta, 225
Clementine-and-Collard Salad, 38
Collard Greens with Garlic and
  Sippets, 242
Creamed Greens with Garlic
  Breadcrumbs, 277
Creamy Chicken-and-Rice Soup
  with Collard Greens, 32
Johnnycakes with Leeks and Collard
  Greens, 219
Oyster Stew, 219
Salmon with Lemony Greens and
  Grains, 66

Cookies. *See also* Bar cookies and brownies
Almond Shortbread, 79
Ambrosia Macaroons, 287
Brown Sugar Cookie Stars, 292
Chocolate-Pecan Biscotti Thins, 292
Chocolate-Praline Thumbprints, 288
Cranberry-Orange Butter
  Cookies, 293
Cream Cheese Cookie Wreaths, 287
Dark Chocolate-Ginger-Molasses
  Cookies, 289
Dipped Pistachio Shortbread, 287
Peppermint Cookie Truffles, 288
Reindeer Gingersnaps, 335
Salted Butter-Pecan Shortbread
  Cookies, 228
Sprinkle Sandwich Cookies, 292
Sugar-and-Spice Rugelach, 289

Corn
Classic Grilled Corn with
  variations, 139
Cornbread Dressing Cakes, 346
Corn Custards with Berry
  Compote, 114
Field Peas, Corn, and Okra in
  Country-Ham Cream, 100
Fluffy Corn Pudding, 249

Quick Shrimp-and-Corn
  Chowder, 106
Shrimp-and-Sausage Skillet
  Corn, 119

Cornmeal
"Any-Berry" Muffins with Cornmeal
  Streusel, 155
Buttermilk Spoon Bread, 252
Cornbread Dressing, 260
Favorite Southern Cornbread, 261
Hot-Water Cornbread, 263
Hurry-Up Homemade Cornbread
  Yeast Rolls, 325
Johnnycakes with Leeks and Collard
  Greens, 219
Orange-Sweet Potato Pie with
  Rosemary-Cornmeal
  Crust, 334
Parmesan Grits Triangles with
  Pesto, 175

Couscous
Toasted Israeli Couscous and
  Shrimp, 65
Tomato-Basil Couscous with
  Chicken Smoked Sausage, 156

Cranberries
Baked Apple-Cranberry-Pecan
  Oatmeal, 231
Candy Roaster Squash with
  Sorghum, Black Walnuts, and
  Cranberries, 242
Cranberry-Apple Pie, 328
Cranberry-Apple Pie Filling, 329
Cranberry-Orange Butter
  Cookies, 293
Cranberry-Pecan Chicken Salad, 335
Cranberry-Pecan Coffee Cake, 303
Cranberry-Pecan Crusts, 338
Cranberry Sangria Punch, 324
Cranberry-Turkey Panini, 338
Fresh Cranberry Congealed
  Salad, 262
Holiday Cranberry Salad, 263
Honey-Curry Glazed Lamb
  with Roasted Grapes and
  Cranberries, 338
Pear-Cranberry Pie with Ginger-
  Almond Streusel, 239
Perky Cranberry Punch, 324
Roasted Grapes and
  Cranberries, 339
Smoky Cranberry-Apple Sauce, 348
Turkey Pot Pie with Cranberry-
  Pecan Crusts, 338
Turkey Salad with Cranberry
  Dressing, 342

Cucumbers
Creamy Feta Phyllo Bites, 273
Turmeric-Dill Cucumbers, 160

D

Desserts. *See also* **Cakes; Pies and tarts**
Apple Brown Betty, 260
Apple-Gingerbread Cobbler, 328
Brandy Alexander Cheesecake, 331
Brown Sugar Bread Pudding with Rich Bourbon Sauce, 333
Chocolate-Coconut Pavlova Cake, 91
Chocolate-Pecan Phyllo Turnovers, 258
Corn Custards with Berry Compote, 114
Creamy Peach Icebox Cake, 158
Favorite Strawberry Shortcakes, 109
Grapefruit Cheesecake, 41
Hazelnut Financiers with Strawberry Jam and Lemon Puree, 79
Hot-Buttered-Rum Bread Pudding, 285
Old-Fashioned Trifle, 283
Orange-Buttermilk Trifle, 220
Persimmon Pudding, 227
Strawberry Gelato with Almond Shortbread and Elderflower Crème, 79
Strawberry-Rhubarb Crisps with Sweet-and-Savory Granola, 80

Dips and spreads
Baked Brie with Honeyed Five-Spice Pecans, 257
Baked Goat Cheese Spread with Pepper Jelly, 270
Beer-Cheese Fondue, 273
Charred Onion Dip, 134
Charred Tomatillo-Avocado Salsa, 142
Colby-Pepper Jack Cheese Dip, 323
Creamy Southwest Black-Eyed Pea Dip, 57
Smoky Field Pea-and-Greens Dip, 101
Smoky Kimchi Pimiento Cheese, 202

Dressings and stuffings
Broccoli Dressing, 260
Chestnut Stuffing, 266
Cornbread Dressing, 260
Cornbread Dressing Cakes, 346
Herby Pecan-Cornbread Dressing, 257
Sausage-Cornbread Dressing, 266
Sheet Pan Chicken with Dressing, 50
Shrimp and Grits Dressing, 344
Spicy Cornbread Dressing with Chorizo, 247

E

Eggs
Asparagus-and-Goat Cheese Quiche, 72
Bacon Deviled Eggs, 204
Basil Fried Rice with Butter Peas, 117
Company Quiche, 86
Creamy Egg Strata, 327
Huevos Rancheros Bake, 84
Leek-and-Mushroom Grits Frittata, 69
Sausage, Egg, and Cheddar Biscuit Sandwiches, 121
Sausage-Hash Brown Casserole, 87
Smoky Pimiento Cheese Deviled Eggs, 345

F

Fennel bulb
Carrot-and-Fennel Salad, 31
Fennel-Potato Gratin, 348
Pickled Shrimp and Citrus Endive Cups, 273
Sheet Pan Chicken with Dressing, 50

Field peas
Field Pea Cakes with Tomato-Ginger Jam, 99
Field Peas, Corn, and Okra in Country-Ham Cream, 100
Field Peas in Herbed Broth, 99
Field Pea-Tomato Salad with Lemon Vinaigrette, 100
Smoky Field Pea-and-Greens Dip, 101

Fish. *See also* **Shellfish; Shrimp**
BBQ-Glazed Cedar-Plank Salmon, 135
Crispy Catfish Tacos with Slaw, 51
Grilled Salmon Panzanella Salad, 151
Honey-Mustard Salmon and Vegetables, 90
Pecan-and-Dill-Crusted Salmon, 340
Salmon with Lemony Greens and Grains, 66

Frostings and icings
Brown Butter-Pistachio Frosting, 114
Cherry-Swirl Frosting, 149
5-Cup Cream Cheese Frosting, 332
Fondant Snowflakes, 329
Fudgy Cola Frosting, 147
Lemon-Buttermilk Glaze, 113
Lemon-Lime Cream Cheese Frosting, 146
Lemon-Vanilla Buttercream, 64
Magnolia or Camellia Cake Toppers, 296
Mascarpone-Whipped Cream Frosting, 148
Rich Fudge Icing, 147
Rose-Vanilla Buttercream, 64
Royal Icing, 292
Strawberry Buttercream Frosting, 330
Swiss Meringue Buttercream, 295
Vanilla Buttercream, 64, 292
Vanilla Buttercream Frosting, 329, 332

G

Grains. *See also* **Cornmeal; Couscous; Grits; Oats**
Fried Red Quinoa, 80
Instant Pot Beef-and-Barley Soup with Mushrooms, 34
Salmon with Lemony Greens and Grains, 66
Strawberry-Rhubarb Crisps with Sweet-and-Savory Granola, 80

Grapefruit
Grapefruit Cheesecake, 41
Pickled Shrimp and Citrus Endive Cups, 273

Grapes
Crispy Chicken-and-Broccoli Salad, 157
Honey-Curry Glazed Lamb with Roasted Grapes and Cranberries, 338
Roasted Grapes and Cranberries, 339

Green beans
Green Bean Casserole with Fried Leeks, 262
Green Beans with Hollandaise Sauce, 347
Oven-Fried Pork Chops with Sweet Potatoes and Green Beans, 52
Pasta with Summer Beans and Bacon, 119
Perfect Green Beans, 343
Sausage-Tortellini Soup, 349
Spicy Green and Yellow Beans, 160

Greens. *See also* **Collard greens; Kale; Spinach**
Field Greens, Crumbled Blue Cheese, and Spicy Pecans, 262
Johnnycakes with Leeks and Collard Greens, 219
Pickled Shrimp and Citrus Endive Cups, 273
Skillet Chicken with Beans and Greens, 56
Stuffed Beef Tenderloin, 341

Grits
Leek-and-Mushroom Grits Frittata, 69
Parmesan Grits Triangles with Pesto, 175
Shrimp and Grits Casserole, 88
Shrimp and Grits Dressing, 344

H

Ham
Baked Ham with Brown Sugar-Citrus Glaze, 281
Baked Smokin' Macaroni and Cheese, 344
Creamy Southwest Black-Eyed Pea Dip, 57
Dinner Mac and Cheese, 336

Field Peas, Corn, and Okra in
Country-Ham Cream, 100
Ham-and-Vegetable Cobbler, 337

K

Kale
Creamed Greens with Garlic
Breadcrumbs, 277
Slow-Cooker Winter Vegetable Soup
with Bacon, 55
Smoky Field Pea-and-Greens Dip, 101

L

Lamb
Honey-Curry Glazed Lamb
with Roasted Grapes and
Cranberries, 338
Roast Leg of Lamb, 264
Leeks
Asparagus-and-Goat Cheese
Quiche, 72
Creamy Chicken-and-Rice Soup
with Collard Greens, 32
Green Bean Casserole with Fried
Leeks, 262
Johnnycakes with Leeks and Collard
Greens, 219
Leek-and-Mushroom Grits Frittata, 69
Savory Bacon-and-Leek Bread
Pudding, 346
Skillet Pot Pie with Chicken and
Spring Vegetables, 89
Lemon(s)
Lemon Broccolini, 348
Lemon-Buttermilk Glaze, 113
Lemon-Coconut Chess Bars, 48
Lemon-Garlic Butter Shrimp and
Broccoli, 53
Lemon-Lime Cream Cheese
Frosting, 146
Lemon-Lime Meringue Pie, 31
Lemon-Poppy Seed Cakes, 333
Lemon Pound Cake, 328
Lemon Puree, 79
Lemon-Vanilla Buttercream, 64
Lemony Potato-and-Beet Salad with
Dill, 81
Meyer Lemon-Ginger Mignonette, 218
"Naked" Lemon Cake with a Flower
Crown, 61
Pan-Roasted Okra and Sweet
Onions with Lemony
Masala, 201
Pork Paillards with Lemony Squash
Salad, 108
Roasted Heirloom Root Vegetables
in Lemon-Horseradish
Butter, 348
Salmon with Lemony Greens and
Grains, 66

Spring Shrimp-and-Orzo Salad with
Lemon Dressing, 70
Sugared Lemon-Lime Zest, 146
Lime(s)
Lemon-Lime Cream Cheese
Frosting, 146
Lemon-Lime Meringue Pie, 31
Lime Sea Salt, 335
Sugared Lemon-Lime Zest, 146
Watermelon-Ginger Mojitos, 127

M

Mushrooms
Cheesy Mushroom Tartlets, 272
Chicken-Mushroom Skillet, 230
Creamed Spinach-Stuffed
Mushrooms, 275
Instant Pot Beef-and-Barley Soup
with Mushrooms, 34
Leek-and-Mushroom Grits Frittata, 69
Mushroom Gravy, 339
Smoked Pork Tenderloins with
Sherry-Mushroom Sauce, 342

O

Oats
Baked Apple-Cranberry-Pecan
Oatmeal, 231
Butter-Pecan Granola, 334
Raspberry-Almond Crumble Bars, 48
Strawberry-Rhubarb Crisps with
Sweet-and-Savory Granola, 80
Okra
Charred Potato-Okra Salad, 135
Field Peas, Corn, and Okra in
Country-Ham Cream, 100
Pan-Roasted Okra and Sweet
Onions with Lemony
Masala, 201
Zesty Okra, 160
Onions
All-Purpose Red Onions, 160
Charred Onion Dip, 134
Charred Scallion Aïoli, 219
Company Quiche, 86
Grilled Steak Salad with Potatoes
and Pickled Red Onion, 120
Pan-Roasted Okra and Sweet Onions
with Lemony Masala, 201
Pickled Onions, 201
Roasted Onions, 347
Spicy Fruit-Stuffed Pork Loin with
Roasted Pears and Onions, 340
Sweet Onion Pudding, 343
Vidalia Onion-and-Vinegar Sauce, 29
Orange(s)
Bacon-Mandarin Salad, 343
Baked Ham with Brown Sugar-
Citrus Glaze, 281
Clementine-and-Collard Salad, 38

Clementine Whiskey Sour, 218
Cranberry-Orange Butter Cookies, 293
Cranberry Sangria Punch, 324
Nehi Orange Curd, 148
Nehi Orange Poke Cake, 148
Orange-Buttermilk Trifle, 220
Orange-Sweet Potato Pie with
Rosemary-Cornmeal Crust, 334
Orange-Vanilla French Toast
Casserole with Bourbon-
Maple Syrup, 85
Pickled Shrimp and Citrus Endive
Cups, 273
Oysters
Grilled Oysters, 218
Oyster Stew, 219
Roasted Oysters with Bacon-
Stuffing Topping, 275
Scalloped Oysters, 250

P

Parsnips
Roasted Heirloom Root Vegetables
in Lemon-Horseradish
Butter, 348
Slow-Cooker Winter Vegetable Soup
with Bacon, 55
Pasta
Baked Smokin' Macaroni and
Cheese with variations, 344
Basil Shrimp Scampi, 104
Beefy Butternut Squash Pasta, 225
Cheesy Beef and Spinach Ravioli, 69
Cheesy Sheet Pan Pasta, 54
Chicken-Tortellini Salad with Basil
Vinaigrette, 140
Classic Lasagna, 340
Creamy Baked Macaroni and
Cheese with Bacon, 244
Creamy Chicken Spaghetti, 107
Creamy Pesto-and-Shrimp Penne
with Peas, 153
Dinner Mac and Cheese, 336
Pasta with Summer Beans and
Bacon, 119
Sausage-Tortellini Soup, 349
Smoked-Pork-Stuffed Shells, 209
Spring Shrimp-and-Orzo Salad with
Lemon Dressing, 70
Tortellini Caprese Bites, 323
Peaches
Creamy Peach Icebox Cake, 158
Peach-Ricotta-Prosciutto Toasts, 135
Tipsy Peach Shortcakes, 109–110
Pears
Basil-and-Blue Cheese Salad, 343
Brussels Sprouts Slaw with Pecans
and Pomegranate Seeds, 277
Pear-Cranberry Pie with Ginger-
Almond Streusel, 239

Spicy Fruit-Stuffed Pork Loin with
Roasted Pears and Onions, 340
Peas. *See also* **Black-eyed peas;**
Field peas
Basil Fried Rice with Butter Peas, 117
Creamy Pesto-and-Shrimp Penne
with Peas, 153
Skillet Pot Pie with Chicken and
Spring Vegetables, 89
Smoky Split Pea-and-Sausage
Soup, 35
Sweet Pea-and-Prosciutto Macaroni
and Cheese, 344
Peppers, bell
Greek Stuffed Peppers, 208
Spicy Pepper Jelly Coleslaw, 131
Spicy-Sweet Refrigerator
Pickles, 134
Peppers, chile
Colby-Pepper Jack Cheese Dip, 323
Creamy Southwest Black-Eyed Pea
Dip, 57
Green Chile-Chicken Soup, 207
Honey-Chipotle Glaze, 139
Hot Pepper Vinegar, 218
Huevos Rancheros Bake, 84
Marinated Olives and
Peppadews, 270
Pepper Jack Macaroni and
Cheese, 344
Spicy-Sweet Refrigerator Pickles, 134
Pies and tarts
Black-and-Blue Buttermilk Tart, 141
Chocolate-Covered Cherry Pie, 330
Cranberry-Apple Pie, 328
Crunch-Top Apple Pie, 261
Dulce de Leche-Cheesecake Pecan
Pie, 238
Fudge Truffle-Pecan Tart, 331
Green Tomato Skillet Pie, 113
Heirloom Tomato Pie with
Parmesan-Buttermilk
Crust, 136
Lemon-Lime Meringue Pie, 31
Old-Fashioned Apple Pie, 195
Orange-Sweet Potato Pie with
Rosemary-Cornmeal Crust, 334
Pear-Cranberry Pie with Ginger-
Almond Streusel, 239
Pomegranate-Chess Tart, 238
Pumpkin Chess Pie, 264
Roasted Granny Smith Apple Pie, 241
Salted Caramel-Apple Hand
Pies, 223
Skillet Vegetable Pie with Goat
Cheese, 40
Spiced Coconut-Pumpkin Pie, 237
Tiramisú Toffee Trifle Pie, 331
Walter's Favorite Pecan Pie, 267
Watermelon Chiffon Pie, 128

Pineapple
Ambrosia Macaroons, 287
Bing Cherry Salad, 342
Pomegranate
Brussels Sprouts Slaw with Pecans
and Pomegranate Seeds, 277
Pomegranate-Chess Tart, 238
Pork. *See also* **Bacon; Ham;**
Prosciutto; Sausages
Oven-Fried Pork Chops with Sweet
Potatoes and Green Beans, 52
Pico de Gallo Pork Chops, 117
Pork Paillards with Lemony Squash
Salad, 108
Smoked-Pork-Stuffed Shells, 209
Smoked Pork Tenderloins with
Sherry-Mushroom Sauce, 342
Spicy Fruit-Stuffed Pork Loin with
Roasted Pears and Onions, 340
Sweet-and-Spicy Meatballs, 272
Potatoes. *See also* **Sweet potatoes**
Butternut Squash Gratin, 344
Charred Potato-Okra Salad, 135
Cheese-and-Carrot Mashed
Potatoes, 336
Classic Parmesan Scalloped
Potatoes, 345
Creamy Cheddar-Potato Soup with
Bacon, 71
Creamy Whipped-Potato
Casserole, 278
Fennel-Potato Gratin, 348
Grilled Steak Salad with Potatoes
and Pickled Red Onion, 120
Honey-Mustard Salmon and
Vegetables, 90
Lemony Potato-and-Beet Salad with
Dill, 81
Next-Day Turkey Bake, 338
Oyster Stew, 219
Pecan Soup, 349
Perfect Mashed Potatoes, 347
Quick Shrimp-and-Corn
Chowder, 106
Roasted Garlic Mashed Potatoes, 346
Sausage-Hash Brown Casserole, 87
Shepherd's Pie, 336
Simple Mashed Rutabagas and
Potatoes, 245
Slow-Cooker Winter Vegetable Soup
with Bacon, 55
Prosciutto
Cheesy Garlic-Herb-and-Ham
Bites, 304
Peach-Ricotta-Prosciutto Toasts, 135
Sweet Pea-and-Prosciutto Macaroni
and Cheese, 344
Pumpkin
Baked Mini Pumpkin-Pecan
Doughnuts, 223

Pumpkin Chess Pie, 264
Spiced Coconut-Pumpkin Pie, 237

R
Radishes
Crispy Catfish Tacos with Slaw, 51
Sautéed Radishes with Bacon and
Cilantro, 83
Raspberries
"Any-Berry" Muffins with Cornmeal
Streusel, 155
Raspberry-Almond Crumble Bars, 48
Raspberry Truffle Shortcakes, 109–110
White Chocolate-Raspberry
Cheesecake Bars, 333
Rice
Basil Fried Rice with Butter Peas, 117
Basmati Rice, 201
Creamy Chicken-and-Rice Soup
with Collard Greens, 32
Greek Stuffed Peppers, 208
One-Pan Hot Honey Chicken and
Rice, 205
Pico de Gallo Pork Chops, 117
Rajma (Punjabi Red Beans), 198
Sea Island Crab Fried Rice, 246
Wild Rice Salad, 347
Rolls and buns
Best-Ever Sticky Buns, 326
Crescent Rolls, 325
Hurry-Up Homemade Cornbread
Yeast Rolls, 325
Mini Bananas Foster Sticky Buns, 39
Refrigerator Yeast Rolls, 265
Sea Salt-Poppy Seed Cloverleaf
Rolls, 326
Sour Cream Pocketbook Rolls, 325
Sweet Potato Rolls with Cane Syrup
Glaze, 254
Rutabagas
Root Vegetable-and-Butternut
Squash Gratin, 279
Simple Mashed Rutabagas and
Potatoes, 245

S
Salad dressings
Apricot Vinaigrette, 343
Basil Vinaigrette, 323
Salads
Bacon-Mandarin Salad, 343
Basil-and-Blue Cheese Salad, 343
Bing Cherry Salad, 342
Brussels Sprouts Slaw with Pecans
and Pomegranate Seeds, 277
Carrot-and-Fennel Salad, 31
Charred Potato-Okra Salad, 135
Chicken Salad-Stuffed Tomatoes, 154
Chicken-Tortellini Salad with Basil
Vinaigrette, 140

Chopped Salad with Buttermilk
    Dressing, 132
Clementine-and-Collard Salad, 38
Cranberry-Pecan Chicken Salad, 335
Crispy Chicken-and-Broccoli
    Salad, 157
Field Pea-Tomato Salad with Lemon
    Vinaigrette, 100
Fresh Cranberry Congealed
    Salad, 262
Grilled Salmon Panzanella Salad, 151
Grilled Steak Salad with Potatoes
    and Pickled Red Onion, 120
Holiday Cranberry Salad, 263
Lemony Potato-and-Beet Salad with
    Dill, 81
Marinated Watermelon-and-Tomato
    Salad, 126
Pork Paillards with Lemony Squash
    Salad, 108
Shaved Carrot, Asparagus, and
    Apple Salad, 83
Spicy Pepper Jelly Coleslaw, 131
Spinach Salad with Apricot
    Vinaigrette, 343
Spring Shrimp-and-Orzo Salad with
    Lemon Dressing, 70
Turkey Salad with Cranberry
    Dressing, 342
Turkey Salad with variations, 268
Wild Rice Salad, 347

Sandwiches
Cranberry-Turkey Panini, 338
Diner-Style Patty Melts, 226
Sausage, Egg, and Cheddar Biscuit
    Sandwiches, 121
Smashed Bacon Cheeseburgers, 134
Smoky Grilled BLTs, 152
Turkey, Brie, and Fig Pressed
    Sandwiches, 223

Sauces. *See also* **Sauces, dessert**
Aïoli, 301
Béarnaise Sauce, 341
Charred Scallion Aïoli, 219
Cheese Sauce, 31
Coconut-Buttermilk Sauce, 199
Giblet Gravy, 266
Holiday Herb Butter, 334
Hot Pepper Vinegar, 218
Make-Ahead Turkey Gravy, 347
Meyer Lemon–Ginger Mignonette, 218
Mint Sauce, 264
Mushroom Gravy, 339
Simple Raita, 201
Smoky Cranberry-Apple Sauce, 348
Spicy Butter, 301
Sweet Hot Honey Mustard, 334
Vidalia Onion-and-Vinegar Sauce, 29

Sauces, dessert
Bananas Foster Sauce, 328
Berry Compote, 114
Cinnamon Whipped Cream, 227
Elderflower Crème, 79
Lemon Puree, 79
Praline Sauce, 264
Rich Bourbon Sauce, 333
Sweetened Whipped Cream, 64

Sausages
Jambalaya Skewers, 105
Leek-and-Mushroom Grits
    Frittata, 69
Sausage-and-Shrimp Pizzas with
    Spinach-Basil Pesto, 132
Sausage-Cornbread Dressing, 266
Sausage, Egg, and Cheddar Biscuit
    Sandwiches, 121
Sausage-Hash Brown Casserole, 87
Sausage-Tortellini Soup, 349
Shrimp-and-Sausage Skillet
    Corn, 119
Smoked Sausage Pretzel Bites, 273
Smoked Turkey-and-Andouille
    Gumbo, 25
Smoky Split Pea-and-Sausage
    Soup, 35
Spicy Cornbread Dressing with
    Chorizo, 247
Spinach-Sausage Turnovers, 322
Tomato-Basil Couscous with
    Chicken Smoked Sausage, 156

Shellfish. *See also* **Shrimp**
Foil-Pack Clams with White Wine
    and Herbs, 133
Grilled Oysters, 218
Lump Crab Mornay, 322
Mini Crab Cakes with Cajun
    Sauce, 270
Oyster Stew, 219
Sea Island Crab Fried Rice, 246

Shrimp
Basil Shrimp Scampi, 104
Creamy Pesto-and-Shrimp Penne
    with Peas, 153
Garlic Butter-Roasted Shrimp
    Cocktail, 323
Garlic-Butter Shrimp, 203
Jambalaya Skewers, 105
Lemon-Garlic Butter Shrimp and
    Broccoli, 53
Pickled Shrimp and Citrus Endive
    Cups, 273
Quick Shrimp-and-Corn
    Chowder, 106
Sausage-and-Shrimp Pizzas with
    Spinach-Basil Pesto, 132
Shrimp-and-Bacon Stir-Fry, 103

Shrimp and Grits Casserole, 88
Shrimp and Grits Dressing, 344
Shrimp-and-Sausage Skillet
    Corn, 119
Shrimp Cakes with Smoky
    Horseradish Sauce, 103
Shrimp Fajita Bowls, 207
Shrimp-Stuffed Mirlitons, 249
Spicy Shrimp with Jalapeño
    Cornbread and Aïoli, 301
Spring Shrimp-and-Orzo Salad with
    Lemon Dressing, 70
Toasted Israeli Couscous and
    Shrimp, 65

Soups and stews
Beef-and-Vegetable Soup with
    Gnocchi, 225
Butternut Squash Soup, 260
Creamy Cheddar-Potato Soup with
    Bacon, 71
Creamy Chicken-and-Rice Soup
    with Collard Greens, 32
Green Chile-Chicken Soup, 207
Instant Pot Beef-and-Barley Soup
    with Mushrooms, 34
Lentil Soup with Sweet Potatoes and
    Bacon, 36
Oyster Stew, 219
Pecan Soup, 349
Quick Shrimp-and-Corn
    Chowder, 106
Roasted Tomato-Cheddar Soup, 33
Sausage-Tortellini Soup, 349
Slow-Cooker Winter Vegetable Soup
    with Bacon, 55
Smoked Turkey-and-Andouille
    Gumbo, 25
Smoky Split Pea-and-Sausage
    Soup, 35
Tomato Bisque, 349
Tortilla Turkey Soup, 349

Spinach
Cheesy Beef and Spinach Ravioli, 69
Creamed Spinach-Stuffed
    Mushrooms, 275
Crumb-Topped Spinach
    Casserole, 345
Grilled Salmon Panzanella Salad, 151
Sausage-and-Shrimp Pizzas with
    Spinach-Basil Pesto, 132
Smoky Field Pea-and-Greens
    Dip, 101
Spinach Salad with Apricot
    Vinaigrette, 343
Spinach-Sausage Turnovers, 322

Squash. *See also* **Pumpkin; Zucchini**
Beefy Butternut Squash Pasta, 225
Butternut Croutons, 339

Butternut Squash Gratin, 344
Butternut Squash Soup, 260
Butternut Squash Triangles, 304
Candy Roaster Squash with
    Sorghum, Black Walnuts, and
    Cranberries, 242
Grilled Chicken with Quick-Pickled
    Squash Salad, 118
Pork Paillards with Lemony Squash
    Salad, 108
Root Vegetable-and-Butternut
    Squash Gratin, 279
Shrimp-Stuffed Mirlitons, 249
Skillet Vegetable Pie with Goat
    Cheese, 40
Squash Casserole, 266
Yellow Squash Bundt Cake, 113

Strawberries
"Any-Berry" Muffins with Cornmeal
    Streusel, 155
Berry Compote, 114
Corn Custards with Berry
    Compote, 114
Favorite Strawberry Shortcakes, 109
Hazelnut Financiers with
    Strawberry Jam and Lemon
    Puree, 79
Strawberry Buttercream
    Frosting, 330
Strawberry Gelato with Almond
    Shortbread and Elderflower
    Crème, 79
Strawberry Jam, 79
Strawberry-Rhubarb Crisps with
    Sweet-and-Savory Granola, 80
Triple-Decker Strawberry Cake, 330

Sweet potatoes
Cornflake, Pecan, and Marshmallow-
    Topped Sweet Potato
    Casserole, 345
Grated Sweet Potato Pudding with
    Pecans, 250
Grilled Sweet Potato Fries, 131
Lentil Soup with Sweet Potatoes and
    Bacon, 36
Melting Sweet Potatoes with
    Walnuts, 278
Orange-Sweet Potato Pie with
    Rosemary-Cornmeal
    Crust, 334
Oven-Fried Pork Chops with Sweet
    Potatoes and Green Beans, 52
Roasted Root Vegetable with Spicy
    Pecan Topping, 258
Rosemary Chicken Thighs and
    Vegetables, 66
Sweet Potato Casserole, 267

Sweet Potato Casserole with
    Marshmallows, 267
Sweet Potato Rolls with Cane Syrup
    Glaze, 254

T

Tomatillos
Charred Tomatillo-Avocado
    Salsa, 142
Green Chile-Chicken Soup, 207

Tomatoes
Chicken Salad-Stuffed Tomatoes, 154
Chicken-Tortellini Salad with Basil
    Vinaigrette, 140
Chopped Salad with Buttermilk
    Dressing, 132
Field Pea-Tomato Salad with Lemon
    Vinaigrette, 100
Green Tomato Skillet Pie, 113
Grilled Salmon Panzanella Salad, 151
Heirloom Tomato Pie with Parmesan-
    Buttermilk Crust, 136
Marinated Watermelon-and-Tomato
    Salad, 126
Mixed Herb-and-Tomato Salad, 133
Roasted Tomato-Cheddar Soup, 33
Smoky Grilled BLTs, 152
Tomato-Basil Couscous with
    Chicken Smoked Sausage, 156
Tomato Bisque, 349
Tomato-Ginger Jam, 99
Tortellini Caprese Bites, 323
Tuscan Cherry Tomatoes, 160

Turkey
Citrus-Grilled Turkey Breast, 337
Cranberry-Turkey Panini, 338
Creole Deep-Fried Turkey, 337
Crispy Fried Turkey with Creole
    Spices, 235
Herbed Turkey, 263
Make-Ahead Turkey Gravy, 347
Next-Day Turkey Bake, 338
Peppered Turkey Breast, 264
Roast Turkey and Gravy, 265
Roast Turkey with Chestnut
    Stuffing, 265
Skillet Turkey Meatballs, 210
Smoked Turkey-and-Andouille
    Gumbo, 25
Spice-Rubbed Smoked Turkey
    Breast with Mushroom
    Gravy, 339
Tortilla Turkey Soup, 349
Turkey, Brie, and Fig Pressed
    Sandwiches, 223

Turkey Pot Pie with Cranberry-
    Pecan Crusts, 338
Turkey Salad with Cranberry
    Dressing, 342
Turkey Salad with variations, 268

Turnips
Pepper Jelly-Glazed Baby
    Turnips, 83
Roasted Baby Turnips with Turnip
    Green Pesto, 83
Root Vegetable-and-Butternut
    Squash Gratin, 279
Wood-Fired Root Vegetables with
    Charred Scallion Aïoli, 219

W

Watermelon
Marinated Watermelon-and-Tomato
    Salad, 126
Watermelon Chiffon Pie, 128
Watermelon-Ginger Mojitos, 127

White chocolate
Chocolate-Peppermint Candy
    Cupcakes, 332
Salty Chocolate-Pecan Candy, 335
White Chocolate-Buttermilk
    Cake, 220
White Chocolate-Raspberry
    Cheesecake Bars, 333

Z

Zucchini
Chocolate-Zucchini Cake, 114
Grilled Chicken with Quick-Pickled
    Squash Salad, 118
Oven-Fried Zucchini Sticks, 132
Sausage-Tortellini Soup, 349

Southern Living
2019 Annual Recipes

MEREDITH CONSUMER MARKETING
Director of Direct Marketing-Books: Daniel Fagan
Marketing Operations Manager: Max Daily
Assistant Marketing Manager: Kylie Dazzo
Content Manager: Julie Doll
Senior Production Manager: Al Rodruck

WATERBURY PUBLICATIONS, INC.
Editorial Director: Lisa Kingsley
Associate Editor: Tricia Bergman
Creative Director: Ken Carlson
Associate Design Director: Doug Samuelson
Production Assistant: Mindy Samuelson
Contributing Copy Editor: Gretchen Kauffman
Contributing Proofreader: Terri Fredrickson
Contributing Indexer: Mary Williams

Recipe Developers and Testers: Meredith Food Studios

MEREDITH CORPORATION
Executive Chairman: Stephen M. Lacy

In Memoriam: E.T. Meredith III (1933–2003)

All of us at Meredith Consumer Marketing are dedicated to providing you with information and ideas to enhance your home. We welcome your comments and suggestions. Write to us at: Meredith Consumer Marketing, 1716 Locust St., Des Moines, IA 50309-3023.

Pictured on front cover:
Chocolate-Buttermilk Cake with Swiss Meringue Buttercream, page 295